D1593254

WRITINGS AND SPEECH IN ISRAELITE AND ANCIENT NEAR EASTERN PROPHECY

SOCIETY
OF BIBLICAL
LITERATURE

SBL
SYMPOSIUM SERIES

Christopher R. Matthews, Editor

Number 10

WRITINGS AND SPEECH IN ISRAELITE AND
ANCIENT NEAR EASTERN PROPHECY
edited by
Ehud Ben Zvi and Michael H. Floyd

Ehud Ben Zvi
Michael H. Floyd
editors

WRITINGS AND SPEECH IN ISRAELITE AND ANCIENT NEAR EASTERN PROPHECY

Society of Biblical Literature
Atlanta

WRITINGS AND SPEECH IN ISRAELITE AND ANCIENT NEAR EASTERN PROPHECY

edited by
Ehud Ben Zvi
Michael H. Floyd

Library of Congress Cataloging-in-Publication Data

Writings and speech in Israelite and ancient Near Eastern prophecy /
Ehud Ben Zvi, Michael H. Floyd, editors.
    p. cm. — (SBL symposium series ; no. 10)
    Includes bibliographical references and index.
    ISBN 0-88414-023-7 (pbk. : alk. paper)
    1. Bible. O.T. Prophets—Criticism, interpretation, etc. 2. Prophets—
Middle East—History. 3. Written communication—Middle East—History.
4. Oral communication—Middle East—History. I. Ben Zvi, Ehud, 1951–
II. Floyd, Michael H. III. Symposium series (Society of Biblical
Literature) ; no. 10.

BS1505.2.W75 2000
224'.06—dc21   00-061877

08 07 06 05 04 03 02 01 00   5 4 3 2 1

Printed in the United States of America
on acid-free paper

Contents

List of Abbreviations

AB   Anchor Bible

ABD   *The Anchor Bible Dictionary.* Edited by D. N. Freedman et al. 6 vols. Garden City, N.Y.: Doubleday, 1992

ABL   *Assyrian and Babylonian Letters Belonging to the Kouyunjik Collections of the British Museum.* Edited by R. F. Harper. 14 vols. Chicago: University of Chicago Press, 1892–1914

ABRL   Anchor Bible Reference Library

AELHF   *Ancient Egyptian Literature: History and Forms.* Edited by A. Loprieno. Probleme der Ägyptologie 10. Leiden: Brill, 1996

AfO   *Archiv für Orientforschung*

ÄIKM   *Ägyptische Inschriften aus den königlichen Museen zu Berlin.* Edited by G. Roeder. Leipzig: Hinrichs, 1901–24

ÄL   *Ägyptische Lesestücke zum Gebrauch im akademischen Unterricht.* Compiled by K. Sethe. Leipzig: Hinrichs, 1924

ANET   *Ancient Near Eastern Texts Relating to the Old Testament.* Edited by J. B. Pritchard. 3d ed. with Suppl. Princeton: Princeton University Press, 1969

AOAT   Alter Orient und Altes Testament

AOS   American Oriental Series

ARM   Archives royales de Mari

ASAÉ   *Annales du service des antiquités de l'Égypte*

ASP   American Studies in Papyrology

BD	Book of the Dead
BEATAJ	Beiträge zur Erforschung des Alten Testaments und des antiken Judentums
BIFAO	*Bulletin de l'Institut français d'archéologie orientale au Caire*
BM	British Museum
BSÉG	*Bulletin de la Société d'égyptologie, Genève*
BWANT	Beiträge zur Wissenschaft vom Alten und Neuen Testament
BZAW	Beihefte zur Zeitschrift für die alttestamentliche Wissenschaft
CAD	*The Assyrian Dictionary of the Oriental Institute of the University of Chicago.* Edited by I. J. Gelb et al. Chicago: Oriental Institute, 1956–
CANE	*Civilizations of the Ancient Near East.* Edited by J. M. Sasson. 4 vols. New York: Scribner, 1995
CBQ	*Catholic Biblical Quarterly*
CBQMS	Catholic Biblical Quarterly Monograph Series
CGC	*Catalogue général des antiquités égyptiénnes du musée de Caire.* Cairo, 1904–
CoffT	Coffin Texts
CT	*Cuneiform Texts from Babylonian Tablets in the British Museum*
Dendera	*Le Temple de Dendera.* Edited by E. Chassinat and F. Daumas. 9 vols. to date. Cairo: Institut français d'archéologie orientale, 1934–
EA	El-Amarna tablets. According to the edition of J. A. Knudtzon. *Die el-Amarna-Tafeln.* Leipzig, 1908–15. Repr., Aalen, 1964. Continued in A. F. Rainey, *El-Amarna Tablets, 359–379.* 2d rev. ed., Kevelaer, 1978
Edfu	*Le Temple d'Edfou.* Edited by E. Chassinat. Paris and Cairo: Institut français d'archéologie orientale, 1892–
FLP	Tablets in the collections of the Free Library of Pennsylvania
FOTL	Forms of the Old Testament Literature
FRLANT	Forschungen zur Religion und Literatur des Alten und Neuen Testaments

GAG	*Grundriß der akkadischen Grammatik.* W. von Soden. Rome: Pontificium Institutum Biblicum, 1952. 3d ed. (*GAG³*) with suppl., 1969
GöM	*Göttinger Miszellen*
HPKM	*Hieratische Papyrus aus den Königlichen Museen zu Berlin.* Leipzig: Hinrichs, 1901–11
HSM	Harvard Semitic Monographs
HTBM	*Hieroglyphic Texts from Egyptian Staelae, etc., in the British Museum.* London, 1912–
ICC	International Critical Commentary
IEJ	*Israel Exploration Journal*
JAF	*Journal of American Folklore*
JAOS	*Journal of the American Oriental Society*
JBL	*Journal of Biblical Literature*
JANESCU	*Journal of the Ancient Near Eastern Society of Columbia University*
JAOS	*Journal of the American Oriental Society*
JARCE	*Journal of the American Research Center in Egypt*
JCS	*Journal of Cuneiform Studies*
JEA	*Journal of Egyptian Archaeology*
JNSL	*Journal of Northwest Semitic Languages*
JSNTSup	Journal for the Study of the New Testament: Supplement Series
JSOT	*Journal for the Study of the Old Testament*
JSOTSup	Journal for the Study of the Old Testament: Supplement Series
JSP	*Journal for the Study of the Pseudepigrapha*
JSS	*Journal of Semitic Studies*
KAI	*Kanaanäische und aramäische Inschriften.* H. Donner and W. Röllig. 3d ed. Wiesbaden: Harrassowitz, 1973
KBo	*Keilschrifttexte aus Boghazköi.* Leipzig, 1916–

KHC	Kurzer Hand-Commentar zum Alten Testament
KRI	Kitchen, K. A., ed. *Ramesside Inscriptions: Historical and Biographical.* Oxford: Blackwell, 1969–
LAI	Library of Ancient Israel
LÄ	*Lexikon der Ägyptologie.* Edited by W. Helck, E. Otto, and W. Westendorf. Wiesbaden: Harrassowitz, 1972–
LDÄÄ	Lepsius, R. *Denkmäler aus Ägypten und Äthiopien.* 12 vols. Berlin: Nicolai, 1849–1913
l.p.h.	Life, prosperity, health
MARI	*Mari: Annales de recherches interdisciplinaires*
MDAI	*Mitteilungen des Deutschen archäologischen Instituts zu Kairo*
MMA	Metropolitan Museum of Art, New York City
MNABU	Mémoires de Nouvelles assyriologiques brèves et utilitaires
MSL	*Materialien zum sumerischen Lexikon.* Edited by Benno Landesberger
NABU	*Nouvelles assyriologiques brèves et utilitaires*
NIB	*The New Interpreter's Bible.* Edited by L. E. Keck et al. 12 vols. Nashville: Abingdon, 1994–
NCB	New Century Bible
NRSV	The New Revised Standard Version
OBO	Orbis biblicus et orientalis
OCD	*The Oxford Classical Dictionary.* Edited by S. Hornblower and A. Spawforth. 3d ed. Oxford: Oxford University Press, 1996
OEAE	*Oxford Encyclopedia of Ancient Egypt.* Edited by D. B. Redford. New York: Oxford University Press, forthcoming
OLA	Orientalia lovaniensia analecta
OLP	Orientalia lovaniensia periodica
Or	*Orientalia*
OTL	Old Testament Library

P.	Papyrus
PT	Pyramid Texts
RA	*Revue d'assyriologie et d'archéologie orientale*
RB	*Revue biblique*
RdÉ	*Revue d'Égyptologie*
RelSRev	*Religious Studies Review*
RGG²	*Die Religion in Geschichte und Gegenwart.* Edited by H. Gunkel et al. 2d ed. 5 vols. Tübingen: Mohr, 1909–13
SAA	State Archives of Assyria
SAAB	*State Archives of Assyria Bulletin*
SAAS	State Archives of Assyria Studies
SAK	*Studien zur altägyptischen Kultur*
SBLDS	Society of Biblical Literature Dissertation Series
SBLMS	Society of Biblical Literature Monograph Series
SBLSBS	Society of Biblical Literature Sources for Biblical Study
SBLSS	Society of Biblical Literature Semeia Studies
SEL	*Studi epigrafici e linguistici sul Vicino Oriente antico*
SJOT	*Scandinavian Journal of the Old Testament*
StudOr	Studia orientalia
Urk.	*Urkunden des ägyptischen Altertums.* Edited by G. Steindorff. Leipzig: Hinrichs; Berlin: Akademie-Verlag, 1903–
UT	Unpublished text
VAT	Vorderasiatische Abteilung Tontafel. Vorderasiatisches Museum, Berlin
VT	*Vetus Testamentum*
VTSup	Vetus Testamentum Supplements
WÄS	*Wörterbuch der ägyptischen Sprache.* Edited by A. Erman and H. Grapow. 5 vols. Leipzig: Hinrichs, 1926–31

YOS	Yale Oriental Series, Babylonian Texts
ZA	*Zeitschrift für Assyriologie*
ZÄS	*Zeitschrift für ägyptische Sprache und Altertumskunde*
ZAW	*Zeitschrift für die alttestamentliche Wissenschaft*
ZDMG	*Zeitschrift der deutschen morgenländischen Gesellschaft*
ZPE	*Zeitschrift für Papyrologie und Epigraphik*

Introduction: Writings, Speeches, and the Prophetic Books—Setting an Agenda

Ehud Ben Zvi
University of Alberta

This volume is the first of several planned by the Prophetic Texts and Their Ancient Contexts Consultation of the Society of Biblical Literature.[1] The consultation serves as a "meeting place" for scholars who wish to deal with some basic issues concerning the study of the prophetic texts and "books"[2] of the Hebrew Bible in their ancient context. It aims to foster dialogue among a wide variety of approaches and viewpoints within the international scholarly community by providing a forum in which different areas of expertise inform each other, rather than talk past each other.

---

[1] The informal steering committee of the consultation for 1998 and 1999 included Alice Ogden Bellis, Ehud Ben Zvi, Lester L. Grabbe, Michael H. Floyd, Chris Franke, Julie Galambush, Robert D. Haak, Peter Machinist, Cynthia L. Miller, and J. Maxwell Miller. The title of the next volume, edited by Lester L. Grabbe and Robert D. Haak, is *The Urban Centre and Prophetic Literature: Social and Textual Constructions, Historical Circumstances and Theological Discourse* (forthcoming in 2001 from Sheffield University Press in the JSOT Supplement Series).

[2] Within this introductory chapter, a "prophetic book" (e.g., the book of Micah) is a "book" that claims an association with a prophetic personage of the past (e.g., Micah) and is presented to its readership as YHWH's word. As such the book claims to communicate legitimate and authoritative knowledge about YHWH. A "book," in this context, is a written work that presents itself as a self-contained unit—with a clear beginning and conclusion—and shows a significant degree of textual coherence and distinctiveness (e.g., the book of Isaiah, the book of Chronicles, the book of Obadiah, the book of Jeremiah). See the relevant terms among the glossary entries in E. Ben Zvi, *Micah* (FOTL 21B; Grand Rapids, Mich.: Eerdmans, 2000), 187-89.

The present volume begins to make the work of the consultation available to a wider audience. It contains revised versions of papers presented at the consultation's 1998 session on "Orality and Writtenness in the Prophetic Books: Textual and Social Considerations" as well as several additional contributions invited specially for this collection. While no single volume can fully address the extent, variety, and complexity of issues connected with this topic, what emerges here is proof positive that questions of "writtenness" and "orality" stand at the heart of issues central to the study of the prophetic books in the Hebrew Bible, prophets and prophecy in ancient Israel, and Israelite history at large. No attempt is made here to shape a "school," or to develop a single, consistent approach to these matters. Rather it is the explicit purpose of the Prophetic Texts and Their Ancient Contexts Consultation to foster a wider academic conversation that takes seriously the present diversity of approaches and methodologies for the study of the past. Because of its focus on historical Israel, and the relation of Israel to larger social, political, cultural, and economic systems in the surrounding area, the consultation also recognizes the necessity of discussing these issues in a manner that is clearly informed by our knowledge of the ancient Near East. The inclusion of the substantial chapters by Nissinen, Redford, and van der Toorn reflects this recognition and suggests trends for further research.[3]

The first three chapters in the volume (by James Crenshaw, Robert Culley, and Philip Davies) had their origin in the 1998 meeting of the consultation. The chapter by John Van Seters is based on his response to these three presentations in that original (oral and aural) venue. Crenshaw focuses mainly on how and why prophecy was transmitted. Issues such as circles of followers, institutional sponsorship—or lack thereof—and whether the transmission was oral or written figure prominently in his paper. Culley substitutes for the terms orality and writtenness the more specific concepts of "oral traditional" diction and "traditional scribal" practices, respectively. Following John M. Foley's development of the Milman Parry–Albert B. Lord approach, Culley reflects on the features of traditional oral language, the influence of oral idioms in written texts, and the process of composition. He also addresses the question of the

---

[3] It is worth mentioning that the speakers who predict the future in Egyptian "prophecies" do not provide a good parallel to Israelite, Neo-Babylonian, or Neo-Assyrian prophets. See R. R. Wilson, *Prophecy and Society in Ancient Israel* (Philadelphia: Fortress, 1989), 124–28; cf. M. Nissinen, "Prophecy against the King in Neo-Assyrian Sources," in *"Laßet uns Brücken bauen . . .": Collected Communications to the XVth Congress of the International Organization for the Study of the Old Testament, Cambridge, 1995* (ed. K.-D. Schunck and M. Augustin; BEATAJ 42; Frankfurt am Main: P. Lang, 1998), 157–58, n. 5. However, the question of whether Egyptian "prophetic texts," as well as the "Akkadian Prophecies," are partially comparable to the biblical books deserves much more elaboration.

reception of prophetic books and considers the conditions that allow them "to survive through many contexts and continue to produce readings." Davies focuses on prophecy as writing. He notes that sociological and anthropological studies show that intermediaries "do not write their words in big books" and, therefore, addresses the question of how the prophetic books came into existence. He also warns about the danger of "monolithic explanations." Van Seters provides a critique of these three papers and introduces nonbiblical Near Eastern parallels into the debate. These parallels also stand at the center of several other contributions to this volume.

Three of the chapters specially commissioned for this volume have a somewhat different character. Donald Redford presents an extensive discussion of written and oral tradition in ancient Egypt,[4] with attention to their interactions and relation to social roles. Although he does not directly address the issue of prophetic literature and prophecy, his study of the social roles and realia involved in written and oral communication in ancient Egypt is of considerable comparative value for the study of similar processes in ancient Israel.[5] Turning to Mesopotamian prophecy and written communication of or about prophecy, Karel van der Toorn focuses on a particular time and place that has figured prominently in previous studies of ancient Near Eastern prophecy, namely, Old Babylonian Mari. He discusses, among other matters, the relation between oral prophetic messages and their transmission in writing. This contribution, along with that of Martti Nissinen, develops a particular subfocus within the volume, one that centers around the Mari evidence and its potential significance for the study of some of the questions to be advanced below. Nissinen himself surveys the evidence for prophecy in the ancient Near East as a whole and focuses on issues surrounding the communication of divine messages. His study of the evidence of Mari and Assyria shows that the transmission of divine messages "was not motivated by the idea of literal inspiration, but rather by the pursuit of appropriate interpretation and application." Nissinen underscores that "the very writtenness of biblical and ancient Near Eastern prophecy shows that prophecy is more than the prophets, their words and personalities."

Two additional invited chapters on prophecy and prophetic texts in Israel complement those that originated in the consultation's 1998 meeting. Ronald Clements focuses on a particular biblical text. He advances the case for a

---

[4] For a study of the Mesopotamian evidence, see M. E. Vogelzang and H. L. J. Vanstiphout, eds., *Mesopotamian Epic Literature: Oral or Aural?* (Lewiston, N.Y.: Mellen, 1992).

[5] To some extent, his work on Egypt may be compared with Vogelzang and Vanstiphout, *Mesopotamian Epic Literature.*

written, original prophetic memoir in Isa 6:1–8:18*, a document that subsequently underwent considerable expansion. He further addresses the implications of his analysis in relation to such issues as the potential of written prophecy to extend its interpretation, the constraints on how additions could be made to a specific passage in a written text, and the theological significance of written prophecy. Michael Floyd provides an ideological-critical and historical analysis of the oral-written distinction and the way in which ideologically grounded assumptions have influenced biblical scholarship on these matters. He stresses that "it is necessary to cease using the oral-written distinction as a binary opposition and to purge from it any connotation of progress derived from theories of social development."[6] The chapter not only deconstructs the binary opposition but also advances stepping-stones for a nonbinary model that deals with performance, composition, and transmission. Moreover, it deconstructs traditional images of scribes and scribal schools and advances substantial elements for a historical reconstruction of their roles and worldviews. Floyd calls for a clear distinction between the history of prophetic literature (i.e., of the prophetic books, which existed only during a particular period of time) and that of prophecy itself. He also underscores the diversity encompassed by the term "prophecy" in both First and Second Temple periods.

The role of an introduction is to pave the way, as it were, for what is to follow.[7] To be sure, at one level, what is to follow is the series of chapters mentioned above. At a different level, it is the editors' hope that what is to follow is the setting of an agenda for the study of the prophetic literature in its ancient contexts that is strongly informed by matters of writtenness, orality, and their social implications. If the volume is approached from this standpoint, the following contributions become illustrative examples of how scholars may contribute to the elucidation of particular issues associated with this research agenda, each from his or her own perspective and each within her or his area of expertise. To pave the way for this understanding of the volume, and for the discussion that will hopefully follow, the volume must be set in its full contextual horizon. To achieve this goal, this introduction will now shift the focus to general issues of writtenness and orality in prophetic literature and the plethora of research questions arising from them. While this volume does not and cannot provide answers to most of them or bring us to a final destination, it does issue an invitation to join and rejoice in a long journey.

---

[6] Despite differences in tone and scope, see R. Finnegan, "What is Orality—If Anything?" *Byzantine and Modern Greek Studies* 14 (1990): 130–49.

[7] Cf. Aristotle, *Rhetoric*, 3.14.

Social Realia, Literati, and Written Prophetic Texts

Issues associated with questions of writtenness and orality lie at the heart of many crucial issues and academic discussions concerning the prophetic books in the Hebrew Bible, the study of prophets and prophecy, and Israelite history in general. Why is this the case?

Before one attempts to answer this question, a few basic and mostly uncontroversial considerations bear particular note, because they provide solid stepping-stones on which a well developed edifice of answers to that question may be built.

First, the immense majority of the population in ancient Israel during the time of the writing of the prophetic books, or at any other time for that matter, did not know how to read, and certainly did not have the high literacy required to read for themselves and study, let alone compose literary texts such as the prophetic books.[8]

---

[8] See I. M. Young, "Israelite Literacy: Interpreting the Evidence. Part I," *VT* 48 (1998): 239–53; idem, "Israelite Literacy: Interpreting the Evidence, Part II," *VT* 48 (1998): 408–22; J. L. Crenshaw, *Education in Ancient Israel: Across the Deadening Silence* (ABRL; New York: Doubleday, 1998), and the bibliography cited in these works. For a different approach, see, e.g., A. R. Millard, "The Knowledge of Writing in Iron Age Palestine," in *"Laßet uns Brücken bauen . . .": Collected Communications to the XVth Congress of the International Organization for the Study of the Old Testament, Cambridge, 1995* (ed. K.-D. Schunck and M. Augustin; BEATAJ 42; Frankfurt am Main: P. Lang, 1998), 33–39. An important distinction to be kept in mind is the one between those who may be able to write only a short note or report and bearers of high literacy. In the ancient Near East, the latter were substantially fewer in number than the former. To illustrate, the less than erudite writer of the letter mentioned by S. Parpola ("The Man without a Scribe and the Question of Literacy in the Assyrian Empire," in *Ana šadî Labnāni lū allik: Beiträge zu altorientalischen und mittelmeerischen Kulturen. Festschrift für Wolfgang Röllig* [ed. B. Pongratz-Leisten, H. Kühne, and P. Xella; Kevelaer: Butzon & Bercker; Neukirchen-Vluyn: Neukirchener Verlag, 1997], 315–24) and others of similar scribal competence could be included among the former, but certainly not among the latter. See also M. Nissinen's comments on this particular "man without a scribe" in his contribution to this volume. Studies of other traditional societies, including the ancient Near East and the classical period, also lead to the conclusion that only a small percentage of the population was literate, and far fewer were bearers of high literacy. See J. S. Cooper, "Babbling on Recovering Mesopotamian Orality," in *Mesopotamian Epic Literature* [ed. M. E. Vogelzang and H. L. J. Vanstiphout; Lewiston, N.Y.: Mellen, 1992], 110–11; J. Baines, "Literacy and Ancient Egyptian Society," *Man*, NS, 18 (1983): 572–99; J. Baines and C. J. Eyre, "Four Notes on Literacy," *GöM* 61 (1983): 65–96; J. Ray, "Literacy in Egypt in the Late and Persian Periods," in *Literacy and Power in the Ancient World* (ed. A. K. Bowman and G. Woolf; Cambridge: Cambridge University Press, 1994), 51–66; W. V. Harris, *Ancient Literacy* (Cambridge: Harvard University Press, 1989); M. Beard et al., eds., *Literacy in the Roman World* (Journal of Roman Archaeology Supplement Series 3; Ann Arbor, Mich.: Journal of Roman Archaeology, 1991); R. Cribiore, *Writing, Teachers, and Students in Graeco-Roman Egypt* (ASP 36; Atlanta: Scholars Press,

Second, nevertheless, the basic mores of Israelite society were surely transmitted from generation to generation.[9] The vast majority of the Israelites, as was true of the peoples of any other ancient society, were educated through a process that at all its stages was based on oral and aural communication. Even the well-off "students" of Ben Sira were asked to learn from listening rather than reading.[10] The goal of their education was not to turn them into scribes or sages like those described in Sir 38:24–39:11 or like Ben Sira himself; nor was it to develop high literacy among them. Rather, it was to socialize them into a world in which they required, and therefore should appreciate, the work of the relatively few scribes and teachers available, such as Ben Sira.[11]

Third, the written word, and above all written texts, enjoyed high status.[12] YHWH was imagined not only as commanding YHWH's scribes to write as

1996); and R. Thomas, *Literacy and Orality in Ancient Greece* (Cambridge: Cambridge University Press, 1992); idem, "Literacy and the City-State in Archaic and Classical Greece," in *Literacy and Power in the Ancient World* (ed. A. K. Bowman and G. Woolf; Cambridge: Cambridge University Press, 1994), 33–50. For information about the mediaeval period, see R. McKitterick, ed., *The Uses of Literary in Early Mediaeval Europe* (Cambridge: Cambridge University Press, 1995). On these matters, see also the chapters by Nissinen and Redford in this volume.

[9] These mores included, of course, social, religious, and ethical aspects, which in any case were not considered separate categories.

[10] On these matters, see J. L. Crenshaw, "The Primacy of Listening in Ben Sira's Pedagogy," in *Wisdom, You are My Sister: Studies in Honor of Roland E. Murphy, O. Carm., on the Occasion of His Eightieth Birthday* (ed. M. L. Barré; CBQMS 29; Washington, D.C.: Catholic Biblical Association of America, 1997), 172–87. Crenshaw's conclusion is worth quoting: "Nowhere in this unit [Sir 6:18–37] does Ben Sira mention the reading of texts or exercises in writing. His students learn by listening to intelligent conversation; Ben Sira still lives in a predominantly oral culture. He himself reads torah and writes what he hopes will be viewed as inspired teaching, yet he transmits his instructions to students orally, and he expects them to learn by astute listening" (p. 187). It follows that Ben Sira's students are not the intended readership of his written work, which consists only of the few other "Ben Siras" (i.e., sages) in Jerusalem.

[11] To be sure, the social and economic reality of Jerusalem and Yehud, or any ancient polity for that matter, was not conducive to the creation of a large class of scribes and students of written texts communicating the divine word and teaching, nor was high literacy a skill that was required of members of the social and economic elite, even in Roman Egypt. In addition, there is a long tradition in the ancient Near East of a manipulated scarcity of bearers of high literacy. This manipulation secured their status. See Crenshaw, "Primacy of Listening," 177–78, among others.

[12] The same holds true for ancient Mesopotamia and for Egypt. Also in the Persian Empire written texts were given much authority. See D. M. Lewis, "The Persepolis Tablets: Speech, Seal and Script," in *Literacy and Power Literacy and Power in the Ancient World* (ed. A. K. Bowman and G. Woolf; Cambridge: Cambridge University Press, 1994), 17–32; and note the

befits a king,[13] but even as one who is personally involved in writing when the matter justifies such action.[14] Significantly, the referent of the term, "the teaching of YHWH"—and similar terms—was a written text,[15] explicitly associated with and composed by human writers.[16] To read (or, in the case of a king, to have someone else read aloud)[17] and to study this written teaching was considered a crucial duty for leaders and pious sages.[18] To do just as "it is written" (ככתוב) in an authoritative document was considered (at least rhetorically) what one should and ought to do.[19]

Fourth, the prophetic books are written texts. They claimed to be, and were considered to be, the word of YHWH. This is how they were regarded, at least

---

hyperbolic references to this matter in Esther. It is worth noting that not all ancient societies in which the vast majority of the population could not read literary texts held written works in high esteem, as the case of Sparta shows. Israelite culture—as well as earlier cultures in the Levant—was an ancient Near Eastern culture that was much influenced by both Mesopotamia and Egypt, where there had been very well established traditions regarding written texts and their high status for at least two millennia by the time the prophetic books were written. Significantly, this fact has called into question whether some of the analyses of orality based on examples from ancient Greece are applicable to Mesopotamia. See J. A. Russo, "Oral Theory: Its Development in Homeric Studies and Applicability to Other Literatures," in *Mesopotamian Epic Literature* [ed. M. E. Vogelzang and H. L. J. Vanstiphout; Lewiston, N.Y.: Mellen, 1992], 7–21, esp. 19–20.

[13] E.g., Exod 17:14; 34:27; cf. Exod 24:4; Mal 3:16. On God as a writer, see Young, "Israelite Literacy," 247–48; on this point see also S. Niditch, *Oral World and Written Word: Ancient Israelite Literature* (LAI; Louisville, Ky.: Westminster John Knox, 1996), 79–82.

[14] See Exod 31:18; 32:16; 34:1; Deut 4:13; 5:22; 9:10; 10:2–4; cf. Exod 24:12. Given that כתב may mean "write" but also "ask someone else to write" (see below), it is unclear whether the texts in Exod 32:32 and Hos 8:12 should be included in this group of examples rather than in the previous one. Personally, I tend to favor the second alternative (cf. Exod 32:32 and the more explicit case of Mal 3:16). Although significantly different from the preceding cases, there are also supernatural writings in such texts as Ezek 2:9–10 and Dan 5:5.

[15] See, among others, Josh 24:26; Neh 9:3; 2 Chr 17:9; 31:3; 35:26; and also Josh 8:31, 34; 23:6; 1 Kgs 2:3; 14:6; Dan 9:11, 13; Ezra 3:2. It is worth mentioning that Josh 24:26 explicitly characterizes Joshua as writing in the "book of God's teaching" (וַיִּכְתֹּב יְהוֹשֻׁעַ אֶת־הַדְּבָרִים הָאֵלֶּה בְּסֵפֶר תּוֹרַת אֱלֹהִים)

[16] E.g., Josh 8:31; 23:6; 24:26; 2 Kgs 14:6; Neh 8:1; cf. 2 Chr 34:14.

[17] This is the likely meaning of קרא in Deut 17:18–19 cf. 2 Kgs 22:10–11, 16. As mentioned above, כתב may also mean to ask someone to write (see Young, "Israelite Literacy," 248–49, 408–9).

[18] See Deut 17:18–19; Josh 1:8; Ps 1:2; and cf. Dan 9:2; Sir 38:24–39:3.

[19] See, for instance, 1 Kgs 2:3; 2 Kgs 14:6; 23:1; Ezra 3:2, 4; Neh 8:15; 10:35, 37; 2 Chr 30:5; and cf. 2 Chr 30:18.

by the readers for whom they were primarily intended. And since these books survived, this was probably how they were also regarded by other groups as well (see below). It stands to reason that these books were read and studied by their primary readership as such.[20]

It follows from the preceding that within a society in which the vast majority is illiterate and the total number of highly literate people is minuscule,[21] the explicitly written character of particular instances of the word of YHWH—that is, "the prophetic books" themselves—cannot be considered a theological or literary feature of secondary importance. Rather, it is one of the most salient features of this literature, and it should be treated as such by historical-critical scholarship. In fact, this feature has a substantial bearing on the social role of these books, the status of their composers and readers (as opposed to those to whom the text must be read), the social function of high literacy,[22] the construction of language and discourse, and the role of writing in the propagation of theological/ideological viewpoints, including particular views of society and its hierarchy.

The choice of the written medium and the accompanying requirement of high literacy, along with the explicit claim that YHWH's word is written discourse, effectively create a world in which YHWH's word is directly accessible only to a few literati in each generation. These circumstances encourage a strong sense of group identity and a self-perception of high status.[23] They also indicate a certain in-group aesthetics[24] and epistemology,

---

[20] It goes without saying that illiterate people did not write the prophetic books, nor could they read them by themselves. On the implications of this self-evident observation, see below.

[21] See E. Ben Zvi, "The Urban Center of Jerusalem and the Development of the Literature of the Hebrew Bible," in *Aspects of Urbanism in Antiquity: From Mesopotamia to Crete* (ed. W. G. Aufrecht, N. A. Mirau and S. W. Gauley; JSOTSup 244; Sheffield: Sheffield Academic Press, 1997), 194–209.

[22] See Hos 14:10; Dan 9:2; and cf. Sir 38:24–29:3. I have discussed these matters elsewhere; see E. Ben Zvi, *A Historical-Critical Study of The Book of Obadiah* (BZAW 242; Berlin and New York: de Gruyter, 1996), 3–6, 96, and passim; idem, *Micah*, passim. Notice also the degree of convergence of the concepts of תורה and דבר יהוה shown in Isa 2:3 and Mic 4:2 (see Ben Zvi, *Micah*, ad loc.). On the תורה and its study, see other references in this chapter.

[23] An important question is whether outsiders shared this inner-group perspective. Certainly as much is required from the outsiders if they are to be convinced of the value of the (religious) teachings that the literati study and communicate to them (see below). But were the literati "effective" teachers? If so, for whom? For all the Yehudite population? The actual status of "the sages" in the rabbinic period may provide some good heuristic suggestions. Yet caution is recommended before advancing clear answers to these questions because of the

particularly since the books are considered YHWH's word rather than a scribe's words. In addition, these factors could not but communicate a stance regarding a divinely ordained, hierarchical order, according to which a small group within Israel is set apart as the rightful "conservers," "learners," and "teachers" of the divine written instruction. Since this group, the literati, is characterized by its high literacy, and, as a result, by its ability to learn directly YHWH's word and teachings, they are the ones who compose, read, reread, and study prophetic books and, of course, other biblical literature as well. To be sure, such considerations raise questions about the actual sociological makeup of the society in which and for which the prophetic books were written.[25] Certainly, these observations are directly relevant to the study of the actual *Sitz im Leben* of the composition, and above all of the reading and rereading of the written prophetic books.[26]

---

pitfall of comparing things that are actually not fully comparable (e.g., the Jewish communities in the rabbinic period and Achaemenid Yehud centered in Jerusalem).

[24] Such aesthetics would determine the choice of features that shape the textual coherence of the book as a whole, including the structure of the book itself, the system(s) of cross-references that communicate textual coherence at the book level, terrace patterns linking one unit to the next, particular and identifying turns of phrase, and the like. (It goes without saying that these choices may also include veiled or even quite clear references [e.g., 2 Kgs 14:6] to other works within the documentary repertoire of the literati.)

On a different level, claims for the high status of "godly documents" probably led to an aesthetics of writing that involved not only legibility (cf. Deut 27:8; Hab 2:2) but also the use of "graceful" handwriting. It is probable that a particular group of skillful "handwriters" was involved in the actual writing. One may keep in mind, too, that writing and reading are two different skills.

Moreover, there is a question of layout. The layout of some biblical texts already at Qumran, particularly with respect to their poetical units, seems to reflect aesthetical and literary sensibilities. It is true that there is no way of knowing how far back the arrangements present in some manuscripts from Qumran (though not all) may go, but in any event there is no reason to assume that an awareness of layout as a significant component of a written text is a new development of the late Hellenistic Roman period. Note the reference to "collections beautifully written with skillful layout . . . prepared for archival purposes" in Nissinen's contribution to this volume. See also H. L. J. Vanstiphout, "Some Remarks on Cuneiform *écritures*," in *Scripta Signa Vocis: Studies about Scripts, Scriptures, Scribes and Languages in the Near East* [Festschrift J. H. Hospers] (ed. H. L. J. Vanstiphout et al.; Groningen: Egbert Forsten, 1986), 217–34. On the evidence from Qumran, see J. L. Kugel, *The Idea of Biblical Poetry* (New Haven: Yale University Press, 1981), 119–21; but cf. E. Tov, "Special Layout of Poetical Units in the Texts from the Judean Desert," in *Give Ear to My Words: Psalms and Other Poetry in and around the Hebrew Bible: Essays in Honour of Professor N. A. van Uchelen* (ed. W. Dijk; Amsterdam: Kamp Societas Hebraica, 1996), 115–28.

[25] See n. 23.

[26] I have discussed these issues in my monograph on Obadiah, and at length in my FOTL commentary on Micah. It will suffice here to mention that the social setting in which these

Unless one assumes that these literati were full-time writers and readers of prophetic literature, an unavoidable historical question emerges: What professional duties were they likely to have had in addition to writing, editing, reading—mainly rereading—and teaching prophetic (or any other) literature that claims to convey YHWH's word? Were they mainly bureaucrats who served the administration of the Achaemenid province of Yehud and the Jerusalemite temple? Did their employment (or lack thereof) vary according to the resources and policies of the temple (and/or the administration)? Did some of them work at least in part for the "private sector," for instance, as teachers or tutors for children of wealthy families, whether individually or at a "school"? Surely the social location, activities, and sources of support and employment (or potentially, lack thereof) of the authors and primary readers of the prophetic books are systemic issues of great relevance for the historical study of the composition and role of these books and of the society from which they emerged.[27]

Turning to the larger societal picture, at any particular point in time the only group in Yehud that had direct access to the prophetic books consisted of a few literati. They therefore turned into absolutely necessary brokers of the knowledge of this divine word who alone could disseminate the teaching associated with it for those who could not and were not required to read the texts for themselves, that is, almost the entire population of Yehud.[28] Since the development and maintenance of these groups of literati required social resources, and since these groups did exist, as the literature they created plainly shows, one has to assume that their role as brokers was, at least to some extent, partially accepted. These observations, in turn, raise further matters concerning the social history of postmonarchic Israel (mainly Achaemenid Yehud) and the role of the prophetic literature among its different strata.

Moreover, the considerations advanced above raise issues concerning the general social structures required to channel resources for the textual activities already mentioned, and the systemic reasons for the social allocation of

---

books—as a whole—were produced is characterized by an authorship and readership able to produce, read, and reread these written texts, that is, by bearers of high literacy who were very few in relative and absolute numbers.

[27] See Ben Zvi, "Urban Center." On unemployed or underpaid scholars at the height of the Neo-Assyrian empire, see S. Parpola, "The Forlorn Scholar," in *Language, Literature and History: Philological and Historical Studies Presented to Erica Reiner* (ed. F. Rochberg-Halton; AOS 67; New Haven, Conn.: American Oriental Society, 1987), 257–78.

[28] Nehemiah 8; cf. Deut 31:11; Josh 8:34; 2 Kgs 23:2; 2 Chr 17:7–9; 34:30. It is unlikely that the prophetic books will be completely "esoteric" as opposed to a torah to be taught (through the intermediation of the literati) to all. See Sirach, Prologue, vv. 1–2.

resources to these purposes.[29] Further, one may focus on particular social structures, such as the location and ownership of "libraries,"[30] the determination of who gets to be a bearer of high literacy, the authorities who

---

[29] I have made a few observations on these issues in Ben Zvi, "Urban Center."

[30] There is ample evidence for the use of written sources in the composition and redaction of biblical books and, needless to say, any redaction of a biblical book implies a written source (see Esther and Jeremiah, to mention two obvious cases). Examples of the use of written sources in the ancient Near East are abundant too (e.g., Gilgamesh, royal inscriptions, Assyrian and Babylonian Chronicles). On these matters see J. Tigay, ed., *Empirical Models for Biblical Criticism* (Philadelphia: University of Pennsylvania Press, 1985). For our purpose here, it is worth stressing that the use of written texts during the composition and redaction of prophetic and other biblical books implies the existence of (personal or institutional) libraries.

It is highly likely that the first and the second temples had libraries. It is reasonable to assume that the library of the first temple perished at the time of the destruction of Jerusalem, but what about private libraries? Did they disappear too? As for the early second temple, was its temple library the only one in Jerusalem? If there were others, how extensive were their holdings of "religious" literary texts? If written sources were used for the composition of the prophetic books in their present form—as many, including myself, maintain—then these questions are most relevant to the understanding of the process of composition. Moreover, they may point to some systemic features that exerted some control over the process itself, such as the possible use of one main library sponsored and controlled by the temple.

Another issue concerns the possibility of retrieval, which is an essential feature of libraries and archives. Which documents were filed, and how? Were some types of documents more likely to be kept than others? Or were some filed better (i.e., were they more easily retrieved) than others? Such questions have a substantial bearing on proposals regarding the transmission of prophetic oracles and their possible role in the eventual development of the prophetic books, as well as implications for any type of writing on the basis of written sources. Cases of this sort are addressed in several of the contributions to this volume, and their study will remain a most important component of future research in this area. (To be sure, the messy type of document retrieval shown in J. M. Sasson, "Some Comments on Archive Keeping at Mari," *Iraq* 34 [1972]: 55–57, is neither meant to further, nor is it conducive to, any long-term literary activity. Other systems of archiving were most likely at work in ancient Israel.)

On libraries in the ancient Near East see, e.g., O. Pedersen, *Archives and Libraries in the Ancient Near East 1500–300 B.C.* (Bethesda, Md.: CDL, 1998); J. A. Black and W. J. Tait, "Archives and Libraries in the Ancient Near East," *CANE*, 2197–201; for Egypt, see Redord's chapter in this volume. On the issue of libraries in Israel, see P. R. Davies, *Scribes and Schools: The Canonization of the Hebrew Scriptures* (LAI; Louisville, Ky.: Westminster John Knox, 1998), and Niditch, *Oral World*, 63–69.

It is worth mentioning that Niditch objects to the process of composition on the basis of written sources. She raises the issue of a problematic "logistics of literacy" (see esp. pp. 113–14). She admits, however, that Chronicles is based on written sources (p. 127). Since there was no technological change that allowed the author/s of Chronicles (or later authors for that matter) to work with scrolls or papyri in ways that were either impossible or impractical in previous generations (e.g., those responsible for the Pentateuchal texts), the argument based on the "logistics of literacy" falls apart.

make this determination,[31] and the definition of the curriculum (including the rules by which certain materials are included or excluded, possible influences on the formation of a repertoire of authoritative texts, and the sense of social cohesion that is created by such a shared curriculum).[32] In addition, one may ask what was the actual place where literati wrote, read, reread, and studied books, prophetic and otherwise.[33] To be sure, these issues must be explored to advance our knowledge of the historical and social processes that led to and were associated with the composition and reception of the prophetic books. Comparative evidence from other places in the ancient Near East is of great importance for this task.

We may further observe that the written text, as it was composed, redacted, studied, stored, read, and reread by the literati of the period was—from their point of view at least—"a word of YHWH." As such, its material presence, in the form of the text to which they had direct access, was likely to communicate symbolically and metaphorically a sense of the divine presence among them. The world of the text reflected and shaped a social memory of YHWH's interaction with Israel in the past; the actual presence of the material text and their dealings with it constructed an image of YHWH's interaction with Israel as it was conducted in their times, from their own perspective.

---

[31] If there is a clear connection between high literacy and priesthood, then a hereditary element is to be taken into account. But were all priests highly literate? Conversely, were all the literati priests? Could, for instance, the son of a wealthy merchant who can afford the cost of training become a writer, reader, and teacher of divine knowledge (cf. *ABL* 1245)? For discussion of the issue of who could study toward full literacy in ancient Egypt, see the chapter by Redford in this volume.

[32] On teaching and the teaching curriculum in Greco-Roman Egypt, see Cribiore, *Writing, Teachers, and Students.* On education in ancient Egypt, see R. J. Williams, "Scribal Training in Ancient Egypt," *JAOS* 92 (1972): 214–21; C. J. Eyre and J. Baines, "Interactions between Orality and Literacy in Ancient Egypt," in *Literacy and Society* (ed. K. Shousboe and M. T. Larsen; Copenhagen: Akademisk Forlag, 1989), 94–97. See also H. L. J. Vanstiphout, "Memory and Literacy in Ancient Western Asia," *CANE*, 2181–96, esp. 2189–90. It is perhaps interesting to mention that some basic learning of writing seems to have preceded that of reading, that copying was a significant instructional activity, and—more important for the present discussion—that "classical" texts were part of the curriculum in ancient Egypt, Greco-Roman Egypt, and Mesopotamia. Did this complex of scribal skills involve the ability to go back and "re-scan" the text? Did copying from tablets and papyrus always involve reading aloud (as opposed to silent reading)? These questions raise significant cognitive issues.

[33] There is no need to assume that the "library" was such a place. Cf. Black and Tait, "Archives and Libraries," 2200.

The materiality of the written text was also often associated with its being "a witness forever"[34] and with textual stability, even if it was copied again and again.[35] Moreover, the well-attested belief—or metaphor—of heavenly, written records of life is consistent with a communally accepted association between written records and textual stability,[36] even if YHWH is conceived as able to make changes in those records.[37] The discursive association of textual stability with writtenness most likely contributed to the legitimacy and authority of the written texts held by the literati, supported the claims of these texts to reflect YHWH's interactions with Israel in the past, and as such helped to create a memory of that Israel. In sum, within this discourse, written texts were a *material* symbol of YHWH's word and teachings, as well as a source of communal memory, and thus their transmission from generation to generation had to be ensured.[38] It is worth stressing, however, that the literati who shared this discourse, copying, storing, retrieving, reading, and rereading these written texts, were the same literati who also redacted, edited, and even composed them.[39] Thus the written character of the prophetic books (among other books of the time) led to both actual textual fluidity and discursive as well as symbolic

---

[34] See Isa 30:8; cf. Isa 8:16; Hab 2:2–3.

[35] Within its discourse, the command in Deut 17:18 implies that each king shall have the same text of (divine) teaching written for him. Here, the copying of a written text is conceived as a process that preserves the already existing written text from generation to generation.

[36] See Exod 32:32; Isa 4:3; Mal 3:16–17; Pss 69:29; 139:16; Dan 12:1.

[37] See Exod 32:32.

[38] By means of this process, the written text becomes a symbol of everlasting permanence (see above). One may note that if texts written to survive for generations were considered to provide some form of immortality to the writers (cf. P. Chester Beatty IV verso 2.5–3.11; M. Lichtheim, *Ancient Egyptian Literature* [2 vols.; Berkeley: University of California Press, 1975–76], 2:175–78), then the written document carrying YHWH's words and teaching at one level associates "immortality" (i.e., full permanence) not only with YHWH but also with these particular instances of YHWH's word and teaching. Moreover, at another level, the actual writer may be seen as one who attained some form of immortality by means of this process, but it should be stressed that this demands his (and less likely her) full identification with the implied author of the text, as well as the partial blurring of the latter's voice with the prophetic (human) and divine voices that resonate within the literary text. In other words, the writer becomes "immortal," as it were, because his (written) words are YHWH's word (i.e., a prophetic book).

[39] From a historical perspective it is most unlikely that these literati (or even a substantial minority of them) were hypocritical in their own eyes. A study of the tension raised here must follow a different path.

permanence.[40] It is possible that the tension between the two was solved by an approach of "writing in the spirit of someone," which may have helped writers to identify themselves as "animators" of the implied authors of the books. If they pragmatically assimilated the implied author with any of a book's main characters, as is probable, they would then see themselves as animators of these characters, and closely identify themselves with prophetic voices from the past, and to some extent even identify themselves with YHWH.[41] In such a scenario, the process of composing, redacting, and editing prophetic books, along with the use of written sources for these purposes, would have had much to do with the literati's self identification as animators of the prophets and YHWH, or in other words, with a quasi-prophetic status.[42] In turn, their quasi-prophetic status introduces into the logic of the discourse a demand for the type of permanency associated with "written documents" because of their quasi-prophetic words. Further, the process does not stop at the level of either composition or redaction. When reading, or reading to someone, the literati voice the "I" of the text, which is more often than not a godly "I," either human or divine. By doing so, they identify with that "I." Moreover, there is a performative aspect to this activity: YHWH and the prophets of old become present—as it were—as the literati utter their words, which are—at a different level—also the words that they (that is, the literati) wrote, edited, and copied.

---

[40] To be sure, on the surface both the authoritative character of the text and indirect admonitions not to add or erase material from a written text (c.g., Deut 4:2; 12:32; Jer 26:2; Prov 30:6; and see Qoh 3:14) may be interpreted as an effort by some bearers of high literacy to convince other, similar literati—who were the only people capable of doing so—to keep texts as they are, that is, to curtail the process of textual fluidity. One might be tempted to explain the issue of textual fluidity versus textual permanence in terms of an internal power conflict among the literati themselves. This may be true to a point, but a full picture of the process that led to the biblical books as we have them cannot be developed in this manner, because this type of explanation cannot explain why full textual stability was to be developed much later than the time of the composers (and first editors) of the texts, nor is "immutability of text" a required component of "symbolic permanence." A different explanation based on other premises is needed (see below).

[41] Cf. N. G. Cohen, "From *Nabi* to *Mal'ak* to 'Ancient Figure,'" *JSS* 36 (1985): 12–24.

[42] This is probably about as close as literati could actually come to being "prophets" because the authority of contemporary prophets will hardly have been accepted by those for whom authority is based on the words and teachings communicated to great individuals of the past, who also serve as "guardians" of such words and teachings (see below). For example, consider the rejection of Montanus, Maximilla, and Priscilla by the "established" church, even though they did not necessarily express "false" doctrine. On the partial shaping of the character of a prophet in the likeness of the author of a prophetic book, see E. Ben Zvi, *A Historical-Critical Study of the Book of Zephaniah* (BZAW 198; Berlin: de Gruyter, 1998), 352–56.

The postmonarchic scribes, who were responsible for the prophetic books in their present form, were careful to characterize the language of prophetic characters set in the monarchic period (with the exception of Jonah)[43] in a distinctive manner. In these books, prophets speak a language that is most likely not identical to the language common in the province of Yehud in the Achaemenid period (cf. the language of Isaiah 1–66 as a whole and that of Jonah or Chronicles; cf. "classical" with "late" biblical Hebrew and consider the use of Aramaic in Yehud).[44] If this is so, interesting matters of language (including lexical choices) and linguistic ideology emerge. The authors or redactors of these books are careful to communicate through linguistic differentiation that the words of YHWH associated with prophets from the late monarchic period did indeed sound different from everyday speech.[45] This feature allows a text, composed or redacted in the not-so-distant past, to convey a sense of distance from the present day, and also a sense of authority that comes from the ancient past. These observations are consistent with the tendency of religious language, particularly that of established communities with a strong sense of their shared past, as well as the language of "classical" texts, to be different from commonly spoken language. This language distinction serves social needs.[46] Although it may be, and often is, conveyed within oral discourse, it is clearly marked in the written discourse of the literati from the Achaemenid period. Moreover, it is worth noting—since even reconstructed oral speech embedded in written texts is different from that present in actual oral communication[47]—that the written character of the text already creates a "language gap" between the literary text and common communication in a predominantly oral society.

It might be suggested that most of the previous discussion is an exercise in circular thinking. That is, one reconstructs elements of the social history of

---

[43] I have discussed the case of Jonah in my paper "Atypical Features, the Meta-prophetic Character of the Book of Jonah and Other Communicative Messages," presented at the 1999 meeting of the Pacific Northwest Society of Biblical Literature held in Tacoma, Washington.

[44] In any event, written language is not identical to oral language, and even reported speech in a literary work is different from actual speech.

[45] Against this background of linguistic differentiation, it is worth mentioning that divine speech and human prophetic speech often tend to merge in these prophetic books. (On this point, see Ben Zvi, *Micah*, passim.)

[46] For a survey of recent scholarship on religious language in general, see W. Keane, "Religious Language," *Annual Review of Anthropology* 26 (1997): 47–71.

[47] See, for instance, D. Tannin, "Introducing Constructed Dialogue in Greek and American Conversational and Literary Narrative," in *Direct and Indirect Speech* (ed. F. Coulombs; Trends in Linguistics: Studies and Monographs, 31; Berlin : de Gruyter, 1986), 311–32.

postmonarchic, and most likely Achaemenid, Yehud on the basis one's understanding of the prophetic books as texts to be read, reread, copied, stored, and the like; and then one uses these reconstructed features for the interpretation of the text. Such an argument would be a serious objection if there were nothing beyond inner coherence to sustain the previous discussion, that is, if there were no claims that could be proven without reference to the other claims advanced in the discussion. But this is not the case. The inescapable fact is that there were written texts of the prophetic books and their existence demands that there were literati able not only to read them and mediate them to the nonliterate majority, but also to compose, edit, copy, and archive them. The existence of these literati required an investment of social resources, and such an investment would only be made for particular reasons by those who channeled or controlled those resources.

Oral/Aural Communication

Oral communication reigned in the society in which the literati lived. This being the case, if they were to serve as brokers of divine knowledge to the vast majority of the population, the literati must have read to the general population and interpreted for them pieces of prophetic literature.[48] If this is so, then the written character of the prophetic books implies not only reading, rereading, and study—as well as composition, editing, copying, and the like—among the literati, but also their oral presentation of the divine message and an audience's aural reception of it. In other words, a written text becomes the starting point for oral communication.[49] Needless to say, the communicative event here involves not only the written text or a portion thereof, but also how it is read or proclaimed and the interaction between audience and speaker. Under these social conditions, it is reasonable to assume that an authoritative written text becomes the starting point for the oral performances of the literati and for the

---

[48] See the examples of reading and interpreting the Torah given above. Jeremiah 36 provides, of course, a classical example of reading from a scroll, that is, of oral communication based on a written text.

[49] Cf. Deut 31:19, 22. On the issue of written texts as sources for oral performances, see E. W. Conrad, "Heard But Not Seen: The Representation of 'Books' in the Old Testament," *JSOT* 54 (1992): 45–59, esp. 47. To be sure, similar considerations are relevant to the study of the consumption or reception of written literature outside the group of literati in the ancient Near East in general. See Vanstiphout, "Some Remarks," and Redford's chapter in this volume.

aurality of an audience.[50] But which audience or audiences? Are we to assume that everyone was informed of the (interpreted) contents of the prophetic books? Or only some? Or perhaps many, but at different levels?

Furthermore, since messages conveyed in oral presentations depend to a great degree on the interaction between presenter and audience, one may ask what emphases were conveyed when the context or text of a prophetic book, or portions thereof, were communicated orally to and interpreted for the audience. And when were these emphases communicated? No doubt one may assume that they probably changed from time to time, according to the occasion and setting-in-life of the reading. Moreover, it is improbable that all the literati were communicating YHWH's word in exactly the same manner. Besides differences in style and content due to either personality or occasion, one has to take into account the issue of the individual skill of the reader/interpreter. Further, given the importance of clear (i.e., persuasive) speech for the communication of the divine message, it is probable and even likely that the literati were also trained for skillful speech. If so, how, where, and by whom were they trained to be good communicators/orators/readers?[51] All things considered, it seems likely that these scribal brokers of YHWH's word communicated to society as a whole a set of related oral "texts," each informing the others, within the general discourse of the period. Any history of the social reception of prophetic texts in the ancient societies in which they were written must deal with these matters.[52]

---

[50] It is worth stressing that whereas one may read a text to oneself aloud or silently (or in an inaudible manner), a text can only be read aloud to those who cannot read for themselves. If one assumes that written biblical literature was communicated beyond the narrow circle of the literati themselves, then the written text must have engendered a performance. On the possibility of silent reading, see below.

[51] See Redford's discussion of comparable matters in his contribution to this volume, and note the previous reference to the Prologue in Sirach (n. 43).

[52] As an aside, and with all the obvious reservations, one may heuristically compare the picture described here with that of our present society in the United States and Canada—and I assume in other geographical areas too. To be sure, our North American society is one of the most literate in the world. Still, today more people hear the Bible than read it, every week. Many hear the Bible read in religious services, in religious schools, in Bible groups, and in religious mass media (TV or radio). Of course, they never hear the entire Bible, but only some texts from it, selected either by the communicator (pastor, rabbi, preacher, priest, evangelist, lay leader, etc.) or by tradition. In all cases, the text communicated is never, and can never be, the bare written words. The text is shaped and interpreted by the communicator, already by intonation of voice, but more often than not by explicit interpretation rhetorically presented as being fully consistent with the text. Since there is clearly no unanimity among the biblical communicators, the social result of this process is a multitude of coexisting "living Bibles" informing each other within the larger matrix of the whole society and, to some extent, competing with each other. In any event, this case shows

This history must also take up the question of the settings in which people who were not fully literate had texts read to them. If one thinks in terms of readings of authoritative religious literature to a large audience, then such occasions were probably characterized by some form of ritual, and organized or promoted by a center of authority in society.[53] The same may hold true even for readings to smaller groups. In any case, the setting of the reading itself, or of the communication of authoritative religious texts by means of speech in ways other than reading, creates expectations and a horizon of pertinence that is certainly relevant to the communicative process that is taking place.

Prophetic Literature and Social Formation

Various features associated with the written character of the prophetic books are comparable to features of the oral/aural performance of prophetic texts noted above. One of the most salient characteristics of the prophetic books is the frequent presence of multivalent words and expressions, generating additional and often multiple connotations, as well as puns and networks of intertextual associations informing one another. These features are expected and coherent in books that are to be read, reread, and studied generation after generation (cf. Josh 1:8; Hos 14:10; Sir 38:24–39:3).[54] These features create a net of partial (re)readings of the text, informing and balancing each other. The different ways in which a particular unit within a prophetic book may be communicated orally—depending on the audience, the identity of the communicator, the social setting, and the particular occasion—are likely to inculcate in the memory of the wider community a network of received texts informing each other. Significantly, all these readings are bound together practically and symbolically to a written text that serves as an anchor of stability and thus as a marker of social and discursive cohesion.

When a social group shares a particular collection of written works, the group memory shaped by these texts through the very act of reading and

---

how a book accepted by a society as authoritative, although it is clearly something written, can begin a process of oral transmission; and it also shows that the reading, rereading, and studying of the text by contemporaneous literati—of different kinds—does not preclude oral communication, but rather leads to it. Oral communication exists at all levels and in many different groups in our society. Those less proficient in reading skills are still the majority. (See the relevant statistical material provided by the National Center for Educational Statistics in *Condition of Education, 1999*, publication number: NCES 1999022; also available at http://necs.ed.gov/pubsearch/pubsinfo.asp?public = 1999022.)

53 Cf. 2 Kgs 23:1–3; Nehemiah 8; 2 Chr 17:7–9.

54 On these matters I have written extensively elsewhere. See Ben Zvi, *Historical-Critical Study of the Book of Obadiah*, passim; and idem, *Micah*, passim.

rereading them creates a sense of identity and continuity with the past; and the same holds true for the group's recollection of text-based speeches they have heard. If the material presence of such books conveys a sense of the presence of divine teaching, and even the presence of the divine itself, among the literati, then it is reasonable to assume that the public reading of portions of the text could have had comparable effects.

In addition, just as written texts can be taken out of their "original" context and brought into a new literary context, the same can be done orally through interpretation. In fact, high literacy and the expectation of continuous rereading led to the composition of written texts that not only furthered but also depended on the ability of readers and rereaders to "extract" literary elements out of their circumstances in the world of the text (e.g., prophetic or divine speeches associated with events in the monarchic period as construed by the text)[55] and "appropriate" them. This process of recontextualization was necessary to allow the rereaders to identify with the (literary) Israel present in the text and to feel as if they themselves were addressed by speakers within the world of the text. Significantly, a comparable but not identical process of recontextualization took place in oral retelling or ritual reading of a prophetic text or portions thereof, or, for that matter, in any oral telling of words and actions attributed to a prophet from the (monarchic) past in any social setting.

From the viewpoint of the postmonarchic communities within which and for which prophetic books, at least in their present form, were written, there is an additional consideration. The prophetic books as a whole provided hope by pointing to an ideal future promised by YHWH. This was one of the most important communicative messages of these texts (cf. Sir 49:10). These books tended to include fulfilled prophecies (usually of doom) as well as unfulfilled prophecies of a great future for the community with which the intended readers (and hearers; see below) identified themselves. Among other things, this combination served a clear rhetorical purpose, reassuring readers (and hearers) that just as the prophecies of doom were fulfilled in the past, so the still unrealized prophecies of salvation will also be fulfilled in the future.[56] This message of hope was meant for *both* the few who were fully literate and the many who were not. Further, there is no reason to assume that the persuasive power of the logic implied in the combination of fulfilled and unfulfilled prophecy was diminished by either the literati's reading for themselves or their

---

[55] On the important distinction between prophets and prophetic characters in literary texts, see the concluding section of this introduction.

[56] I have written about these issues elsewhere. See Ben Zvi, *Historical-Critical Study of the Book of Zephaniah,* 149, 298–306, 351; *Historical-Critical Study of the Book of Obadiah,* 172.

reading to the ones who could not read.[57] This is a clear example of the way in which different patterns of communication likely conveyed a similar and most prominent message to the community/ies. It is most significant that this message is precisely the thing that clearly sets apart the prophetic books—whether read, reread, and studied among the literati themselves or treated as textual material to be communicated and interpreted to social groups other than the literati—from both the oral oracles generally typical of the ancient Near East and the Assyrian written collections of oracles.[58]

In sum, in spite of the different social mechanisms and the involvement of audiences other than the primary, highly literate readership of the prophetic books in the oral scenarios mentioned above, some of the features that characterize one of the communicative processes are certainly comparable to those that characterize the other. In principle, these similarities should not be surprising, because all these processes may be seen as subsystems of communication and theological, ideological, and social formation within the larger social system of Yehud in the Achaemenid period. It is obvious, however, that further studies in this area will clarify these matters and substantially contribute to our understanding of the interrelation between the processes involved in written and oral communication of prophetic texts in antiquity, particularly those that occurred simultaneously in a single society.[59]

---

[57] One may notice that, to large extent, this basic persuasive pattern is found also in the so-called Akkadian Prophecies. See A. K. Grayson and W. G. Lambert, "Akkadian Prophecies," *JCS* 18 (1964): 7–30, esp. 10a; cf. W. W. Hallo, "Akkadian Apocalypses," *IEJ* 16 (1966): 231–42. Much of Hallo's discussion about the uniqueness of the biblical prophets reflects some of his basic assumptions and need not be discussed here. I would only underline his comments (as well as those of Grayson and Lambert) about the employment of the topos of the fulfilled prophecy in the service of legitimizing a still unfulfilled prophecy, which seems to lead from prophecy into apocalyptic; see H. Ringgren, "Akkadian Apocalypses," in *Apocalypticism in the Mediterranean World and the Near East: Proceedings of the International Colloquium on Apocalypticism, Uppsala, Aug. 12–17, 1979* (ed. D. Hellholm; Tübingen: Mohr, 1983), 379–86. Apocalyptic is precisely the type of discourse that seems to have replaced that of prophetic book, for the former can be seen as characteristic of Achaemenid Yehud and the latter of Ptolemaic, Seleucid, and Roman Judah. This issue and the heuristic role of partial comparisons between prophetic books and Akkadian Prophecies (as well as Egyptian "prophecies" [see below]) is another topic that requires further study and may affect the way in which one understands the production and reception of prophetic books, as well as the end of these social practices.

[58] On the latter see S. Parpola, *Assyrian Prophecies* (SAA 9; Helsinki: Helsinki University Press, 1997).

[59] To be sure, there are also important differences between the two processes. For one thing, those who read for themselves may go back to the text, rescan it, as it were, and ponder textual polyvalences. They may jump from place to place in the text, and also perceive larger

The Symbiosis of Literacy and Orality

It is naïve to think that orality and aurality are relevant only for understanding the process of communicating YHWH's (written) word to those who could not read. If the literati themselves were immersed in an oral and aural world, it is certainly reasonable to suppose that they were strongly influenced by it in their lives and in their writing. Oral patterns of speech and discourse could have influenced their writing, and most likely did so, in ways known or unknown to them.[60] Significantly, this holds true whether or not the literati read their written sources silently as they composed their works. To be sure, it is often believed that ancient literati only read aloud, but this claim is to

---

structures of textual coherence spanning the book as a whole (e.g., the book of Isaiah, the book of Jeremiah) and the like, in addition to reading the text in a manner informed by their world of knowledge. When the process is based on aurality, then the audience does not have access to the whole text. They can only address the oral text advanced by the communicator and interpret it in terms of their world of knowledge, which may of course include the memory of other readings of the text. Further, the oral/aural communication of YHWH's word most likely involved an element of "composition-in-performance" that was probably not present in the composition of the prophetic books in their present form.

[60] It has to be stressed that the validity of this statement does not depend on controversial claims about an "oral mind-set" or an "oral mentality"—cf. and contrast with R. F. Person Jr., "The Ancient Israelite Scribe as Performer," *JBL* 117 (1998): 601–9; S. Niditch, *Oral World*, esp. 108–9. It does not require us to assume that the composition of a prophetic book took place orally, and certainly not to imagine that there were no written version(s) of the text of prophetic books, but rather in-performance representations of the text. This statement simply expresses the obvious, viz., that people, including the literati, were children of their own times and were influenced by their social and cultural circumstances. For the rejection of the concept of "oral mentality" and the like, see Finnegan, "What is Orality?" esp. 141.

The term "oral residue" (W. J. Ong, S.J., *Rhetoric, Romance and Technology: Studies in the Interaction of Expression and Culture* [Ithaca, N.Y.: Cornell University Press, 1971], 23–48; A. B. Lord, "Oral Composition and 'Oral Residue' in the Middle Ages," in *Oral Tradition in the Middle Ages* [ed. W. F. H. Nicolaisen; Medieval & Renaissance Texts and Studies 112; Binghamton, N.Y.: Center for Medieval and Early Renaissance Studies, State University of New York at Binghamton], 7–29) is probably not appropriate to describe this phenomenon because the term "residue" implies a diachronic development toward an increasingly written medium, even if oral residue is aimed at habits of thought related to the prevalence of the oral medium of communication in a particular culture (Ong, *Rhetoric, Romance and Technology*, 25–26; cf. Lord, "Oral Composition," 7). The society of the writers of the prophetic books (and for that matter, all but the very first Mesopotamian and Egyptian writers too) did not live in a society that saw the introduction or substantial and consistent furthering of literacy, particularly high literacy. The systemic factors contributing to both the existence and the very low percentage of high literacy remained basically stable for millennia in the ancient Near East.

be rejected.[61] Although undoubtedly less common than reading aloud, as expected in an overwhelmingly oral society, silent or inaudible reading was most likely not an unknown practice, and it could have played a role in, or somehow facilitated, written composition on the basis of written sources.[62] In any case, written texts in a society in which communication is primarily oral, whether read aloud or not, tend to show some aural (and oral) features. For instance, under these conditions they may exhibit a tendency towards sound repetition and word repetition, a feature that appears in both oral and written texts.[63] Moreover, even silent reading may evoke "sounds" in the mind of the reader, so that silent reading becomes essentially inaudible but still mentally vocalized reading.[64]

We may also ask, if the prophetic books known to us underwent processes of redaction, could the oral interpretations of the literati not have affected some of these books by eventually finding places in the texts themselves? Further,

---

[61] See B. M. W. Knox, "Silent Reading in Antiquity," *Greek, Roman and Byzantine Studies* 9 (1968): 421–35; F. D. Gilliard, "More Silent Reading in Antiquity: *Non Omne Verbum Sonabat*," *JBL* 112 (1993): 689–94; J. Svenbro, *Phrasikleia: An Anthropology of Reading in Ancient Greece* (trans. J. Lloyd; Ithaca, N.Y.: Cornell University Press, 1993), 163–68 and passim; Cribiore, *Writing, Teachers, and Students,* 150; cf. M. Slusser, "Reading Silently in Antiquity," *JBL* 111 (1992): 499. To be sure, these works refer to the situation in the Greek/Hellenistic world, but the evidence they present is strongly suggestive, all the more so because *scriptio continua,* which is a serious obstacle to reading in general and to silent reading in particular (see Cribiore, *Writing, Teachers, and Students,* 9, 47–48, 148–49; Svenbro, *Phrasikleia,* 166–67), was most likely not a problem for the readers and rereaders of biblical books (see E. Tov, *Textual Criticism of the Hebrew Bible* [Minneapolis: Augsburg, 1992], 208–9, and bibliography). In any event, it is worth mentioning that the assumption that the ancient literati read only aloud is based mainly on a particular interpretation of the evidence from the classical period and late antiquity.
    To be sure, reading and singing aloud in ancient Egypt were very common educational practices in the training of new scribes (Williams, "Scribal Training"; Lichtheim, *Ancient Egyptian Literature,* 2:168–78). Yet this practice does necessarily imply that scribes, particularly highly literate scribes, could only read aloud and did so under any and all circumstances, in contrast with the way in which writing and reading are mostly taught today. Incidentally, in one text students are asked to do their calculations silently. Silent reading most likely existed in Egypt (see Eyre and Baines, "Interactions," 102).

[62] Knox, "Silent Reading," 421–22; Svenbro, *Phrasikleia,* 167–68.

[63] For reasons mentioned in n. 60, I think it is misleading to refer to these features as "oral residue" or the like.

[64] Needless to say, this is the case if texts were composed in written form but "published" both in writing and by reading them aloud. See H. L. J. Vanstiphout, "Repetition and Structure in The Aratta Cycle: Their Relevance for the Orality Debate," in *Mesopotamian Epic Literature* [ed. M. E. Vogelzang and H. L. J. Vanstiphout; Lewiston, N.Y.: Mellen, 1992], 247–64, esp. 263–64.

even if direct access to the written text was the exclusive realm of those who could read it for themselves, once oral interpretations were given, they may have developed a life of their own, turning into "traditions" that through different channels may have influenced the composition or redaction of written literary works.[65] The same holds true even for ever-changing "traditions" about heroes of the past, particularly if they are (or are made) popular within the community at large. The question of how to identify such instances, or whether identifying them is possible at all, deserves more research.

To be sure, none of these considerations leads to the conclusion that the prophetic books are not the product of the high literacy of the literati themselves. Rather, they show that literacy in general, and the work and world of the literati, should be considered as integral parts of a larger social system. In the context of that integrated system, prophetic books were not only composed, read, reread, studied, and interpreted to others, but they were also produced and maintained with direct or indirect social support and investment.

It is worth noting that the present discussion clearly leads to an image of "restricted, high literacy" and "general orality" as two deeply interwoven social phenomena. Within the proposed historical matrix, one does not and cannot take over and replace the other; rather, they complement (and sustain) each other. Moreover, literacy here does not lead to the development of (objective) history as opposed to (communal) myth, nor necessarily to detachment, distance, or analytic thinking. This being so, one may ask how the already mentioned traits of ancient Israelite literacy relate to other features of literacy in other cultures, and what the identification of these traits can contribute to current studies of literacy/ies.[66]

All in all, if the considerations advanced in this section hold, then the study of the written and oral aspects associated with the prophetic books is deeply connected to the study of the social system within which prophetic literature was not only written, read, reread, and studied by the literati but also

---

[65] Comparable processes may have influenced the production of the Targums, which are written texts too. In any event, translations have always been influenced by the interpretation of biblical texts. The phenomenon of "converse translations" is perhaps the most telling example. On the latter, see R. P. Gordon, "'Converse Translation' in the Targums and Beyond," *JSP* 19 (1999): 3–21 and the bibliography; also A. Shinan, תרגום ואגדה בו (Jerusalem: Magnes, 1992), esp. 164–67, 190–91. There is no reason to assume that this type of process, that is, from oral interpretation to written text, could not have influenced, directly or indirectly, the editing of prophetic books, or, if they are based on written sources, the manner in which these sources were interpreted and appropriated.

[66] For a survey of these matters, see J. Collins, "Literacy and Literacies," *Annual Review of Anthropology* 24 (1995): 75–93. See also the sharp remarks on the danger of mistaken generalizations in Finnegan, "What is Orality?" 144–45.

communicated and taught to the nonliterati who comprised almost the entire population. This perspective also offers a window through which light may be shed on the nonoppositional relation between literacy/ies and "orality" in the ancient Near East.

Literary and Oral Prophets:
An Additional Set of Issues and Questions

Questions about orality and writtenness stand at the center of another set of issues. It is obvious that, on the one hand, there were prophetic books in Israel, at least in the Achaemenid period; and surely there are prophetic characters in the prophetic books (e.g., Isaiah, Jeremiah, Amos). On the other hand, there were also prophets in monarchic and postmonarchic Israel/Judah who are comparable, for instance, to those in Mari and Assyria.[67] These prophets primarily communicated their word orally. This two-foci situation has led to a plethora of research issues.

Of course, some scholars have focused mainly on the postmonarchic prophetic books as such (i.e., as "textuality" whose purpose is to advance and reaffirm some particular theological, social, and moral tenets, as well as to shape a certain group identity), and others have focused on the historical figures of monarchic prophets. Whereas some scholars stress the difference between these two foci and warn that they should be kept apart in historical-critical studies, many others sense that the two are not too distant—for instance, that the prophetic books are at least in part some form of "transcribed orality" or that the world described in the literary text resembles in the main the actual historical world of the monarchic prophets.[68] Yet it seems that all scholars working in the area of prophetic literature and its historical contexts struggle with and—at least for heuristic purposes—implicitly or explicitly take a stand on such matters.

---

[67] Significantly, the Neo-Assyrian prophets are more or less contemporary with the late monarchic period, the time in which most of the prophetic characters mentioned in the prophetic books are set. For Neo-Assyrian prophecy, see Parpola, *Assyrian Prophecies,* and M. Nissinen, *References to Prophecy in Neo-Assyrian Sources* (SAAS 7; Helsinki: Neo-Assyrian Text Corpus Project, 1998). The bibliography on prophecy at Mari is extensive. See the chapters by van der Toorn and Nissinen in this volume, and among recent works see also J. M. Sasson, "The Posting of Letters with Divine Messages," in *Florilegium marianum II: Recueil d'études à la mémoire de Maurice Birot* (MNABU 3; ed. D. Charpin and J.-M. Durand; Paris: Société pour l'étude du Proche-Orient ancien, 1994), 299–316.

[68] For the distinction between textuality and transcribed orality and its possible implications, see B. W. Henaut, *Oral Tradition and the Gospels: The Problem of Mark 4* (JSNTSup 82; Sheffield: Sheffield Academic Press, 1993), 115–18.

It would be fair to say that issues arising from this two-foci situation have been, explicitly or implicitly, at the forefront of the study of prophecy and prophetic literature, and that in somewhat different forms they are likely to remain so for the foreseeable future. Within the frame of an introduction to this volume of collected essays, it suffices to point out some prominent research questions that relate to this two-foci situation.

(1) Which attributes are prophets of the monarchic period likely to share, and which not, with the prophetic characters created in the prophetic books and set in the monarchic period? What characterizes a (literary/theological) "prophet" in the prophetic books, and what characterizes a (living and oral) "prophet" in the historical context of the ancient Near East and ancient Israel? What are the similarities and differences between the oral prophets and the quasi-prophets represented by the literati who composed, redactéd, read, reread, studied, and transmitted the prophetic books[69] that were eventually included in the Hebrew Bible? To mention an obvious difference, oral prophets did not have to be literate at all, but the quasi-prophets had to be highly literate.[70] The main social role of the ancient Near Eastern prophet was not to write books, but to proclaim oracles; but the writing of books is just what characterizes the quasi-prophets. Yet there are also similarities between the two, as the term quasi-prophets already implies. Related to the immediately foregoing set of issues, did the quasi-prophets begin to shape their portrayal of past prophets, either entirely or partly, in their own image?[71] If so, do we then have a process, or at least the beginning of a process, in which the characteristic of high literacy is anachronistically attributed to figures who were mainly or exclusively associated with oral prophetic proclamation? [72]

(2) What were likely the systemic similarities and dissimilarities between the messages of oral prophetic pronouncements in monarchic Israel and the message of prophetic books from the postmonarchic period? To illustrate,

---

[69] Given the fact that these literati played a most active role in the communication of the word of YHWH (i.e., a prophetic book), whether as composers, editors, readers, rereaders, brokers, and the like, and given that society accepted their involvement in these capacities, they may at least be called "quasi-prophets" (see above).

[70] This does not, of course, mean that they were not able to communicate in oral/aural terms. See B. Alster, "Interaction of Oral and Written Poetry in Early Mesopotamian Literature," in *Mesopotamian Epic Literature* (ed. M. E. Vogelzang and H. L. J. Vanstiphout; Lewiston, N.Y.: Mellen, 1992), 49–50; and see Ezek 31:32–33, which also seems to convey an implicit call to the readers and rereaders of the book of Ezekiel not to treat it as literature read (only or mainly?) for the joy of reading, but as YHWH's word.

[71] As I maintain in Ben Zvi, *Historical-Critical Study of the Book of Zephaniah*, 352–56.

[72] See Davies's contribution to this volume.

whereas one may assume that a substantial prophetic role during the monarchic period was to express and to gather support for (or foment opposition to)[73] the reigning Israelite/Judahite king and his policies, this is certainly not the social role of the prophetic books. However, these books did communicate a clear message of support for, and exaltation of, the heavenly king, YHWH, as well as a call for his subjects (i.e., Israel) to be brought close to their king and to follow his commands.[74]

(3) The oral prophecies from Mesopotamia suggest that oracles dealt with the relatively close future, not with an ideal future set far away from present reality. The same holds true for the written collection of Assyrian oracles.[75] As mentioned above, one of the prominent messages of the prophetic books is to advance an image of an ideal future, and to reassure society that this future will become reality, by the will of YHWH, at some indefinite point in the future. Does this matter raise the issue of the comparability of the prophetic books—in their present form—with those texts?[76] Significantly the same

---

[73] See, for instance, Jer 26:20–23. For a prophecy aimed against Esarhaddon, the reigning king, see *ABL* 1217 recto 2–5; also Nissinen, "Prophecy against the King," 157–70; idem, *References,* 108–53, esp. 110–11, 120–21; and for Old Babylonian examples of prophets proclaiming a condemnation of the deeds of the king, see Sasson, "Posting of Letters," 311–12.

[74] This being the case, there was a very high potential for the development of a discourse that considered opposing the prophetic books (i.e., YHWH's word) tantamount to disloyalty to YHWH, the king, and as such liable to punishment (cf. Deut. 13:2–6; see among others, Nissinen, "Prophecy against the King"). Moreover, since the prophetic books had to be read to (and therefore interpreted to) the rest of the population, one wonders if the same discourse did not apply to their interpretation. The question of whether this potential discourse did develop is of much significance in the case of prophetic literature (as distinct, for instance, from the Pentateuch). As for the latter, cf. Neh 8:13–17; and see M. Fishbane, *Biblical Interpretation in Ancient Israel* (Oxford: Clarendon, 1985), 109–13; for the important distinction between pentateuchal books (i.e., Torah) and other biblical books in Chronicles, see, for instance, I. L. Seeligman, "The Beginning of *Midrash* in the Books of Chronicles," *Tarbiz* 49 (1980): 14–32 (Hebrew; English summary, pp. ii–iii). Moreover, even if this discursive potential developed, the issues of the extent to which and the way in which it actually influenced life in postmonarchic Yehud (especially the Achaemenid period) are further topics that deserve considerable study. All these matters bear directly on the issue of the social reception and role of the prophetic books in society at large.

[75] See Parpola, *Assyrian Prophecies.*

[76] Elsewhere I have developed the idea that prophetic books are a particular (written) genre developed only in Israel for a very limited time, and a genre whose unique character contributed to—among other things—the construction of a sense of religio-cultural identity all during the postmonarchic period, but mainly the Achaemenid period (cf. the later development of the rabbinic Midrash). See E. Ben Zvi, "Looking at the Primary (Hi)story

question may be raised on the basis of, for instance, (a) the sheer length of the larger prophetic books and (b) the tendency of some literary, prophetic characters (e.g., Micah) to couch their words (in the world of the text) in general terms that are good for every generation and closely related to other sayings in the book, rather than terms that are particular to a historical situation and audience.[77]

(4) Are there traceable, compositional relations linking oral utterances by monarchic-period prophets and the prophetic books associated with their names in their present form? Since there is clear evidence from Mari and Assyria that at times reports about prophetic (oral) performances were written close to the event and then archived or organized in collections, do these models provide a good starting point for the study of the composition of the prophetic books in the Hebrew Bible?

(5) What do these models suggest about the possibility of recovering the *ipsissima verba* of prophets? Related to the three previous questions, do the prophetic books in their present form contain much, some, or no material at all that can be traced back to an oral, "speaking" prophet? And at a more basic, methodological level, how can one trace that material?

(6) What is the relevance of well-known studies of orality—particularly in view of recent developments within what one may label the Parry-Lord school—for the study of orality (and writtenness) in ancient prophetic literature in general, and more specifically for the study of the prophetic books eventually included in the Hebrew Bible? If one maintains that such studies are at least heuristically helpful for analyses of the particular literary genre called prophetic book, what can be learned from them, and how? [78] With regard to the so-called markers of oral diction (e.g., formulaic language, repetition, and the density in

---

and the Prophetic Books as Literary/Theological Units within the Frame of the Early Second Temple Period: Some Considerations," *SJOT* 12 (1998) 26–43, esp. 42.

[77] See my commentary on Micah (FOTL).

[78] To be sure, debates about their relevance for biblical studies, as well as debates about oral traditions and their faithfulness, are surely not limited to prophetic literature. See, for instance, J. Van Seters, *Abraham in History and Tradition* (New Haven: Yale University Press, 1975); idem, "Review of *Oral World and Written Tradition* by Susan Niditch," *JAOS* 118 (1998): 436–37; H. M. Wahl, *Die Jakobserzählungen* (BZAW 259; Berlin: de Gruyter, 1997); Henaut, *Oral Tradition and the Gospels;* cf. Niditch, *Oral World;* W. H. Kelber, *The Oral and the Written Gospel: The Hermeneutics of Speaking and Writing in the Synoptic Tradition, Mark, Paul, and Q* (Philadelphia: Fortress, 1983). Nor are such debates limited to biblical studies. See the critique of the Parry-Lord thesis advanced by Thomas (*Literacy and Orality*, 29–51), particularly in regard to ancient Mesopotamia, as exemplified by the general tone of Vogelzang and Vanstiphout, *Mesopotamian Epic Literature*; see, for instance, the contributions of Cooper, "Babbling," 103–22, and P. Michalowski, "Orality and Literacy in Early Mesopotamian Literature," 227–45.

which such phenomena appear in a text) most would argue that they may and do appear in written texts,[79] but that their presence in any text is not necessarily an indicator that it was composed or transmitted orally (e.g., the Assyrian royal inscriptions and the Amarna Letters). If so, why do such markers still figure so prominently in much of the biblical research on these matters? What can the presence or absence of these markers actually prove, besides the occurrence or even prevalence of some stylistic features in a particular set of texts that—at least in their present form—are certainly written texts? Those interested in theology and in present-day sociology of knowledge may also raise questions about what is at stake in the search for the oral roots of written (prophetic) books? And conversely, what may be the theological significance of "written prophecy"[80] and the "written character of YHWH's word"? Related to the two previous questions, in a relatively recent study Lord wrote: "The fundamental assumption with which the following contribution has been written is that the oral traditional vernacular literatures of Europe in the Middle Ages were formed and had attained a level of sophistication before the introduction of writing among the people who created and practiced them."[81] Is the search for oral roots associated somewhat with a theological or ideological desire to believe that the prophetic texts were created and reached their sophistication among people who were not fully literate, i.e., "common folks" as opposed to a few (elite) literati? Is the attempt to disassociate the prophetic books from "high culture" related in some manner to a tension between contemporaneous uneasiness about "high culture" and a desire to maintain the theological

---

[79] The "classical" study on that matter is still L. D. Benson, "The Literary Character of Anglo-Saxon Formulaic Poetry," *Publications of the Modern Language Association* 81 (1966): 334–41. Further, some of the more recent distinctions advanced by J. M. Foley have faced strong criticism. For instance, J. Martínez-Pizarro wrote as follows in his review of Foley's "The Implications of Oral Tradition": "Foley's main example, taken from Serbo-Croatian poetry, is a phrase that describes a character jumping to his feet: taken by itself, it is a simple account of a physical movement, but within the tradition and in the understanding of a traditionally-trained audience it is a gesture of heroic readiness in the face of tremendous odds. The problem is that this sort of metonymic reference also works in literature, which after all has traditions of its own, within the framework of which it is produced and understood. The rich intertextuality that Foley attributes to his formulas and themes can be achieved in literature by the choice of a stylistic register or level, or by the use of a generic convention (e.g. the choice of either Greek or English names for the characters in Renaissance pastoral)" (see J. Martínez-Pizarro, "Review of *Oral Tradition in the Middle Ages*, ed. W. F. H. Nicolaisen," *The Medieval Review*, 96.11.16, [http://www.hti.umich.edu/b/bmr/tmr.html]). In their contributions to the present volume, Culley and Van Seters address some of these issues, each from a different viewpoint.

[80] Crenshaw addresses this issue at the conclusion of his contribution to this volume.

[81] Lord, "Oral Composition and 'Oral Residue,'" 8.

legitimacy of these books? Is it associated in some manner with "that romantic but at the same time guilt-ridden projection onto others of our own wishes and nostalgias, apparently so typical of recent Western culture"?[82]

This introduction has surveyed a range of complex issues connected with the investigation of orality and writtenness in the prophetic books within the larger context of studies of writings and speech in Israelite and ancient Near Eastern prophecy. It has also laid out some of the key questions that must appear on the agenda for future research. The following chapters already address in diverse ways, directly and indirectly, many of these issues and will hopefully lead to further studies and questions in the future. Let the journey begin!

---

[82] See Finnegan, "What is Orality?" 144. It is worth mentioning here that although it is probably true that some of the supporters of the oral-formulaic school had an "aversion to the ancient Near East" and perhaps a very ethnocentric view of non-Indo-European cultures in general, coupled with romantic views of the latter (see, for instance, Cooper, "Babbling," 107–9), I think that these considerations do not apply to the current proponents of these methods in the area of Hebrew Bible, and that they therefore have no place in the questions mentioned above.

Transmitting Prophecy across Generations

James L. Crenshaw
Duke University

According to Mikhail Bakhtin, every utterance arises as a response to something that has preceded it. To the extent that this observation accords with reality, the task of interpretation entails the discovery of the earlier word evoking a reply, which in turn necessitates getting back to its social context. Such a search is severely compromised by an axiom in critical scholarship, specifically that biblical prophets addressed their own historical community to announce divine judgment, to stimulate repentant action in the face of anticipated calamity, and to encourage the downtrodden by pointing beyond their misery to improved conditions in the near future.[1]

---

[1] John Barton, *Oracles of God: Perceptions of Ancient Prophecy in Israel after the Exile* (New York and Oxford: Oxford University Press, 1986), has highlighted the sharp disjunction between the modern critical interpretation of ancient Israelite prophecy and the way it was understood before the development of historical criticism. He explores four modes of reading ancient prophecy: (1) as halakah, or ethical instruction; (2) as eschatological promise, containing foreknowledge of the present moment of interpreters; (3) as prognostication but without a sense of an imminent inbreaking of the divine; and (4) as speculative theology about God's character and the heavenly realm. Interpreters after the exile, both Jewish and Christian, viewed prophets as recipients of divine secrets, and this understanding of prophecy spurred them on to develop hermeneutical principles capable of unlocking the mystery pertaining to the present situation. They did not employ distinctions of genre, however, and that failure allowed them to discover prophecy in Torah, Psalms, wisdom literature, indeed in any sacred book. The decisive issue was whether or not God spoke in the text; if so, it was prophecy. Merely warning people of their own day required no word from God; prediction in its true sense did depend on revelation, in the view of ancients. Using the image of looking into a well of the past, Barton accuses precritical readers of seeing their own reflection rather than the great classical prophets: Amos, Hosea, Isaiah, and Jeremiah. Has Barton exaggerated the differences between "lone laymen" and postexilic prophecy? Perhaps the promised sequel to *Oracles of God* will address this important

Because this principle of interpretation fails to take into consideration the transmission of prophetic traditions across generations, it must be judged inadequate. Why would anyone be inclined to preserve prophetic teachings if they only addressed the immediate audience? A purely antiquarian interest hardly explains this phenomenon; other motives must have inspired individuals to keep the prophetic words alive in changing social circumstances.[2] Visions and oracles were thought to have possessed lasting value irrespective of the historical situation in which they initially burst on the scene.[3]

A comparison with wisdom literature may be instructive.[4] The sages preserved the teachings of predecessors primarily because of their pedagogic worth, whether in the form of short sayings, instructions, sustained dialogue, or monologue. The intrinsic value of such assessments of the human situation transcended space and time, partly because they lacked anything pertaining to a specific group or historical era, and partly because they focused on humankind in general.[5] Although originating in specific times and places, the sapiential

---

question in the light of the extensive redaction of older prophetic literature during the postexilic period.

[2] Those shifts in fortune include the termination of the northern kingdom, the exile of a large segment of Judah, and the eventual return of a small group to a province lacking the power of self-rule. These momentous events, spanning more than two centuries, witnessed a growing chasm between rich and poor, subjects and kings. Older family structures gave way to executive privilege, which in turn collapsed before foreign rule. In the restored community priestly hierarchy emerged, and competition for inherited land ruled the day, along with struggles to determine rights of inclusion. Given the scope of these changes, the formidable task of describing social characteristics in any given historical situation is humbling. Determining motives for the actions of an ancient group of people poses an even more daunting challenge.

[3] The distinction between mantics and visionaries became blurred over time, as did the various terms designating prophetic figures: *rōʾeh, ḥōzeh, ʾîš ʾĕlōhîm, ʾîš hārrûaḥ,* and *nābîʾ.* The superscription to the book of Amos deftly combines the visionary and the oracular types of intermediation ("The words of Amos which he saw . . ."). The decisive issue pertained to the source of the prophecy, regardless of its form. If the prophecy derived from the deity, it was thought to have permanent relevance for individuals who possessed sufficient insight to decode it.

[4] This shift is more than a retreat to familiar territory when in doubt. The move occurs because sages reflected openly about the potential of cited words to immortalize their dead source. To put the matter succinctly, "when the dead are quoted their lips move." Stated another way, the written tablet keeps the memory of its scribe/author alive long after death has silenced the teacher. Similarly, the quoted prophetic oracle amounted to a death-defying act, a refusal to concede that the spirit infusing that word or vision has abandoned the religious community.

[5] When Miriam Lichtheim wrote that "Egyptians, Mesopotamians, and Israelites, all three had the same approach to retaliation, vengeance, and forgiveness," she did not superimpose

CRENSHAW: Transmitting Prophecy across Generations   33

traditions give the impression of timelessness. The teachings of the eighth century were just as compelling in the second century; otherwise Ben Sira could not have made free use of the book of Proverbs, both as a model and as a source of material.[6]

The preservation of familial instruction and professional debate about life's meaning makes sense. In the interest of shaping character in youth,[7] parents needed an arsenal that had been tested over the years and could effectively combat the twin foes of lust and laziness. Furthermore, those who trained advanced scribes also needed classic examples of intellectual engagement with mind-stretching questions. Institutional necessity thus led to the transmission of wisdom literature from one generation to the next. The family[8]

---

modern concepts of forgiving one's enemies upon ancient texts (*Moral Values in Ancient Egypt* [OBO 155; Fribourg: University Press; Göttingen: Vandenhoeck & Ruprecht, 1997], 46). Nor was she a victim of the evolutionary approach adopted in interpreting ancient literature. Instead, she simply called attention to one feature of ancient thought that transcends space and time. One can concur with her that contemporary research has fallen into a terminological muddle as a result of a too-free use of the category "wisdom literature" by specialists in Egypt and Mesopotamia. At the same time, one need not surrender the insight that both these civilizations had a corpus of literature that reflected on the most efficient means of attaining success and shaping character, while seriously pondering life's deeper mysteries.

[6] This sentence presupposes a central core of proverbial teachings during the monarchy, as well as accurate historical memory lying behind the superscription in Prov 25:1 ("These, too, are proverbs of Solomon that the men of Hezekiah, king of Judah, transmitted" [הֶעְתִּיקוּ]). The latter view has recently come under attack (M. Carasic, "Who Were the Men of Hezekiah [Proverbs XXV:1]?" *VT* 44 [1994]: 291–300), and the former has been reinforced (C. Westermann, *Roots of Wisdom* [Louisville, Ky.: Westminster John Knox, 1995]). On Ben Sira's reliance on earlier wisdom literature see J. L. Crenshaw, "Sirach," *NIB* 5:601–867.

[7] Concomitant with modern societal interest in "family values" has come renewed attention to the formation of character in the ancient world. The first full-scale analysis, W. P. Brown, *Character in Crisis: A Fresh Approach to the Wisdom Literature of the Old Testament* (Grand Rapids, Mich.: Eerdmans, 1996), juxtaposes the efforts at community maintenance in the book of Proverbs with more crisis-centered approaches within the books of Job and Ecclesiastes. For him, the move of the self charts a journey outward but does not end there. The final resting place entails a return to the communal ethos by one whose journey has brought fresh insights and growth in moral fiber.

[8] The familial locus of teachings in the initial collection of Proverbs, chs. 1–9, is no mere literary fiction. The memory of parents' role in formulating earlier collections of sayings exercised remarkable power over later traditionists, for whom professional *ḥăkāmîm* may have been a reality (see J. L. Crenshaw, *Old Testament Wisdom* [Rev. and enl. ed.; Louisville, Ky.: Westminster John Knox, 1998]; idem, *Urgent Advice and Probing Questions: Collected Writings on Old Testament Wisdom* [Macon, Ga.: Mercer University Press, 1995]; and Westermann, *Roots of Wisdom*).

and the scribal guild, perhaps eventually also the school,[9] gave impetus to the collection and maintenance of prized teachings.

With the collapse of the monarchy and temple cult in Judah, what social institution provided refuge for prophetic traditions? That question motivates this exploration into the preservation of oracles and stories about prophets. Every attempt to locate a group responsible for transmitting prophetic traditions comes up against a formidable claim that prophecy fell into disrepute for some reason in the view of those responsible for Zech 13:2–6, which goes beyond the attempt in Deut 18:15–22 to regulate prophecy and endeavors at some level to stamp it out.[10] Moreover, the form in which traditions were transmitted, whether oral or written, complicates the picture. Recent examinations of the persistence of orality as late as Ben Sira[11] and of the meager evidence of literacy[12] suggest that older paradigms may need to be replaced.

---

[9] A weakness of the argument from analogy with Mesopotamia and Egypt arises from distinct differences in urban complexity and cultural development. N. Shupak's stimulating analysis of affinities between Israelite and Egyptian concepts of education does not give sufficient attention to this important detail (*Where Can Wisdom be Found? The Sage's Language in the Bible and in Ancient Egyptian Literature* [OBO 130; Fribourg: University Press; Göttingen: Vandenhoeck & Ruprecht, 1993]). F. W. Golka, *The Leopard's Spots* (Edinburgh: T&T Clark, 1993), has seen this disjunction between Israel and her more advanced neighbors with sharp clarity.

[10] I have explored the primary reason for this prophetic decline, namely, the people's inability to distinguish between authentic intermediaries and religious charlatans (*Prophetic Conflict: Its Effect upon Israelite Religion* [BZAW 124; Berlin and New York: de Gruyter, 1971). The scope of disenchantment with prophecy in this astonishing snippet within Zechariah is unclear; some interpreters view it as absolute, and others think it pertains only to a certain type of prophecy.

[11] When this early second century teacher issues specific advice to his audience, he instructs them to enter into lively dialogue with thoughtful people, not to pick up a scroll and read it—notwithstanding the present reality of that counsel in written form. The long tradition of teaching by means of oral instruction has persisted to the twenty-first century, despite frequent attacks on lecture as a pedagogical method. The importance of hearing did not immediately vanish from education with the rise of reading texts, for people usually read aloud. By this means the two senses, seeing and hearing, heightened understanding. I have discussed Ben Sira's manner of teaching in J. L. Crenshaw, "The Primacy of Listening in Ben Sira's Pedagogy," in *Wisdom, You Are My Sister: Studies in Honor of Roland E. Murphy, O. Carm., on the Occasion of His Eightieth Birthday* (ed. M. L. Barré; CBQMS 29; Washington, D.C.: Catholic Biblical Association of America, 1997), 172–87.

[12] Recent assessments of literacy in ancient Greece (W. V. Harris, *Ancient Literacy* [Cambridge, Mass.: Harvard University Press, 1989]) and in Egypt (J. Baines, "Literacy and Ancient Egyptian Society," *Man*, NS, 18 [1983]: 572–99) occasion little surprise when they estimate that less than 10% of citizens in classical Greece and about a half of one per cent in Egypt were literate. The complex writing systems in both countries only partially explain this

Similar reassessment has already begun in regard to the reliability of the biblical record pertaining to the prophets.[13] The recognition that texts bear witness first and foremost to the time of their composition, together with growing awareness that most of the prophetic canon achieved literary expression in exilic and postexilic times, places a huge question mark before every reading of events prior to 587 B.C.E. To what extent did later editors retroject their own culture into descriptions of earlier events? Modern interpreters, ranging from minimalists to maximalists, adopt varying positions on this issue. The paucity of nonbiblical evidence (e.g., the three types of prophets at Mari,[14] the ecstatic prophet mentioned in the Egyptian Tale of Wen Amun, and the reference in the Lachish letters to a prophet whose behavior resembles that of Jeremiah) does little to settle this debate.

The position one takes on this issue determines the historical focus of discussion about the manner in which prophetic texts were "read." If an interpreter refuses to accept as reliable any information about preexilic prophets, the time-span of transmission is shortened by several centuries. In that case, an interpreter focuses on the social circumstances in the province of Judah during Persian and Hellenistic times. Those who adopt a less stringent attitude to the traditions take into consideration the two centuries before the exiled Judeans returned to the land from which they had been taken when Babylonian soldiers sacked Jerusalem.

An Inner Circle of Followers ("Disciples")

Perhaps a starting point for either analysis can be found in the immediate followers of holy persons. The last of the poems designated by Bernhard Duhm

---

phenomenon. The alphabetic system in ancient Hebrew was much simpler, but the Israelites possessed few incentives to master it, and a number of disincentives (J. L. Crenshaw, *Education in Ancient Israel: Across the Deadening Silence* [ABRL; New York: Doubleday, 1998]).

[13] Postmodernism functions as a healthy reminder that assured results of a previous generation's scholarship reflect biases of the elite and powerful. The many substitutes being offered today—feminist, Marxist, Afro-Americanist, liberationist, fundamentalist—only replace the white male bias with others equally one-sided. Their value consists in bringing a whole range of issues to the table where, one hopes, rational assessment will eventually occur. Debate also rages over the most effective method by which to illuminate the prophetic literature: an evolutionary history of ideas or a sociological model. Each of these methods has serious drawbacks.

[14] The ecstatic, the cultic diviner, and lone layperson at Mari correspond to the prophetic types referred to in biblical literature. Similarly, several literary expressions link the two prophetic phenomena despite their distance in time and place (e.g., "fear not"; "the God X has sent me"; and "thus you shall say").

as Servant Songs (Isa 52:13–53:12) implies devoted disciples,[15] and this exilic text may lend credence to a similar phenomenon in earlier times, although one could argue that the socioeconomic context of Deutero-Isaiah's era has been read back into the stories about followers of Elijah and Elisha.[16] The same applies to Isa 8:16, which refers to the practice of preserving prophetic testimony among those who have been instructed, a sealing up of the divine word communicated through the prophet until it comes to fruition.[17] Similarly, the deity tells Habakkuk to write the visionary prediction on tablets in clear letters for ease of reading, but also as a sign that the vision will definitely become reality.[18] The principle underlying this practice comes to expression in Isa 55:10–11, which asserts that the word of YHWH is no less reliable than fructifying rain and snow.[19]

These texts both provide a plausible social location for the transmission of prophetic teachings and identify the most likely motive for such preservation. The immediate followers of prophets had a vested interest in authenticating a message and assuring faithfulness in its transmission. In addition, they may have wanted to supply fresh interpretation in light of changing circumstances, confident that they were acting in the spirit of their teacher. In their view,

---

[15] The most plausible reading of this poem chronicles the astonishing journey of these disciples from a position similar to that of Job's three friends to a directly opposing viewpoint. The author gives no hint as to the basis for the decisive shift from viewing the servant as suffering for his sins to understanding his affliction as vicarious, redemptive, and undeserved.

[16] The episodes involving these two prophets have more affinities with postexilic understandings of earlier prophecy than do the oracles and visions attributed to classical prophets. In the case of Amos, Hosea, Isaiah, Jeremiah and Micah one observes a radical disjunction between the preserved traditions and the view of prophecy in postexilic Judaism. That element of discontinuity may suggest that authentic memories have survived the reinterpretation of later editing.

[17] A legal background seems to be implied, e.g., the sealing of official documents for subsequent validation, if necessary. Such a practice would naturally apply to prophetic predictions so long as one accepts Deuteronomy's criterion of fulfillment as a mark of genuine prophecy.

[18] Who does the reading? If the prophet, then the text describes a herald rapidly scurrying about in order to proclaim a word to the entire citizenry. The alternative interpretation is less plausible because it presupposes an ability to read on the part of the populace.

[19] Such thinking carries within itself a fundamental core of eschatology, the conviction that the divine word will inevitably attain closure. Israel's experience with partial fulfillments gradually gave rise to expectations of final resolution some day, a tying up of all loose ends. F. Kermode, *The Sense of an Ending* (Oxford: Oxford University Press, 1967), writes of the tic/toc movement in linear thought, an inevitable anticipation of something that is yet to arrive on the scene.

predictions that seemed to have gone awry, for some unknown reason, retained their power, making it necessary to wrest their hidden meaning by hook or crook.[20] Daniel's use of Jeremiah's prediction about the lapse of seventy years between exile and return (Dan 9:1–27; cf. Jer 25:11–12; 29:10) offers a specific instance of this practice.[21]

To some extent, the essential nature of prophetic mediation enhanced its durability, if one can trust the hint in Num 12:6–8. In that author's view, Moses alone received clear messages from YHWH, whereas all other prophets experienced the divine word as enigma (*běḥîdôt*). This elusive, and allusive, feature of intermediation infused the word with multivalence, leaving it completely open-ended.[22] Six components seem to characterize the activity of prophets from the reception of a message to its proclamation: (1) the putative revelatory moment during which an enigmatic vision or word captures the imagination; (2) a period of reflection about the meaning of this captivating message; (3) the articulation of the message in terms of a religious tradition deemed authoritative; (4) the refining of that word or vision by means of poetic language and/or rhetorical style; (5) the addition of supportive arguments, either threatening or comforting; and (6) the actual proclamation, complete with gestures and tone of voice, and occasionally accompanied by prophetic symbolic actions.[23]

---

[20] This endeavor to rescue all predictions by any available means led to extensive hermeneutical development of interpretive strategies, which come to light in various communities (e.g., Qumran, the New Testament, intertestamental Judaism, rabbinic Judaism, the Church Fathers). M. Fishbane, *Biblical Interpretation in Ancient Israel* (Oxford: Clarendon, 1985), treats the interpretive tradition in prophecy under the title of mantological exegesis (443–524).

[21] The problem with becoming specific is acute, for the generation affected by the prophecy experiences its disconfirmation and is forced to explain the failure. Religious people have remarkable resilience when confronted with cognitive dissonance (R. P. Carroll, *When Prophecy Failed* [London: SCM, 1979]).

[22] In the ancient writer's view, Moses had direct access to the deity, whereas every other prophet received the divine word derivatively—that is through riddles that had to be interpreted. Similarly, later readers believed that classical prophets received divine oracles and postexilic prophets worked with derivative traditions, interpreting them rather than transmitting oracles directly from the deity. E. F. Davis, *Swallowing the Scroll: Textuality and the Dynamics of Discourse in Ezekiel's Prophecy* (JSOTSup 78; Sheffield: Almond, 1989), may be correct that Ezekiel brought about a decisive shift to the *text* as opposed to a word spoken by the deity to a prophet. "Nostalgia, not theocracy, was the death of prophecy" (Barton, *Oracles of God*, 115).

[23] This description, largely conjectural, relies on information gleaned from visionary accounts in the books of Amos and Jeremiah.

As I have argued elsewhere,[24] that enigmatic feature also contributed to prophecy's decline, for it encouraged differing interpretations that placed prophets in conflict with one another. Discerning the divine will in a given situation could not be divorced from the principles by which a prophet lived or from the understanding of history/metahistory that seemed to be at work. Moreover, unprincipled charlatans may also have complicated the situation, although base motives could easily be concealed, as various confrontations between prophets demonstrate and different views within the prophetic literature attest.

Competing understandings of divine intention increased the need for institutional backing. Those prophets whose reading of history placed them at odds with the Davidic dynasty and its theopolitical agenda were thrust to the perimeter, forcing them to become outsiders fending for themselves. Their opposites found favor in high places and enjoyed a central position in society, which carried both prestige and power.[25] Neither type of prophetic activity was devoid of risk, for royal interests did not always correspond to what the prophets proclaimed.

The sometimes hot, sometimes cold, relationship between a given prophet and king in the biblical record has a ring of authenticity, for rulers would probably have wished for divine protection in perilous confrontations—as ample testimony from ancient Near Eastern texts demonstrates.[26] Similarly, prophets may have wanted to influence policy and transform society from above. Such a favorable assessment of this gravitation toward the places of power may also be supported by the assumption that higher ethical expectations

---

[24] Crenshaw, *Prophetic Conflict*.

[25] R. R. Wilson, *Prophecy and Society in Ancient Israel* (Philadelphia: Fortress, 1980), employed this concept of central and peripheral prophecy as a means of clarifying the power structures of competing groups.

[26] On Assyrian prophecy, see M. Nissinen, *References to Prophecy in Neo-Assyrian Sources* (SAAS 7; Helsinki: The Neo-Assyrian Text Corpus Project, 1998), and S. Parpola, *Assyrian Prophecies* (SAA 9; Helsinki: Helsinki University Press, 1997). Nissinen concludes that prophecy functioned in imperial ideology to provide divine directions for the king and propaganda for royal policies (164), although he adduces an example of a private citizen, Urad Gula, consulting a prophet. Parpola explains the paucity of prophetic texts by the oral nature of the phenomenon, stresses its ecstatic character, notes that only Esarhaddon and Assurbanipal mention prophetic oracles in their inscriptions, lists several similarities with biblical prophecy, and offers a translation and extensive notes of twenty-eight oracles from thirteen different prophets (four male, nine female). Collection 2.4 has a notably striking reference to sealing the writing of the Urartian (cf. Isa 8:16). Parpola's account of the worship of Ishtar of Arbela as monotheistic, indeed his description of Assyrian religion in general, is highly speculative.

apply to the upper class than to peasants (see Jer 5:4–5).[27] If these observations have any basis in reality, the charge that prophets courted royal favor for selfish reasons may miss the mark completely.

What social group had a vested interest in promoting the well-being of a small conclave of prophetic disciples?[28] The temple cult? Prophecy's institutionalization must surely have been problematic, for a definite anticultic bias permeates the oracles attributed to such individuals as Amos, Isaiah, and Jeremiah.[29] Its presence would have discouraged sponsors from priestly circles, who could find considerable opinion in this prophetic literature with which to take issue. They may have been persuaded to overlook this polemic, however, because of compensating features favorable to the king, under whose beneficence they themselves found shelter.

This ambivalent attitude could explain the presence of glosses in various prophetic books that employ the kind of language usually attributed to the Deuteronomist.[30] The lofty ethical ideals of this book rest comfortably with those articulated by eighth- and seventh-century prophets.[31] If the thesis has

---

[27] The elitist attitude represented by the author of this text attributed to Jeremiah may at first strike readers as strange, given the prophet's ill treatment by certain elements in power. The issue is more complex than that, however, for the biblical record also suggests that Jeremiah enjoyed considerable support from highly placed persons in Jerusalem. The contemptuous view of the poor contrasts with the equation elsewhere of the poor and the devout, an attitude with a long history.

[28] J. Blenkinsopp, *Sage, Priest, Prophet: Religious and Intellectual Leadership in Ancient Israel* (LAI; Louisville, Ky.: Westminster John Knox, 1995), offers a thorough evaluation of the dominant social roles in the biblical world. His analysis of prophecy pays scant attention to the problem posed by competing voices and the struggle to escape the dilemma arising from an inability to distinguish between an authentic and a bogus prophet.

[29] Interpreters have understood the harsh attacks on the cult as either absolute or conditional. The infusion of Roman Catholic scholars into the mix, as well as renewed appreciation among Protestants for liturgy, has brought about a shift in favor of the latter interpretation, i.e., criticizing certain features of the cult but coming short of rejecting it entirely.

[30] On this complicated issue see my article "The Deuteronomist and the Writings," in *Those Elusive Deuteronomists: The Phenomenon of Pan-Deuteronomism* (ed. L. S. Schearing and S. L. McKenzie; JSOTSup 268; Sheffield: Sheffield Academic Press, 1999), 145–58.

[31] Scholars would do well to avoid the assumption that a single group held a monopoly on lofty ethics (cf. M. Weinfeld, *Deuteronomy and the Deuteronomic School* [Oxford: Oxford University Press, 1972; repr. Winona Lake, Ind.: Eisenbrauns, 1992]). Israelite society was not so insular as to yield specialists in morality; instead, fundamental values found champions among priests, prophets, and sages. Not every piece of legislation in the book falls into the category of humane. The law about recalcitrant sons seems particularly harsh,

merit that a levitical hand can be detected behind Deuteronomy,[32] then a link between prophecy and torah may exist. Traditions that associate certain prophets, particularly Jeremiah and Ezekiel, with priests may not be easily dismissed, given the affinities between priests and the postexilic prophets Zechariah, Joel, and the unknown author of Malachi.[33] Moreover, the prophetic attack against cultic ritual may not be absolute, functioning rather to purify the cult by elevating ethics above ritual (note the juxtaposition of ritual language and its rejection in Psalm 51).[34]

Was sponsorship by an institution necessary for the survival of prophetic oracles? The marginal existence of prophetic bands associated with Elijah and Elisha does not encourage such speculation about their survival. The less dire social circumstances of later classical prophets make it possible to imagine a self-sustaining group of followers bent on preserving the teachings of their leader. Such a collection of avid disciples could even have persisted without institutionalization, given the extent of their devotion and the scope of their vision.[35] Caught up in a view of metahistory and anticipating decisive divine action in the near future, they could certainly have kept the prophetic dream alive for generations.

---

even when one takes into account the concept of honor and shame, as well as the importance of protecting communal solidarity.

[32] G. von Rad championed the view that levitical preaching lay behind the text of the book of Deuteronomy. See *Deuteronomy* (OTL; Philadelphia: Westminster, 1966), *Das Gottesvolk im Deuteronomium* (BWANT 47; Stuttgart: W. Kohlhammer, 1929), and *Studies in Deuteronomy* (trans. D. Stalker; London: SCM, 1953).

[33] Priestly features of these prophetic books abound (e.g., the importance of the temple, the role of the priest, the centrality of ritual and mediation by the ministers of the altar, the significance of adjudicating matters of purity and impurity). For Blenkinsopp, prophecy was swallowed by the cult, a view that D. L. Petersen challenges ("The Temple in Persian Period Prophetic Texts," in *Second Temple Studies 1: Persian Period* [ed. P. R. Davies; JSOTSup 117; Sheffield: JSOT Press, 1991], 125–44).

[34] The juxtaposition of Psalms 50 and 51 makes this issue all the more interesting. The rejection of sacrificial worship in Psalm 50 gives rise to copious ritual language in Psalm 51, together with language pointing beyond the penitential ritual to a shattered spirit.

[35] The nature of the Israelite family is the subject of a recent monograph by L. G. Perdue et al., *Families in Ancient Israel* (Louisville, Ky.: Westminster John Knox, 1997). The discussion does not encourage one to think that ordinary families devoted themselves to such things as preserving religious traditions for posterity. Their chief aim was survival in a hostile environment.

Oral or Written Transmission?

In what form was the prophetic tradition transmitted across generations, oral or written? That question has returned to the forefront of discussion, thanks to recent research on literacy in the ancient Near East. Susan Niditch's efforts to isolate oral features within the biblical canon and to contrast them with characteristics of literary production illustrate the complexity of this problem,[36] and Michael Fishbane's magisterial analysis of innercanonical interpretation shows indirectly how pressing the issue has become.[37] What if the *traditum* existed in oral form? How different things would look from the description he has provided! My own study of ancient Israelite education[38] suggests that Fishbane's approach to the dynamic process within the canon of interacting with earlier views rests on the highly dubious assumption of widespread literacy and ready access to written materials. Such convenient texts for consultation strike me as a figment of the imagination, given the agrarian society of Yehud and the limited population of Jerusalem in the Persian period.[39]

Sparsely populated villages had little need for literate persons, and the scribal guild zealously guarded its monopoly on writing.[40] In such an oral culture, written words (icons) shimmered with the power of the sacred,[41] and

---

[36] S. Niditch, *Oral World and Written Word: Ancient Israelite Literature* (LAI; Louisville, Ky.: Westminster John Knox, 1996), proposes four models for evaluating biblical material on the literacy/orality continuum: (1) oral performance, (2) slow crystallization of a pan-Hebraic literary tradition, (3) written imitation of oral-style literature, and (4) the production of a written text excerpted from another.

[37] Fishbane, *Biblical Interpretation.*

[38] Crenshaw, *Education in Ancient Israel.*

[39] See the conclusions of C. E. Carter, "The Province of Yehud in the Post-Exilic Period: Sounding in Site Distribution and Demography," in *Second Temple Studies 2: Temple Community in the Persian Period* (ed. T. C. Eskenazi and K. H. Richards; Sheffield: JSOT Press, 1994), 106–45, and E. Ben Zvi, "The Urban Center of Jerusalem and the Development of the Literature of the Hebrew Bible," in *Aspects of Urbanism in Antiquity* (ed. W. G. Aufrecht, N. A. Mirau, and S. W. Gauley; JSOTSup 244; Sheffield: Sheffield Academic Press, 1997), 194–209.

[40] The term "managed scarcity" aptly describes scribal practices in ancient Egypt. The secret was to train just enough scribes to handle the demand for their services. The existence of too many scribes at a given time would compromise their employment and reduce their income appreciably. Presumably, a similar practice characterized Mesopotamian scribes.

[41] B. Holbek ("What the Illiterate Think of Writing," in *Literacy and Society* [ed. K. Shousboe and M. T. Larsen; Copenhagen: Akademisk Forlag, 1989], 183–96) writes that written letters and words shimmered with the very power of the gods. For most people, then,

religious figures used popular awe to their own advantage.[42] That is why one detects a growing emphasis on heavenly books, a registry for the names of those destined for life,[43] as well as mystical language of swallowing scrolls[44] and visions about a huge scroll in the sky.[45] In this realm of discourse, divine scribal activity is thinkable,[46] ranging from incising texts in stone (Exod 31:18) to writing on the human heart (Jer 31:33), or even forming ominous letters of the alphabet on a wall while humans revel in drunken debauchery (Dan 5:5).[47]

To be sure, certain indications of literacy exist within prophetic texts, but all these must be examined on their own merit. Apart from permanent testimonials to authenticate memorable predictive oracles, such reports may be retrojections of a later culture. If writing played a minimal role among the

---

words functioned as icons. Their magical character did not escape those in power, who benefited most from royal stelae.

[42] Much nonsense has been written about the magical power of the spoken word to bring about what it proclaims. This claim overlooks the instances in which the biblical text acknowledges the failure of oaths and curses, supposedly the most power-laden of all speech.

[43] See the exhaustive treatment of this phenomenon by S. M. Paul, "Heavenly Tablets and the Book of Life," *JANESCU* 5 (1973): 345–53 (with a postscript by W. W. Hallo), and the comments of H. Wildberger, *Isaiah 1–12* (trans. T. H. Trapp; Minneapolis: Fortress, 1991), 169–70. Besides listing a book in which was recorded the name of everyone destined for life, the Bible also refers to a book of memorable deeds (Ps 139:16), one in which the tears of the righteous are recorded (Ps 56:9), and a book of remembrance (Mal 3:16). The idea of a book of life (Exod 32:32–33) has a long history (cf. the Babylonian concept of the Tablets of Destiny).

[44] Davis, *Swallowing the Scroll*, underestimates the symbolic aspects of such language and overplays the written character of prophetic traditions.

[45] According to D. L. Petersen (*Haggai and Zechariah 1–8* [OTL; Philadelphia: Westminster, 1984], 245–54), the unrolled scroll portends punishment for violations of two laws, theft and false swearing. Thus old values persist in a new community, the diarchy that has replaced monarchy. Punishment falls to YHWH, and it hovers over all. C. L. Meyers and E. M. Meyers (*Haggai, Zechariah 1–8* [AB 25B; New York: Doubleday, 1987], 277–93) emphasize the correspondence of size between the temple vestibule and the scroll. They also consider the oath administered by priests to be important.

[46] "Beware of saying:
    'Everyone is according to his nature (*bi 't*)
    ignorant and learned ones alike,
    Fate and fortune are graven in the nature
    in the god's own writing. . . .'"
    (P. Chester Beatty IV; the translation is taken from Lichtheim, *Moral Values in Ancient Egypt*, 32.)

[47] Is their offense the abuse of wine or sacrilege involving sacred vessels obtained through victory over Jerusalem?

Israelite sages, is it likely that things were different in prophetic circles? Never does a wisdom teacher in Israel advise anyone to consult a written text; instead young men are urged to observe what transpires before their eyes and to listen eagerly to intelligent people.[48] That is how one acquired knowledge. To go a step further and gain wisdom, the student had to embody that information in the context of religious devotion.

Oral transmission of valued teachings has a distinct advantage, one recognized by Plato, who observed that a written text cannot choose its readers. Once put in writing, a text is subject to manipulation by literate interpreters.[49] While the same is true to some extent of orally transmitted teachings, access can be controlled to a greater degree. The person who wishes to pass along vital lore can choose those deemed worthy of receiving it. Even though accuracy of transmission may not have been a hard and fast rule, reformulation within an acceptable realm of discourse would have been a desideratum. In such circumstances, limited circulation among a fictive family of select disciples makes good sense. Did prophetic circles isolate particular ideas for further reflection by subsequent generations?

Thematic Emphases

Those who preserved biblical prophecy underlined the significance of several themes by various means. For example, they frequently cited an ancient credo, often in new and bold associations (Exod 34:6–7);[50] they developed a particular idea in increasingly complex ways (the day of YHWH);[51] they reflected on mythic adumbrations of familiar notions (the garden or vineyard of YHWH);[52] they elevated the linguistic register to the lyrical (utopian visions of

---

[48] Crenshaw, "The Primacy of Listening."

[49] For Plato's insight, see *Phaedrus* 274b–78b. One may compare a Yoruba proverbial saying: "The white man who created writing also created the eraser."

[50] I have examined the use of this confessional expression in "Who Knows What YHWH Will Do? The Character of God in the Book of Joel," in *Fortunate the Eyes that See: Essays in Honor of David Noel Freedman in Celebration of his Seventieth Birthday* (ed. A. Beck et al.; Grand Rapids, Mich.: Eerdmans, 1994), 185–96.

[51] See J. L. Crenshaw, *Joel* (AB 24C; New York: Doubleday, 1995), 47–50 and passim, for analysis of this expression.

[52] On the importance of this theme, see N. Frye, *The Great Code: The Bible and Literature* (New York: Harcourt Brace Jovanovich, 1982). Note also the different treatments of the vineyard of YHWH in Isaiah 5 and 27.

Zion);[53] they stoutly resisted apparent empirical disconfirmations (the growing body of oracles against foreign nations); and they developed a form of lively debate (an end of suffering at YHWH's hand). Whether or not these thematic emphases correspond to the unresolved social issues of colonial Judah such as status, inclusion, and theodicy will need to be investigated.

By pondering these themes and developing them further, the successors to the prophets both honored their predecessors and kept the vision alive in new circumstances. Even though persuaded that their own insights were largely derivative, these descendants of YHWH's servants the prophets contributed to the prophetic tradition in important ways. The dynamic process of testing ancient words by the standards of their own age and making necessary changes inaugurated a movement that persists to this day. Nevertheless, a decisive difference has taken place; that process has become two-pronged, with one group transmitting the *traditum* from within the circle and with another group standing aloof and evaluating it from afar. The interaction of both approaches to the prophetic literature holds enormous potential, for it balances two distinct passions, subjective involvement and attempted scholarly detachment.[54]

---

[53] I treat this phenomenon in "Freeing the Imagination: The Conclusion to the Book of Joel," in *Prophecy and Prophets: The Diversity of Contemporary Issues in Scholarship* (ed. Y. Gitay; SBLSS; Atlanta: Scholars Press, 1997), 129–47.

[54] The goal of objectivity has come under attack by those who wish to replace it with passionate involvement similar to that of religious communities. I continue to value objective reading insofar as possible, chiefly as a means of dealing with the tower of Babel resulting from contemporary voices.

Orality and Writtenness in the Prophetic Texts

Robert C. Culley
McGill University

The topic of orality and writtenness in prophetic texts brings together two large areas of study, the question of oral versus written and the study of the prophetic tradition. Over the past fifty years or so, the study of the oral and the written has been investigated in many different texts stemming from numerous language communities and from various historical periods from the distant past to the present. The amount of scholarship on oral studies is now substantial and is expanding by the year. Then, there is the prophetic tradition. Prophetic texts form a substantial collection within the Bible, and investigation of them has produced a daunting number of commentaries, monographs, and articles, the number of which continues to increase at a robust pace. The scope of the present topic which puts together the notion of oral/written and the prophetic collection poses the immediate need of finding a way to narrow the focus and reduce the discussion to manageable proportions, at least for an essay of this size. In order to do this, I shall substitute for the key words "orality" and "writtenness" two terms that are more restricted in their range, and I shall develop my investigation along these narrower lines. On the prophetic side, only a very limited range of material will be referred to. The discussion will unfold in four stages: introduction of the more restricted terms for orality and writtenness; development of some general observations from these terms; application of these observations to a small amount of prophetic material; and, in conclusion, brief comments on some of the implications the discussion might have on issues like text, reading, author, and context.

The study of orality and writtenness in connection with the biblical texts is no small undertaking. The general, interdisciplinary discussions of the nature of oral and written, which have been going on for so many years now, are complex and cannot be reduced to simple axioms. On the biblical side, matters are no more encouraging. Evidence from biblical texts of the sort that could be used to determine unequivocally their origin in oral or written composition is by no means abundant or unambiguous. Consequently, given the range of theoretical perspectives and the limited evidence from biblical texts, we are compelled to engage in educated guesswork using various kinds of general models of, or sets of assumptions about, orality and writtenness. The game, then, is to apply models or assumptions that appear to be appropriate to biblical material in order to see if they help us to understand the nature of these texts more fully and to gain useful clues about how to read them. Over the years, different models, some leaning toward oral and some leaning toward written, have surfaced in biblical scholarship. One only has to think of Wellhausen's decision to abandon the search for oral background in order to focus on written documents and authors and then compare it to Gunkel's willingness to look behind the documents for the shapes of oral genres. In our present studies, we all make our choices according to the larger frameworks we have adopted. How we make choices and show preference for one model of oral/written over another has a lot more to do with our larger assumptions and perspectives, whether conscious or unconscious, than with the force of the evidence or the clarity of the theoretical discussion. In what follows, I shall simply adopt one way of looking at oral and written, and see where it leads when applied to prophetic texts.

Terminology

The first step, then, is to reduce the broad scope of the terms *orality* and *writtenness,* to a more restricted focus. My way of doing this is to substitute *oral traditional* for orality and *scribal* for writtenness.[1] This will need further explanation. A lot has happened in the study of oral tradition over the last forty years or so. In referring to this complex discussion, I shall be very selective and direct my comments to one particular kind of oral (traditional oral) and one kind of written (scribal). When I first began to comment on oral tradition, in an article from 1963, I suggested that a review of general research on oral tradition up to that time pointed to five possible ways that texts in the Hebrew Bible may have come into existence.[2] The five options ranged from orally composed works taken down by dictation right up to composition of texts with the use of writing. Although the five stages I mentioned would have to be revised and

---

[1] The terms *oral traditional, traditional scribal, written,* and *s cribal* will thus appear—rather ungrammatically but economically—as substantives.

[2] R. C. Culley, "An Approach to the Problem of Oral Tradition," *VT* 13 (1963): 124–25.

restated today, the basic idea of a range of options between oral and written still remains for me a valid summary of the possibilities, and it forms one of the assumptions I work with, as will be seen later. One of the five positions I mentioned in the 1963 article requires further comment because it will play a role in how I discuss the problem of oral tradition and the Bible. In the middle of the spectrum just mentioned, I placed the *transitional text,* a term used at the time by a few scholars in the oral field. They proposed that some texts, for example Beowulf, may have been composed with the aid of writing yet still in an oral traditional style.[3] This notion is important because it opens up a way of relating oral and written, the features of oral composition, and the practice of writing, and this relationship has significant implications for the larger question of orality and writtenness. It should be added that one of the key figures in oral studies at that time, Albert Bates Lord, rejected the notion of transitional text in *The Singer of Tales,* his most influential book.[4] Based on his experience in the field, he argued that one must maintain a sharp distinction between orally composed texts and texts produced in writing.

This was the situation thirty years ago, when the approach developed by Lord and Milman Parry, generally known as the oral-formulaic theory, was being debated, sometimes quite vehemently. This theory concentrated mainly, but by no means exclusively, on epic poetry and examined particularly the presence of traditional material like *formulas* (fixed and varied phrases), *themes* (variable, recurrent descriptions, and stock scenes), and *story-patterns* (tale types). Great emphasis was placed on how much of this kind of traditional material was present in a given text because the amount was thought to be a key factor in determining whether a given text was orally composed or not. Over the years, the theory found wide acceptance and support but also substantial criticism. For example, two important books on oral poetry, one by Ruth Finnegan and the other by Paul Zumthor both raise important criticisms of Lord's work, although they do not deny the importance of his contribution.[5]

---

[3] For some of this early discussion, see R. C. Culley, *Oral Formulaic Language in the Biblical Psalms* (Near and Middle East Series 4; Toronto: University of Toronto Press, 1967), 25–27.

[4] A. B. Lord, *The Singer of Tales* (Harvard Studies in Comparative Literature 24; Cambridge, Mass.: Harvard University Press, 1960).

[5] R. Finnegan, *Oral Poetry: Its Nature, Significance, and Social Context* (Bloomington: Indiana University Press, 1992); P. Zumthor, *Oral Poetry: An Introduction* (trans. K. Murphy-Judy; Theory and History of Literature 70; Minneapolis: University of Minnesota Press, 1990).

In recent times, one of the most interesting critics of the oral-formulaic theory is John Miles Foley.[6] Although he is among those who have worked extensively with the oral-formulaic theory, his familiarity and experience with the approach have led him to see the need for substantial correction and restatement. For example, Foley agrees with critics like Finnegan that one cannot simply universalize the details of the oral-formulaic theory to cover all oral poetry.[7] How oral composition and transmission works varies from tradition to tradition. More significant for the present discussion, Foley also challenges "the untested assumption that 'oral' could always and everywhere be distinguished from 'written.'"[8] Essentially, he accepts the notion of transitional texts as part of a spectrum of possibilities, although he refers to such texts as "orally-derived texts" to stress the interplay of oral and written. In my own thinking, the category of orally-derived texts seems more and more to be a likely possibility for the composition of a significant amount of biblical material. Orally-derived texts are still to be viewed within the full range from oral composition to written composition. This range, or continuum, from oral to written composition has been mapped out very well and the issues stated clearly by Susan Niditch in her book *Oral World and Written Word*, where she argued that "ancient Israelite literacy has to be understood in the context of an oral-traditional culture."[9]

In the following discussion, I will work within this general perspective but only elaborate some particular issues relevant to prophetic texts. I have chosen to use the terms *oral traditional* and *scribal* (which can be highly traditional as well) because they will serve to open up two lines of discussion. The one, *oral traditional*, will allow me to say something about a certain kind of oral style that has been studied rather widely. The other, *scribal*, will permit a discussion of a mode of composition that involves writing but that nevertheless may employ a style much closer to oral than to writing, at least as we know and practice it today in our print culture.

---

[6] See, for example, his comments in "Traditional Signs and Homeric Art," *Written Voices, Spoken Signs: Tradition, Performance, and the Epic Text* (ed E. Bakker and A. Kahane; Cambridge, Mass.: Harvard University Press, 1997), 56–82.

[7] Ibid., 60.

[8] Ibid., 59.

[9] S. Niditch, *Oral World and Written Word: Ancient Israelite Literature* (LAI; Louisville, Ky.: Westminster John Knox, 1996), 99.

General Observations

We now need to look at each of these terms in more detail. First, oral traditional. The term *oral traditional* has been widely used for many years in oral research and has been applied to biblical texts by Niditch, myself, and some others. The word *traditional* is important because it indicates that we are talking about the kind of oral composition that involves traditional material. At this point, all I mean to convey by *traditional* is that oral traditional performers usually repeat material that is already familiar to listeners. They reproduce, although in ever-varying form, well-known stories and poems. This means that the same stories, or stories with similar patterns, or the same poems, or poems of the same genre, are repeated over and over again, yet with constant variation. The important point is that this traditional material, both in its general content and language, is well known not only to the poets but also in varying degrees to the listeners. When poets say something new and different, which they do all the time, they work it out within the possibilities offered by traditional language. In other words, the listeners expect to hear what is familiar, and this is apparently just what the poets and storytellers want to give them. Traditional oral style is marked by repeated language, imagery, themes, and patterns, as I indicated earlier.

Initially studies of poetic texts thought to be oral or related to oral tradition concentrated on identifying formulas and themes in the material because these features were understood primarily as devices oral poets needed in order to compose orally. The presence of large amounts of formulaic material was taken to mean that the poems may have been composed orally or were very close to oral tradition. Smaller amounts of repeated language might suggest some relationship with oral tradition. This kind of approach was used in my own work on the Psalms.[10] There, I simply collected phrases that were repeated exactly or with variations. These I then listed and showed how they clustered in a few psalms. The results were modest and it was clear then, and even clearer now, that any conclusions drawn would necessarily be limited. At the very least, it seems likely that most of the phrases collected represent traditional language rather than copying. It is also possible that this traditional language gained its shape in an oral tradition where traditional language was used by the poets. However, since this language may have continued in a period of scribal composition, the presence of what appears to be oral traditional language says little about whether or not the poems had been composed orally or in writing.

In recent discussion the presence of the various elements of traditional language has been considered from another angle, how they function as

---

[10] Culley, *Oral Formulaic Language.*

traditional language rather than simply how they assist poets to compose. While this aspect of the function of tradition has been recognized by a number of scholars, John Miles Foley has developed this line of investigation in some detail, and so I will use his proposals to fill in some of the background for the way in which I will be looking at prophetic texts. According to Foley, the significant features of traditional oral style like formulas, themes, and story-patterns are important not so much because of their role as devices for composition by oral poets but because of their role in forming a body of traditional language shared by poets and audiences.[11] He argues that the relationship between performers and audiences, within which performers produce works based on a larger tradition shared with the audience, leads to a particular kind of referentiality, which he simply calls traditional referentiality.[12] He combines this idea of referentiality with a notion of metonymic meaning, a kind of convention in which the parts, traditional elements that appear in any particular poem, stand for a larger sphere of reference in the tradition known and shared by poets and audience.[13] This means that any given performance of a traditional poem or story necessarily evokes, through specific expressions of traditional language, imagery, themes, and patterns, the larger body of stories and poems in the common store of material familiar in varying degrees to performer and audience. From this angle, composition and reception are intimately linked and depend on each other. What may strike us as stereotyped and repetitious is integral to this bond. Even though skilled poets and storytellers seem to be able to work more freely and creatively with traditional language than poets with less ability, the familiarity with the tradition on the part of poets and audiences is a critical factor.

In Foley's view, then, the oral traditional idiom involves a fluency both on the part of performers and listeners. In his discussion, he identifies three features that, for the sake of interest, may be worth mentioning here: performance arena, register, and communication economy. These features concern the place where performer and audience meet and the nature of the familiar, traditional language known to both. *Performance arena*, or place, refers to the actual locations where performance occurs, but—and this is important—place is defined ultimately by the language of the tradition rather than specific settings. The speech act defines the place, not vice versa. This means that when the performance arena, or place, changes from situations

---

[11] Foley, "Traditional Signs," 56–82; idem, *Immanent Art: From Structure to Meaning in Oral Traditional Epic* (Bloomington: Indiana University Press, 1991), 2–60.

[12] Foley, *Immanent Art*, esp. 39–60.

[13] Ibid., 7–8.

where actual performances of poems and stories are heard to situations where they are read as texts, the poems or stories still invoke the same place, so that "there is no wholesale dislocation when the performance arena changes from an actual site to a rhetorically induced forum in a text."[14] *Register* refers to the kind of literary or poetic speech developed in those repeated settings where performance occurs. This would be language appropriate to performance and expected by audiences—in other words, the traditional language we have been discussing. Such language is layered and brings a lot of the past with it as it mixes older forms, expressions, and images with newer ones. *Communicative economy* refers to the potential of particular instances of traditional language to evoke elements of the tradition as a whole. I have mentioned these three features because they bear a certain similarity to three important issues pursued by Gunkel and subsequent form critics when they talked about the *Sitz im Leben* or the repeated settings from which various genres arose, the special language associated with different genres, and the way this language maintained itself and became traditional.

While Foley has gone further than most in developing a theory about oral traditional language and how it works, others have recognized the importance of traditional language and commented on different aspects of the issue. The contributions of two scholars can be mentioned briefly. In a recent article, Lauri Honko has discussed how epic poems function as tales of identity in that they are able "to convey extra textual meaning to those groups who recognize them as 'our story.'"[15] This author suggests that epics in fact create the "us" of the audience and, indeed, in doing so create the "them" who are different from the "us." I simply note this in passing because at a later point it will be asked whether the prophetic tradition functions in a similar way so that the collection of prophetic texts plays a role in establishing identity.

A case of traditional language functioning in nonepic poetry can be found in a study by Anna Caravelli of orally performed folksongs collected recently in Greece.[16] Some of her comments about performance and social context are relevant. One of the features of these songs is that, while written versions of songs appear complete, performed versions appear fragmentary. Caravelli argues that, with these incomplete songs, it is the world outside the song that completes the song. By world she means things like the knowledge that the

---

[14] Foley, "Traditional Signs," 69.

[15] L. Honko, "Epic and Identity: National, Regional, Communal, Individual," *Oral Tradition* 11 (1996): 21.

[16] A. Caravelli, "The Song Beyond the Song: Aesthetics and Social Interaction in Greek Folksong," *JAF* 95 (1982): 129–58.

audience has of the traditional forms of expression and the understanding of how the traditional themes relate to the community. She suggests that the incompleteness of these versions can be explained in the following way:

> A significant factor is that almost all present were familiar with the local song repertory, such that a line or two was sufficient for them to recall other lines not sung. . . . In a way then, each sung line and stated idea is mentally complemented by contextual meaning created by the audience's knowledge of other lines, themes, or words that complete the idea.[17]

In referring to Foley, Honko, and Caravelli, I do not mean to suggest that their work can be applied directly to prophetic texts, only that their work offers a few suggestions and, in Foley's case, some theory about how traditional oral composition works and can be understood in terms of poetics.

There has, of course, been a long discussion of the many aspects of oral tradition in biblical studies. The important contributions are noted in Niditch[18] and in my earlier reviews, especially the one in *Oral Tradition*, which also covers attempts to apply her approach to biblical texts. [19]

We turn now to *scribal*, another term that covers a lot of ground. Just as oral tradition is a very complex and varied phenomenon, so is scribal. The common factor in scribal activity is, of course, that writing is employed. Still, this could mean anything from writing down something from oral dictation to composition in writing. I will not attempt to cover the whole spectrum of possibilities but would like to think specifically of a kind of scribal practice that seems to develop in close relationship to oral traditional composition and transmission. If it is so that traditional, oral idioms exist and are deeply rooted in particular cultures (Niditch's "oral mentality"), then what happens when individuals begin to use writing in an oral traditional context? As we have seen, Foley has suggested that the traditional language developed in an oral tradition does not necessarily come to an end when poets begin to use writing to compose traditional poems. If, as many suggest, the move from orality to literacy proceeds along a continuum,[20] then the kind of scribal I am talking about would refer to a situation in which the oral idiom continues even when writing is used to inscribe texts.

In a recent book, Egbert Bakker has proposed a useful set of variations to employ when mapping out oral and written features. When considering oral and

---

[17] Ibid., 133.

[18] Niditch, *Oral World.*

[19] R. C. Culley, "Oral Tradition and Biblical Studies," *Oral Tradition* 1 (1986): 30–65.

[20] Niditch, *Oral World;* E. Bakker, *Poetry in Speech: Orality and Homeric Discourse* (Ithaca, N.Y.: Cornell University Press, 1997), 9.

written texts, he argues that it is important to make a distinction between medium and conception, that is to say, whether a text is produced in an oral or written form (medium) and whether a text is conceived in oral or written terms (conception). For example, in an oral-traditional setting, composition occurs during oral performance using the traditional idiom (orally conceived and orally presented). In contrast, we ourselves compose in writing because writing is "a way of organizing thought and texts"[21] and, even if we prepare everything in our heads before we write, we generally conceive of it as something that will end up in writing or, more likely, print (conceived as writing and put into writing). It is true that we can also produce oral presentations or write for oral presentation, but this is only in limited ways like oral-traditional composition in that we do use some conventional forms and language. Orally-derived texts would mean traditional texts conceived largely in oral terms but still produced in writing.

An attempt to apply this perception of orally-derived, traditional material to medieval texts can be found in an article by A. Doane, a specialist in Anglo-Saxon, who has proposed that the scribes who wrote vernacular Anglo-Saxon texts could be described as performers.[22] By this, Doane wants to suggest that the role of the scribe of traditional texts was somewhat analogous to the role of the oral traditional performers of traditional poems, described above, who employed variations of traditional language when they composed. Doane's proposal is based on an examination of a few poetic texts that are preserved in two copies. Apart from some obvious scribal errors, the copies still show variations. Doane concludes that variation was the norm when copying poetic texts. He contrasts this with the practice of scribes writing Latin texts, a language in which they were not necessarily fluent, where copying involved more care and a sense of textual fixity. With traditional, vernacular texts, scribes were conscious of both the obligations they had toward the tradition and the responsibility they felt toward their contemporary audience. As Doane puts it: "The scribe-as-performer would see the rewriting as enhancing the traditional text by giving it life in the present, by making it 'more real.'"[23] The extent to which this proposal is valid for the Anglo-Saxon texts will have to be left to the specialists who control the material. However, if Doane is on the right track, his description of the work of scribes working with traditional texts is worth keeping in mind.

---

[21] Bakker, *Poetry in Speech*, 25.

[22] A. Doane, "The Ethnography of Scribal Writing and Anglo-Saxon Poetry: Scribe as Performer," *Oral Tradition* 9 (1994): 420–39.

[23] Ibid., 434.

Discussion of scribal activity has long been a part of the study of biblical texts, and this seems reasonable since, however they were conceived, biblical texts were first written down on scrolls. General overviews of the problems in describing this writing process have been given by Susan Niditch, Philip Davies, and most recently Ian M. Young,[24] and they refer to the abundant scholarly literature relevant to this issue. As with the study of oral tradition in biblical studies, the range of approaches is considerable and it may be helpful to indicate something of this variety with a few selected examples.

There are those interested in the work of scribes as redactors. Michael Fishbane starts from the question of inner biblical interpretation and searches out, in a very detailed discussion, evidence of scribal activity in the biblical text. His main interest is to explore the way scribes interpreted the texts that came into their hands.[25] Michael Fox, in the final chapter of his book *The Redaction of the Books of Esther*, is also concerned with redactors.[26] On the basis of his study of Esther texts, he suggests that editors range all the way from copyists to "aggressive redactors," and this latter is the kind he is primarily interested in. What intrigues him is the problem of how to read redacted texts so that the earlier and later elements in them are allowed to have their say, without either removing redactions to get the "original" text or suppressing the earlier parts in favor of a supposed "final form." Fox attempts to explore how "multiple, sequential voices *interact*—and not only tell their own stories—within a single work."[27] As a historical critic, however, he does want to take the sequential seriously in his reading of the different voices in composite texts. He also distinguishes between the intentions of ancient redactors and the perceptions of modern readers. He argues that, even though redactors may try to suppress the older text they are working with, critical readers do not have to accept this suppression but may expose it and work with the tensions created by the earlier and later.[28] Finally one might mention Raymond Person's use of Doane's idea of the scribe as performer when he applies it to the ancient

---

[24] Niditch, *Oral World;* P. R. Davies, *Scribes and Schools: The Canonization of the Hebrew Scriptures* (LAI; Louisville, Ky.: Westminster John Knox, 1998); I. M. Young, "Israelite Literacy: Interpreting the Evidence. Part I," *VT* 48 (1998): 239–53; idem, "Israelite Literacy: Interpreting the Evidence. Part II," *VT* 48 (1998): 462–81.

[25] M. Fishbane, *Biblical Interpretation in Ancient Israel* (Oxford: Clarendon, 1985), esp. 23–88.

[26] M. V. Fox, *The Redaction of the Books of Esther: On Reading Composite Texts* (SBLMS; Atlanta: Scholars Press, 1991), 142–53.

[27] Ibid., 149.

[28] Ibid., 152 n. 28.

Israelite scribes whom he sees, following Niditch, as "literate members of a primarily oral society." [29]

A rather different perspective can be found in the work of John Van Seters, who highlights the role of major authors and makes this a governing factor in his understanding of how texts were written. For him, J is a compiler/author. Van Seters's model for this approach is the ancient, antiquarian historiographer like those found in the Greek tradition who "takes up the extant traditions, written and oral, and reshapes them, edits them, compiles and incorporates them into an extensive work."[30] A similar focus on the author/compiler, this time the writers of the gospels of the New Testament, is evident in the writings of Werner Kelber, although he works very much along the lines of Foley and Doane and wants to give considerable weight to the nature of the extant traditions selected and to the way they were used by the gospel writers.[31] He adds the dimension of cultural memory to the process, and it may be useful to quote him at length on this topic:

> Contrary to the assumptions of historical criticism, a text's substantial and multifaceted investment in tradition does not suggest intertextuality in the sense of scanning through multiple, physically accessible scrolls but, more likely, accessibility to a shared *cultural memory*. When Mark, like many other writers, operated with a plurality of oral and written traditions, reclaiming and citing some, revising others, responding critically, even deconstructively to the stimuli provided by various traditions, dislodging some even as he built upon them and orchestrating the chorus of polyphonic voices into a narrative addressed to followers of Jesus in the period after 70, he was plugging into a copious reservoir of memories, retrieving and reshuffling what was accessible to him memorially. In the end I venture the suggestion that the gospel composition is unthinkable without the notion of cultural memory which serves ultimately not the preservation of remembrances per se but the preservation of the group, its social identity and self image.[32]

The general observations on oral traditional and scribal practice that I have just presented were developed largely from the interdisciplinary discussion about oral tradition that has been going on for some time. In drawing on this I have been selective and concentrated on one particular stream of discussion,

---

[29] R. F. Person Jr., "The Ancient Israelite Scribe as Performer," *JBL* 117 (1998): 602.

[30] J. Van Seters, *The Life of Moses: The Yahwist as Historian in Exodus-Numbers* (Louisville, Ky.: Westminster John Knox, 1994), 457.

[31] W. H. Kelber, *The Oral and the Written Gospel: The Hermeutics of Speaking and Writing in the Synoptic Tradition, Mark, Paul, and Q* (Bloomington: Indiana University Press, 1997; repr., with a new introduction, of the 1983 edition [Philadelphia: Fortress]).

[32] Ibid., xxiii.

one that assumes an oral–written continuum and holds the notion open of an overlapping of oral and scribal composition in the middle of the continuum. This is nevertheless a serious line of research based on the work of several scholars over many years—investigations that have ranged from contemporary oral settings to ancient texts. However, the question still remains: can this model, or general perspective, be applied with profit to the biblical texts? Some of us would like to think that it can, and in ways that may be helpful and suggestive in thinking about the nature of biblical texts, which, as we have recognized for some time, are quite complex. While I have given some importance to the idea of transitional or orally-derived texts in which oral and written both play a role, this option still remains a part of a spectrum that runs all the way from oral composition at one end to written composition at the other. For example, it is possible that there may be biblical texts that remain rather close to oral performance, in which there are multiple and varied versions of traditional poems and stories, which are dense with language carried along and mixed together from different stages in the past. Since this density of language may continue when writing is used, we may have orally-derived texts that conserve oral style. As the use of writing increases, the exploitation of the potential it offers will have its effect on the composition and collection of traditional materials. The existence of manuscripts allows for a kind of collecting and building of traditional texts that would seem to me unlikely in an oral setting. Writing allows scribes to combine, interweave, and expand received material, increasing the density and complexity even more.

The Bible represents a remarkable example of a composite document, for which it is difficult to find close parallels. There is such a profusion and variety of material that at the same time is held together on higher levels by numerous syntagmatic (plots, storylines) and paradigmatic features (repeated language, imagery). The work of the biblical scholars that I mentioned above when talking about scribal activity—scholars such as Fishbane, Fox, Van Seters, and Kelber—illustrates the intricate and manifold nature of the biblical text and the problems of exploring its complexity. Producing composite texts involves putting different materials side by side, revising, and adding further comments. Even if scribes continued to conceive of composition in an oral way, they were doing so within the framework of the production of composite texts from materials already in existence.

Applications

We now turn to prophetic texts. My description of oral traditional, traditional scribal, and the way they may interact will not mean much to the discussion of prophetic texts if we can find no clues to them in the biblical texts. I say clues because we do not have a lot of material, considering the time span of prophetic activity. What we have combines elements scattered over long periods of time. Then too, I move into the prophetic material with considerable caution because of the complexity of the texts and substantial body of critical literature. Still, with oral tradition, it is not a matter of starting completely from scratch. The idea of viewing the texts in the Hebrew Bible as traditional is hardly new. Long ago, Hermann Gunkel spoke of the constraints of tradition.[33] It has already been noted how the elements of his general definition of traditional genre (use of traditional language and the role of a setting in the life of the people) bear some similarity to the elements used by Foley in his description of traditional fluency, although Gunkel and subsequent form critics handled them differently. Furthermore, Gunkel went in a somewhat different direction with the prophets.[34]

When the whole prophetic tradition is kept in view, two major themes stand out: rescue and punishment. These themes are not only important in prophetic tradition but they are also prominent in psalms and narratives.[35] The theme of rescue, or restoration, that becomes dominant in Deutero-Isaiah also plays a role in most of the other prophetic books. In these books the theme of punishment, whether announced against Israel or other nations, emerges as the overpowering concern. This theme embraces a cluster of images and language that includes features like the description of the wrongs that make punishment necessary and elaborate depictions of the punishment itself. While punishment could come in the form of famine, drought, or plagues, it was often portrayed as destruction by an invading army marching against Israel or other nations like Egypt or Babylon. As a consequence, military imagery came up often and, within the poetic language, seemed to take on a life of its own, even though it was often applied to specific occasions like an Assyrian invasion.

All this is quite evident and has by no means been overlooked by commentators. For example, imagery about a foe from the north found in the book of Jeremiah was examined in a 1959 article by Brevard Childs, "The Enemy from the North and the Chaos Tradition,"[36] although he took a different slant on the material than I am using here. Childs began with the references in

---

[33] H. Gunkel, *Die israelitische Literatur* (Darmstadt: Wissenschaftliche Buchgesellschaft, 1963), 2–3.

[34] M. H. Floyd, "Prophecy and Writing in Habakkuk 2,1–5," *ZAW* 105 (1993): 462–81.

[35] See the discussion of narrative patterns in R. C. Culley, *Themes and Variations: A Study of Action in Biblical Narrative* (SBLSS; Atlanta: Scholars Press, 1992).

[36] B. S. Childs, "The Enemy from the North and the Chaos Tradition," *JBL* 78 (1959): 187–98.

Jeremiah 1, 4, 5, and 6. Here an invading army, never identified, is described as being foreign and powerful, well supplied with horses, chariots, and various weapons, and coming from the north, from a distant land. To these Jeremiah references he added Isaiah 5 and Habbakuk 1, recognizing also some similarities in Nahum 2–3. Childs further noted the military language in the oracles against foreign nations of Jeremiah 46–51, Ezekiel 38–39, Isaiah 13, and Joel, and that it raises the military imagery to a broader cosmological level, which he called a chaos tradition. I only want to note here that this military imagery of Yahweh's punishment, whether the attack of an army on the human level or a larger cosmological battle, seems to be a complex, traditional, image-cluster available to those who adopted the prophetic idiom. If it had its origins in oral tradition, then it was the kind of image shared by poets and audiences and continued in the production of scribal texts, and so elements of this image cluster are found in several variations in prophetic books.

I would like now to look more closely at some of the language of this imagery of a battle involving the deity by examining more carefully some repeated or similar motifs and phrases. In what follows, Isaiah 13 is taken as a base and used to trace motifs and similar phrases in other related texts. The motifs from Isaiah 13 discussed here are: (1) the announcement of an attack, (2) a day of Yahweh, (3) darkness, (4) shaking, (5) anger, (6) the reaction of people to this event, and (7) the subsequent desolation. Most of the examples come from texts with a similar theme like Isaiah 18; Jeremiah 4, 6, 49, 50 and 51; and Joel and Zephaniah. I will simply quote some of the relevant lines and add further references.

The announcement of an attack in Isaiah 13 (against Babylon) is "raise a signal":

Isa 13:2	עַל הַר־נִשְׁפֶּה שְׂאוּ־נֵס הָרִימוּ קוֹל לָהֶם
Jer 51:12	אֶל־חוֹמֹת בָּבֶל שְׂאוּ־נֵס הַחֲזִיקוּ הַמִּשְׁמָר

In other texts, a phrase is added about blowing the trumpet:

Jer 4:5, 6	וְתִקְעוּ שׁוֹפָר בָּאָרֶץ קִרְאוּ מַלְאוּ
	שְׂאוּ־נֵס צִיּוֹנָה הָעִיזוּ אַל־תַּעֲמֹדוּ
Jer 6:1	וּבִתְקוֹעַ תִּקְעוּ שׁוֹפָר וְעַל־בֵּית הַכֶּרֶם שְׂאוּ מַשְׂאֵת
Jer 51:27	שְׂאוּ־נֵס בָּאָרֶץ תִּקְעוּ שׁוֹפָר בַּגּוֹיִם
Isa 18:3	כִּנְשֹׂא־נֵס הָרִים תִּרְאוּ וְכִתְקֹעַ שׁוֹפָר תִּשְׁמָעוּ

Joel 2:1 only mentions trumpet.

In Isaiah 13 the attack of nations from afar involves Yahweh as leader so that the event becomes a cosmological day of Yahweh when darkness and anger prevail. For the phrase "the day of Yahweh is near":

Isa 13:6	הֵילִילוּ כִּי קָרוֹב יוֹם יְהוָה כְּשֹׁד מִשַּׁדַּי יָבוֹא
Isa 13:9	הִנֵּה יוֹם־יְהוָה בָּא אַכְזָרִי וְעֶבְרָה וַחֲרוֹן אָף
Joel 1:15	כִּי קָרוֹב יוֹם יְהוָה וּכְשֹׁד מִשַּׁדַּי יָבוֹא
Joel 2:1	יִרְגְּזוּ כֹּל יֹשְׁבֵי הָאָרֶץ כִּי־בָא יוֹם־יְהוָה כִּי קָרוֹב
Joel 4:14	כִּי קָרוֹב יוֹם יְהוָה בְּעֵמֶק הֶחָרוּץ

See also Ezek 30:2; Obad 15; and Zeph 1:7, 14.

This is accompanied by darkness:

Isa 13:10	כִּי־כוֹכְבֵי הַשָּׁמַיִם וּכְסִילֵיהֶם לֹא יָהֵלּוּ אוֹרָם
	חָשַׁךְ הַשֶּׁמֶשׁ בְּצֵאתוֹ וְיָרֵחַ לֹא־יַגִּיהַ אוֹרוֹ
Joel 2:2	יוֹם חֹשֶׁךְ וַאֲפֵלָה יוֹם עָנָן וַעֲרָפֶל
Joel 3:4	הַשֶּׁמֶשׁ יֵהָפֵךְ לְחֹשֶׁךְ וְהַיָּרֵחַ לְדָם

See also Ezek 32:7, 8; Zeph 1:15; Joel 4:15; Hab 3:11.

There is also a shaking:

Isa 13:13	עַל־כֵּן שָׁמַיִם אַרְגִּיז וְתִרְעַשׁ הָאָרֶץ מִמְּקוֹמָהּ
Jer 8:16	מִקּוֹל מִצְהֲלוֹת אַבִּירָיו רָעֲשָׁה כָּל־הָאָרֶץ
Joel 2:10	לְפָנָיו רָגְזָה אֶרֶץ רָעֲשׁוּ שָׁמָיִם

See also Jer 50:34; 51:29; Joel 2:1; 4:16.

The anger of Yahweh is sometimes mentioned as well:

Isa 13:3	גַּם קָרָאתִי גִבּוֹרַי לְאַפִּי עַלִּיזֵי גַּאֲוָתִי
Isa 13:9	הִנֵּה יוֹם־יְהוָה בָּא אַכְזָרִי וְעֶבְרָה וַחֲרוֹן אָף
Isa 13:13	בְּעֶבְרַת יְהוָה צְבָאוֹת וּבְיוֹם חֲרוֹן אַפּוֹ

See also Jer 4:8, and perhaps Jer 25:37, 38.

The reaction of the people about to be attacked is described in Isaiah 13 as a state in which hands will fall helplessly, hearts will melt, and agonizing pangs will seize them like a woman in childbirth:

Isa 13:7	עַל־כֵּן כָּל־יָדַיִם תִּרְפֶּינָה וְכָל־לְבַב אֱנוֹשׁ יִמָּס
Isa 13:8	צִירִים וַחֲבָלִים יֹאחֵזוּן כַּיּוֹלֵדָה יְחִילוּן
Jer 6:24	שָׁמַעְנוּ אֶת־שָׁמְעוֹ רָפוּ יָדֵינוּ צָרָה הֶחֱזִיקַתְנוּ חִיל כַּיּוֹלֵדָה

See also Jer 50:43; Jer 49:24 mentions the woman; cf. Isa 21:3, Ezek 7:17 and 21:12 (prose).

There is the subsequent desolation of the place attacked. Humans will no longer inhabit it but only the jackal, the ostrich, and strange creatures. On this, see Isa 13:19–22 and Jer 50:39–40, but also Isa 34:13, 14 (for jackals, Jer 9:10; 10:22; 51:37).

It is interesting to observe how this imagery of Yahweh's punishment is worked out in the book of Joel. In the first chapter, a visitation of locusts is described and portrayed as divine punishment. The second chapter seems to retain the basic notion of punishment by a plague of locusts but transposes most of the language into the two-level imagery of a day of Yahweh and invading army that we have just been considering. It seems that, once the plague of locusts is understood as divine punishment, the other traditional imagery associated with punishment can be drawn in. In his discussion of the performance arena or place referred to earlier, Foley remarked that the traditional language defined this rather than the situation outside the text. Something like this may be happening here in that the visitation of the locusts, already understood as a typical form of punishment, is further defined by the imagery of the day of Yahweh and the invading army. At any rate, the example of Joel illustrates how traditional imagery and language defines and characterizes an event on the human plane. From this angle, the text may not find its context so much in a particular infestation of locusts at a particular time and place as in the cluster of traditional imagery around the theme of punishment that defines and ties together many such events.

Implications

The images, motifs, and language from prophetic texts that I have just listed are fragmentary and cannot be offered as clear evidence of oral composition. Still, this collection of material is suggestive. From my perspective, it looks like traces of oral-traditional style and displays the features I would expect to find in oral style. At the very least, the presence of this kind of similar language suggests that those who produced these texts liked to say things in a traditional way, sticking with the familiar, which is how I defined tradition earlier. So the possibility of oral style continuing in scribal composition is a genuine consideration. In fact, the presence of elements of oral tradition is recognized by many at least to some degree, although there is the inclination to put most of the weight on scribal activity and written style. By way of example, the views of three scholars may be briefly noted. James Crenshaw has described the style of the Book of Joel as anthological, the work of a learned scribe who was "familiar with a wide range of sacred tradition, either oral floating traditions or written texts."[37] Philip Davies accepts the notion of traditional style, which he sees in passages like the oracles against

---

[37] J. L. Crenshaw, *Joel* (AB 24C; New York: Doubleday, 1995), 36.

foreign nations "that recur to the point of tedium."[38] He describes these texts as conceivably examples of scribal exercises in learning to write in a traditional style. Ehud Ben Zvi also thinks in terms of scribes and their repertoire but seems to lean strongly in the direction of writing and texts.[39] At least it is significant that all three note the role of tradition, what has gone before, in shaping texts.

On the basis of my discussion of traditional oral and scribal given above, I would be inclined, if I were to make an educated guess, to support the idea that oral style had a fairly large influence on the work of scribes. This is in line with the proposals of those who argue that scribal composition may well have continued in an oral style and at the same time begun to exploit the potential of writing. If this was so, it may be important, in any consideration of scribal composition, to keep the notion of oral traditional style as a significant part of the picture. This still leaves room for other styles of composition in what is clearly a very complex process about which decisions are difficult to make. For example, Davies' suggestion of scribal exercises in traditional style cannot be excluded, but the matter can be turned around and viewed from the other direction. What we consider tedious repetition is the core of oral-traditional style and is integral to the bond of common tradition shared and negotiated by performers and audience. The question of how exactly prophetic texts came into existence probably needs to remain open.

But suppose we turn from how things may have happened in the history of composition and consider another angle: the nature of the texts we are now left with and how we may read them. The discussion of traditional oral and scribal practices has at least placed us in a position to ask different questions about reading these ancient texts, and here, I think, is the most valuable contribution of a study of orality and writtenness. It encourages us to look at prophetic books a little differently, especially when we think about text, reading, author, and context. At the moment I am rather more interested in gaining some insight into this side of things, the nature of biblical texts and how they may be read, than in trying to reconstruct exactly what may have happened at any particular stage of the composition of prophetic material.

---

[38] P. R. Davies, "The Audiences of Prophetic Scrolls: Some Suggestions," in *Prophets and Paradigms: Essays in Honor of Gene M. Tucker* (ed. S. B. Reid; JSOTSup 229; Sheffield: Sheffield Academic Press, 1996), 60.

[39] E. Ben Zvi, "Twelve Prophetic Books or 'The Twelve': A Few Preliminary Considerations," in *Forming Prophetic Literature: Essays on Isaiah and the Twelve in Honor of John D. W. Watts* (ed. J. W. Watts and P. R. House; JSOTSup 235; Sheffield: Sheffield Academic Press, 1997), 155; see also his comments in *A Historical-Critical Study of the Book of Obadiah* (BZAW 242; Berlin and New York: de Gruyter, 1996), 1–9, 260–67.

I have no particular problem with historical reconstruction, especially because I have been doing some of this in my discussion of the oral traditional and scribal. We are free to ask how texts may have been read in the various settings associated with the stages of their growth, whether it be the original, the final, or somewhere in between. Still, even if we were sure about how texts were understood at any of these stages, it is not clear why any particular stage should become the key to reading the text, whether this means isolating part of the text as an original or essential core or privileging the final form as the key to how one reads the text as a whole. These are valid choices but not necessary ones, acceptable but not inevitable. There is at least one disadvantage in selecting some particular point in a text's development and using a historical context reconstructed from this as a point from which to view the rest. This procedure subordinates, or perhaps even suppresses, other possible readings which may have taken place, or could take place, in different historical contexts. The richness of the text may be closed down. The problem is not in discerning different voices in a text, they are there, but in how one chooses to deal with them critically. Since texts survive through many contexts and continue to produce readings, it may be worth considering what it is about texts that enables them to do this. My concluding comments will simply list a few suggestions about how the perspective on orality and writtenness I have outlined may raise questions about text, reading, author, and context.

As with most biblical material, prophetic texts seem to be composite in one way or another, either in the sense that through redaction already existing material has been attached or in the more nebulous sense that traditional style brings the past with it and juxtaposes earlier and later perceptions, although later material may still sound a lot like the earlier. If oral traditional texts exist only in versions such that no "original" or "final" version functions as a key to the others, what could this suggest about prophetic books? By way of analogy, one could suggest that in a complex, composite text, such as a prophetic book, the various stages may be something like a series of performances or versions that play with the same themes, so that the potential of important themes like punishment and rescue are explored and worked out in different ways. Rather than separating the stages of the text into a historical series, I would rather think of a cluster of versions or partial versions. The word "cluster" suggests that the relationships between the various elements can be worked out in all directions and not just a single, linear direction. A cluster implies alternatives, choices, even tensions, contradiction, and conflict within the same traditional stream. Even moving back and forth from one level to another, as in the interplay between historical and cosmic noted in the examples given above, suggests how important it may be in reading traditional texts to foster the ambiguity offered rather than reducing it.

If we are prepared to allow this kind of complexity to remain in play as we read, then texts cannot be seen as closed, determined by a strict notion of textual unity that absorbs everything and leaves no remainder. At the same time, allowing the complexity to remain in play does not mean that texts are open to any and all interpretations that readers may wish to place upon them, since the bundle of traditional themes, images, and language seems to mark out certain limits and boundaries within which and from which reading is played out. One might even think of a prophetic book, or even the prophetic books as a whole, as a cluster or bundle of differing explorations of major themes, explorations that never resolve themselves into a unity or strict harmony and that even resist readings that try to produce this.

As we have seen, traditional authors, while original and creative in their own way, often express the new by reworking and restating known traditional themes, imagery, and language. If this were true of the contributors to the prophetic books, then to what extent would it be useful to think of the different voices we encounter as performers of traditions that were familiar to them and to their listeners or readers? From a historical perspective, it may have been necessary, in order to be recognized as a genuine prophetic voice, to employ recognizable prophetic language. This may have been a question of validation or legitimation. To be accepted as a prophetic voice, one needed to sound like a prophet, to enter into a relationship with the audience through the shared tradition, even if the message might in the end not be acceptable to the audience. A similar situation could be true at later stages as well, even for authors who used writing. In a sense, the persona of "prophet" was a given, even though a given capable of shifting and changing as old themes were explored and new themes were introduced. Whether a prophetic text reflects the words of a prophet or the words of a scribe, the language continues to function rhetorically, relating readers to the text in a certain way, or at least inviting them to do so, because the texts can still be read counter to or against this intention.

This leads us to the idea that traditional texts play a role in creating their own context—something that is probably true of all texts to some degree. One may indeed speak of the specific historical, religious, and social context of particular contributors to a prophetic book and of their audiences, because this certainly applies for all texts. But there is also the context of *tradition* which seems to have been strung out over longer stretches of time and may have played an important role in determining and defining the particular situations as they arose. Versions of traditional prophetic language were achieved in a number of settings over time, resulting in an interplay between specific realizations and the continuing cluster of tradition. It is in this longer perspective of tradition that the prophetic collection fosters an identity not only for the prophets and those who wished to speak like prophets but also for the listeners and readers who shared an understanding of the larger tradition to which the individual versions of it pointed.

"Pen of iron, point of diamond" (Jer 17:1): Prophecy as Writing

Philip R. Davies
University of Sheffield

Prophecy as Literature

Sometimes the obvious is not obvious, and not least in biblical studies. Of the sociological/anthropological studies of "Israelite prophecy,"[1] few if any have noted that intermediaries do not write their words in big books; few have followers who write down their words, and fewer still have schools of editors reworking their verbal legacy for later generations. The phenomenon of "prophecy" in ancient Israel and Judah is not essentially a social one but a literary one: what makes the case of these societies unique is that they produced "prophetic" scrolls. From these scrolls (and some others) emerges the idea of a single institution of "prophecy," and in some of the less critical literature, even of our own day, this literary and ideological invention has been reverted to historical description: one speaks of "the prophets" as if dealing with a historical institution.

But ancient intermediaries do not as a rule keep records of their intermediations, nor are these preserved over centuries. Still, written transcriptions of prophetic speeches are occasionally found—for example at Mari, in the Sibylline literature, or among the Mormons—and one should thus not deny a

---

[1] The most influential of these is R. R. Wilson, *Prophecy and Society in Ancient Israel* (Philadelphia: Fortress, 1980). See also the work of T. W. Overholt (*Prophecy In Cross-Cultural Perspective: A Sourcebook for Biblical Researchers* [Atlanta: Scholars Press, 1986]; idem, *Channels of Prophecy: The Social Dynamics of Prophetic Activity*, [Minneapolis: Fortress, 1989]).

priori that the literature later canonized as the Jewish scriptures could possibly be an exception to this rule. Nevertheless, the indisputable evidence that the so-called "prophetic" books were created as literary artifacts, and indeed were mostly brought into their present shape by scribal editing, surely places a burden of proof on those who want to associate them primarily with the spoken words of named individuals.

"Biblical prophecy" presents us *prima facie* with a literary phenomenon, and the insistence that any connection between these scrolls, each one marked by the name of an individual, and their eponyms needs to be analyzed rather than assumed. This premise will surely be taken as yet another manifestation of revisionist scepticism, of the kind that adamantly refuses to accept both the plain statements of Holy Scripture (or even of other similar ancient texts) and the accumulated wisdom of theological commentators and historians of ancient Israelite religion looking for material to write about. But I simply regard such a stance as good methodology: what we can see is what we know, and what we would like to think needs to be argued for. It would be convenient to assume that the "prophets" of the four scrolls of Isaiah, Jeremiah, Ezekiel, and the Twelve really existed and had some influence on the behavior of their society, because without them most of the dominant portraits of that religion (notably that of Romantic Protestantism, which flourished in Germany in the nineteenth century and North America in the twentieth century) collapse. But analysis of the books (in nearly every case the only evidence we have for these characters) suggests considerable caution.

What Do the Books Know of the Prophets?

Let us start with the connections made between prophets and the books named for them. I shall confine myself to the Book of the Twelve for the moment, since the other three prophetic scrolls clearly present a different phenomenon by virtue of their length and compositional history—and indeed Isaiah, Jeremiah, and Ezekiel each need to be taken separately with regard to their composition. Their shape, structure, and indeed, their existence, may well arise from individual and not identical causes.

Here is a table of the correspondences between the individual prophetic "books" of the Twelve and the historical data about their eponyms:

Prophet	Date	Detail
Hosea b. Beeri	"in the days of Uzziah, Jotham, Ahaz, and Hezekiah of Judah, and Jeroboam of Israel"	
Joel b. Pethuel		
Amos	"in the days of Uzziah king of Judah and Jeroboam of Israel, two years before the earthquake"	"among the herdsmen of Tekoa"
Obadiah		
Jonah b. Amittai	(dates can be inferred from 2 Kgs 14:25 but not actually given in the book itself)	
Micah of Moreshet	"in the days of Jotham, Ahaz and Hezekiah"	
Nahum the Elkoshite		
Habakkuk		
Zephaniah b. Cushi, b. Gedaliah, b. Amariah, b. Hizkiah	"in the days of Josiah b. Amon of Judah"	
Haggai	"in the second year of Darius"	
Zechariah b. Berechiah	"in the second year of Darius"	
Malachi		

The sequence of prophets here has probably been arranged, as Barry Jones has argued, following others, not just in a chronological order, but in such a way as to reflect the kind of scheme we see in Daniel: a division of history into epochs of world empires.[2] The earliest collection apparently comprised nine prophets, three assigned to each of three empires (Assyria, Babylonia, and Persia). Jones's suggestion is based on the variable placement of Jonah, Joel and Obadiah in the LXX and the Qumran texts. Accordingly, Hosea, Amos, and

---

[2] B. A. Jones, *The Formation of the Book of the Twelve: A Study in Text and Canon* (SBLDS 149; Atlanta: Scholars Press, 1995), 54.

Micah are the three assigned to the Assyrian period. That these three, and not Joel, Obadiah, or Jonah, have chronological assignations (correlated with 2 Kings) supports his contention that they form a distinct group; but on the same hypothesis, two of the prophets of the Babylonian period (Nahum, Habakkuk) and one of those from the Persian period (Malachi) do not have any chronological assignments at all, which raises a question about the coherence of any overall editing with such a chronological scheme in mind. The rather uneven interest in the precise dating of these prophets may betray the fact that precise chronology was not of particular importance; was a broader interest in world history what mattered, or was such a schematization self-evident?

But I am not here much concerned about the redactional arrangement of these prophetic collections, since it certainly belongs already to a literary stage. What is important for my purpose is to note that apart from the occasional bits of chronological information, which in some cases are the result of an editing concerned to link the books to the history now in the books of Kings, there is very little indeed of biographical information about any of these characters. Hence, we have no basis for deducing that any transmission of assumed "traditions" about such prophets contained biographical information about them. This strikes me as worthy of explanation. When transmitted orally, material about an individual generally accumulates legendary stories about the character. Were the presumed "disciples" of Hosea, Micah, or Amos never asked about their hero?

Is this general lack of information about the individuals in itself an indication that in the composition of these books oral transmission did not play any significant role? I suppose that many will deny such an inference. However, it is probably fair to draw a comparison, or rather, a contrast, with the cycle of stories about Elijah and Elisha. Here we have material that is widely regarded as redolent of oral storytelling. Without necessarily endorsing or denying that impression, we can accept that the text associates, with Elisha at least, a "circle" of prophets to whom the preservation of such legends might be attributed. Yet the contrast between such narratives, which are biographical (I do not necessarily mean they are reliably so), and the sayings that make up the bulk of the Minor Prophets is vivid: on the one hand are legends and hardly any *nota dicta*; on the other, the opposite. If any analogies are to be drawn at all between the intermediaries described in the Elijah and Elisha (and related) materials in aid of positing circles of disciples who transmit prophetic words, the marked contrast in the character of the material thus (*ex hypothesi*) produced is eloquent.

Apart from the superscriptions, personal information about the prophets in the Book of the Twelve is meagre. The marriage of Hosea hardly counts as such information, and the episode in Amos 7 shows clear signs of a literary construction that makes it doubtful that the story arose from oral (or written) traditions traceable to the time of the prophetic character himself. We can conclude that any disciples of such prophets, if they ever existed, would have remembered little about the individuals they revered and that they transmitted (or even invented) minimal information, if any, about their persons and lives. There appear, of course, occasional firm connections between the time of the eponymous prophet and the content of the book assigned to him: references to Assyrians or Babylonians or Edomites.[3] But while these might tempt a scholar to suggest a solid traditional linkage between a named prophet and the words connected to him, such a suggestion is not really required. The assignation of a date to a prophet may as well be the result of an editorial inference (correct or otherwise) from the contents. In this case, linkage between a prophetic scroll, an eponymous prophet, and a historical context may as plausibly arise within a literary editorial and compositional process as from a tradition linking a historical prophet with the book named after him. Once a collection is attached to a prophet with an assigned date, the aggregation of further material will correspond to the characteristics of the existing material in that scroll. In other words, to posit a "tradition" that links a body of material to a prophet of a particular historical moment is not always necessary.

The issue, however, will not be fruitfully debated by asking for proof; my own experience shows that this only invites the charge of "sceptic" or "minimalist." A necessary condition for debate about the origin and growth of "prophetic" literature must be the existence of an alternative but realistic model for the creation of prophetic literature which does not substantially go back to an oral performance, orally transmitted by hearers and acolytes before being committed to writing. I shall therefore propose an alternative model, not with the claim that it is definitive or resolves all problems, but in order to challenge the theory of oral transmission by "disciples" so as to show that such a challenge is necessary as well as plausible.

Oral Distinct from Written?

In her discussion of orality and writtenness in biblical literature, Susan Niditch comments as follows:

> Especially for the compositions of the classical prophetic corpus, oral performances that are written down through dictation or later recreated via notes by someone at home in the oral-compositional medium seems a

---

[3] However, I exclude considerations of social contexts. Abuse of wealth, cultic and religious laxity, and so on are capable of being applied to almost any period from the early Israelite and Judean monarchies to the Greco-Roman period.

distinct possibility, not only because of the style of the works of the classical prophets—*which, granted, could have been created by a writer familiar with formulaic composition*—but also because of the assumed life setting or social context behind the literature.[4]

She later quotes John Niles,

> It sometimes happens that people who are not born into a dominantly oral culture, or whose education has led them into very different realms, imitate the style and content of an oral poetry and compose new songs that read like traditional ones,

and comments:

> It is possible that *some* works of the Hebrew Bible were composed in writing by writers who are fully conscious of and immersed in the oral culture. *It is, of course, extremely difficult if not in many cases impossible* to distinguish between oral-traditional imitative written works and orally-performed works that were then set in writing.[5]

The italicized words point to the presence of an assumption, namely, that even while we cannot actually tell oral from written composition, we must assume that the former is to some degree present.

But the issue is not of modern invention, of course. In the 1970s it was highlighted in a debate between David Gunn and John Van Seters about the presence of oral traditional composition in the court history of 2 Samuel.[6] It has been a hallmark of Van Seters's work that what has often been taken as evidence of *oral* composition can be shown, on close analysis, to be the result of literary composition. In his view, oral techniques may well underlie literature that is nevertheless both originated and transmitted in written form.

One can go still further back to view this debate. As Michael Floyd has recently pointed out,[7] Gunkel proposed that transcriptions of the prophets'

---

[4] Susan Niditch, *Oral World and Written Word: Ancient Israelite Literature* (LAI; Louisville, Ky.: Westminster John Knox, 1996), 117–120, emphasis added.

[5] Ibid., 125, quoting J. Niles, "Understanding Beowulf: Oral Poetry Acts," *JAF* 106 (1993): 131–55, emphasis added.

[6] D. M. Gunn, "Narrative Patterns and Oral Tradition in Judges and Samuel," *VT* 24 (1974): 286–317; "David and the Gift of the Kingdom (2 Sam 2–4, 9–20, 1 Kgs 1–2)," *Semeia* 3 (1975): 14–45; "Traditional Composition in the 'Succession Narrative'," *VT* 26 (1976): 214–29; "On Oral Tradition: A Response to John Van Seters," *Semeia* 5 (1976): 155–61; J. Van Seters, "Oral Patterns or Literary Conventions in Biblical Narrative," *Semeia* 5 (1976): 139–54; "Problems in the Literary Analysis of the Court History of David," *JSOT* 1 (1976): 22–29.

[7] M. H. Floyd, "Prophecy and Writing in Habakkuk 2,1–5," *ZAW* 105 (1993): 462–81. Gunkel's views on the development of written prophecy are conveniently set out in "Propheten II.B.," *RGG²* 4:1538–54.

oracles were collected and circulated by the prophets themselves following a lack of success in their oral pronouncements. These formed the raw material from which scribal redactors in the exilic and (chiefly) postexilic periods not only generated prophetic scrolls, but also *created* further scrolls on the same pattern. One of the cardinal errors of intervening research on prophecy follows the pattern of what Mowinckel did to Gunkel's work in respect of the Psalms: just as Mowinckel argued that the existence of discrete genres (oracle of salvation, messenger speech, lawsuit accusation, lament, dirge, oracle against foreign nation, etc.) arose directly out of specific occasions in the cult and thus enabled that cult to be reconstructed, so also the "ministry" of a "prophet" has not infrequently been reconstructed from the literary genres that the book bearing his name employs. As with a great deal of biblical scholarship, we may need to go back to the beginning of the twentieth century to retrace our steps.[8] The idea that prophecy is largely a literary phenomenon is both chronologically and logically a fine place to start. And, in my view, with some modification, Gunkel's model will work quite well.

Oracles in Writing

It seems, or should seem, strange to the modern critic that the sayings of prophets in a preindustrial society should develop into the literary form of the prophetic book. We have ample evidence from Uruk,[9] Mari,[10] and

---

[8] One could, of course, go earlier still. Late antiquity and medieval portraits of the prophets typically depict them as writing directly from divine dictation. They are authors of books, not oral declaimers. See, for instance, the fifteenth-century depiction of Isaiah from the Bridgeman Art Library that appears in J. Rogerson and P. Davies, *The Old Testament World* (Englewood Cliffs, New Jersey: Prentice-Hall, 1989), 325, and cf. the images in pp. 282–83. See also the images of prophetic figures made available electronically through the École Initiative (http://cedar.evansville.edu/~ecoleweb/images.html), many of which also tend to associate written texts with prophets. The image of the prophet in rabbinic Judaism shows several traits. The prophet may be a writer (see *b. B. Bat.* 14b–15a in relation to figures such as Jeremiah or Samuel), though significantly, according to this source, The Book of the Twelve and Ezekiel (along with Daniel and Esther) were written in the Persian period by "the men of the Great Assembly." For the preaching/teaching aspects of the image of the prophet in rabbinic literature, see, for instance, *Pesiq. Rab.* 26, 129b. All in all, it seems that prophets were constructed mainly as a kind of "earlier sages" in Rabbinic Judaism (cf. *m. 'Abot* 1.1, and Rambam, *Mishne Torah,* Introduction 6). My thanks to Ehud Ben Zvi for raising this issue with me.

[9] Presented in *ANET*, 604.

[10] *ANET*, 623–32. See, among others, A. Malamat, "A Forerunner of Biblical Prophecy: The Mari Documents," in *Ancient Israelite Religion: Essays in Honor of Frank Moore Cross* (ed. P. D. Miller, P. D. Hanson and S. D. McBride; Philadelphia: Westminster, 1987), 33–52.

Assyria[11] that some intermediaries would write messages and send them to a king or perhaps a client.[12] That practice is portrayed in 2 Chr 21:12, where Elijah is said to have sent to Jehoram a letter that was composed in true Deuteronomistic style. I do not, of course, conclude that Elijah sent a letter to anyone, but the details suggest that the writer and reader would not have found such behavior strange. Such letters, if sent to the palace or temple (or even generated within it), were, upon receipt, obviously filed by those very orderly scribes responsible for archiving anything and everything. Thus, the very notion of literarily preserved oracles catalogued in archives is reasonable. We may well think of an intermediary dictating an oracle to be sent to the court or temple, or even dictating it in the palace or temple itself. And while it is likely that such people did speak publicly (as the books sometimes have them do, though explicit reference is not very usual), it need not be assumed that written words sent to the recipient were also proclaimed publicly. Conceivably they were never spoken except by the scribe to the recipient.

From Scrap to Scroll

But a collection of written oracles in a royal or temple archive does not lead automatically to the production of a prophetic scroll. How would such individual communications come to be collected into larger literary units? Before attempting an answer, it is probably worth considering briefly a non-answer, prompted by Jeremiah 36.[13] The story of Jeremiah's scrolls, effortlessly

---

The relevant literature is published by J.-M. Durand, *Archives épistolaires de Mari I/1* (ARM 26; Paris: Éditions Recherche sur les civilisations, 1988).

[11] I might add the reference to a prophet in Lachish 16 (see, conveniently, D. Pardee, *Handbook of Ancient Hebrew Letters* [SBLSBS 15; Chico, Calif.: Scholars Press, 1982], 110–11; G. Davies, *Ancient Hebrew Inscriptions* [Cambridge: Cambridge University Press, 1991], 6). But the very fragmentary nature of the text really permits no inferences about written oracles of Judean prophets. I also leave out of consideration literature that is better described as "mantic"; it may, indeed, be relevant to some of the biblical "prophetic" literature but can be generally agreed as literary from the beginning. Such literature includes *vaticinia ex eventu* and divinatory texts.

[12] It seems probable that most if not all of the examples stem from intermediaries attached to the court.

[13] I apologize for repeating myself here. I have dealt with this before in the following works: P. R. Davies, *Scribes and Schools: The Canonization of the Hebrew Scriptures* (LAI; Louisville, Ky.: Westminster John Knox, 1998), 119–20; "The Audiences of Prophetic Scrolls: Some Suggestions," in *Prophets and Paradigms: Essays in Honor of Gene M. Tucker* (ed. S. B. Reid; JSOTSup 229; Sheffield: Sheffield Academic Press, 1996), 48–62, esp. 52–53.

misread by many scholars,[14] explains that the scrolls came into existence (a) because the prophet was incapacitated, and (b) in order to be read aloud by Jeremiah's understudy. It also appears to imply that the oracles had all been spoken by God to Jeremiah but had not yet been uttered (as v. 3).[15] No doubt the story is intended to account for a lengthy scroll of Jeremiah (containing all his words, each one of them dictated by God). But the narrative is not interested in giving an account of why there are prophetic scrolls in general; on this level, indeed, it would fail, since Jeremiah's scroll is merely an accident arising from Jeremiah's incapacity. The main thrust of the story seems to be not on the creation of the scroll, but on its status. The repetition of the sequence—Yahweh spoke, Jeremiah dictated, Baruch read, the people heard—runs throughout the narrative, illustrating the fact that written prophetic scrolls, though actually produced by people like Baruch (scribes), originate from the mouths of people like Jeremiah and ultimately from deities like Yahweh. By insisting that it came about by divine dictation, via Jeremiah to Baruch, the story effectively puts the book on a par with the scroll(s) of Moses as divine words.[16] Prophecy (at least Jeremiah's) has the status of torah.[17]

Yet another claim is being made here. Like their patriarch, Baruch, the copiers of prophetic scrolls do not originate but faithfully transmit the divine revelation that the divinely called prophet received. That they did in fact add material to these scrolls made their claim to be writing the words of a prophet

---

[14] W. Holladay, *Jeremiah 2. A Commentary on the Book of the Prophet Jeremiah Chapters 26–52* (Hermeneia; Minneapolis: Fortress, 1989), 253–62: "This chapter has attracted great attention, in that it allows one to see the process by which oral tradition becomes written text" (p. 253). Holladay continues: "It therefore becomes particularly important to inquire as to the authenticity of the narrative," but he proceeds not to do so. Instead we get the assertion, "Since Baruch took part in the events narrated, one may presume that it is composed by him" (pp. 253–54)!

[15] It is possible that the "house of Judah" is supposed to have heard them before and is being given a second chance. Why they would hear oracles "against Israel" (v. 2) is unexplained, and the LXX reading "against Jerusalem" is more coherent.

[16] See L. Alonso Schökel, "Jeremías como anti-Moisés," in *De la Torah au Messie: Mélanges Henri Cazelles* (ed. M. Carrez, J. Doré, and P. Grelot; Paris: Desclée, 1981), 245–54. I assume a single scroll, probably of Deuteronomy (so Ben Sira), but the possibility of a five-scroll or four-scroll collection is not ruled out.

[17] On this thesis, see J. Blenkinsopp, *Prophecy and Canon: A Contribution to the Study of Jewish Origins* (Notre Dame, Ind.: University of Notre Dame Press, 1977). However, I dissent from his treatment of Jeremiah 36 with the statement: "It would be widely agreed that the process of which we are speaking began with the activity of disciples who either committed to memory or wrote down the words of the master as the occasion warranted" (p. 100). However, in typically sage fashion, he also asks soon afterwards, "Is it not possible, for example, that even at an early stage propheticism and scribalism were quite closely related?"

all the more important. The rabbis later effected a similar move in representing their words as Mosaic Torah.

But now I return to the thread: if Jeremiah 36 tells us nothing about how prophetic scrolls came into existence, what explanation can be offered for such a development? Let me return to the story in Chronicles that Elijah wrote a Deuteronomistic oracle to the king. The Chronicler was probably not unaware of people who acted in such a fashion; possibly he had to deal with them every now and then—with some misgivings, since he took the view that all prophets should be members of the levitical caste and thus able to deliver prophetic messages personally within the Temple and under priestly control (as was likely the custom in major city–temple states in the ancient Near East). But whether or not the Chronicler was aware of, or concerned with, prophetic activity in fourth-century B.C.E. Jerusalem (or whenever he wrote), he was probably aware that archives surviving from the monarchic period contained prophetic messages in the form of letters, thus commencing with the name of the writer.[18] The so-called "messenger form" seems to have been standard for such correspondence. It would thus have seemed reasonable to invent such an activity for Elijah.

How does one file such letters? Most likely under the name of the sender. Oracles from persons with the same name will be filed in sequence. Where there are several such files, a corpus already begins to build up along the shelves or in the boxes. Should these files ever need copying, they would probably be copied onto a single piece of leather (more probably than onto papyrus), and that single piece would bear the name of the writer. Lo and behold, a prophetic scroll can very easily be created by archivists!

This procedure, though I suggest it seriously, is not intended to account for the origins of all the "prophetic" books in the Jewish scriptures—though it does explain the incoherence of many of them even after several copyings (and in this case, as usual, copying entails editing). I suggest it only as an evolutionary stage. On the model of prophetic book production I am advancing, material is grouped into single scrolls for convenience and is intended to be consulted or retrieved or scanned by the curious—if intended to be read at all. For the scrolls of Isaiah and Jeremiah, and also many of the "Minor Prophets" (before their assemblage at some point onto a single scroll), do not really seem intended to

---

[18] The extent of survival of archives from the monarchic period into the Persian period must be a matter largely of inference, but in principle it is unlikely that the Babylonians destroyed such valuable material, much of it necessary for continued administration. It can be argued with some plausibility that minimal details of the reigns and activities of Judean and Israelite monarchs were derived by the writers of the books of Kings from such archives, surviving into the Persian period.

be read for edification or pleasure—though we may have to reckon with the possibility of oral performance, perhaps in liturgical contexts.

I would not care to say how much of the material in the prophetic books was assembled by the mechanical process of copying onto a single scroll. I suggest nevertheless that the archiving mentality may have been responsible for a key element in the process, namely, the production of books of oracles, attached to names. By indexing larger scrolls, putting similar kinds of material together—oracles of doom, of hope, against foreign nations—and bringing together smaller scrolls into larger ones, the archiving process proceeds. And what would be the value of such scribal work, apart from keeping records in good condition? Within the context of a culture concerned to assemble whatever it could about the history to which it was laying claim, these materials would provide a useful resource.

Creating Prophets and Prophecy

But there is a further process implicated in the production of prophetic scrolls that extends beyond the archival (though it is partly a continuation of the same process), and this is a compositional one. Subsequent copying of that single scroll will have contributed in most cases to that scroll's acquiring further attributes, whether of detail, expansion, or structural organization. I am not sure how sufficient our literary-critical methods are for determining such processes with precision, but the accumulated work of scholarship has shown that the evidence is there, even if that evidence allows many and differing interpretations. At all events, our literary-critical methods and sensibilities are, in several instances, adequate to detect with some probability cases where a text has undergone expansion, whether internally or by means of supplementation. Some scribe *has* read the material and, in copying it, tried to explain it, interpret it, create from it some kind of message, give it some purpose and coherence, etc. But the motivation for such intervention seems to me both crucial and problematic for our understanding of the emergence of a kind of scroll that is unique in the literature of the ancient Mediterranean–Near Eastern world. We can learn from Ben Sira that "ancient prophecies" were studied along with law and proverbs by the educated person in the second century B.C.E. We can infer the same from the ending to the book of Hosea. But how and why did collections of prophetic sayings ascribed to ancient individuals attract the kind of interest that would ultimately condemn them to canonization? We need to posit another distinct phase.

The problem is perhaps approached by means of the analogies provided by Ben Sira: laws and proverbs—to which we can add psalms. The collection of instructions forms a well-known ancient Near Eastern genre, and such collections were effectively canonized by being repeatedly copied and perhaps used and enjoyed by the restricted literate class around the court and temple, as well as, most probably, studied and coined in schools, as part of scribal education (to read, learn, copy, take to heart, and add to, etc.). The editing of scrolls such as Proverbs is thus a minimal exercise; mostly it is a canon of collections of sayings gathered onto a single scroll and archived in, as it were, the "Solomonic shelf" (together with Song of Songs and Qoheleth, and, if a Greek library, with yet more "Solomonic" works). The Psalms scroll is also a canon of collections of liturgical poetry, gathered onto a single scroll and housed in the "David shelf."[19] Here, a little more editing has happened: some copyists and archivists have suggested links between some of the poems and the life of David as narrated in other canonical writings (on the "Samuel shelf"?). This, however, is a rather marginal form of interference and does not result in scrolls that exhibit a great deal of literary organization.

The books of law are a much more complicated matter. Here, various legal collections have become bound up with what I think is an essentially historiographical enterprise.[20] The combination of law and narrative is not surprising, since the laws are a vehicle for political philosophy, tracing the contours (and filling in some of the spaces) of an ideal "Israelite" society: militaristic (Numbers), ordered by grades of holiness (Leviticus) or construed as a client society governed by a political treaty with its divine patron (Deuteronomy). That these lists of laws should be integrated with a history of the nation—its national and tribal ancestors, its constitution, and its acquisition of land—is not hard to understand but extremely hard to reconstruct in detail.[21]

If the scrolls of the Mosaic canon evidence a greater level of literary editing than those of the Davidic and Solomonic canons, the prophetic scrolls (which I would prefer to see as canons in themselves, a well-defined "prophetic canon" being a creation only of the Common Era)[22] exhibit in many cases at

---

[19] This is merely a variation on the idea of "colleges" somewhat playfully presented in my *In Search of Ancient Israel* (JSOTSup 148; Sheffield: JSOT Press, 1992), 120–23.

[20] Here I should explain that I use "historiography" as a metageneric classification, and do not wish to become involved in distinctions, real or otherwise, between "history writing" and other forms of narrative set in a "realistic" past (discussed, e.g., by J. Van Seters, *In Search of History: Historiography in the Ancient World and the Origins of Biblical History* [New Haven: Yale University Press, 1983]).

[21] The reader is again referred for detailed consideration of biblical historiography and its design to Van Seters, *In Search of History*.

[22] J. Barton, *Oracles of God: Perceptions of Ancient Prophecy in Israel after the Exile* (New York and Oxford: Oxford University Press, 1986).

least as much complexity, but less obvious principles of organization and less telling indications of purpose.

The development of a historiographical corpus within the scribal schools facilitated reference to such "prophetic" compositions (although most of these prophets are unknown to the historiographical corpus, another argument against a theory of long oral tradition) and permitted the contents of these scrolls to be read against a definite and specific context: the fall of the Northern kingdom, the law book of King Josiah, the siege of Jerusalem by Sennacherib, the rebuilding (or lack) of the "second Temple," etc. This historiographical picture emerging from the work of Judean historians enabled the "prophetic" books to develop various kinds of contextualizing. The insertions of what is now Isaiah 36–39 or Jeremiah 52 into the "prophetic" scrolls are merely striking (and unusual) examples of explicit utilization of historiography by the compilers of the prophetic literature. The superscriptions (which do not provide historical references in every case) are further instances. But many of the materials have relatively clear contexts: a story in Amos 7 places the prophet as operating during Jeroboam's reign; Ezekiel flits between Tel Abib and Jerusalem in the aftermath of the first deportation; the poems of "Isaiah" and "Jeremiah" are integrated with stories that put them under specific rulers and in particular political situations.

A further aspect of this negotiation between historiographical and "prophetic" literary collections is the *production of the idea of "prophecy" as an institution of divine guidance of national history*, an idea visible in the "Deuteronomistic" materials. Whether that was in any way inspired by the "prophetic" materials or influenced the development of them may be an irrelevant or unanswerable question. But it seems plausible that, just as historiography provided a context for some of the prophetic scrolls, so the idea of a "succession of prophets" that we find in both the prophetic scrolls and the Deuteronomistic history provides a further, and probably fundamental, link between the two corpora.[23]

In other words, we have evidence of various processes of "historicization" within these "prophetic" collections. Such evidence needs to be examined carefully from the perspective not of a tradition history that places the historical context at the beginning of the process, but of a history of literary production that sometimes accumulated "historical" contexts.

---

[23] The notion of a "Deuteronomistic" edition of prophetic scrolls is one explanation of this phenomenon, but it may be too crudely formulated.

The Dangers of Monolithic Explanations

Before these suggestions gather too much momentum, it is important to appreciate that the prophetic books came into existence in several different ways (we must remember again that the category "prophetic" is a purely canonical one) and as the result of a number of processes. There is a danger, perhaps, of assuming that the result of a process (in this case, four prophetic scrolls) is the deliberate outcome of a consistent purpose. (One outstanding example of this is the assumption that Judean literature is the history of growth of a single canon.) The truth may be messier: that at different times and in the case of different literary materials there were varying motives, and that the emergence of large prophetic scrolls, let alone a canon of prophetic literature, was not foreseen or intended from the beginning. For instance, the book of Jonah is a "prophetic" scroll only by virtue of being copied onto a prophetic scroll and thus classified and canonized accordingly. I still prefer to think of Isaiah as a collection of collections; Jeremiah shows evidence of more consistent editing, though to what end remains elusive. The greater the length of a scroll containing unconnected (or loosely connected) material, the more difficult it is to introduce coherence. Thus two of the three "major prophets," Isaiah and Jeremiah, still seem to me to attain the kind of coherence that, given a single scroll, a copyist/editor may try, with limited success, to introduce; the scroll of Ezekiel may, on the contrary, have begun its life as a coherent piece of writing, a coherence that it arguably retains in large measure. Among the smaller units of the "minor prophets" scroll, Obadiah and Nahum may have originated as single poems rather than as collections of oracles from intermediaries, though if so, Obadiah has been transformed by means of vv. 1–4 into a prophetic oracle.[24]

It is therefore a mistake to assume that the process of production is driven by a consistent theological, ideological, or literary purpose. Just as the raw materials may have been written messages from historical intermediaries, or individual poems (as contained in Isaiah 40–55, for example), so the material may have been expanded for reasons of archival economy, scribal commentary and clarification. Yet do even these processes alone explain the bulk of the *material* in Isaiah, Jeremiah, or Ezekiel? Did so many oracles against foreign nations find their way into the royal or temple archives? Were more added by the copyists/editors? If so, why? In my opinion (and it cannot be more than an opinion) we ought to reckon with an ongoing process of literary composition. "Prophetic" oracles continued to be composed and were incorporated, either

---

[24] Note also the (added?) phrase נאם יהוה at v. 8a.

immediately or at some later stage, onto existing scrolls alongside the already existing material.

Prophecy as Political and Social Critique

What would be the motivation for extensive further composition? What is the reason for continuing to "write prophecy"? We need to discover a further motivation and some elaboration for these products. Why write in the style of intermediaries? Why cultivate (and even create) eponymous "prophets"? The answer is not easy to provide, and can only be conjectural in any event. But the contents largely express social critique. Or, to put it another way in terms of the position being constructed here, the form of messages from intermediaries offers a pretext for political and social critique. By preserving criticisms of ostensibly dead "prophets" on ostensibly past monarchs and past societies, a writer/copyist/editor could express his own frustrations, ideas, and sentiments, if he wanted, as well as (more safely) have another go at writing a poem condemning or threatening Egypt or Edom. Because of the pseudonymity, such sentiments avoid being read explicitly as direct attack upon contemporary society, but also gain authority, when read as such an attack, because of the antiquity of the prophet.

To understand "biblical prophecy" as an expression of social critique, then, I think we need to address less the functions of intermediaries, be they "central" or "peripheral," and consider the social and ideological climate of the scribal class in Second Temple Jerusalem. How did they relate to the ruling class—Persian administrators, Judean aristocracy, priestly families? Did these professional writers typically adopt any particular religious opinions or practices? Were they underemployed, giving them time for composing in their leisure? Were they relatively homogeneous in their political, social, or religious affiliations? Research into the highly intriguing problem of the genesis of "prophetic" literature needs to clarify the motivations of these groups, for it is only among them, I suggest, that we can find any plausible explanation of why there are such things as the scrolls of Isaiah, Jeremiah, Zechariah, and Hosea.

Prophecy and World Order

There is one further aspect of the matter that ought not to be ignored. It is frequently remarked that many of the prophetic books seem to follow different orbits around the theme of world order. Is Israel to have final victory over its enemies, or will they all come to Zion? Will the world-ruling Yahweh finally vanquish them all, or forgive them all? The debate between the "prophetic" word and wise counsel, which may or may not have been a reality in the monarchic state, becomes sterile under a world empire. But the claims of a monotheistic cult whose local deity is also identified as the high god provoke the question whether Yahweh's anointed, the descendant of David the Temple-builder, may not be a foreign king. In much of the "prophetic" literature one can detect the kind of interest in the political implications of a colonial monotheism that fits perhaps better with the scribes employed by the administrative center, be that the colonial governor's or the high priest's, than with intermediaries. Among the motives for the generation of the material in the prophetic scrolls—and perhaps for the editing of these scrolls—may lie an intellectual agenda, allied to historiography.[25] It is an agenda more apparent in some apocalyptic literature, where the course and order of world history is more explicitly addressed. But, as mentioned earlier, the arrangement of the Book of the Twelve may betray the interest in a system of successive world empires that the book of Daniel also shows.

Summary

I have not attempted here (and I do not feel myself able) to propose a detailed account of the generation of prophetic scrolls. I have tried only to sketch a model (essentially Gunkel's) that regards "prophecy" as a literary phenomenon throughout. But the model also recognizes that the processes involved in the preservation, archiving, copying and enlargement of such literary artifacts may be varied and not driven by the intention of producing a prophetic "canon," or even producing the large documents that have resulted.

Comprising such a model are a number of suggestions. I have suggested that behind the generation of prophetic material lies social critique, but it is the critique of the literate, the servants of the established governing class. Also embedded in the process may be an interest in the ordering of history, specifically in terms of what will happen in the future. I have suggested, finally, that the emergence of the notion of "prophecy" as a social and theological institution (a series of men sent by God to remind his people of their covenant obligations and warn them of impending consequences) was a result of scribal activity in both the Deuteronomistic history and some of the prophetic scrolls (e.g., Zechariah and Amos).

None of the suggestions made in this paper is original. I have conceived my project so as to promote discussion of the many issues rather than to

---

[25] I have discussed such an agenda in more detail in "The Audiences of Prophetic Scrolls."

propose a firm hypothesis. I hope that the above sketch will contribute to productive discussion, though it may be in the correction of many of these suggestions that the real progress will be made.

Prophetic Orality in the Context of the Ancient Near East: A Response to Culley, Crenshaw, and Davies

John Van Seters
University of North Carolina at Chapel Hill

The papers by Robert Culley, James Crenshaw, and Philip Davies raise a number of important questions worth discussing, and I will try first to identify them and then to make some modest suggestions.

1. To what extent is oral or scribal composition reflected in the prophetic texts of the Hebrew Bible, and are there ways of identifying orally derived texts?

This is primarily the concern of Robert Culley's essay and is not addressed by the others. In this Culley, along with Susan Niditch,[1] stands in the Parry-Lord school of oral composition analysis, which has been continued and championed by John Miles Foley. Yet the method has been severely criticized by Ruth Finnegan and Jack Goody, and the issues have been excellently reviewed by Rosalind Thomas.[2] Thomas concludes: "It is exceedingly hard to

---

[1] S. Niditch, *Oral World and Written Word: Ancient Israelite Literature* (LAI; Louisville, Ky.: Westminster John Knox, 1996).

[2] R. H. Finnegan, *Oral Poetry: Its Nature, Significance and Social Context* (Cambridge: Cambridge University Press, 1977); J. Goody, *The Interface between the Written and the Oral* (Cambridge: Cambridge University Press, 1987); R. Thomas, *Literacy and Orality in Ancient Greece* (Cambridge: Cambridge University Press, 1992). See also Thomas, *Oral Tradition and Written Record in Classical Athens* (Cambridge: Cambridge University Press, 1989), and "Orality," *OCD,* 1072.

identify a clear-cut 'oral style.'"[3] Virtually everything that one can identify as a feature of oral composition can also be found in written composition, and it always ends up as a question of degree, with no way of drawing a line between oral and written style. (In the Pentateuch, P is the most formulaic and repetitious and J the least.) The use of tradition as a criterion is especially treacherous because so much of ancient literature is very traditional in form and subject matter. And one can trace themes from the early prophets to the later ones that seem consciously to take up the earlier and develop them in new ways.

2. To what extent is orality or literacy involved in the original oracular delivery of the prophet to a particular audience and in the transmission and collection of his/her words to subsequent audiences/readers?

Crenshaw seems to place his emphasis on the oral nature of both delivery and transmission, based on the limits of literacy in ancient Israel. Davies argues that prophecy as a whole is a literary activity regardless of biblical suggestions to the contrary. Culley focuses primarily upon performance and its relationship to audience. This question is very important, and again Thomas has much to say about the comparable situation in ancient Greece, as have Finnegan and Goody on African oral performance. The fact that much of early literature was used for oral performance, given the reality of very limited literacy, suggests that the larger prophetic books may well consist of a collection of short oral performances whether they were composed orally or in writing.

3. What is the social or institutional context of prophecy and its transmission?

Crenshaw suggests the "band of disciples" model and the transmission of prophetic *teaching* on the analogy of the wisdom teacher and his following. There is some support for this in Isa 8:16, which treats prophecy as instruction (*torah*) entrusted to disciples, but whether the prophecy in question is a written collection (as the reference to "sealing" suggests) is not certain. Yet various methods of prognostication were the concern of scholars, and in later periods this extended to the study of prophetic collections. Crenshaw also discusses the degree to which prophecy may relate to the institutional context of temple and priesthood, for which there is a lot of comparative support (more below). Based on the Chronicler's account of Elijah's letter to a Judean king (2 Chr 21:12–15), Davies posits archival collections produced by court scribes from the alphabet-

---

[3] Thomas, *Literacy and Orality*, 50.

ized files of prophetic letters! The example is clearly spurious. Culley notes that the context of prophecy becomes complex and varied as the corpus of prophetic texts develops. The audience and the context of preservation change from the single oracle to the collection, and from the collection to the written book.

4. What role does prophetic conflict play in the preservation of collections that are for or against the king and state?

Crenshaw allows for the distinction between central and peripheral prophetic groups. Davies, on the other hand, suggests that the court bureaucracy made no distinction. It just filed them and then compiled them.

5. Should we make a distinction on degrees of orality between preexilic prophetic oracles and exilic/postexilic prophetic books?

Crenshaw and Culley treat the orality of both preexilic and exilic/postexilic prophecy alike. Davies emphasizes the writtenness of all prophecy and so disputes that any distinction between early and late prophecy is possible.

6. What help are the nonbiblical Near Eastern parallels in addressing these issues?

This question is not treated by these three presentations, so it leaves me a niche to fill in the present discussion. And furthermore, in spite of all the dangers of the comparative method, it still gives us some control over sheer fantasy in addressing the other issues. We could include Greek prophecy as helpful, but we do not have space for that. The literature on Near Eastern prophecy is quite large, and I have no intention of reviewing it here. But I want to call special attention to the recent volume by Simo Parpola on Assyrian prophecies.[4] It deals specifically with texts containing single oracles and collections of oracles from the Nineveh archives. It is therefore most relevant to Davies's remarks.[5]

The two types of prophetic tablets from Assyria published by Parpola, the *single oracle report* and the *collection of oracles*, are quite distinct.[6] The single

---

[4] S. Parpola, *Assyrian Prophecies* (SAA 9; Helsinki: Helsinki University Press, 1997).

[5] There are no extant Iron Age archives from Syria-Palestine, but one can say a lot about cuneiform archives. See esp. K. R. Veenhof, ed., *Cuneiform Archives and Libraries* (Leiden: Nederlands Historisch-Archaeologisch Instituut te Istanbul, 1986).

[6] See esp. Parpola, *Assyrian Prophecies*, liii–lxxi, from which my observations are drawn.

oracle type of tablet is in the style of a report or docket intended for temporary, immediate use. Such texts were used as sources for other documents and then discarded. The more permanent documents containing oracles could be collections of oracles, royal inscriptions in which an oracle is quoted, or various other third-hand accounts. The single oracle report contains the words of an oracle that were uttered *orally* and copied by a scribe. All the extant single-oracle-type texts are recorded by different scribes. They all identify the prophet (male or female) who uttered the prophecy and follow a very similar style, although they often use highly poetic and elevated language.

The collection-of-oracles type belongs to a class of tablet with multiple columns for several oracles, designed for "archival storage and reference purposes," much like treaties, royal decrees, etc. All those in this class are by a single scribe of the royal chancellery. They are compilations of single oracles in a sequence with almost no additional material. However, there is some evidence that such collections were dated at the time of compilation.

Here we clearly have a process of prophetic speech and transmission that seems relevant for our discussion. *All* of the Near Eastern prophecies that are in the form of oracles consistently point to oral utterance. Yet this utterance may be immediately committed to a written form by a professional scribe, who identifies the prophet of the oracle ("by the mouth of PN"). When these are compiled into collections—and Parpola has three collections with multiple oracles—two of them are not assembled as the oracles of a particular prophet (contra Davies) but consist of several different prophets whose oracles deal with a particular set of events or circumstances. One collection has a group of closely related oracles dealing with the "covenant of Assur" that may come from a single prophet. Each collection therefore deals with a fairly short period of time. Prophets in one collection may show up in another collection. What determines inclusion are the particular circumstances of concern to the court which the various oracles addressed at the time the collection was made.

This speaks to the first issue, that of orality and literacy. The oral utterance of an oracle that is immediately written down and that soon becomes part of a collection of such oracles, as we seem to have reflected in Isaiah and Jeremiah, has nothing inherently improbable about it. Even the dating or association of a collection with a particular king's reign may not be something that is very late and redactional but something that is inherent in the collection process. Parpola tries to reconstruct the particular use of the collections as support for the monarchy of Esarhaddon at the beginning of his reign or support for the crown prince Ashurbanipal or similar situations of great political importance, based on the historical allusions in the oracles. This is very similar to the oracles of Isaiah related to the crisis of the Syro-Ephraimite war (Isaiah 7–8) or of Jeremiah concerning the final days of Judah. The issuing of oracles of confidence—salvation oracles—is most common in such situations. They could be treated as covenants between the god and king and set up in the temple.[7]

Another large body of textual references to oracles are those quoted third-hand in documents such as royal inscriptions, correspondence, etc. Some of these certainly use the oracle reports or collections as sources. But some examples of fairly stereotyped "quotes" may also be imitations in prophetic style.[8] All the references to prophecy in Mari, primarily in letters, are of this type. There are no oracle reports or archival collections at Mari. The third-hand quotes give a good view of the situations in which the oracles were delivered, but they also may be subject to some interpretation by the scribe of the letter.[9]

As for the social or institutional setting of the prophets, in Assyria they are most often closely associated with the cult of Ishtar, and Parpola makes much of this. Of course, Ishtar of Arbela was strongly in support of the dynasty in power. A prophetic opponent of the king would belong to a different cult. The Mari texts show the prophets to belong to a number of different social contexts; thus, no one social setting accounts for all prophecy, although the association of some with the temple seems clear enough. So also in Greece, the most famous examples are those of the oracles issue by the temple of Apollo in Delphi.

The official royal collections of Assyria are all, of course, in support of the king, the royal ideology of the state, and its politics. One cannot really separate the temple from the palace. We do not have the oracles of the prophets who supported Esarhaddon's brothers. The prophets who supported the king in power were the true prophets. As M. Nissinen points out, prophecy that is directed against the king is false and could be reported in correspondence to the authorities, but of course never preserved in an archival collection.[10] The fate of such oracles as that described in Jer 36:11–26 would have been typical. That Jeremiah had a scribe like Baruch seems entirely appropriate for the particular historical period and circumstances.

Thus, dissident prophecy could have been preserved by those opposed to the dominant policy of the state. There is no need to think of a single model of prophet–disciples group. Many of Jeremiah's supporters seem to have been

---

[7] See ibid., collection 3, 22–27.

[8] M. Nissinen, *References to Prophecy in Neo-Assyrian Sources* (SAAS 7; Helsinki: Neo-Assyrian Text Corpus Project, 1998).

[9] J. M. Sasson, "The Posting of Letters with Divine Messages," in *Florilegium marianum II: Recueil d'études à la mémoire de Maurice Birot* (MNABU 3; Paris: Société pour l'étude du Proche-Orient ancien, 1994), 299–316.

[10] See Nissinen, *References to Prophecy*, ch. 6, for records of royal correspondence about an opposition prophet.

highly placed in Jerusalem society. Nor is there any reason to suppose that among such supporters there was not a trained scribe who could record the oracles. Indeed, it is altogether likely that there were many other prophets who uttered their oracles but did not have the scribal support to preserve their words. Those groups whose oracular collections were confirmed by the final outcome of events were the ones who survived, and the others were then false and perished. Furthermore, preexilic prophecy was always as much political as it was religious. The prophets in favor at the court gave the king and his policy legitimacy while the dissident prophets had their support in the rival factions. Both no doubt preserved collections of oracles, but we retain primarily one side only. Yet note the report of Jonah ben Amittai on King Jeroboam II in 2 Kgs 14:25–27 and compare this with Amos.

Of course, once collections of certain prophets were gathered into a single corpus, these could be subject to interpretive expansion. And they could become models for literary prophetic works in later periods. I think the Greek model (e.g., the Sibylline Oracles) has much to teach us here. Yet the last two centuries of the Judean monarchy are, I believe, vital to the understanding of the origins of the prophetic literature, and the Near Eastern context is important for clarifying these issues.

However, I think there was an increased tendency towards the literary creation of prophecy from the exilic period onwards. Yet we must not think in terms of someone writing a book, but rather of a series of compositions for oral presentation. It need not even be the prophet himself who put the separate pieces together. This is not too different from the Greek evidence of public speeches and declamations made by orators and the like. Culley and Niditch, following Thomas, are right to stress the continuum of oral to written with gradual sophistication in the use and development of the latter medium.

The Prophet as an Author:
The Case of the Isaiah Memoir

R. E. Clements
Cambridge, United Kingdom

Even in a period of scholarship when it was widely accepted that prophets were essentially preachers and that the transition from speech to written text of prophecy marked a departure from the norm, the case for believing that the prophet Isaiah had left a written memoir (*Denkschrift*) appeared a strong one. In my commentary of 1980 I expressed strong confidence in the case for such a conclusion, and I would still defend such a position.[1] The arguments for and against this have remained divided, and clearly it must now be conceded that some of the arguments in favor call for closer examination. Nevertheless the belief that Isaiah did compose a written memoir and that parts of it, if not its entirety, are still to be found embedded in the text of Isaiah 6–8 is firmly defensible. Many of the objections to making such a recognition can be accommodated by defining the scope of the memoir more narrowly than was earlier claimed.

It is with respect to the question of a transition from orality to literacy in a socioreligious context that the identification of an Isaiah prophetic memoir can be illuminating.[2] It may provide clues as to the circumstances and interests that encouraged the writing down of prophetic messages. In a society in which it was accepted that prophecy, on account of its divine inspiration with the prophet acting as the very mouth of God, should properly be spoken, written

---

[1] R. E. Clements, *Isaiah 1–39* (NCB; London: Marshall, Morgan & Scott, 1980), 70–101.

[2] For the broader issues regarding this see the recent work of Susan Niditch, *Oral World and Written Word: Ancient Israelite Literature* (LAI; Louisville, Ky.: Westminster John Knox, 1996).

prophecy marked an innovation. Accordingly, for sayings of an oracular nature to be given a written form lent to them a fresh potential, beyond that which their original spoken form allowed. This new potential in turn opened up possibilities for new ways of discerning the intentions of God, thereby making written prophecy a far more theologically diverse medium than its earliest form possessed. How this diversity is to be judged is not within the remit of this present examination.

The identification of a written memoir from the prophet Isaiah is most closely associated with the name of Karl Budde, whose monograph of 1928 discerned its presence in Isa 6:1–9:6.[3] According to him the account of the prophet's call in chapter 6 marked its beginning, and the royal coronation oracle of 9:1–6 formed its conclusion. The note regarding the role of the prophet's sons and their sign-bearing names in 8:17–18 declared the memoir's overall purpose.

In effect the entire memoir is comprised of a record of the prophet's call, the conveying of a sequence of messages to King Ahaz through the sign-bearing names of three children (Shear-jashub, Immanuel, and Maher-shalal-hashbaz) and the declaration of the coming of a new king of the Davidic royal line in 9:1–6. The declaration in 8:17–18 reads like a summarizing conclusion, suggesting either that it has been misplaced or, as is argued below, that what follows it was added later.

To each of the children's names are added interpretations, thus removing the ambiguity implicit when the bare name was left without fuller explanation. These interpretations show each of the names originally to have been positive and reassuring so far as the future of the king and his royal throne were concerned. Not until we are informed of the rejection of the prophet's message in 8:5–8 does the potential ambiguity implicit in the names allow them to be understood differently. What was meant as assurance is now turned into threat. That this is now the message of the completed memoir is expressed openly in 8:11–15. In order to make sense of the memoir therefore, it is necessary to recognize that the message of the name-interpretations required their revision and reappraisal in light of the rejection of the message they were originally meant to convey.

This is spelled out clearly in the pictorial language typical of prophecy. Clearly some active response on the part of the king was expected to the assurances contained in the names, but no indication is given as to what this action was. Nevertheless, it is the negative and absolute character of the royal

---

[3] K. Budde, *Jesajas Erleben: Eine gemeinverständliche Auslegung der Denkschrift des Propheten (Kap. 6,1–9,6)* (Gotha: Leopold Klotz, 1928). Budde's thesis was earlier outlined by him in 1885.

rejection which explains the purpose of the memoir. Because God's assurance had been refused, judgment must follow. This word of judgment is then elaborated in warnings of depredations from Assyria in both Israel and Judah (8:7–8). Outside the scope of the original memoir the same message is conveyed incontrovertibly in 5:26–30, although the identity of the enemy is left unclear. Within the compass of the memoir itself the message appears again in 7:18–20, but here it must certainly be regarded as an addition to the original text, as also in the gloss added to 7:17.

The prophet's summary in 8:17–18 provides a conclusion to the memoir by noting that he will await God's future action, which by implication is expected to confirm the correctness of the warnings that God had "hidden his face" from the house of Jacob. There is an overall chronological and theological coherence in the memoir, once it is recognized as such. The period of time that had elapsed between the giving of the original prophecies through the sign-names and the writing of the memoir is undisclosed but need not have been more than two or three years. What is of utmost importance is that the purpose of the memoir is different from the purpose of the messages attached to the children's names. It is very much a part of the memoir's *raison d'être* to show how and why this was so. These names had been reassuring and positive, whereas the message of the memoir as a whole is of divine threat. The situation had been changed on account of the rejection of the original assurances given by the prophet to the royal house of David.

It has to be conceded that the essential core of Budde's case does not require that everything that is currently to be found in Isa 6:1–9:6 was authentic to Isaiah, even though Budde himself was relatively positive on this point. By far the most important of the expansions to the original text is to be found in 9:1–6 (NRSV 9:2–7), which reinterprets the significance and application of the Immanuel prophecy of 7:10–17. As I have dealt with this problem in an earlier essay, there is no need for a repetition here of the arguments to which I still adhere.[4] The name, which was originally applied to Isaiah's soon-to-be-born second child, has been secondarily applied to a royal prince who will replace the faithless Ahaz. That this royal prince was Hezekiah may be regarded as assured. In this process of reinterpretation the original situation presupposed by the memoir has been left behind and the assurance of the Immanuel name has been reapplied to meet a new concern. Already in this fact the novel flexibility

---

[4] R. E. Clements, "The Immanuel Prophecy of Isa 7.10–17 and Its Messianic Interpretation," in *Die Hebräische Bibel und ihre zweifache Nachgeschichte: Festschrift R. Rendtorff* (ed. E. Blum, C. Macholz, and E. E. Stegemann; Neukirchen-Vluyn: Neukirchener Verlag, 1990), 225–40; repr. in R. E. Clements, *Old Testament Prophecy: From Oracles to Canon* (Louisville, Ky.: Westminster John Knox, 1996), 65–77.

of written prophecy reveals itself—a feature to which the completed Isaiah scroll bears abundant testimony.

The whole sequence of sayings in 8:19–23, whether taken as one single unit or, more probably, as a series of additions, must be held as later additions, added to provide exegetical reinterpretations of the importance of heeding God's "instruction" and "testimony" referred to in 8:16. Yet these additions are of particular interest because v. 16 appears misplaced from an original location after 8:2. The words *testimony* and *teaching* undoubtedly originally applied to the name Maher-shalal-hashbaz written on the tablet referred to in 8:1 as the solemn act of legal attestation shows. Yet its relocation to 8:16 strongly suggests that it has been secondarily applied to the written memoir as a whole and has, accordingly, been moved to link with the prophet-author's concluding remark regarding this in 8:17–18.

Yet 8:20 understands the reference to God's "teaching and instruction" more widely than this, thus occasioning the warning against the false teachings of v. 19. So a strong case exists for regarding all that occurs between 8:18 and 9:6 as an expansion of the original Isaiah memoir.

However we must reckon with yet more extensive additions than this. The most prominent of these is to be seen in the expansion of the account of the prophet's commissioning in 6:12–13. This looks beyond the situation of Judah and Jerusalem in the eighth century to contemplate the disasters that fell in the sixth. Similarly Isa 7:1, which provides a general historical introduction to the circumstances relating to the course of the Syro-Ephraimite war, has undoubtedly been introduced from 2 Kgs 16:5 and serves to clarify the context of the prophecies which follow. So also, the evident gloss in 7:8b and the elaborations detailing how God's judgment will fall in 7:18–25 are later insertions. As a feature of literary significance we should note the unlikelihood, on account of their varied form, content, and historical reference, that these additions were all made at the same time. It seems that we are faced with a sequence of miscellaneous additions made at different times that would, if taken as a single attempt at reinterpretation, be self-contradictory.

The key warning in 8:8–9, addressed not to Israel but to unnamed nations who threaten her, must also be regarded as a later addition. It has been located at this point on account of the ideas of God's protection of Jerusalem attached to the promise of the name Immanuel (8:8; cf. "for God is with us" in 8:10). It stands in line with the more extensive level of editorial redaction in the Isaiah scroll on the same theme. It proclaims a warning to Israel's potential enemies as expressed in Psalms 2, 46, and 48 (cf. Isa 14:24–27; 17:12–14).

Overall, therefore, we are left with a strong case for an original Isaiah memoir, subject to the proviso that this memoir has subsequently undergone a considerable amount of expansion. When these additions were made is, for the most part, unclear, but we can best assume that they were made after the memoir had been incorporated into the larger collection of Isaianic prophecies. We are then left with a memoir which is basically comprised of Isa 6:1–11, 7:2–17 (apart from 7:8b), and 8:1–8, 11–18. Overall it is relatively brief, has a clear theme, and most importantly has a recognizable and congruent theological purpose. Nor is it unimportant that the memoir relates closely to the situation of the Syro-Ephraimite conflict in which the threat to the royal house in Jerusalem was a paramount issue.

Objections to the claim that Isaiah wrote, or caused to have written, such a memoir of his prophetic interventions with King Ahaz have ranged widely over virtually every part of the text that is included in these three chapters. Some scholars argue that only some parts of the extant text can have emanated in the form of a memoir from the prophet Isaiah, others that virtually none can have done so and that the so-called "memoir" must be regarded as a fictive construction by a late editor. In the latter case, the memoir no longer offers an authentic autobiographical record from the prophet, nor does it provide reliable evidence relevant to the history of the Syro-Ephraimite conflict. Instead, it has been made to appear so for reasons that arose later regarding concerns over the future of the Davidic royal house. A late author writing after the exile had fresh reasons for presenting a given portrait of an eighth-century B.C.E. prophet and his message, namely in order to account for a state of affairs concerning the future of the Davidic royal house when no such king any longer reigned.

Both Otto Kaiser and Uwe Becker have argued that there are traceable fragments of a memoir that was authentic to Isaiah but that these fragments have been heavily overlaid.[5] They regard the memoir as primarily to be found in Isaiah 6 but as having been extensively elaborated and reconstructed in order to address issues far removed from those which concerned the original prophet. By contrast, H. G. M. Williamson, while defending the authenticity to Isaiah of much of the content of Isaiah 6–9, regards the attempt to reconstruct an original written and independent memoir as unhelpful and unnecessary.[6]

More far-reaching questions have now arisen than Budde's thesis that the main core of material in Isa 6:1–9:6 once formed an independent memoir, authentic to the eighth-century prophet Isaiah. The form in which Budde originally proposed the reconstruction is scarcely defensible in view of the many additions we have noted. Yet, that a core memoir did once exist in the

---

[5] O. Kaiser, *Isaiah 1–12* (new ed.; trans. J. Bowden; OTL; London: SCM, 1983), 118ff.; U. Becker, *Jesaja – von der Botschaft zum Buch* (FRLANT 178; Göttingen: Vandenhoek & Ruprecht, 1997).

[6] H. G. M. Williamson, *Variations on a Theme: King, Messiah, and Servant in the Book of Isaiah* (Carlisle: Paternoster, 1996), 73–112.

scope we have outlined, and that it once formed what is almost certainly the oldest part of the extant Isaiah scroll, is both wholly credible and defensible as a literary hypothesis. If so, then it touches directly on issues concerning how and why prophetic books came into existence at all. The case for identifying a memoir from Isaiah demonstrates that at least some small part of the present book of Isaiah was actually written by the prophet himself in order to function as a piece of prophetic testimony. This was a secondary action, contingent on the fact that the prophet's earlier spoken messages had been rejected. If a good case can be made for the identification of such a written testimony, or "memoir," as conventional practice has come rather misleadingly to describe it, then we have an instructive example of written prophecy fulfilling a role significantly different from that of a more conventional spoken message.

We may focus our attention on the three main points of criticism and objection raised by Williamson in regard to the identification of such a memoir text. Although Williamson's argument is directed in the first instance against Budde's specific hypothesis, he raises issues that relate more widely to whether any case at all can be retained for it, or whether the memoir hypothesis should not now be abandoned. His main criticisms are three in number.

First, chapters 6 and 8:1–18 are couched in the first person, whereas chapter 7 (in vv. 3 and 13) refers to Isaiah in the third person. Probably the reference to Yahweh in v. 10 would also need to be reverted back to the prophetic use of the first person for divine speech. The issue is of additional significance since vv. 10 and 13 occur in the passage (7:10–17) dealing with the sign-name of the second child. If this is a child belonging to the prophet and is to be included among those referred to in 8:18, then we should certainly have expected the first-person form to be retained at this point.

Second, the location of the memoir in 6:1–8:18 disturbs and interrupts the continuity between units that precede and follow it, especially the woe oracles of 5:8–24 and the refrain from 9:8–10:4. Contrastingly 10:1–4a appears more appropriate as a further woe-saying belonging to chapter 5, which deals with the authorities in control in the city of Jerusalem.

Third, the narrative of chapter 6, usually described as the prophet's call narrative, might have been expected to form the opening unit of the present book taken as a whole, as the opening narratives of Ezekiel and Jeremiah do in their respective books. The question has long been raised whether Isaiah 6 really reports the experience of the prophet's call and not another, later experience that rather served as a special act of commissioning in regard to a particular political situation.

Clearly all three objections take note of significant literary facts, but it is not clear that they amount, either individually or taken together, to a case for rejecting the identification of a memoir altogether. They vary in their relative impact on the theory as a whole, and it may be convenient to deal with them in a reverse order of their importance. Overall, it must be remarked, the issues are modified by recognition of the presence of expansions and additions to what we regard as the original memoir text.

We may begin with the second of Williamson's points, since it is the least prejudicial to the thesis as a whole. This relates to the fact that the identification of the memoir in 6:1–8:18 disturbs the structure and flow of ideas and reference between 5:8–24 and 9:8–10:4. This point must certainly be acknowledged. But does this tell us anything at all about the memoir? Awareness of the likelihood of a disrupted text explains the dislocation of the refrain of 5:25 which really belongs to 9:8–10:4. However no altogether satisfactory explanation is forthcoming to show why this occurred. In any event, the compositions of 5:8–23 and 9:8–21 look as if they were incompletely preserved, if we assume that they were once uniformly structured poetic units.

The observation that 10:1–4a appears to belong with chapter 5 must certainly be conceded. Similarly, 5:26–30 is a separate, if undoubtedly highly important, addition to chapter 5. But this too, like the so-called memoir, disrupts the expected sequence of the text between chapters 5 and 10, although it is easy to see why it should have been inserted in its present location for thematic reasons. Throughout the entire section of Isa 5:1–10:34 the disrupted flow of themes and images and the separation of exegetical comments from the texts to which they refer is a feature that is prominently evident. The cause of such apparent disconnections and dislocations is sufficiently unclear to allow of more than one explanation. On balance, the theory that 6:1–8:18 contains a once-separate memoir text provides a useful, if only partially adequate, explanation as to why there appear to be dislocations and disruptions between the units of chapters 5 and 10. Even if it does not wholly explain these, the argument for a memoir that was at one time separate provides a useful starting point for doing so. On what principles prophetic texts were compiled and edited into scrolls still remains much of a mystery throughout the entire Old Testament corpus of written prophecy.

The truth is that in prophecy generally and the prophetic book of Isaiah in particular there are many instances where the identification of units, of possible fragmented texts, and of dislocations and relocations from other contexts need to be considered. Many identifications of this sort evince a high level of plausibility but hardly ever carry any explicit manuscript support. Evidently the techniques and copying safeguards of the written preservation of prophecy were fraught with limitations that gave rise to problems of this kind. The critic can only seek to suggest possibilities and strive for the best sense available. That preserved written prophecy also shows itself to have been a complex and vulnerable type of material for later scribes and copyists to deal with cannot be denied. The practice of combining copying with redacting and interpreting a given text gave rise to many problems. So we cannot draw too many conclusions one way or another by identifying where probable and possible dislocations occurred as a consequence of these procedures. The surviving piecemeal form in which one can discern the reconstructed Isaiah testimony text is simply one product of a search to trace the earliest stages of the formation of the biblical scroll. Among the biblical writings, the scroll of Isaiah has aroused as much discussion as any because of its evident stages of growth. The substructure still shows!

The third of Williamson's reasons for questioning the attempt to identify a separate Isaianic memoir concerns the role of the narrative of Isaiah 6. We have argued that this originally extended only as far as v. 11. Popularly it has been regarded as Isaiah's call narrative, leading to the expectation that it ought properly to have appeared at the beginning of the book. Yet this is to mistake its proper function as a text recalling the prophet's claim to be the recipient of a divine commissioning. It is the mistake of titling it a call narrative that has made its present location problematic. The opposite is the case, once its proper literary function is granted. Far from weakening the interpretation of the function and nature of Isa 6:1–11, the memoir hypothesis greatly strengthens it!

Only the desire to interpret written prophecy "biographically" has brought about the feeling of difficulty over the present location of Isaiah 6. It is wholly coherent, both from a literary and theological perspective, when it is read as the opening affirmation of the prophet's claim to have been commissioned by God to bring a message to the king. This is how the memoir begins. Since we know nothing of Isaiah's life and activities before this event, nor anything concerning the relationship between his inner psychological experience and the production of this written text, we cannot verify its authenticity. We take it on trust, noting its extensive appeal to traditional imagery concerning the heavenly divine court. We are therefore hardly in a position to comment on the preceding background to this experience of Isaiah's. For us it is a text that makes excellent sense as a claim that the message following it had a divine origin. That is its purpose, and that is what it achieves.

The desire to regard Isaiah 6 as a call narrative rather than a narrative of commissioning, is at best unhelpful. Nothing at all is said or even implied regarding Isaiah's earlier activities. The narrative gains immeasurably in meaning and intelligibility when we link it directly to what follows in chapter 7. In this regard it is a matter of paramount importance that the text includes a very skillfully articulated awareness of anticipated, or more probably already experienced, opposition to the message that is to be the main burden of the prophet's task. It gives a clear intimation that the eventual outcome of events will prove disastrous for the nation. Failure to recognize this feature leaves us confused and baffled by the prophet's inconsistency. Only when we link the warning note sounded in this commissioning to the information provided by chapters 7 and 8, that God's assurances given through the prophet were spurned by the king, is this tension relieved. Only then do we have a credible place for the note of promise attached to the interpretation of the name Shear-jashub in 7:3–9. The warning of 6:11 explicitly anticipates disaster, but only the amplification provided by the unfolding sequence of actions in chapters 7–8 shows why this inevitability of national catastrophe has come about. What Isaiah 6 reveals to us is that, in writing afterwards of his God-given task, Isaiah has anticipated the end result from the beginning. There is a heavy and unmistakable note of irony in his having done this.

There has admittedly been much scholarly discussion over the ambiguities between assurance and threat that Isaiah's preaching reveals. The presence of names, themes, and words of hope and reassurance read strangely against the prophet's claim given in 6:9–11 that his message throughout will be one of unremitting disaster to the nation. The fact that such intimations of hope and reassurance appear in the interpreted names of the children referred to in chapters 7–8 provides the strongest possible reason for coupling Isaiah 6 with the narratives that contain them. Only then does their inclusion within the larger structure of the memoir explain their reversal. This alone explains the circumstances that have turned such glowing promises into bitter warnings. Far from providing an argument against the memoir hypothesis, the presence of Isaiah 6 as a narrative of divine commissioning supports such a hypothesis to the hilt. Seen for what it is, as a narrative of legitimization for the prophet's unwelcome and unfruitful mission, the passage provides one of the strongest reasons for embracing that hypothesis. The separate composition of a written testimony serves, better than any other theory, to resolve the tensions and incongruities latent in Isa 6:1–8:18.

Throughout these chapters we encounter the prophet's unusual insistence on the truths of divine sovereignty and foreknowledge with a demand for human obedience and responsiveness. Only when rejection of God's word is chosen is there a warning of the inevitability of disaster. The prophet claims, by his exploitation of ironic language and imagery, to know that national disaster will be the outcome of his mission and that this fact was revealed to him at the beginning! Only the unfolding sequence of encounters in the memoir between the prophet and the king uncovers a theologically consistent timetable for this claim. The theology of Isaiah 6 is well explained once the chapter is seen as the beginning of a narrative telling a story of the prophet's experience of rejection.

Seen in this light, the belief that the prophet was responsible for producing a written memoir, composed at an interval of two or three years after his first approach to the king, makes excellent sense. The theory serves to explain the nature of the commissioning narrative, with all its theological and psychological eccentricities, and throws much-needed light on the use of irony to convert images of assurance into threats. The designation of Isaiah 6 as a call narrative ought, then, to be dropped altogether and replaced by a recognition of its function as a text of authorization. It does no more than assert the prophet's claim to have experienced an act of divine commissioning for the immediate task in hand. He may have been, and probably was, an established prophetic personality long before this time. Certainly his polished artistic skills warrant such a conclusion.

We must still deal with the first of Williamson's reasons for questioning the usefulness of the memoir hypothesis as a means of interpreting and resolving the difficulties in the text of Isa 6:1–8:18. This concerns the point that chapter 7 presents the prophet and his message by use of the third-person form, in contrast to the first-person form used in chapters 6 and 8. This objection weighs heavily with many who have considered the memoir hypothesis in the form Budde adumbrated.

To alter the text so as to revert back to a presumed first-person usage in 7:3 and 13, and probably 7:10 also, may at first appear to be a rather high-handed action. It looks like a case of adjusting the facts to fit the theory rather than the other way round. Yet it is not a difficult assumption to make, once one takes into account the extent of the many glosses and additions that, on any reckoning, appear in the memoir text. The complex nature of prophetic literature and its literary development into a form of liturgical scripture has to be recognized. It was the very hallmark of prophetic speech in ancient Israel that it employed the otherwise presumptuous idiom of using the first-person speech-form of God addressing the people. Much of the extensive debate concerning the use of divine speech in psalmody and its origin with the so-called "cult-prophets" has hinged on the distinctive nature of this form. A subsequent adaptation to a less authoritative, but more familiar, third-person form in the recording of prophetic messages allowed freer citation of prophetic words in public worship. Clearly this is precisely the kind of change that the shift from oral to written prophecy would have encouraged. The phenomenon is well attested in the book of Jeremiah, where the use of the original prophetic first-person form for divine speech is adapted into a third-person form.

Yet this is only part of the general background to the problems present in Isaiah 7. If, as I have argued in my essay already noted,[7] the addition of 9:1–6 as a royal coronation oracle arose in conjunction with a change in the interpretation concerning the identity of the child to be named Immanuel in the

---

[7] Clements, "The Immanuel Prophecy."

prophecy of 7:10–17, then such minor changes are readily explicable. Whether or not Isaiah himself may have been responsible for this shift of reference is another issue altogether, but this appears unlikely. The relatively minor alterations to the presentation of 7:3, 10, and 13, took place either at the same time as this addition or as a consequence of it. Reluctant as any scholar must be to posit unsupported changes to a text, no matter how difficult, the suggestion in this case involves a far less radical change than supposing that later authors deliberately composed additions, making them appear as biographical, or autobiographical, elaborations. Their extraordinary clumsiness in failing to hide their secondary role would be amazing.

Overall the question of the possible change in the personal form of address from the first to the third person in Isaiah 7 has to be considered in relation to the much broader recognition that a number of intelligible interpretive additions have been made to the original memoir text. It is no longer in precisely the compass and shape that the prophet himself gave to it. Once this point is conceded, as it must be, then the change in the form of address becomes a relatively minor point.

In summary, it would appear that the identification of what was apparently a separate written testimony text in Isa 6:1–8:18* belongs as a hypothesis along with the many plausible explanations for the disorderliness of the written prophetic scrolls. Many complex literary features need to be considered in regard to Isaiah 1–12, when read as a finished unit, and our explanation of 6:1–8:18 still appears to be one of the most plausible of the many hypotheses about the origin and growth of these chapters. Its ultimate claim to recognition must rest on its ability to make better sense of a difficult sequence of prophecies and narratives than the alternative explanations have been able to do. It shows the figure of Isaiah as an accomplished speaker, and probably also author, although the use of a professional scribe should not be ruled out.

Taken as a separate unit the memoir shows how written prophecy could fulfill a function beyond what was possible with oral prophesying. It is best described as a testimony text, since it is not autobiography except in a secondary and accidental manner. Its purpose as a witness to future generations of Israelites and Jews that God is both faithful and just is evident. It ensured that the future generations who were destined to suffer the disasters that Isaiah had foretold would understand why they were doing so and on whom the responsibility for this rested.

Overall, therefore, there remains a good case for identifying a written memoir as the original basis of the text of Isa 6:1–8:18, as Karl Budde proposed. This memoir has, however, certainly received many subsequent additions, the most plausible of which we have noted. The identification of such a memoir strengthens and supports the case for regarding the child bearing the second of the sign-names, that is, the Immanuel child of 7:14, as a child soon to be born to the prophet in the same way as the first- and third-named children were his.

A further point of interest concerns how far the case for such a piece of literary analysis in the book of Isaiah contributes towards understanding the nature of written prophecy more widely. In this regard, we may suggest the two following points.

Of first importance is the recognition that the awareness that the purport of the prophet's message had been rejected by the king, who undoubtedly was regarded as acting on behalf of the people more generally, explains the need to write prophecies down. The act of recording the message in a brief text was not necessarily an action contemporaneous with the original spoken declaration, but a second step, aimed at giving to prophecy an additional, and more lasting significance. It turns prophecy into a theodicy for the downfall of a nation. The record of Jeremiah's action in Jeremiah 36 bears a closely similar stamp. The generally recognized fact that the preserved sayings of preexilic prophets are judgmental in their tone is therefore no accident. In essence, the experience of rejection and the belief that by acting in this way the prophet's hearers are themselves responsible for choosing doom rather than deliverance go hand in hand with the resort to written preservation. The written text testifies against them. If the present generation does not listen and heed the prophet's message, then future generations will do so under a very different set of circumstances.

Secondly, the written form of prophecy greatly increases the potential for extending its interpretation. The reinterpretation of the sign-names of Isaiah's children provides a nearly classic example of this. So do the expositions of the importance of Isaiah's "torah-testimony" in 8:19–23 and the many further examples of key names and themes being given new interpretations in other parts of the book. It is a feature relevant to our study of the literary intricacies and frequent disorderliness of the prophetic books that they display such complexities. In the book of Isaiah, expositions of key words and images occur out of conjunction with the texts from which they originate, as the exposition in 10:20–23 of the name of Shear-jashub from 7:3 shows. Similarly, and certainly of direct relevance to the memoir hypothesis, is the presence in 7:23–25 of theme-expositions of the subject of "briers and thorns" relating to 5:6.

Once committed to a scroll the needs and exigencies of writing imposed constraints on how and where additions could be made to a specific passage. The whole phenomenon of intertextuality opened up a rich vein of enlarged interpretations in which the accepted authority of a given text could be utilized to create further messages. So a certain kind of sensitivity was required in reading a prophetic text, since it was seldom possible for it to maintain the type of poetic or literary structure that other formal texts required. Neither chronology, nor poetic structure and balance, nor even consistency of theme and subject matter could give a single overriding shape to any prophetic scroll. Disturbances and out-of-sequence intrusions abound, dooming any attempt to present an all-encompassing "message" of a book.

A final point of theological significance may be noted. By its very nature written prophecy was a different proposition from what its origins in oral prophesying had been. It could seek to defeat the tyranny of time by giving future generations the chance to hear messages from the past that had failed to enjoy the response their authors sought. More especially it could hope to counter the despair engendered by the seemingly irreversible nature of past follies. Disasters that had become inevitable as a result of past mistakes could serve as lessons and warnings so that future generations might not suffer the same fate as their forebears. The search to find meaning in a hostile and unpromising history could then hope to build a new future on the ruins of the past.

"Write the revelation!" (Hab 2:2): Re-imagining the Cultural History of Prophecy[1]

Michael H. Floyd
Episcopal Theological Seminary of the Southwest

The Bible's narrative descriptions of prophets hardly ever involve written documents. Israelite prophets are generally portrayed as persons who make oracular speeches in the name of Israel's God, Yahweh. When prophecy is occasionally described as an activity that involves writing, the documents tend to function as a substitute for oral delivery rather than an alternative to it. For example, Jeremiah dictated a series of oracular speeches to Baruch and ordered him to read them aloud in the temple because the prophet himself was not allowed to go and speak there (Jer 36:1–8). Similarly, Jeremiah had other prophecies written down so that they could be read to the exiles in Babylon because the immense distance prevented him from speaking to them in person (Jer 29:1–32; 51:59–64).

Although it is conceivable that the documents described in these incidents may have become incorporated into the book of Jeremiah, it is unlikely that they provide the model for the production of prophetic literature in general. These documents are qualitatively different from prophetic books. Jeremiah's transcriptions of oracular speeches provide him with a substitute means of addressing his contemporaries about Yahweh's activity in their own time. In

---

[1] This essay was completed while the author was on a sabbatical leave, taking part in the annual Taller Socio-Teológico y Pastoral, Departamento Ecuménico de Investigaciones, San José, Costa Rica. I would like to acknowledge the influence of the participants on the conclusions reached in my research, to express my appreciation to Pablo Richard and the entire DEI staff for their hospitality, and to thank those who supported me in this endeavor: the Trustees of the Episcopal Theological Seminary of the Southwest, the Conant Fund, and the Seminary Consultation on Mission.

contrast, prophetic books have introductions showing that they serve to draw out the implications of what prophets once claimed about Yahweh's activity at various times in the past.

Despite this major difference, there seems to be some connection between prophetic speech and prophetic writings. As Hermann Gunkel (1862–1932) noted, the prophetic speeches quoted in narratives have typical rhetorical forms that are also evident in many parts of the prophetic books. The question is how to explain this connection. Until recently, the explanation given by Sigmund Mowinckel (1884–1965) was accepted by the majority of biblical scholars. He suggested that prophets had disciples who preserved their speeches, that these traditional collections of prophetic speeches were transcribed, and that these transcriptions were subsequently edited by scribal redactors to produce the kind of prophetic books found in the Bible. Many analyses have been done on the basis of this theory, attempting to distinguish original prophetic speeches from subsequently added redactional material. Now, however, questions are being raised about Mowinckel's theory and the kind of analysis that is based on it. Although original prophetic speeches can sometimes be distinguished from redactional additions with relative certainty, such distinctions are more often made in a highly speculatively way using ad hoc criteria. Taking Mowinckel's approach, scholars have seldom been able to agree on the parts of the text that supposedly make up the prophet's original words. Moreover, the role that Mowinckel assigned to prophetic disciples is purely hypothetical. There is very little evidence that prophets ever had disciples and virtually no evidence that disciples played the crucial role assigned to them by Mowinckel.[2]

The relationship between prophetic speech and prophetic writings is thus once again an open question. Some scholars have attempted to avoid it, either by treating prophetic writings simply as transcriptions of prophetic speeches or by returning to the concept of prophets as authors of the books named for them, but both kinds of avoidance are problematic.[3] The former approach ignores the fact that there are significant discrepancies as well as significant similarities between the rhetorical forms of prophetic speeches as they are described in narratives and the rhetorical forms of prophetic writings. The latter approach ignores the fact that prophets are infrequently said to be writers of anything, let alone documents like the prophetic books. If these facts are not to be ignored, some alternative to Mowinckel's theory must be found.

---

[2] I have reviewed elsewhere in greater detail the history of this research; see M. H. Floyd, "Prophecy and Writing in Habakkuk 2,1–5," *ZAW* 105 (1993): 462–69.

[3] As examples of these two tendencies compare two recent commentaries on Amos: J. H. Hayes and S. I. Irvine, *Amos, the Eighth Century Prophet: His Times and Preaching* (Nashville: Abingdon, 1987), and S. Paul, *Amos* (Hermeneia; Minneapolis: Fortress, 1991).

The Oral-Written Distinction as an Ideological Concept

In reopening the question of orality and prophetic writings, we should be aware that our own cultural situation affects the way we frame the issues. The question itself reflects a peculiarly modern concern. As careful readers of scripture, the so-called "precritical" interpreters were also confronted with the fact that prophets are more often described as speakers than as writers, but this discrepancy seems not to have posed for them the same kind of problem that it does for us. As long as the technology of writing was limited to handwritten manuscripts, commentators did not conceive of such a great separation between the oratorical skill with which prophets are typically characterized in biblical narratives and the scribal literacy that was undoubtedly necessary to produce prophetic writings. Partly for this reason, the "precritical" interpreters had no difficulty imagining that prophetic books were written by the same prophets for whom they were named, or at least by prophetic authors very much like them.

The printing press increased the production of writing to such an extent that the world of books became sharply distinguished from any form of human existence without books. Print-based literate scholarship could thus objectify more clearly the difference between literacy and oral tradition, as well as the difference between itself and the earlier manuscript-based literate scholarship that was more closely tied to oral tradition. By developing the disciplines of source, form, tradition, and redaction criticism, modern biblical scholarship has attempted to reckon with both of these differences in explaining how biblical literature was produced. More recently, the electronic media have deprived writing of its longtime monopoly on communication over time and space. The telecommunication of sound has made it possible for us to imagine a kind of "literature" that is designed to be heard aloud as well as read silently, whether or not it is reproduced by any means of electronic transmission or recording. Biblical scholarship has thus begun to reckon with the possibility that the scriptures might have originally fit this description.[4]

Although the oral–written distinction is potentially significant for biblical interpretation, the phenomenon is much more complicated than any simple dichotomy, and our understanding of it is not culturally neutral. Our use of the oral–written distinction inevitably reflects the way in which modern Western

---

[4] See, e.g., S. Niditch, *Oral World and Written Word: Ancient Israelite Literature* (LAI; Louisville, Ky.: Westminster John Knox, 1996); R. F. Person Jr., "The Ancient Israelite Scribe as Performer," *JBL* 117 (1998): 601–9; P. J. Achtemeier, "*Omne verbum sonat:* The New Testament and the Oral Environment of Late Western Antiquity," *JBL* 109 (1990): 3–27; L. H. Silberman, ed., *Orality, Aurality, and Biblical Narrative* (Semeia 39; Atlanta: Scholars Press, 1987); and J. Dewey and E. S. Malbon, eds., *Orality and Textuality in Early Christian Literature* (Semeia 65; Atlanta: Scholars Press, 1995).

culture has defined itself in contrast with premodern and non-Western cultures. This fact does not necessarily preclude a more or less accurate description of the differences between writing and oral tradition in particular cases. It nevertheless raises the possibility that our attempts to imagine the biblical social world in terms of the oral–written distinction may become unwittingly anachronistic. If we remain unaware of the conceptual baggage that the oral–written distinction carries with it, we run the risk of uncritically projecting our Eurocentric presuppositions about cultural "otherness" onto the biblical past. With regard to prophecy in particular, such projections may lead to unwarranted assumptions about the way in which oral prophetic speech was related to the scribal activity that produced the prophetic writings. In order to raise our awareness of the potentially prejudicial implications of the oral–written distinction, a review of its history is in order.

The aim of this essay might be described as ideological criticism. Like the ambiguous term "myth," the word "ideology" has a wide range of both positive and negative meanings, some of them antithetical. In this case, "ideology" is being used in a rather negative way. Here the word applies to terminology that is loaded, in the sense that it pretends only to describe a particular phenomenon and yet at the same time implies a particular way of viewing the world. More specifically, "ideology" can be defined as discourse in which such terminology is used to maintain the worldview that it implies even though it evidently does not give an accurate impression of the phenomenon that it pretends to describe. This essay will attempt to show that the oral–written distinction, as it has been used in the modern study of biblical prophecy, is "ideological" in this sense. The discussion will also explore various ways in which the oral–written distinction might be reconceived so as to avoid or minimize this problem.

The History of the Oral–Written Distinction

The Early Modern Phase

Modern usage of the oral–written distinction is rooted in Enlightenment theories of social development. By the time of the Enlightenment, European explorers had been going on voyages of discovery to all parts of the world for more than two hundred years. From this accumulated experience of other peoples, it seemed self-evident to eighteenth-century Europeans that theirs was the most advanced society on earth. Other societies could thus be classified on the basis of how closely they resembled modern European society, and those that least resembled this ideal norm could be regarded as vestiges of humanity in its original, primitive state. The social theorists who elaborated this basic scheme assumed that universal literacy was characteristic of the most advanced form of society, and they identified oral tradition with the most primitive form of society. The transition from a predominantly oral to a predominantly written culture became regarded as the primary indication of progress, on which any society's advancement in all the arts and sciences depended.[5] Universal literacy became one of the main criteria of civilization.

According to most variations on this scheme, the growth of literacy was closely connected with two other aspects of social progress. First, it coincided with the development of literature and of language itself. The least civilized (i.e., illiterate) peoples had only the most rudimentary grammar and thus tended to express themselves in the paratactically juxtaposed words and sounds characteristic of poetry. In contrast, the most civilized (i.e., literate) peoples had a well-developed grammar and thus tended to express themselves in the precise diction and syntactically well-formed sentences characteristic of prose.[6] Second, the growth of literacy also coincided with the increased differentiation of social roles. In the least civilized (i.e., illiterate) form of human society, the entire group was collectively involved in eking out a subsistence living through hunting and gathering, and it was not possible for many to devote themselves to more specialized tasks. Primitive communities thus tended to have only a few designated leaders, such as kings to keep order, priests to regulate relations with the sacred, bards to recount popular traditions, and warriors to lead the people in battle. In the most civilized (i.e., literate) form of human society, however, roles became more distinctly and more hierarchically defined in terms of specialized functions. The broader range of social roles, each with its own expertise, eventually came to include a variety of professions and occupations

---

[5] "In all countries where the people are barbarous and illiterate, the progress of arts is wofully slow" (Henry Home, Lord Kames, *Sketches of the History of Man* [2d ed.; 4 vols.; Edinburgh, 1778], 1:179; cf. Adam Ferguson, *An Essay on the History of Civil Society* (4th ed.; London, 1773), 280–85; also John Brown, *A Dissertation on the Rise, Union and Powers, the Progressions, Separations, and Corruptions of Poetry and Music* (2d ed.; London, 1773), 26–46. On such theorizing and its social and intellectual context see L. Whitney, "English Primitivistic Theories of Epic Origins," *Modern Philology* 21 (1924): 337–78; also M. M. Rubel, *Savage and Barbarian: Historical Attitudes in the Criticism of Homer and Ossian in Britain, 1760–1800* (Amsterdam: North-Holland, 1978), 7–38.

[6] "Writing and language, throughout all their various modes, ran exactly the same fortune" (W. Warburton, *The Divine Legation of Moses Demonstrated* [3 vols.; London, 1738–1741], 2:215); "Prose composition came to be of a later date [than poetry], introduced perhaps with the use of Writing, which brought with it Arts and Philosophy. . . . [We can] fix the common familiar use of an alphabet in Greece, and prose Writing, to pretty much the same period" (R. Wood, *An Essay on the Original Genius and Writings of Homer* [London, 1775], 241, 257; Home, *Sketches* 1:222–59; T. Blackwell, *An Enquiry into the Life and Writings of Homer* (London, 1735), 36–46.

such as farmer, herder, metal worker, soldier, trader, artisan, builder, musician, and scribe.[7]

In eighteenth-century theories of cultural development, the symbol of humanity in its original state was the "noble savage," and the primitive stage had the positive as well as the negative characteristics connoted by this figure. On the one hand, the primitive stage was an age of savagery. It was a rude kind of existence without many comforts and full of danger, and the goal of human history was to progress beyond it. On the other hand, the primitive stage was also an age of nobility. It was idyllic in its simplicity, and progressing beyond it entailed an unfortunate loss of innocence.[8] Moreover, as the initial stage of human development, the primitive stage was the formative period. It contained within itself the seeds of future growth, and a society could truly progress only if it developed in accord with the roots growing out of its primitive stage. Many societies obviously did not progress very far, and this failure could be due to their not developing in accord with their roots.[9]

For eighteenth-century Europeans, such developmental theories provided more than just a way of understanding their privileged status in relation to the rest of the world. These concepts also provided the basis on which modern European society came to understand its own historical antecedents and its own social class structure. The history of Western civilization was schematized in terms of a grand analogy between its three main periods of history and the three main stages of human cultural development. Ancient Greco-Roman society and the Christian Middle Ages became, as it were, the primitive and transitional stages leading up to the Modern Age of the Enlightenment. As the third and culminating stage, European modernity was assumed to constitute the apex of human development.[10] On the basis of this analogy, the seemingly amazing progress of European society was thought to proceed from the rediscovery of its ancient Greco-Roman roots. The age leading up to the modern era of the Enlightenment would eventually come to be known as "the Renaissance," that is, a rebirth including a renewal of interest in Greco-Roman cultural forms and

---

[7] "A people can make no great progress in cultivating the arts of life, until they have separated, and committed to different persons, the several tasks, which require a peculiar skill and attention" (Ferguson, *Essay*, 301; this statement introduces his discussion "Of the Separation of Arts and Professions," 301–14); Brown similarly traces the process of social diversification as it relates particularly to poetry and music (*Dissertation*, 27–46).

[8] H. N. Fairchild, *The Noble Savage* (New York: Columbia University Press, 1928).

[9] L. Whitney, *Primitivism and the Idea of Progress in English Popular Literature of the Eighteenth Century* (Baltimore: Johns Hopkins Press, 1934), 137–67; Rubel, *Savage and Barbarian*, 23–35.

[10] Rubel, *Savage and Barbarian*, 32–35.

themes. The Greco-Roman age became regarded as the formative period of Western civilization, and Greco-Roman culture became the "classical" model to emulate in order for the West to make true progress. Literature and literary criticism thus entered an age of neoclassicism.

By means of a similar analogy, social class distinctions could also be viewed in terms of the various stages of human cultural development. Because the communal life of the country people and the growing working class was characterized by such oral traditions as ballads and folk tales, the lower classes could be seen as representative of the primitive stage. Because the communal life of the upper class was characterized by the kind of literacy gained through a "classical" education, they were representative of fully realized modern humanity. And the urban middle class, which gained in importance as well as size through the Industrial Revolution, could be seen as representative of the transitional stage moving from the primitive to the most developed stage.[11] From the perspective of this analogy popular folk traditions had a formative role to play in the development of culture, even though the advancement of society as a whole depended on the promotion of universal literacy.[12]

These concepts penetrated the modern European mind so deeply that other terms of discourse were scarcely possible. The Romantic reaction to the Enlightenment was based at least partly on the recognition that its theories of development implied an ideology of sociopolitical and cultural domination. Romantic dissent was nevertheless expressed largely in terms of the very same theories. When colonialism was justified as a means of advancing civilization and when the capitalistic exploitation of labor was justified with reference to the progress of society, critics objected by extolling the human dignity of the tribes that were being colonized and the workers who were being exploited. In other words, the nobility of these dominated groups was emphasized over their savagery. But since these peoples and classes were illiterate, they were still thought to be at the primitive stage of social development—in effect "noble savages"—even by their Romantic defenders. Similarly, when neoclassical odes and lyrics were held up as the most advanced forms of poetry and the fullest expressions of the human spirit, poets and literary critics objected by claiming that modern poets could find better models than the Greco-Roman authors. Some, like William Blake (1757–1827), sought to emulate biblical poetry; others, like William Wordsworth (1770–1850), sought to emulate

[11] Ibid., 18–20.

[12] The extension of the analogy between ancient and primtive, to include among the ancients the ancestors of each people as well as the ancestors of humanity as a whole, is evident, for example, in the two theoretical "dissertations" that preface James Pinkerton's *Scottish Tragic Ballads* (London, 1781).

popular folk poetry. In either case, the Romantics still thought of themselves as developing poetic roots that grew out of some relatively primitive age or society. They differed from the neoclassicists only in claiming that these primitive roots were other than Greco-Roman.

Biblical scholarship became influenced by Enlightenment theories of social development in the context of the growing Romantic reaction to them. The earliest versions of these theories tended to take no account of the Bible at all. Such developmental schemes were initially conceived as "natural history" precisely in order to differentiate them from the kind of supernaturalism associated with traditional Christianity and its Holy Scriptures. This situation changed, however, as literary critics began to elaborate on the grand analogy between the three main stages of social development and the three main periods in the history of Western civilization. Some scholars ventured to suggest that the Bible—considered from a purely human point of view—belonged together with the Greco-Roman classics in the primitive and hence formative period in the history of Western literature.[13] Viewed from this perspective, the Bible began to attain greater literary respectability even in the eyes of rationalists and neoclassicists. It then became possible for Romantics to argue that modern poets should emulate the Bible as well as Greco-Roman authors because biblical poetry was an even more genuine expression of primitive humanity.[14] In the context of this discussion about the Bible's place in the developmental history of Western literature, Robert Lowth (1710–1787) and Johann Gottfried Herder (1744–1803) published their seminal treatments of biblical poetry, Lowth's *De sacra poesi Hebræorum* (1753) and Herder's *Vom Geist der ebräischen Poesie* (1782–1783), writing not as theologians but as literary critics.

For present purposes, two of Lowth and Herder's dominant themes are noteworthy. First, both scholars attempted to show that much of the Bible belongs to the category of primitive poetry. For Lowth, this attempt entailed demonstrating that the Hebrew rhetorical phenomenon of *parallelismus membrorum*, found in the Psalms and elsewhere, implies a kind of linguistic

---

[13] E.g., H. Blair, *Lectures on Rhetoric and Belles Lettres* (2 vols.; London, 1783) 2:385–405.

[14] "Can any Man, who pretends to a Relish of the Classicks, read the loftiest Passages that were ever writ, without being Affected by them, merely because They are in the Bible? If He can, it must proceed from a great Corruption of Taste, as well as a great Depravity in his Manners" (J. Husbands, "Preface," *A Miscellany of Poems by Several Hands* [Oxford, 1731], n.p.); see V. Freimarck, "The Bible and Neo-Classical Views of Style," *Journal of English and German Philology* 51 (1952): 507–26.

rhythm that is as marked as the "classical" Greco-Roman meters.[15] For Herder as well as Lowth, it also entailed showing that biblical poetry utilizes genres that are appropriate to the various social occasions typical of a primitive stage of human development.[16] Second, both scholars further identified prophecy with primitive poetry. For Lowth, this identification was based on showing that prophetic books were characterized by the same *parallelismus membrorum* as the Psalms.[17] For Herder as well as Lowth, it was also based on showing that the role of the Hebrew prophets was in many respects analogous to the role of the bard in other primitive societies.[18]

Having come thus far in our brief history of the oral–written distinction, from the eighteenth into the early nineteenth century, three themes relevant to the discussion of orality and prophetic writings are already evident. First and foremost is the very concept of ancient literature—whether biblical or Greco-Roman—as an "oral" kind of literature. Second is the Romantic identification of the prophet as bard, that is, as primitive oral poet. And third is the implication entailed in this identification, namely, that the role of the prophet has some kind of developmental priority in relation to the role of the scribe. Before turning to the next phase in the history of the oral–written distinction, which extends from the nineteenth into the twentieth century, let us briefly explore some problematic aspects of these three themes.

In view of how it was invented, the notion of ancient literature as "oral literature" must be seen as a purely ideological concept with very little descriptive value. Ancient texts—whether biblical or Greco-Roman—are of course no less "written" than *The Meters of Boethius, In Praise of Folly, Paradise Lost,* or *Moby Dick.* And the ancient cultures that created the Bible and the Greco-Roman "classics" could hardly have produced such writings if they were anything less than literate. It became necessary to think of ancient literature as somehow more oral and somewhat less literate than modern literature only because of the way in which modern European intellectuals chose to define the superiority of their culture in relation to the rest of the

---

[15] R. Lowth, *Lectures on the Sacred Poetry of the Hebrews* (trans. G. Gregory; London: Thomas Tegg & Son, 1835), 28–36.

[16] Lowth, *Lectures,* 189–392; J. G. Herder, *The Spirit of Hebrew Poetry* (2 vols.; trans. J. Marsh; Burlington, Vt.: Edward Smith, 1833), 1:190–286; M. H. Floyd, "Falling Flat on Our Ars Poetica, or, Some Problems in Recent Studies of Biblical Poetry," in *The Psalms and Other Studies on the Old Testament Presented to Joseph I. Hunt* (ed. J. C. Knight and L. A. Sinclair; Cincinnati: Forward Movement Publications for Nashotah House Seminary, 1990), 120–23.

[17] Lowth, *Lectures,* 189–216.

[18] Lowth, *Lectures,* 194–97; Herder, *Spirit* 2:35–53.

world. They first presupposed that print-based literacy made them superior to the peoples they were colonizing, whose cultures were in many cases based primarily on oral tradition. They then speculated that the illiteracy of these peoples made them vestigial representatives of humanity in its original state. They finally concluded that the ancient Hebrew and Greco-Roman societies, which they assumed to be among the oldest communities on earth, must have been culturally analogous to the peoples that were presently being colonized. Unlike contemporary primitives, the ancient Hebrews, Greeks, and Romans could not be characterized as backward by virtue of their limited literacy because such limited cultural development was appropriate for their stage of human history. Indeed, as any forebears of Western civilization must have been, these ancient folks were relatively advanced for their own time. In relation to modern European society, however, they also must have been—like contemporary primitives—somehow more oral and somewhat less literate.

Even in its heyday this analogy was somewhat forced. Ancient Hebrew and Greco-Roman culture could be regarded as comparable with contemporary primitive culture only by playing down the considerable similarities between ancient and modern literature while also giving exaggerated emphasis to those ancient literary forms that most closely resembled the modern European stereotype of primitive oral tradition. Because European critics reckoned the cultivation of prose narrative and exposition among the defining characteristics of modern literate culture, they paid little attention to the fact that Greco-Roman and biblical authors had also developed prose narrative and exposition to a high art. They instead emphasized such ancient poetic genres as the epic, the ode, and the lyric, because these forms of expression more nearly fit their preconception of oral tradition in primitive society. In accord with this preconception, such genres belonged to the category of primitive poetry because they were characterized by metrical or otherwise markedly rhythmic language, by highly figurative diction, and by the paratactic juxtaposition of ideas. Ancient oratory was also brought under the rubric of primitive oral poetry because it was generally supposed to share the same defining characteristics. Although not strictly metrical, ancient oratory was cadenced to the point of being quasi-poetic. Many of its rhetorical devices were highly figurative, and many of its rhetorical effects were achieved by means of juxtaposing rather than logically connecting ideas.[19] In order to maintain the

---

[19] "[The Hebrews] had undoubtedly some regard to the Structure and Contrivance of the Poem, They observ'd a peculiar Harmony, Smoothness, and Propriety in the Turn of the Periods, which cannot be without some kind of Numbers; yet such Numbers are no more than Aristotle thinks requisite in a good Oration. In other respects the Style of their Poetry (to

identification of ancient literature with primitive oral poetry, critics of the eighteenth century thus had to arbitrarily exclude from consideration many ancient works that did not fit this description. And at the same time, they also had to extend the concept of primitive oral poetry to include nearly anything ever spoken in a more than casual way.[20]

This rather far-fetched extension of the concept of primitive oral poetry led not only to a conflation of the Greco-Roman orator with the bard. It also led to a similar conflation of the Hebrew prophet with the bard.[21] Regardless of whether biblical prophets and oral poets may be comparable in some ways, the Romantic identification of these two roles was not motivated by any intention to discover the actual similarities and differences. It was instead based on the desire to construct an alternative lineage and status for modern poetry. In reaction to the concept of modern poetry as neoclassical poetry, which made it merely an effete ornament of the other arts and sciences, the Romantics asserted that modern poetry was rooted in biblical and popular folk culture. It therefore had a vital role to play in contemporary affairs. If the prophet and the bard were the modern poet's true ancestors, then modern poetry could claim to have revealed knowledge that would affect the public life of the community as a whole. This line of thought was already implicit in Blake's composition of poems called prophecies (beginning with *The Four Zoas*, 1795–1804) and became explicit in the *Defense of Poetry* (1821) by Percy Bysshe Shelley (1792–1822). On the basis of the purely ideological Romantic concept of poets as prophets, it could be conversely assumed that prophets were poets. And on the basis of this assumption, together with the assumption that the ancient Hebrews represented human society in its more or less original state, scholars like Lowth and Herder had begun to describe the biblical prophets specifically as oral poets.

---

speak a little paradoxically) seems to have been Prose" (Husbands, "Preface," *A Miscellany of Poems*, n.p.).

[20] It was thus often held that the ancients actually spoke poetry in their everyday activities. For example, Blackwell approvingly cites Longinus's assertion that "the Ancients in their ordinary Discourse delivered themselves rather in Verse than Prose" (*Enquiry*, 39); "[Poetry is] the original language of men in an infant state of society in all countries" (J. Pinkerton, "Dissertation on the Oral Tradition of Poetry," *Scottish Tragic Ballads*, x).

[21] E.g., "[Among the ancient Hebrews] their Prophets were indeed their Bards; and appear to have been invested with all the Dignity belonging to that Office in its most honoured State. But as the Almighty God, and the great Events of his Providence, were the continued Object of their Songs; so, the poetic or musical Character was but secondary to the religious: Therefore the Name of Bard was swallowed up and lost in the higher Title of 'The Prophet of the Most High'" (Brown, *Dissertation*, 181–82).

In the context of Enlightenment theories of social development, the description of prophets as oral poets had specific implications with regard to defining the relationship between prophets and scribes. By being described as oral poets, prophets were assigned one of the elemental leadership roles that pertained to the earliest stage of society. In contrast, the role of the scribe emerged in the process of social differentiation that was characteristic of the later stages. As a by-product of the Romantic poets' need for a prophetic ancestry, it thus became assumed that the role of the prophet was socially incompatible with the role of the scribe. Moreover, according to many developmental theories the process of social differentiation was also a process of secularization. For society to progress it was necessary for the literati to move away from religion into a sphere of their own, where they could exercise their rational capacities without the limitations imposed by traditional beliefs. Intellectuals of the Enlightenment, having experienced liberation from the restraints of traditional beliefs in the struggle to make the modern university a place of free inquiry, could hardly refrain from projecting their own secularist attitude onto their ancient counterparts. Biblical scholars who adopted the concept of the prophet as an oral poet thus also tended to view the ancient scribe as a protorationalist. The incompatibility between prophet and scribe then became defined not only in terms of oral versus written, but also in terms of religious versus secular. Prophets were religious reformers, whereas scribes were secular intellectuals.[22]

By the early nineteenth century the complex of categories in which we are still accustomed to think about prophecy and writing had already begun to take shape. Some important modifications were made in the later nineteenth and twentieth centuries, which will be discussed further below, but the foundational assumptions laid down in the context of the Enlightenment itself are already recognizable. Before going on to consider the later modifications, it bears reiterating that these foundational assumptions were not defined through any systematic consideration of how to approach the phenomena in question. They

---

[22] In most of the developmental schemes, the transition from illiteracy to literacy was not only a transition from poetry to prose but also a transition from emotion to reason. As Home puts it, "When people began to reason . . . they were obliged to descend to humble prose" (*Sketches* 1:230). Using examples of Old Testament as well as Greco-Roman narrative, he goes on to show that this transition also entails a progression from "dramatic" prose narrative, in which God himself is frequently introduced into the dialogue, to a more straightforward representation of "the bare historical facts" (pp. 231–59). Wood similarly states that the transition from oral/poetic to written/prosaic "brought with it Arts and Philosophy, and a more chaste and faithful mode of recording facts" (*Essay,* 241). The introduction of writing produced a mode of narrative description without supernatural agency. Scribes were thus, in effect, deists.

were largely defined by the ways in which modern European culture chose to imagine itself as distinctly different from other cultures and by the internal logic of the conceptual system within which these differences were speculatively categorized. In the form in which we have inherited it, the oral–written distinction is a binary opposition that has been used primarily to reinforce another binary opposition, the we–they distinction. In the process, it has become arbitrarily associated with several other distinctions, such as primitive–advanced, early–late, prophet–scribe, and religious–secular. The emerging challenge is to develop a way of thinking about prophecy and writing that does not fall into this ideological complex, but we must first consider more recent developments in the history of the oral–written distinction.

The Late Modern Phase

As we have seen, the two crucial postulates of Enlightenment theories of social development were that contemporary primitive society represented humanity in its original state and that contemporary primitive society was therefore analogous to ancient Greco-Roman and Hebrew society. Both of these assumptions were plausible only if one could also assume that the earth and the human race were not very old. Because we take evolutionary cosmology so much for granted, it is perhaps easy for us to forget that in the late eighteenth and early nineteenth centuries even self-consciously modern, self-avowed rationalists held the same kind of geological chronology that we now associate with religious fundamentalism. In those days, even *philosophes* thought that the earth was not much more than five thousand years old. Only on the basis of such a chronology could one suppose that the Hebrews, Greeks, and Romans were but one step removed from the earliest stage in the development of the human race, or that vestiges of humanity in its original state could still be seen in non-European parts of the world. The publication of *The Origin of Species* (1859) by Charles Darwin (1809–1882) and *The Principles of Geology* (1850–1855) by Charles Lyell (1797–1875) made it necessary to think of the earth's age and of human history in terms of many millions of years, not just a few thousand. The superiority of Western civilization could thus no longer continue to be conceived in the same developmental terms.

The increasing awareness of humanity's great diversity in time and space made it impossible to think of human history as a single, unified process moving in a direct, linear fashion from its relatively recent crude beginnings to its culmination in modern European society. The new evidence did not, however, lead nineteenth-century Europeans to doubt that their society was indeed the culmination of human history. The Enlightenment theories of social development, which sustained this presupposition, thus had to be modified rather than abandoned. In a similar way, medieval astronomers had artificially maintained the Ptolemaic cosmology for centuries, incorporating into its geocentric system the contrary evidence that they themselves accumulated. When heavenly bodies were seen not to behave as if they were circling the earth, such anomalies were explained in terms of epicycles, that is, deviations from the geocentric pattern that did not destroy the pattern itself. Because medieval society had such a great ideological investment in the Ptolemaic cosmology, it was not abandoned until the multiplication of epicycles became extreme enough to make the theory's self-contradictions evident. Only then did the Copernican view of the solar system win wide acceptance.[23] When human history proved too long and too diverse to fit the Enlightenment's developmental schemes, nineteenth-century social theorists similarly devised a concept analogous to the epicycles of the medieval astronomers. Because modern European society had such a great ideological investment in the theory of primitive-to-modern development, its intellectuals found a way of explaining humanity's evidently anomalous variations from this Eurocentric pattern as digressions that did not destroy the pattern itself. The success of their efforts is still evident in the persistence of their modified theory of primitive-to-modern development in so many fields, including biblical scholarship. As we shall see, however, biblical scholarship itself has accumulated enough contrary evidence to reveal the self-contradictions in its own commonly held version of this theory.

In order to incorporate the rapidly multiplying evidence of human diversity into the theory of primitive-to-modern development, nineteenth century social theorists devised the metaphorical concept of each society's passing through a life cycle. In eighteenth-century versions of the theory, the ancient Hebrew and Greco-Roman cultures were "classical" in the sense that they constituted Western civilization's primitive and hence formative stage. The nineteenth-century innovation of the life-cycle concept brought with it a new use of the term "classical" in a somewhat different sense. According to this concept, each society went through its own stages of development analogous to the stages through which a living being passes. Every human community was thus born into the time of its relatively primitive infancy, grew into the "classical" stage of its prime, and then suffered the decline and decadence of its old age.[24] As

---

[23] T. S. Kuhn, *The Copernican Revolution: Planetary Astronomy in the Development of Western Thought* (Cambridge, Mass.: Harvard University Press, 1957).

[24] This notion is still evident in T. S. Eliot's dictum that "a classic can occur only when a civilization is mature" (*What Is a Classic? An Address Delivered before the Virgil Society on the 16th of October, 1944* [London: Faber & Faber, 1945], 10); cf. R. Wellek, "The Term

each society rose and fell in this way, it left behind some legacy—great or small—that was gathered up into the ongoing progress of humanity as a whole. The progress of humanity as a whole was still conceived in terms of a primitive-to-modern pattern of development, with European society as its goal and culmination, but at any given point in this overall progression individual societies would be at various points in their own life cycles. The Hebrews, Greeks, and Romans were still regarded as the founders of Western civilization, but not in the sense that they were the main proto-Westerners among the first human beings on earth. By means of the life-cycle concept, they could be recognized as having had a "classical" stage of their own in which they made some cultural achievements nearly rivaling those of modern Europe, thus contributing to and setting precedents for the progress of humanity toward its modern European culmination. By the same means, non-Western societies like China and India could also be recognized as having made significant cultural achievements while still relegating these societies to a subsidiary place in human history as a whole.[25]

This modification of the Enlightenment theories of social development affected the oral–written distinction in a particular way. When human history was seen in terms of millions rather than thousands of years, the development of language itself could no longer be tied to the development of writing. Anthropological investigation showed that human beings could have a fully developed capacity for speaking a language, with a complete system of grammar and an extensive range of rhetorical expression, even without becoming literate. It was evident that human beings must have developed their capacity for language long before they developed any systems of writing. When this realization was synthesized with the metaphorical concept of each society's passing through its own life cycle, the oral–written distinction came to function in a somewhat different way. The development of humanity as a whole continued to be conceived in terms of the transition from oral tradition to universal literacy, but each society was also thought to partially recapitulate this same transition as it progressed through its own life cycle. As each society moved through its primitive, classical, and decadent stages, it also made the

---

and Concept of Classicism in Literary History," *Discriminations: Further Concepts of Criticism* (New Haven: Yale University Press, 1970), 55–89.

[25] As Rubel points out (*Savage and Barbarian*, 35–38), the notion of a culture's having a "rise and fall" was already worked out in various eighteenth-century British theories of social development. It was somewhat later, in the early nineteenth century, that German Romantics began describing this dynamic orgainically in terms of a life cycle (A. K. Wiedmann, *The German Quest for Primal Origins in Art, Culture, and Politics 1900–1933: Die "Flucht in Urzustände"* [Studies in German Thought and History 16; Lewiston, N.Y.: Mellen, 1995], 47–80).

transition from oral tradition to writing—but without ever becoming quite as literate as modern European society. As societies continued to rise and fall the project of universal literacy was advanced little by little, until it was finally brought to completion in modern European society.

Married to the concept of the life cycle, the oral–written distinction came to have a somewhat ambiguous significance in relation to the primitive–advanced distinction. On the one hand, orality could no longer be identified entirely with primitiveness. Cultural progress did not depend entirely on writing, and there could thus be at least some advancement without literacy. Although primitiveness entailed orality, orality did not necessarily entail primitiveness. Orality could also be part of the cultural dynamic that moved each society from its primitive to its classical stage. On the other hand, writing could no longer be identified entirely with advancement. Literacy was an important factor in each society's development into its classical stage, but literacy was also symptomatic of each society's decline. Advancement entailed writing, but writing did not necessarily entail advancement. Writing could also be part of the cultural dynamic that moved each society from its classical to its decadent stage.

As modern biblical scholarship was founded on Enlightenment theories of social development, it was also profoundly shaped by nineteenth-century modification of these same theories. The influential work of Julius Wellhausen (1844–1918) and Hermann Gunkel can be seen in this context. Both scholars simply took it for granted that the cultural history of ancient Israel fit the life-cycle pattern. This assumption was the basis on which Wellhausen's documentary hypothesis, stated in his seminal *Prolegomena zur Geschichte Israels* (1878), attributed significance to the succession of sources from which the Pentateuch was compiled—the Yahwistic (J), Elohistic (E), Deuteronomic (D), and Priestly (P) documents.

The life-cycle concept is especially evident in Wellhausen's view of the first and last of these sources, the Yahwist and the Priestly writers. The former marked the beginning of Israel's transition from its primitive to its classical stage. As early writing, J was still in touch with the primitive vitality of the tribal period's oral traditions and reflected the emerging sophistication of the early monarchy as Israel began to progress into its classical period. The Priestly writer marked Israel's decline from its classical stage into the decadence of the postexilic period. As late writing, P was at the other end of the sociocultural continuum from J, far-removed from the vitality of Israel's primitive origins and thus symptomatic of the religious rigidity and cultural sterility that marked

Israel's final stage. The succession of sources thus reflects the process through which Israel's cultural development blossomed and then withered.[26]

The life-cycle pattern was also the basis for Gunkel's formulation of his theory of the history of literary forms. He supposed that the genres of biblical literature first took definitive shape during Israel's primitive period as oral forms of speech, and that they retained their definitive shape as they began to be written during Israel's classical period. After being subjected to writing for a long time, however, the genres lost their primitive roots and their definitive shape. Late biblical literature, produced during the time of Israel's cultural decline, was thus characterized by the disintegration and confusion of once distinct literary forms in *Mischgattungen*.[27]

Three of Wellhausen and Gunkel's shared views of prophecy and writing are noteworthy. First, both scholars assumed that prophecy went through the same life-cycle stages as Israelite culture in general. We have thus come to think of primitive, classical, and late phases in the development of prophecy. Second, the introduction of writing was assumed to be a positive factor marking the advancement of prophecy into its classical stage. Primitive prophets, who continued to be cast in the Romantic role of the oral poet, were those who preceded the emergence of prophetic literature in the eighth century. Classical prophets, beginning with Amos, were oral poets who also had something to do with the books named for them. Gunkel's theory, that the classical prophets actually had a hand in transcribing their own oracular speeches, was eventually displaced by Mowinckel's theory of transmission through prophetic disciples. The terms "writing prophets" and "classical prophets" are nevertheless still used more or less interchangeably, even by scholars who follow the theory of Mowinckel and thus do not believe that the books named after prophets were actually written by them. Third, the increased use of writing was assumed to be a negative factor marking the decline of prophecy into its late, decadent stage. Beginning with Ezekiel, prophecy became scribalized and lost its nerve as Israelite religion became priest-ridden and law-bound in the postexilic period.

The use of the life-cycle concept as a model for Israel's cultural history was always a bit forced, even when it was first introduced. For example, the

---

[26] J. Wellhausen, *Prolegomena to the History of Ancient Israel* (Gloucester, Mass.: Peter Smith, 1973). The life-cycle concept, which underlies the entire discussion, is sometimes described in botanical terms as when, e.g., the historical development of the cult is compared with the growth and further fate of a tree: "We may compare the cultus in the olden time to the green tree which grows up out of the soil as it will and can; later it becomes the regularly shapen timber, ever more artificially shaped with square and compass" (p. 81).

[27] H. Gunkel, *Die israelitische Literatur* (Darmstadt: Wissenschaftliche Buchgesellschaft, 1963).

life-cycle concept never made particularly good sense of the data gathered and affirmed by historical-critical scholarship regarding Israel's beginnings. As a people formed by emigration from the two main centers of ancient civilization, Mesopotamia and Egypt, why did the Israelites have to start the cycle of cultural development all over again at the primitive stage? The life-cycle concept also never made very good sense of the canonization process. Why would Israel's greatest legacy, the canon of sacred scripture, begin to flower precisely at the time when religious and cultural decline supposedly set in? And if scribes performed a basically secular role, how did they come to play such a crucial part in the *spätjudische* priestly theocracy? Such gross inconsistencies show that this use of the life-cycle model was basically a conceptual ruse, similar to the use of the epicyle in medieval Ptolemaic astronomy. The main function of such historiography was to prop up modern European society's view of itself as the most advanced representative of the progression from a primitive oral to an advanced literate culture. It soon became evident that there was an even greater inconsistency on the most general level of this theory of human social development. The theory applied the life-cycle model to the history of every society except modern Europe. Even if modern Europe was the most advanced representative of the progression from primitive oral to advanced literate culture, why would it not progress through its life cycle too? The theory was thus turned back on itself to become the basis for anxious speculations about the decline of the West in, for example, *Jenseits von Gut und Böse* (1886) by Friedrich Wilhelm Nietzsche (1844–1900), and *Der Untergang des Abendlandes* (1918–1922) by Oswald Spengler (1880–1936).

Despite the limitations that have long been apparent, biblical scholarship is still working with the stereotypes of prophet and scribe that took shape in the work of Wellhausen and Gunkel. According to these stereotypes, based on Enlightenment theories of social development as later modified by the life-cycle concept, prophets and scribes played social roles that were altogether different and completely incompatible. On the one hand, prophets were active in Israel's history from its primitive beginnings. They were basically oral poets or orators, not writers. Oral prophetic speech could be secondarily represented in written form, but prophecy itself could not authentically be written. The identification of prophecy with a canonical collection of writings meant that scribes had usurped the role of prophets and that prophecy had in effect died. On the other hand, scribes became active in Israel's cultural history at a relatively late date. They were basically rationalistic intellectuals at home in academic institutions or schools. The scribal usurpation of prophecy was part of the process by which Judah's postexilic priestly theocracy imposed its control on Israel's religious life, reducing it to ritualistic legalism.[28]

With such broad generalizations, the work of these two great scholars is at best caricatured. Such generalizations are nevertheless useful in laying bare the fact that these still predominant views of the prophetic and scribal roles are indeed only stereotypes. Our current notions of ancient Israelite prophets and scribes are primarily informed by the speculations of Enlightenment social theorists regarding the relationship between social diversification and literacy. To these theorists we owe the assumption that religious oral poets necessarily preceded secular literate intellectuals in the overall development of human society. Our notions of these two roles are further informed by the way such developmental schemes were modified when evolutionary cosmology became the dominant modern worldview. To this modification we owe the assumption that the same pattern had to be recapitulated as Israel's cultural history progressed through stages resembling a life cycle. Both of these assumptions have the same underlying ideological function. They establish and reinforce a cultural analogy between the ancient peoples regarded by the modern West as its ancestors and the so-called primitive peoples treated by the modern West as its subjects. The myth of Western superiority has thus been well served by the way in which modern biblical scholarship has imagined the oral and written dimensions of Israelite prophecy.

In reaching such a judgment, I do not mean to imply that we biblical scholars of the present are better or smarter than our predecessors. Most of the scholars named above were known for their character as well as their intellect. Perhaps the worst that can be said of them is that they were people of their own time; and if no worse can be said of us when we are dead and gone, we are fortunate indeed. We have no other way of knowing the past than they had, that is, by imaginatively comparing it to situations with which we are already directly or indirectly familiar. If we can think of richer alternative scenarios for the development of the oral–written distinction in Israel's cultural history, this may only be due to the fact that our imagination is—as I mentioned at the outset—informed by our experience of electronic communications media as well as the printing press. And our conclusions will of course be affected by our own ideological commitments, both consciously and unconsciously, just as theirs were.

---

[28] The characterization of emergent Judaism in such negative terms unfortunately helped to perpetuate a secularized form of the traditional Christian "teaching of contempt" regarding Judaism, but this concern lies beyond the scope of this essay. I have addressed it elsewhere; see M. H. Floyd, "Zechariah and Changing Views of Second Temple Judaism in Recent Commentaries," *RelSRev* 25 (1999): 260–62.

Although we are neither morally nor epistemologically superior to our predecessors, we can nevertheless learn something from their mistakes. To imagine the biblical past in terms of modern Europe's encounter with so-called primitive peoples was not altogether mistaken. It was an error, however, to substantiate the comparison with a highly speculative developmental theory that took into account only the supposed similarities and ignored major differences. If the developmental analogy had been treated as a heuristic device rather than a foregone conclusion, it might have served a more than merely ideological function. To reimagine the cultural history of prophecy in a way that does not make the same mistake, we first need to take into account the differences between the biblical past and societies that depend only on oral tradition. And second, we also need to look at the information regarding prophecy that has been documented but largely ignored because it does not fit the conventional picture. We may then be able to formulate a theory that can serve as a heuristic device for investigating the phenomenon of spoken and written prophecy without its becoming just a cipher for our own postmodern assumptions that will inevitably underlie it.

Toward a Postmodern Concept of the Oral–Written Distinction

First of all, it is necessary to cease using the oral–written distinction as a binary opposition and to purge from it any connotations of progress derived from theories of social development. Throughout human history there have been societies whose culture can truly be described as "oral" in the sense that they neither know nor use any writing at all. In all other cases, however, societies use all sorts of writing systems in all sorts of ways. It is practically useless to describe all these possibilities in terms of a binary contrast, as pertaining to societies with a "written" culture, and to think of cultural development simply in terms of a progression from oral to written. If the oral–written distinction is to serve a descriptive purpose, as opposed to the merely ideological purpose it has often served in the past, it must be more fully defined in terms that can categorize the various possible ways of using writing.[29] Moreover, although cultural developments widely regarded as "advances" may be broadly connected with changes in the technology of

---

[29] In Susan Niditch's recent work, *Oral World and Written Word,* she recognizes the inadequacy of conceiving the oral–written relationship in terms of a binary opposition, but her analysis does not succeed in breaking out of this limitation. She advocates defining the distinction along a continuum, which allows some flexibility in her analysis. Because the continuum is still defined as extending between the polar opposites of oral and written, however, the distinction remains in effect a binary opposition.

communication, changes in a society's writing habits and patterns of literacy do not necessarily indicate "progress" or the lack of it. Assessments on this score will surely vary, depending on how one conceives of social advancement and whether one thinks that there is any such thing as progress in the modern sense. If the oral–written distinction is to be more than merely ideological, it must also be capable of describing changes in the way a society uses writing without necessarily implying that such changes indicate either a cultural advance or a cultural decline.

In the ancient Near Eastern context, there were probably societies with a truly oral culture. The peoples known to us, however, are largely those that have left some written record. Ancient Israel falls in this category, for we know about this people because they were born into a cultural context that had long made use of writing. As an ancient Near Eastern society, the Israelites had a technology of writing very different from the ones with which we are familiar. They probably used written documents to a lesser extent than we do, and the ways in which they typically used writing may well have been very different from ours. Ancient Israelite literacy was also sociologically different from the "universal" literacy to which many western societies still aspire. It makes no sense, however, to describe all these differences *in the use of writing*—known to us precisely *through a body of writings*—as differences somehow characteristic of an *oral* traditional society. The task is rather to describe more specifically what these differences are and how they affect the composition of particular kinds of documents. In carrying out this task, we must also reckon with the probability that Israel's writing habits and patterns of literacy changed over time. The Israelites first formed some kind of tribal league in the land of Canaan, which eventually became a pair of small monarchial nation states. Then, as a result of defeat and exile, expatriate descendants of the southern kingdom formed a religious community dispersed throughout the ruling empire and centered on the restored sanctuary in Jerusalem. All of these major sociopolitical transformations were no doubt accompanied by changes in the function and use of writing, but these changes cannot be adequately described in terms of either a progression from oral to written or the rise and fall of the Israelite cultural life cycle. The task is rather to correlate sociopolitical transformations with changes in the function and use of writing, without implying that such changes are in themselves either positive or negative.

As a preliminary indication of what the task just described might entail, I propose that the oral–written distinction be categorically expanded by applying it to three aspects of biblical documents, namely, their composition, transmission, and performance. In societies that know nothing of writing, all verbal art is inevitably oral with respect to all three of these aspects. Epic poetry, for example, can evidently be composed, transmitted, and performed in a purely oral form.[30] Societies that know something of writing sometimes choose to continue such purely oral traditions. In addition, however, they tend to develop other kinds of verbal art that can be distinguished in terms of the different ways in which writing and speaking figure in these three aspects of their use. Drama, for example, is obviously oral with respect to its performance, but it is generally written with respect to its composition and transmission. Modern playwrights still follow the patterns of their ancient predecessors, writing scripts from which actors read and thereby learn their lines in order to speak them before an audience.[31] As an example of a type of literature that is written with respect to its composition, transmission, and performance, one might cite the modern novel. In this classificatory scheme the alternatives are not mutually exclusive. Ballads are orally composed and performed, but they can be transmitted in either oral or written form. Balladeers can learn songs from one another, in person or nowadays from a recording, but they can also learn them from the printed versions that circulated formerly as "broadsides" and nowadays as sheet music. Moreover, the two forms of transmission have been known to interact when balladeers have incorporated variations taken from the printed version into a song they first learned orally.[32] As is evident from these examples, the expanded oral–written distinctions often correspond with genre distinctions. Many other factors, however, can also be constitutive for genre definitions.

Using this kind of oral–written analysis, historical changes in the use and function of writing cannot be described in terms of sweeping cultural typologies or shifts from one kind of mentality to another. The categories of composition, transmission, and performance are more useful for understanding particular cases of historical change and adaptation. For example, when the Homeric epic tradition was eventually transcribed in the form of two standardized texts, *The Iliad* and *The Odyssey*, there was not simply a transition from oral to written.

---

[30] The classic studies of the oral epic are M. Parry, *The Making of Homeric Verse* (ed. A. Parry; Oxford: Clarendon, 1971), and A. B. Lord, *The Singer of Tales* (Harvard Studies in Comparative Literature 24; Cambridge, Mass.: Harvard University Press,1960). The Parry-Lord theory becomes problematic, however, when it is untenably extended into a general theory of oral tradition and oral culture.

[31] It is not clear whether ancient actors themselves read scripts in order to learn their parts or whether they were rehearsed in their parts by other readers, but in any case they learned their lines from scripts written by playwrights. See, e.g., M. Bieber, *The History of the Greek and Roman Theater* (Princeton: Princeton University Press, 1961), 80–86; also J. M. Walton, *Greek Theatre Practice* (Contributions in Drama and Theatre Studies 3; Westport, Conn.: Greenwood, 1980), 33–80.

[32] See, e.g., A. Friedman, *The Ballad Revival: Studies in the Influence of Popular on Sophisticated Poetry* (Chicago: University of Chicago Press, 1961).

Even in transcription the poetry retained many features characteristic of oral composition, and for centuries these epics were still orally performed by rhapsodes. Although Homeric epic became written with respect to its transmission, it retained a kind of orality with respect to both its composition and performance. The standardized written version served as an *aide-mémoire* for the rhapsodes, limiting the variations they might introduce in their oral performance.[33] On a broad level, historical change can be described in terms of an association between a particular case—like this development in the Homeric epic tradition—and some change in the sociopolitical context. In this case, the shift to written transmission can be related to changes in the Greek school curriculum, which made Homer an object of study as well as a source of popular entertainment.[34]

This proposed expansion of the oral–written distinction may finally prove to be an inadequate means of analyzing biblical literature and describing how the use and function of writing changed in ancient Israel. It may nevertheless be heuristically useful if it only manages to show that the oral–written distinction is entirely too complex to be reduced to a binary opposition, and thus points the way to a better set of categories.

Culturally Diverse Models of Prophetic Activity

If the oral–written distinction were revised along the lines just suggested, expanding it beyond the limits of a binary opposition and ridding it of developmental connotations, the study of prophecy would be affected in two particular ways. First, the prophetic role would have to be defined in terms of greater diversity. As a result of the intellectual history summarized above, biblical scholarship still reckons largely with just one model of the prophetic role, namely, the oral poet/orator whose oracular speeches were subsequently written down. This model would certainly continue to be regarded as a major possibility, but other models of prophetic activity entailing other patterns of speaking and/or writing would also have to be considered. Second, the history of prophecy would no longer be conceived in terms of an oral–written progression which advanced from its primitive to its classical phase when prophetic speeches began to be transcribed, and declined from its classical to its decadent stage when prophecies began to be put straight into writing. Phases in the history of prophecy might well entail changes in the overall patterns of

---

[33] M. L. West, "Rhapsodes," *OCD*, 1311–12.

[34] R. Lamberton, "Homer in Antiquity," in *A New Companion to Homer* (ed. I. Morris and B. Powell; Leiden: Brill, 1997), 33–48.

speaking and/or writing, but not a transition from just speaking to just writing. Moreover, such changes would not in themselves be indicative of any sort of sociocultural advance or decline.

To put it another way, a clear distinction would have to be made between the history of prophecy itself and the history of prophetic literature in the narrower sense (i.e., most of the books now grouped together as "the Latter Prophets" in the Jewish canon). Judging from the extant examples, it seems that this type of literature resulted from documentation that began around a particular time (i.e., the eighth century), and that books of this sort ceased to be produced around a particular time (i.e., the fifth century). Before, during, and after this length of time, however, prophecy continued to express itself in other ways. Although this type of prophetic literature had a kind of "rise and fall," the history of prophecy itself cannot be reduced to or gauged solely in terms of this phenomenon. The production of such prophetic books may have "died out," and one kind of prophetic activity along with it, but prophecy itself hardly died. The whole notion of "the end of prophecy" is the result of categorical confusion between the history of this one particular kind of prophetic literature and the related but still distinct history of the prophetic phenomenon itself.[35]

With regard to the prophetic role, modern biblical scholarship has shown two somewhat contradictory tendencies. On the one hand, for the reasons described above, it has remained ideologically committed to the single model of the oral poet/orator whose oracular speeches were subsequently written down. Scholars have developed various explanations of the psychological conditions under which such revelatory speeches were composed and delivered, but the various theories of prophetic religious experience have all assumed pretty much this same model of the prophetic subject. On the other hand, driven by its preoccupation with historical reconstruction, modern biblical scholarship has also relentlessly documented the diversity of Israelite prophecy. When these two tendencies are compared, the contradiction becomes evident. The diversity is too great to be contained within just one model of the prophetic role.

The diversity of prophecy is evident in the terminology for it. The various designations, such as *rōʾeh, ḥōzeh, nābîʾ*, and *ʾîš ʾelōhîm*, have been studied extensively.[36] The problem is that the texts which have preserved these terms have also begun to subsume them all within a single homogenous concept of

---

[35] The fact that "the death of prophecy" is a very old notion does not obviate its having resulted from this kind of categorical confusion; see J. Barton, *Oracles of God: Perceptions of Ancient Prophecy in Israel after the Exile* (New York and Oxford: Oxford University Press, 1986), 105–16.

[36] E.g., by D. L. Petersen, *The Roles of Israel's Prophets* (JSOTSup 17; Sheffield: JSOT Press, 1981).

what a prophet is, namely, the Deuteronomistic concept of the *nābîʾ*. In this regard, the narrator's parenthetical remark in 2 Sam 9:9 is telling: "He who is now called a *nābîʾ* was formerly called a *rōʾeh*." In other words, in the texts that have preserved the memory of the differences that once existed, the differences themselves have largely been effaced. For this reason, it is probably impossible to reconstruct the various social roles and different divinitory practices underlying the Deuteronomistic concept of the *nābîʾ*. (And thus we are similarly stuck with using the one term "prophet" for this complex of phenomena.) We must nevertheless reckon with the fact that there once was this variety, and with the probability that it was not eliminated by the Deuteronomistic attempt to propagate a single, theologically normative view of the prophetic role.

The diversity of prophecy is also evident in the various social locations in which prophets lived. Despite the fact that the prophetic books themselves show relatively little concern for the life and times of the prophets for whom they are named, modern biblical scholarship has taken a basically biographical approach to the study of this literature. The limits of this approach are now becoming evident, but it has nevertheless shown beyond doubt that prophets could come from many different sectors of community life, ranging from the center to the periphery of Israelite and Judean society.[37] Elijah lived a quasi-monastic life mostly withdrawn from society, sometimes as a hermit and sometimes in community with other "sons of the prophets." Nathan was a public official on the staff of David's royal court, and Haggai and Zechariah analogously served under the ruling partnership of the governor and high priest in postexilic Yehud. As some kind of farmer, Amos cultivated orchards and maintained herds of cattle. Isaiah seems to have come from the inner circles of upper-class Jerusalem society against which Micah, the rural rustic, railed. Jeremiah and Ezekiel were from priestly families, etc. Among such diverse social locations there is no simple common denominator with which to define a single prophetic role.

The contradictory tendencies within the modern study of prophecy are glaringly evident in the case of cultic prophecy. On the one hand, a large body of data has been accumulated concerning this phenomenon.[38] Much of this

---

[37] R. R. Wilson (*Prophecy and Society in Ancient Israel* [Philadelphia: Fortress, 1980]) has suggested that the diverse social locations of prophets be described on a continuum ranging from central to peripheral, which at least captures the fact of their diversity; but the various social locations may be too disparate to be schematized in terms of such a continuum.

[38] The concept, first fully formulated by S. Mowinckel (*Psalmenstudien 3: Kultprophetie und prophetische Psalmen* [Oslo: Dybwad, 1922], 4–29), was subsequently given

information is indirect, and it has thus been impossible to form a precise impression of the ways in which prophecy functioned in the cultic sphere. It is nevertheless evident that some kinds of prophetic activity did indeed take place in cultic contexts. And yet, on the other hand, modern scholarship has been unable to incorporate this fact into its general description of the prophetic role. When it has not been simply ignored, cultic prophecy has been equated with "false prophecy," dismissed as nothing more than an expression of religious nationalism, characterized as an aspect of "primitive" prophecy subsequently outgrown by "classical" prophecy, etc. The Deuteronomistic, theologically normative definition of the *nābîʾ* was expansive enough to include the personnel of the high places and their musical activities (e.g., 1 Sam 10:5–13). From the modern perspective, however, any such cultic prophecy seems anomalous. Modern biblical scholarship has been unable to reconcile its single model of the prophetic role—the oral poet/orator whose oracular speeches were subsequently written down—with its own discovery that biblical prophecy also included other, specifically cultic activities perhaps not characterized by the same kind of oral–written distinction.[39]

This single model also has considerable deficiencies with respect to its implications for the categorization of prophetic literature. Because modern scholarship has imagined the role of the prophet in only one way, it has also reckoned with just one kind of prophetic literature. If the prophetic role is defined only in terms of an oral poet/orator whose speeches subsequently became written down, then prophetic literature can only consist of documents based on the transcription of such speeches. On this assumption it is difficult to explain why many other kinds of literature—which modern biblical scholarship has rightly distinguished from literature that is prophetic in this narrower sense—were also considered prophetic by Second Temple Jews. This problem surfaces in the form of questions about canonical classification. In the Jewish canon, with its threefold classification of the Law, the Prophets, and the Writings, why are books like Jonah and Joshua–Kings counted among the Prophets? From a modern viewpoint, such narratives might seem better categorized as short story and historiography, respectively. And similarly in the Christian canon, whose Old and New Testaments reflect the older or alternative twofold classification of the Law and the Prophets, why are even more disparate kinds of books, like Psalms and Daniel, also regarded as prophetic?

---

comprehensive treatment by A. R. Johnson (*The Cult Prophet in Israel* [2d ed.; Cardiff: University of Wales, 1962]).

[39] See, e.g., R. Coggins, "An Alternative Prophetic Tradition?" in *Israel's Prophetic Heritage: Essays in Honour of Peter R. Ackroyd* (ed. R. Coggins, A. Philips, and M. Knibb; Cambridge: Cambridge University Press, 1982), 77–94.

From a modern viewpoint these two documents might seem to be better categorized as cultic poetry and apocalyptic literature, respectively. As a result of imagining the prophetic role in only one way, it has often been assumed that documents other than those based on oracular speeches could not be prophetic in any real sense. Other kinds of literature could only have come to be considered prophetic secondarily, as a result of conceptual distortions that arose in the canonization process. This hypothesis is dubious, however, because the canonization process began while these various other kinds of literature were still being produced: narratives both historiographical and legendary, annotated collections of liturgical lyrics, and apocalypses, etc., as well as books based on oracular speeches. It is highly unlikely that books of a kind that were still being produced got drastically and mistakenly recategorized in the process of becoming canonically normative. It is more likely that such books were included within the canonical category of prophecy because the books themselves were already conceived and recognized as prophetic in some sense.[40]

As we have previously noted, the Jewish and Christian canons vary in their delimitation of "the Prophets," reflecting different concepts of prophetic literature that already existed within Second Temple Judaism. This difference does not imply, however, that an original and relatively limited concept of prophetic literature—corresponding to the modern scholarly concept—became corrupted and expanded. For present purposes, two aspects of this canonical difference are noteworthy. First, it does not indicate a dispute about whether prophecy is a diverse and varied phenomenon. It is rather symptomatic of the concern, already evident in the Deuteronomistic material, for defining a theologically normative concept of prophecy amidst all the diversity and variety. Second, even if one were to argue that the Tanak's relatively limited view of prophetic literature is in some sense more basic than the relatively expansive view represented by the Christian Bible—which is doubtful[41]—the Tanak itself does not limit the Prophets to documents based on oracular speeches (i.e., the Latter Prophets). It also includes the historiographical narratives conventionally known to modern scholarship as the Deuteronomistic history (i.e., the Former Prophets). No matter how the differences between the Jewish and Christian canons are explained, Second Temple Jews had a broad concept of prophetic literature that included more than books based on oracular speeches. This does not mean that authors and readers of this period could not tell the difference between a book like Isaiah and books like Samuel or Psalms.

---

[40] See the discussion of this matter in Barton, *Oracles of God.*

[41] Ibid., 35–95.

It means that for them such differences could be subcategories within a larger category of prophetic literature, which in turn implies that their concept of the prophetic role included various possibilities with respect to the use of writing.

The modern study of prophecy can begin to resolve its contradictory tendencies and fill its explanatory gaps by ceasing to resist the conclusion toward which its own efforts have led. Prophecy was too diverse to be limited to a single model of the prophetic role defined in terms of one particular version of the oral–written distinction. Prophecy probably did include the oral delivery of oracular speeches that were subsequently transcribed and edited, but it also must have included other kinds of divinatory activity that entailed other combinations of speaking and writing. Before these other possibilities can be described, it is first necessary to consider the other social role that is relevant to the question of prophecy and writing, namely, that of the scribe.

Culturally Diverse Models of Scribal Activity

Just as modern biblical scholarship has inherited from Enlightenment theories of social development several assumptions about prophets, it has also inherited from the same source several complementary assumptions about scribes. As noted above, these two social roles have been regarded as incompatible because the primitive oral phenomenon of prophecy is supposed to have been developmentally prior to the more advanced practice of writing. Scribes, moreover, are supposed to have emerged through a process of social differentiation and secularization to become the rationalistic intellectuals of ancient society. These assumptions are still operative in the study of wisdom literature, just as they are in the study of prophecy. They are evident, for example, in modern biblical scholarship's historical placement of the books it has relegated to the category of wisdom literature. Although most of these books cannot really be dated, they are nevertheless presumed to be "late." As examples of scribal literature par excellence, they could hardly have been "early." This is a purely ideological tautology, based on little more than the speculative logic of the Eurocentric developmental social theory described above. Wisdom literature was produced in the ancient Near East long before Israel became a nation, and it continued to be produced long after the traditions of Israel took the form of the Jewish religion. All during this time scribes fulfilled a wide variety of functions in ancient Near Eastern society. Why must it be assumed that in Israel scribes only came "late," or that Israel ever went through a time in which scribes were not an integral part of its cultural life? Unless one affirms the ideological axiom that Israel's cultural history followed a life-cycle pattern in which it had to recapitulate the cultural developmental of the human race, progressing from primitive orality toward universal literacy, there is no reason for such assumptions. This is not to say that scribes in the tribal league would have held the same social positions that they held during the monarchy or the Second Temple period. Their role and writing's function would certainly have changed and may well have gained importance over time, but it is highly unlikely that the Israelites ever lived in a truly oral culture.

A complete deconstruction of the stereotype of the scribe, inherited by modern biblical scholars from Enlightenment theories of social development, lies beyond the scope of this essay. Several aspects of this stereotype, however, are particularly relevant to our reconsideration of the prophetic role. In accord with the Enlightenment theories surveyed above, scribes have conventionally been viewed as intellectuals whose function in ancient society was roughly analogous to the function of intellectuals in modern society. Scribes must therefore have been a basically secular and rationalistic group of fellows, primarily at home in the institutional context of the academy where they did objective research and taught others to read and write.[42] This view of scribes as

---

[42] This view is implied in G. von Rad's influential concept of "the Solomonic Enlightenment," which he took to be manifest in the historiographical innovations made during Solomon's reign: "Now this completely new way of picturing Jahweh's action in history . . . was merely an expression of a more profound spiritual transformation. For an era which no longer experienced Jahweh's working mainly in the sacral form of miracles . . . its whole relationship to the reality surrounding it . . . became secularised, and was, as it were, overnight released from the sacral orders sheltering it. In consequence, the figures in the stories now move in a completely demythologized and secular world. Unquestionably, we have here to do with the traces of an Enlightenment on a broad basis, an emancipation of the spirit and a stepping out from antiquated ideas" (*Old Testament Theology* [2 vols.; trans. D. M. G. Stalker; New York: Harper & Row, 1962], 1:52–53). As S. Herrmann noted, von Rad's description of this development presupposes its connection with Solomon's promotion of the role of the *sōpēr*, which in turn implied that its impact was limited to the then very small scribal class (*A History of Israel in Old Testament Times* [trans. J. Bowden; Philadelphia: Fortress, 1975], 182). Regardless of whether scribes are connected with such a historical development, they are nevertheless often described as the kind of secular rationalists produced by modern Western universities, and thus not very interested in religious matters. J. Blenkinsopp, for example, describes the social location of the Israelite scribal class as "comparable to the English establishment in the nineteenth and early twentieth centuries recruited from families wealthy enough to send their sons to the public schools and universities. The essential first step was literacy." In the course of their training, Israelite scribes studied proverbs that were "for the most part secular in tone and substance." The references to Yahweh in such material must therefore be secondarily "due to an editorial theologizing of this kind of proverbial instruction" (*Sage, Priest, Prophet: Religious and Intellectual Leadership in Ancient Israel* [LAI; Louisville, Ky.: Westminster John Knox, 1995], 33–34). In other words, theologizing could not have been an integral part of scribal instruction since scribes are by definition secular fellows. Although Blenkinsopp perpetuates this stereotype of the scribe, his overall description of the sage goes beyond it; and other recent descriptions of the scribal social role have similarly begun to push beyond such stereotypical limitations. L. L. Grabbe, for example, concludes: "The learned tradition was

a skeptical academic class has directly affected modern theories about the production of prophetic literature in two ways. First, the assumption that scribes functioned primarily in an academic institutional context has made it difficult to imagine that prophetic activity could ever entail writing. If the ability to write was largely imparted through formal schooling, most prophets would probably fail to qualify. Second, the assumption that scribes had a basically secular outlook has led scholars to view the production of prophetic literature as a basically nonprophetic activity. Prophets, as entranced speakers of poetic oracles, made inspired claims about God; but their speeches were then written down and edited by academics who, as intellectual skeptics, had no particular self-investment in such mystical matters. These views of scribal schools and scribal secularism are both debatable.

With regard to the issue of scribal schools, it is necessary to distinguish and consider separately three assumptions that are sometimes insufficiently differentiated: (1) that there was no culturally significant scribal activity in Israel until there were scribal schools, (2) that scribal schools were primarily devoted to teaching literacy, and (3) that the teaching of literacy in schools served primarily to create a reading public. This combination of assumptions provides a particularly good example of the way in which the modern European ideology of the oral–written distinction has used the ancient past as a screen on which to project the image of its own origins. These are, after all, variations on the basic suppositions underlying the modern Western view of the relationship between literacy and schooling, but it is doubtful that any of them apply in the ancient Israelite context.

With regard to the question of scribal activity and schools, there are very few direct references to schools and schooling in biblical times, and all of them are relatively late. For example, Sir 51:23 mentions a "house of learning" (*bêt midraš*). Daniel 1:4 describes what several young Jewish exiles were taught at the Babylonian royal court as "the letters and language of the Chaldeans" (*sēper ûlĕšôn kasdîm*). In 2 Macc 4:9–14 the establishment of a Greek *gymnasion* in Jerusalem is recounted. Although Jews are involved in all three instances, the schooling itself is Jewish only in Sirach. Aside from such examples, there are no clear references to either group instruction in literacy or the kind of place in which such activity might happen. In the Bible there are many references to someone who writes (a "scribe"; *sōpēr*) or to the action of writing (*ktb*). In some cases (e.g., Prov 22:20–21) the setting is conceivably

---

not confined to one group or institution. Scribes, priests, some diviners and some prophets will have intersected with the intellectual stratum of society" (*Priests, Prophets, Diviners, Sages: A Socio-Historical Study of Religious Specialists in Ancient Israel* [Valley Forge, Pa.: Trinity Press International, 1995], 180).

academic, but in general neither the person nor the activity is explicitly described in the context of a school. Several extrabiblical texts have been discovered at archeological sites, but neither their contents nor the conditions under which they were found necessarily leads to the conclusion that there were schools in these places.[43]

Much of the extrabiblical textual evidence—for example, the many brief inscriptions on clay seals—indicates only that lettering could be used as a kind of identification tag. One could certainly make and recognize such tags without a very profound grasp of reading and writing. Some other kind of graphic symbol might just as well have been used instead of lettering. In other cases, however, the extrabiblical documents and inscriptions show a relatively high level of literacy, that is, an ability to create, materially represent, and decode novel verbal compositions. Such texts are not numerous, they are of very different kinds, and their geographical distribution is spotty. They nevertheless show beyond doubt that scribal skills of a sophisticated sort were practiced here and there in Israel, from the tenth century off and on.[44]

Because most of the biblical documents were written long after the time they describe, it is difficult to assess the significance of their descriptions of scribal activity. It would not necessarily be anachronistic to attribute writing to any time in Israel's history. In any given case, however, a biblical document might actually be describing a particular use of writing that was conventional at the time when it was composed, anachronistically projecting that particular use of writing back into a time when it had not yet become conventional. Each case must therefore be carefully weighed on its own merits.

The interpretation of Judg 5:14b provides an interesting case in this regard. The Song of Deborah (Judg 5:2–31a) is commonly acknowledged to be one of the oldest texts in the Old Testament. Many scholars believe that its composition is virtually contemporaneous with the event it celebrates, the victory of the Israelite tribal militia over the Canaanite forces of King Jabin. In describing a less than complete rally of the tribal militia (vv. 13–18), v. 14b refers to members of the Zebulon contingent as *mōškîm běšebet sōpēr*. This phrase, which includes the word that ordinarily means "scribe" (*sōpēr*), might be translated as "handlers of the scribal stylus." Scribes seem to have been involved in the mustering of troops, at least in the time of the monarchy (e.g., 2 Kgs 25:19; 2 Chr 26:11; and Jer 52:25). Apparently assuming that a similar use

---

[43] D. W. Jamieson-Drake, *Scribes and Schools in Monarchic Judah: A Socio-Archaeological Approach* (JSOTSup 109; Sheffield: Sheffield Academic Press, 1991), esp. 156–57.

[44] See Niditch's summary review of the extrabiblical evidence of writing in preexilic Israel (*Oral World*, 45–58).

of writing would not be out of place in the time of the tribal league, the translators of the LXX rendered this phrase as a reference to such military record-keepers, as did Luther and the translators of the King James Version despite the somewhat different precedent set by the Vulgate.[45]

In the late eighteenth and early nineteenth centuries, however, opposing tendencies began to emerge with regard to the interpretation of this verse. As Enlightenment theories of social development gained force in modern biblical scholarship, some translators and commentators came to assume that any reference to scribes under the primitive cultural conditions of the tribal league was unthinkable.[46] Most recent English versions have therefore translated the phrase in question as a description of persons exercising a generally military function rather than a specifically scribal role (e.g., "those who bear the marshal's staff" [NRSV]). After weighing all the philological evidence, however, various commentators have continued to affirm just the opposite. Scholars from various camps, including those on both sides of the debate between orthodoxy and modernism, have concluded that this text probably shows that scribes kept records regarding the deployment of the tribal militia.[47] Here again we have a case of conflict between general claims made on ideological grounds and the facts in a particular case. Once it is recognized that general claims about the absence of scribes in Israel's early history are largely ideological, references to writing in the days of the judges cannot be arbitrarily discounted even if the culture of the tribal league was in some sense relatively "primitive." References to writing like the one in Judg 5:14b (including, e.g., Judg 8:14) may not be anachronistic, even if some other descriptions of writing during this time probably are (e.g., Josh 24:26).

In any case, as a starting point for historical analysis we can affirm that there were scribes in Israel as early as the tenth century, and perhaps even earlier. From this fact we can deduce that these scribes had to learn their skills in some particular social setting(s). The problem is how to imagine their social role, as well as the context in which they were trained to play this role, in light

---

[45] The Vulgate reads: *qui exercitum ducerent ad bellandum.* This appears to be based on a Hebrew original different from MT rather than a variant of MT itself.

[46] K. Budde's influential commentary is symptomatic of this trend. He argues that, because it is difficult to imagine a scribal role being played so early in Israel's history, it would be better to take the root *spr* in the sense of "count" and make it the main verb in the next verse (*Das Buch der Richter* [KHC 7; Tübingen: Mohr, 1897], 45).

[47] E.g., G. F. Moore, *A Criticial and Exegetical Commentary on Judges* (ICC; Edinburgh: T&T Clark, 1895), 151–53; C. F. Keil and F. Delitzsch, *Biblical Commentary on the Old Testament: Joshua, Judges, Ruth* (trans. J. Martin; Grand Rapids, Mich.: Eerdmans, 1950), 318; and J. Gray, *Joshua, Judges and Ruth* (NCB; London: Nelson, 1967), 286.

of whatever else we may specifically know about the Israelite context and whatever else we may generally know about its ancient Near Eastern background. As noted above, modern biblical scholarship has imagined the scribal role primarily in terms of an academic guild made up of professional scholars, following Enlightenment theories of social development. In line with this model, it has been assumed that scribes were trained primarily through formal schooling and that there could not have been culturally significant scribal activity until the advent of schools, archives, and libraries. On the basis of this assumption, any scribal activity prior to the advent of such institutions is anomalous and thus to be discounted as a kind of cultural false start.

Schools, archives and libraries were undoubtedly centers of scribal activity in the ancient Near East. It is questionable, however, whether we should think of culturally significant scribal activity as something necessarily or exclusively focused in such an institutional setting. The limitations of relying primarily on the Eurocentric stereotype of the scribe are evident in the debate about the advent of scribal schools in Israel. On the assumption that culturally significant scribal activity could only take place in schools, it has been difficult to reconcile the evidence concerning writing with the evidence concerning schools. As we have seen, there are signs of fairly sophisticated writing skills from at least the tenth century on. There are no indications of scribal schools, however, until much later, perhaps as early as the eighth century but perhaps not until the sixth century or even later.[48] The problem is how to make sense of this discrepancy.

It has been argued, on the one hand, that where there was writing there must also have been schools, and therefore an extensive system of scribal or even general education existed as early as the tenth century. This argument does not reckon adequately with the lack of evidence concerning schools. It has also been argued, on the other hand, that until there were schools there could have been no culturally significant writing, and therefore the production of "canonical literature" could not have begun until the postexilic period. This argument arbitrarily discounts the material evidence of skilled and relatively sophisticated writing in preexilic times. The evidence seems not to lead to this kind of either–or, but to the conclusion that culturally significant scribal skills could have been learned and practiced by means other than schooling. Writing

---

[48] See the summary discussion of this question and the bibliography cited in Grabbe, *Priests, Prophets, Diviners, Sages,* 171–74.

could also have been learned through apprenticeship in nonacademic settings where it would have been used for nonacademic purposes.[49]

From the archeological remains of the ancient Near Eastern background, there is ample evidence that scribes did indeed function in many settings besides schools and that writing was used for many nonacademic purposes. In the public sphere scribes worked in the areas of international relations, civil administration, military deployment, law courts, religious cults, trade and commerce, etc., and in the private sphere they provided domestic records and facilitated personal correspondence. Many documents have been found on the sites of ancient archives and libraries, but many have also been recovered from other kinds of settings, including temples, commercial establishments, military installations and private houses. Because the material evidence shows scribal skills to have been so widely dispersed in different social settings, it is difficult to suppose that either their acquisition or practice was primarily concentrated in the relatively small realm of the professional scholastic class and its academic institutions. Just as the single model of the prophet as oral poet/orator cannot adequately explain the fact of great diversity in prophetic activity, the single model of the scribe as professional academic cannot adequately explain the fact of similar diversity in scribal activity. Within the social system there must have been some kind of symbiotic relationship between the relatively specialized forms of scribal activity practiced by the academic guild and the more general forms of scribal activity practiced in the community at large. The guild's role can hardly be characterized in terms of having a monopoly on scribal skills, however, despite the frequent assertions of modern scholars to this effect.

Just as literacy does not necessarily entail schooling, in the ancient cultural context schooling does not necessarily entail literacy. Even though scribal schools undoubtedly specialized in teaching the skills of reading and writing, it is probably a distortion to think of them as institutions primarily concerned with literacy for its own sake. Biblical wisdom literature exhorts young men to learn, but not necessarily to become literate. The learning to which they are called is generally described as "wisdom and understanding," and in order to attain such learning they are to follow the advice of parents and elders, meditate on proverbs, master the rules of etiquette, identify positively with examples of prudent behavior and negatively with examples of foolish behavior, etc. The necessary parental directives, lists of aphorisms, tips, and moral exempla are all

---

[49] E. Lipiński, "Royal and State Scribes in Ancient Jerusalem," *Congress Volume: Jerusalem 1986* (ed. J. A. Emerton; VTSup 40; Leiden: Brill, 1988), 157–64; C. Meyers, *Discovering Eve: Ancient Israelite Women in Context* (New York: Oxford University Press, 1988), 154; cf. R. N. Whybray, *The Intellectual Tradition in the Old Testament* (BZAW 135; Berlin and New York: de Gruyter, 1974), 33–43.

contained within the written text of books like Proverbs and Sirach, and in order to gain access to this material someone obviously has to be able to read it. The students themselves, however, are not assigned this task. Such books thus probably reflect a pedagogical process in which the teacher has the only "textbook," knows how to read its previously written lesson material, and conducts the class by reading the text aloud and commenting on it. (In terms of the expanded oral–written categories presented above, such wisdom literature can be described as another kind of document that is written with respect to composition and transmission, but oral with respect to performance.)

As attentive and responsive participants in this process, students would be able to learn through the literacy of their teacher without necessarily having to be literate themselves. In this sense each student is exhorted figuratively to "write [the teacher's] directives on the tablet of your heart" (Prov 7:3b). Of course some or all of the students who took part in such an educational process may have also become literate. It is nevertheless important to recognize that they would not need to use literacy skills—and by implication would not even need to have such skills—in order to participate in the process. Wisdom literature reflects a concept of formal education that entails the use of written texts, but this concept does not simply equate formal education with literacy. Scribal skills are helpful in the pursuit of wisdom, but one can be wise without having scribal skills, and being a scribe does not necessarily make one wise. [50]

This example of wisdom literature in the setting of the scribal school shows the necessity of making a distinction not only between education and literacy (even in the context of schooling) but also between the audience and the readership of texts composed and transmitted in writing. In the kind of pedagogical process just described, the teacher is the only one who actually reads the text, but the teacher reads it to an audience of students. The author of such a text can thus aim to reach a relatively large audience through a relatively small readership because there are situations in which those able to read the text can mediate its contents to those who may not be able to do so. Above and beyond this academic example, it is possible to identify nonacademic settings in which texts might function similarly. For example, ritual settings—whether one thinks of the sacrificial cult or the emerging synagogue—also provided occasions on which readers could relate the contents of writings to an audience of listeners. Texts used in this way could be purely written compositions but they might nevertheless use many of the same rhetorical devices as orally

---

[50] J. L. Crenshaw, "The Primacy of Listening in Ben Sira's Pedagogy," in *Wisdom, You Are My Sister: Studies in Honor of Roland E. Murphy on the Occasion of His Eightieth Birthday* (ed. M. L. Barré; CBQMS 29; Washington, D.C.: Catholic Biblical Association of America, 1997), 172–87.

composed speeches, and thus sound like orally composed speeches, because they were intentionally designed to be orally performed.

From the assertion made above, that scribal skills were widely dispersed in ancient Israelite society, it does not necessarily follow that literacy was very common. The question of the extent of literacy in ancient society has been much studied and much debated.[51] For present purposes, it is sufficient to make some broad generalizations about the ancient Israelite context in the light of the distinction just made between readership and audience. On the one hand, the evidence seems to show that literacy was not highly restricted to a particular group. As is generally the case with any information technology, the wealthy probably had potentially greater access than others. But because the skills of reading and writing could be acquired in other contexts besides schooling, and because various economies could be made with respect to the necessary materials, these skills were also more widely available. On the other hand, literacy was not widely sought. Although various degrees of competence in reading and writing were necessary in a variety of occupations, one could participate knowledgeably in most major aspects of community life without such skills. Israelite and Jewish society may have become increasingly literate in the sense that most of its basic cultural information came to be stored in written form, but in a variety of social settings this information could reach a public audience through a relatively small readership. It eventually became necessary to identify with a particular body of writings in order to be Jewish, and Jewish identity thus came to entail the existence of a scribal class. Because of the distinction between readership and audience, however, it never became

---

[51] See I. M. Young, "Israelite Literacy: Interpreting the Evidence. Part I," *VT* 48 (1998): 239–53; idem, "Israelite Literacy: Interpreting the Evidence. Part II," *VT* 48 (1998): 408–22; J. L. Crenshaw, *Education in Ancient Israel: Across the Deadening Silence* (ABRL; New York: Doubleday, 1998); and the bibliography cited in these works. With regard to the surrounding cultures see, e.g., J. S. Cooper, "Babbling on Recovering Mesopotamian Orality," in *Mesopotamian Epic Literature: Oral or Aural?* (ed. M. E. Vogelzang and H. L. J. Vanstiphout; Lewiston, N.Y.: Mellen, 1992), 110–11; J. Baines, "Literacy and Ancient Egyptian Society," *Man*, NS, 18 (1983): 572–99; J. Baines and C. J. Eyre, "Four Notes on Literacy," *GöM* 61 (1983): 65–96; J. Ray, "Literacy in Egypt in the Late and Persian Periods," in *Literacy and Power in the Ancient World* (ed. A. K. Bowman and G. Woolf; Cambridge: Cambridge University Press, 1994), 51–66; W. V. Harris, *Ancient Literacy* (Cambridge, Mass.: Harvard University Press, 1989); M. Beard et al., eds., *Literacy in the Roman World* (Journal of Roman Archaeology Suppl. Ser. 3; Ann Arbor, Mich.: Journal of Roman Archaeology, 1991; R. Cribiore, *Writing, Teachers, and Students in Graeco-Roman Egypt* (ASP 36; Atlanta: Scholars Press, 1996); and R. Thomas, *Literacy and Orality in Ancient Greece* (Cambridge: Cambridge University Press, 1992); idem, "Literacy and the City-State in Archaic and Classical Greece," in *Literacy and Power* (ed. Bowman and Woolf), 33–50.

necessary or even desirable for most Jews to be able to read those writings for themselves. It is thus a distortion to characterize the function of scribal schools, even in the Second Temple period, in terms of creating a reading public. It can nevertheless be said that one function of scribal schools was to create a small readership through which writers could reach a wider public audience.

From this reconsideration of scribal schools and their function, it is evident that the Enlightenment theories of social development have bequeathed to us a rather too simplistic concept of the role of the scribe. Just as the role of the prophet cannot be limited to the single model of the oral poet/orator, the role of the scribe cannot be limited to the single model of the academic intellectual. One could become a scribe (i.e., attain more than perfunctory reading and writing skills) without necessarily attending a school where such skills were taught. Writers commonly produced documents for use in settings other than academic ones (e.g., religious settings). In both academic and nonacademic contexts, documents were not necessarily written in order to reach a reading audience. These observations hardly begin to map out the various possible models of the scribal role and their various functions, but they are enough to show that the question of whether prophets used writing cannot be reduced to the question of whether they belonged to scribal schools. There were also nonacademic areas of society in which writing and prophecy might overlap. For example, if writing and prophetic activity could both take place in a cultic setting, it is possible that the activities associated with cultic prophecy might well entail writing. Whether prophets belonged to scribal schools is nevertheless an open question that has considerable bearing on how one imagines the production of prophetic literature. In order to deal with this question we must also reconsider another aspect of the conventional stereotype of the scribe, namely, that scribes were secular skeptics.

Here again we have a good example of the way in which the logic of Eurocentric ideology has led biblical scholarship to make statements that are at odds with its own documentation of the facts. Introductory treatments of the cultural background of the Old Testament often report that ancient Near Eastern scribes were generally involved in the production of texts containing—among other things—mythology, oracles, incantations, omens, and materials relating to divinatory practices of all sorts. In the very same discussion, it is not uncommon to find also the inconsistent conclusion that scribes were typically secular, pragmatic, and skeptical, etc. For example, in a recent work Philip Davies asserts that "religion for the scribe will have been, professionally, an instrument of political ideology and of intellectual reflection, but not the wellspring of political or social behavior, in which the scribe was guided increasingly by rational and empirical considerations." In the next sentence he says that the writing skills possessed by scribes were "often regarded as magical, divine in origin, occult."[52] He then proceeds to report that "some [Mesopotamian scribes] were specialists in one or another arcane branch of lore, such as spells,"[53] and that the library of Ashurbanipal at Nineveh included among its five thousand tablets "[not only] myths, but also omen lists, magical . . . and ritual compositions."[54] Moreover, many Egyptian scribes were associated with temples where they occupied themselves with texts "mainly of a religious kind, intended for cultic use, but including magical texts." These Egyptian temple scribes not only wrote didactic books of instruction, but also "attempted to predict the future."[55]

It is difficult to reconcile Davies's generalization with the data that he himself reports. On what basis can we suppose that divinatory activities, such as attempts to predict the future using the "magical" skill of writing, were guided only by "rational and empirical considerations"? And on what basis can we suppose that divinatory activity was only "an instrument of political ideology," something not viewed as a "wellspring of political or social behavior"? Judging from the many extant documents relating to divination, both biblical and extrabiblical, it is much more probable that attempts to predict the future were generally based on a mystical religious desire to discern the involvement of the gods in human affairs, and this work was typically undertaken in order to determine a particular concrete course of action for individuals and communities. In his generalization about scribal religious sensibility, or lack thereof, Davies seems to be projecting anachronistically onto ancient writers the agnosticism of modern academics, in accord with the scribal stereotype invented by Enlightenment theories of social development. His own research shows that even if some scribes might have fit the ideological stereotype of the secular skeptic, many others were deeply involved in what might be called the mantic arts and viewed the results of their practice as socially foundational knowledge.

The attribution of secularity to Israelite scribes is often substantiated by noting that the biblical wisdom literature makes few references to theological themes, but this hardly explains anything. A secular outlook is hardly shown by the fact that there are few references to God in one among the many types of

---

[52] P. R. Davies, *Scribes and Schools: The Canonization of the Hebrew Scriptures* (LAI; Louisville, Ky.: Westminster John Knox, 1998), 18.

[53] Ibid., 20.

[54] Ibid., 22.

[55] Ibid., 25.

literature produced by Israelite scribes.[56] What about the rest of the wisdom literature in which the central concerns are theological? And what about the rest of the Bible? In the final analysis it is all scribal literature—who else but scribes made literature?—and it is difficult to suppose that canonical scriptures were produced by a group who were in principle indifferent to matters of divination, ritual, and theology, etc. It is more probable that Israelite scribes were generally like those of the cultural context to which they belonged.[57] Of course there were many scribes whose duties never entailed writing or thinking anything about the gods, and some were no doubt personally indifferent in religious matters. But judging from the form and content of many texts they left behind, ancient Near Eastern scribes were generally steeped in the religious practices and beliefs characteristic of their culture and age.

Some scholars have recently located the origins of apocalyptic literature in a setting described as "mantic scribalism."[58] With regard to such a setting, however, there is no need to think only in terms of apocalyptic literature. This phrase is an appropriate description of the setting that produced all the kinds of literature that were conceived as prophetic in the broader sense, including histories, apocalypses, and psalters, as well as edited collections of oracular speeches. If modern biblical scholarship had not inherited the stereotype of the secular scribe from the Eurocentric ideology of literacy, there would be no reason to qualify any reference to scribes with the modifier "mantic." This does not mean that each and every scribe was in effect a diviner, but rather that the concerns of scribes and prophets could and often did readily converge.

The Interrelationship of Prophetic and Scribal Activity

In view of the extent to which modern biblical scholarship's views of prophecy and writing have been ideologically determined by the myth of Western superiority, there is an obvious need to reconstruct the categories in which we conceptualize this subject. The foregoing attempt to do so may well prove deficient in various respects, but unless it completely misses the mark,

---

[56] E.g., W. McKane, *Proverbs: A New Approach* (OTL; Philadelphia: Westminster, 1970), 451.

[57] "Biblical wisdom is basically religious, not secular" (R. Murphy, "Wisdom in the OT," *ABD* 6:922).

[58] E.g., H.-P. Müller, "Mantische Weisheit und Apokalyptik," *Congress Volume: Uppsala 1971* (VTSup 22; Leiden: Brill, 1972), 268–93; J. C. VanderKam, "The Prophetic-Sapiential Origins of Apocalyptic Thought," in *A Word in Season: Essays in Honour of William McKane* (ed. J. D. Martin and P. R. Davies; JSOTSup 42; Sheffield: Sheffield Academic Press, 1986), 163–76.

we shall eventually have to reorganize what we generally know about prophets and scribes so as to recognize that the following range of possibilities is at least theoretically possible. There could certainly be prophetic activity that had nothing directly to do with writing, as well as scribal activity that had nothing directly to do with prophecy. However, prophetic activity and scribal activity could also overlap to a considerable extent. Various types of prophetic activity might entail direct use of writing, whether in a nonacademic setting like the cult or in the context of a scribal school. And conversely, various types of scribal activity, whether in or out of an academic context, could be prophetic in the sense that documents were written and studied in order to discern divine involvement in contemporary human affairs. Further study will be necessary in order to discover which of these possibilities may have been realized in specific cases and whether there were changes over time in this regard. I have argued elsewhere that Habakkuk's report of a divine command to "write the revelation" (Hab 2:2) exemplifies a kind of prophetic activity that makes direct use of writing.[59] I have similarly argued that Haggai exemplifies a specifically prophetic kind of scribal historiography (namely, a written narration of the past, based on a study of extant sources, providing its readers with a model of how to divine God's involvement in the events of their own time).[60]

Whether or not these particular arguments hold, it is necessary to suppose that prophetic and scribal activity could overlap in order to explain adequately two of the central developments in biblical prophecy. First, the oracular speeches of apparently nonwriting prophets were recorded, studied, annotated, and expanded. In this editorial process oracular speeches were not simply transcribed so as to document what prophets once said. In the process of being rewritten, oracular speeches were also prophetically reinterpreted. It is difficult to imagine how such rewriting could have happened unless one supposes that prophets who could write took an interest in the oracles of prophets who could not, and that writing prophets collected and reworked oral prophetic speeches in the various written forms to which they were accustomed. Scribes without prophetic concerns might perhaps have been motivated to make copies of oracles that were for some reason notable, but they would hardly have been motivated to engage in the kind of reinterpretation that is evident in documents like Amos and Isaiah. Second, from a relatively large group of documents produced by writing prophets, a few documents were eventually singled out as canonical, that is, as theologically normative models of how God's involvement

---

[59] Floyd, "Prophecy and Writing," 470–81.

[60] M. H. Floyd, "The Nature of the Narrative and the Evidence of Redaction in Haggai," *VT* 45 (1995): 470–90.

in human affairs could be discerned. In the process of canonization, documents were not simply classified and catalogued so as to serve a particular political or social agenda. The range of canonical selection defined the array of historical and theological lenses through which the Jewish community had come to view various aspects of exile and restoration as transformative events. It is difficult to imagine how such a range of selections could have been made unless one supposes that there were scribal groups with the prophetic desire to discern from those transformative events the patterns of God's involvement in their own time. Scribes without such prophetic concerns might perhaps have been motivated to define a literary canon that was educationally normative—as was the case in Hellenistic schools—but not a literary canon that was also cultically and theologically normative.

In the final analysis, there is no contradiction in the Bible's presenting us, on the one hand, with prophetic writings and, on the other hand, with narratives that mostly describe prophets as speaking rather than writing. A discrepancy appears only when biblical scholarship makes the same ideological assumptions about the oral–written distinction that modern Eurocentric theories of social development have made since the eighteenth century. When these assumptions are exposed and replaced by a more adequate—if still only heuristic—set of conceptual categories, the apparent discrepancy tends to recede. The description of oracular speeches in writing results from an overlap in the diverse range of prophetic and scribal roles in the biblical social world. Modern biblical scholarship has long resisted such a conclusion, even as it has amassed the information that points strongly toward it, thus showing its considerable ideological investment in the myth of Western superiority. The positions taken in this essay can hardly pretend to set the standard for nonideological correctness, but they are indicative of the kind of self-questioning that is necessary for biblical scholarship to enter the postcolonial era.[61]

---

[61] Along this same line, see the essays in L. E. Donaldson and R. S. Sugirtharajah, eds., *Postcolonialism and Scriptural Reading* (Semeia 75; Atlanta: Scholars Press, 1996); also R. S. Sugirtharajah, ed., *The Postcolonial Bible* (The Bible and Postcolonialism 1; Sheffield: Sheffield Academic Press, 1998).

Scribe and Speaker

Donald B. Redford
Pennsylvania State University

The Interface between Written and Oral Tradition
in Ancient Egypt

It is a commonplace that the *scribal tradition* among the ancient Egyptians held primacy of place in the complex society that emerged in the early third millennium B.C.E. While modern scholarship sometimes confuses *writing* with *authorship*, and misconstrues the latter as revealing itself first and foremost in the putting of signs in a visible medium, the profession of scrivening in the ancient world resides completely within archival practice. As the cohesive element in the administration of the state, the scribal art constituted a logonomic system designed for a kind of hegemonic discourse that could control regimes of production and reception.[1] In particular, the tradition displays an archival penchant wholly antithetic to orality, and one that, as we shall see, set about actively to denigrate oral composition and transmission. Both traditions in fact approximate "two solitudes," each proceeding according to its own lights, but impinging from time to time one upon the other in an interaction at once hostile yet accommodating. The mechanics and consequences of this interaction will be the subject of the present paper.

The Problem of Literacy

Those who have written recently on "literacy" in ancient Egypt have displayed a tendency towards quantification worthy of a modern "number

---

[1] See R. Hodge, *Literature as Discourse* (Baltimore: Johns Hopkins Press, 1990), 12–13.

145

cruncher."[2] The need of those caught up in the Industrial Revolution of the past two and one-half centuries for employees who could read simple alphabetic texts and compose minimally in the same medium, has led to a new and dominant concern among archivists to rank communities on the basis of a percentage who are "literate." The lower the percentage abroad the more comfortable the condescension of the Western world. The higher the percentage at home the more justified the missionary zeal to preach literacy to the underprivileged Third World. (Only within the past generation with the coming of the computer age and its crying need for computer "literacy" and workplace automatons, does traditional literacy appear to be gravitating out of its former central position.)[3]

Studies of literacy, insofar as they attempt to assess its extent, fall wide of the desirable mark. It is a nonissue for us moderns (and wholly irrelevant to the ancients) whether 0.4%, 4.4%, or 84.4% of a total population was able to read a text;[4] for the degree of literacy had little to do with the efficiency, accomplishment or technological sophistication of a culture. Much more to the point are the answers to three questions that constitute a necessary prolegomena to the whole topic: (1) Why was a visible code invented in the first place? (2) What type of literacy is in question in Ancient Egypt? And (3) who was obliged to read and write?

One should remember that the invention of script is but the latest and most obvious stage in a process of corporate self-consciousness. This began far in the past with individual, and later communal, awareness of the world round about as a separate entity that could be observed and confronted in a conscious sense as something *other*. This incipient consciousness distanced the community from

---

[2] E.g., J. Baines, "Literacy, Social Organization and the Archaeological Record: The Case of Early Egypt," *State and Society: The Emergence and Development of Social Hierarchy and Political Centralization* (ed. J. Gledhill, B. Bender, and M. T. Larsen; London and Boston: Unwin Hyman, 1988), 192–214; B. Bryan, "Evidence for Female Literacy from Theban Tombs of The New Kingdom," *Bulletin of the Egyptological Seminar* 6 (1984): 17–32; cf. the trenchant observations of L. H. Lesko, "Some Comments on Ancient Egyptian Literacy and Literati," in *Studies in Egyptology Presented to Miriam Lichtheim* (ed. S. Israelit-Groll; 2 vols.; Jerusalem: Magnes, 1990), 2:656–59; idem, ed., *Pharaoh's Workers: The Villagers of Deir el-Medina* (Ithaca, N.Y.: Cornell University Press,1994), 186 n. 18.

[3] Cf. the horrors of the "Minimalist Language" (Min Lan) and the abandoning of literacy which Kubrick's films presage: "Books, newspapers, if they survived at all, would be for an elite, and regarded in an urgent world as irrelevant as mediaeval manuscripts" (*The Economist* [March 13–19, 1999]: 102).

[4] Cf. J. Baines, "Literacy and Ancient Egyptian Society," *Man*, NS, 18 (1983): 572–99, esp. 582; J. Baines and C. J. Eyre, "Four Notes on Literacy," *GöM* 61 (1983): 65–96, esp. 65–70.

entities of the environment, and made it possible if not obligatory to invest them *as signs* with meaning. The result was an evolving *gestural* discourse in which writing (for the ancients) was but the latest and most sophisticated result.[5]

The full-blown semiotic system[6] of the hieroglyphic script was invented by and served the needs of a civil service, and from the outset was highly innovative.[7] It appeared relatively suddenly, the time from the earliest figurative discourse to the appearance of an agreed-upon code being only a few generations, and scarcely more than two centuries.[8] In its final stages it showed a quantum leap forward and a degree of inventiveness that presupposed a code-maker, conscious of his inventive task.[9] The needs addressed by the new,

---

[5] Cf. C. Falck, "Original Language," *Myth, Truth, and Literature: Towards a True Postmodernism* (2d ed.; Cambridge and New York: Cambridge University Press, 1994), 34–54.

[6] That is, one in which icon, metonym, and phonetic metaphor have combined in a complex of preferred signifiers, to borrow the apt term of Goldwasser (O. Goldwasser, *From Icon to Metaphor: Studies in the Semiotics of the Hieroglyph* [OBO 142; Fribourg: University Press; Göttingen: Vandenhoeck & Ruprecht, 1995], 10). One is reluctant, however, to rely heavily on Saussurean/Derridean theory in the analysis of the Egyptian script, as it has now come under such devastating fire on both philosophical and linguistic levels (cf. D. D'Souza, *Illiberal Education* [New York: Free Press, 1992], 176–90; Falck, *Myth, Truth, and Literature*, 4–33). Exponents' own verbiage approaches the absurd at times, as in the "'primal process' where only signifier-signifying signifiers exist" (G. Hartman, *Saving the Text: Literature, Derrida, Philosophy* [Baltimore: John Hopkins Press, 1981], 60–61).

[7] The same situation obtains in the late Uruk Period in Mesopotamia (see R. F. G. Sweet, "Writing as a Factor in the Rise of Urbanism," in *Aspects of Urbanism in Antiquity from Mesopotamia to Crete* [ed. W. E. Aufrecht, N. A. Mirau, and S. W. Gauley; JSOTSup 244; Sheffield: Sheffield Academic Press, 1997], 35–49).

[8] That there was a prior stage of development cannot be denied, but that it assumed the proportions assigned to it by some scholars (e.g. J. Vercoutter, "La Predynastie égyptienne: Anciens et nouveaux concepts," *Cahiers de Recherches de l'Institut de Papyrologie et d'Égyptologie de Lille* 13 [1991]: 137–46, esp. 143–46; W. Kaiser, "Zur Entstehung des gesamtägyptischen Staates," *MDAI* 46 [1990]: 287–300, esp. 288–90; cf. P. Vernus, "La Naissance de l'écriture dans l'Égypte ancienne," *Archéo-Nil* 3 [1993]: 86) taxes credulity. Of course iconic representations of Badarian or Amratian date occasionally survived to be admitted into the script—many did not!—but this simply means that the "inventor(s)" drew on material from a long-standing decorative tradition (W. S. Arnett, *The Predynastic Origin of the Egyptian Hieroglyphs: Evidence for the Development of Rudimentary Forms of Hieroglyphs in Upper Egypt in the Fourth Millennium B.C.* [Washington, D.C.: University Press of America, 1982]).

[9] Cf. J. Ray, "The Emergence of Writing in Egypt," *World Archaeology* 17 (1986): 307–16. The function of "code-maker" may have to admit a plurality of participants; but the unity of effort and purpose points unmistakably to a single need and venue. To a significant

visible code comprised three: the need to commemorate, the need to enumerate, and the need to identify.[10] These were exigencies created by the birth of a complex society centered upon something quite new, namely, the *Ḥnw*, the "residence," the "Center,"[11] with its paramount chief metamorphosed into the Horus-avatar living on earth. The capacity of script-cum-image to commemorate[12] met the need of this new political configuration, the nation state, to establish its presence *in time* in a timeless and durable statement, and *in space* more extensive than the length of a day's journey for purposes of power-statements and unity through intimidation. It also fulfilled the requirement of memorializing events through time, so self-conscious was the *Ḥnw* of its role in a rapid sequence of events ever replicating themselves.[13] This involved a

---

extent the linguistic affiliation of the inventors may have to be sought in a northern, non-Egyptian community (W. Helck, *Untersuchungen zur Thinitenzeit* [Ägyptologische Abhandlungen 45; Wiesbaden: Harrassowitz, 1987], 138–43; D. B. Redford, "Some Observations on the Northern and Northeastern Delta in the Late Pre-dynastic Period," in *Essays in Egyptology in Honor of Hans Goedicke* [ed. B. Bryan and D. Lorton; San Antonio, Tex.: Van Siclen, 1994], 201–10).

10 See D. B. Redford, "Historical Sources: Texts," *OEAE*. That the needs were essentially unitary at the outset does not preclude the fact that very shortly multiple uses suggested themselves (W. Schenkel, "Wozu die Ägypter eine Schrift braucthen?" in *Schrift und Gedächtnis* [ed. A. Assmann, J. Assmann, and C. Hardemeir; Beiträge zur Archäologie der literarischen Kommunikation 1; Munich: W. Fink, 1983], 46–53, esp. 49–50).

11 On *ḥnw* see *WÄS* 3:372.10; D. Meeks, *Année lexicographique* (3 vols.; Paris: Imprimerie de la Margeride, 1980–82), 1 (1980): 292; 2 (1981): 295; 3 (1982): 229; P. Posener-Krieger, *Les Archives du temple funéraire de Neferirkarê-Kakai* (Bibliothèque d'étude 65; Cairo: Institut français d'archéologie orientale, 1976), 263; O. Goelet, "The Term *stp-sȝ* in the Old Kingdom and Its Later Development," *JARCE* 23 (1986): 90; cf. also G. Husson and D. Valbelle, *L'État et les institutions en Égypte des premiers pharaons aux empereurs romains* (Paris: A. Colin, 1992), 22–25. The application of "Center/Periphery" theory to the history of ancient Egypt is particularly elucidating (cf. T. C. Champion, ed., *Centre and Periphery: Comparative Studies in Archaeology* [London and Boston: Unwin Hyman, 1989]).

12 D. B. Redford, *Pharaonic King-lists, Annals, and Day-books: A Contribution to the Study of the Egyptian Sense of History* (Mississauga, Ont.: Benben, 1986), 86–88, 130–31; J. Assmann, *Das kulturelle Gedächtnis: Schrift, Erinnerung, und politische Identität in frühen Hochkulturen* (Munich: C. H. Beck, 1992), 169–70; idem, *Ägypten: Eine Sinngeschichte* (Munich: Hanser, 1996), 47–50.

13 The desire to memorialize and remember, rising almost to a national trait, is conveyed by the common verb *sḫȝ*, "to remember" (*WÄS* 4:232–34) in contradistinction to *sḫm*, "to forget, commit to oblivion" (H. G. Fischer, "*sḫȝ.sn [Florence, 1774]*," *RdÉ* 24 [1972]: 64–71, esp. 64–66), early crystallized into a divine hypostasis, *Sḫȝt*, the bovine presence who cares for Horus (PT 1375b; K. Sethe, *Übersetzung und Kommentar zu den altägyptischen Pyramidentexten* [5 vols.; Glückstadt: J. J. Augustin, 1935–62], 5:309; cf. also J. Leclant, *Montouemhât, quatrième prophet d'Amon et prince de la ville* [Bibliothèque d'étude 35; Cairo: Institut français d'archéologie orientale, 1961], 11 n. *w*).

practical need as well as prestige present and future: the new phenomenon, a human community occupying space 700 miles from one end to the other, could only prosper through prognostication, and this entailed an ability to reckon the future on the basis of the past.[14] The Nile flood must be predicted in advance; but this meant judging its performance in the past. In short, annals and archives rapidly proved to be indispensable.[15]

The need to enumerate arises pursuant to a new situation created by the unification of the Nile Valley and (later) the union with the Delta under a single authority. The *Ḥnw*, by the very nature of its creation, is larger than any community seen heretofore, and cannot be sustained by the small-scale food-producing strategies of a village. As both the *Ḥnw* as a human community and the territory on which it must rely for food production expand, exigencies of control and coercion arise involving a growing mass of population in the "periphery." This mass of the "great unwashed," in contrast to the closely knit and mutually recognized members of a prehistorical farming hamlet, have never been seen or identified by new authorities, the *Ḥnw*. Now, however, their production must be noted, quantified, and remembered. The iconic use of graphic signs combined with a code of quantification must replace oral notification and acceptance if the social organization of the *Ḥnw* is not to lapse into hopeless confusion.[16]

But the need to identify those (for the *Ḥnw*) faceless and nameless members of the periphery posed an even greater problem. The use of some such means as exchange or deposit of palpable talismans would involve such volume and differentiation that it would prove logistically impossible to carry through. Far better to use the phonemic pattern whereby people identify themselves, namely, their *names*, to provide graphic permanence to a body of individuals as

---

[14] Egyptian *sr*, which means basically "to announce in advance," later "to predict" (*WÄS* 4:188–89; see C. Cannuyer, "Brelan de 'Pharaons' Ramses XI, Thoutmosis III et Hatschepsout," in *Studies in Egyptology Presented to Miriam Lichtheim* [ed. S. Israelit-Groll; 2 vols.; Jerusalem: Magnes, 1990], 1:98–115, esp. 104–5).

[15] D. B. Redford, "The Meaning and the Use of the Term *gnwt*, Annals," in *Studien zu Sprache und Religion Ägyptens zu Ehren von Wolfhart Westendorf* (ed. F. Junge; Göttingen: F. Junge, 1984), 327–42; idem, *Pharaonic King-lists*, 65–96; Helck, *Untersuchungen zur Thinitenzeit*, 144–67; J. Goody, *The Interface between the Written and the Oral* (Cambridge: Cambridge University Press, 1987), 54–55.

[16] For a similar need to keep accounts that prompted the adoption of the Phoenician script by the Greeks in the eighth century B.C.E. see G. Glotz, *Ancient Greece at Work: An Economic History of Greece from the Homeric Period to the Roman Conquest* (trans. M. R. Dobie; London: Routledge & K. Paul, 1965 [1st ed. 1926]), 116. Interestingly, even as late as the mid-fourth century B.C.E. three of the four uses of writing given by Aristotle have to do with the practicalities of business, accounting, and civics (*Politica* 8.3.1338A 15–17)!

a production unit. Such a demand, however, puts a burden on a purely iconic script that it cannot sustain. Only a limited number of names are based on visible traits reducible on a one-to-one or metonymic basis to picture-signs, and still fewer on the lucky chance of homonyms. Many names derive from sentential statements by mother or midwife, or from pure abstractions for which homonyms (to be used rebus fashion) do not exist. It is in the face of this final requirement that a great leap forward catapults the entire semiotic system onto a plane where all sounds can be immediately and without ambiguity rendered by graphemes. At this point the inventing urge has divorced itself from considerations of meaning, and focuses, not on "sound pattern" or "psychological impression"[17] (if they even exist), but on sounds articulated by any orifice. Since few practice communication by flatulation,[18] the universal orifice of human choice is the mouth. Partly by the rebus-principle, partly by metonym, a limited set of graphic images is devised solely to render *single sounds* of oral articulation of tongue, lips, teeth, palate, glottis, and pharynx.

At this juncture the new script has endowed itself inherently with the capability of rendering any *"paroles"*;[19] but in fact its initial use resides within

---

[17] F. de Saussure, "The Object of Study," in *Modern Criticism and Theory* (ed. D. Lodge; London and New York: Longman, 1988), 1–9.

[18] The mechanism is conceivable (cf. Peter Jay, ed., *The Greek Anthology and Other Ancient Epigrams: A Selection in Modern Verse Translations* [Harmondsworth: Penguin, 1981], no. 409). Communication by gestural discourse is even more likely (Rabellais, *Pantagruel* Bk. 2 [Thaumast vs. Panurge]), and figurative art suggests that it was sometimes employed.

[19] Even though the infelicitously named "(auto)biographical statement" does not appear before the early Fifth Dynasty (Schenkel, "Wozu die Ägypter eine Schrift brauchen?" 59; N. Kloth, "Beobachtungen zu den biographischen Inschriften des Alten Reiches," *SAK* 25 [1998]: 189–205), it is totally misleading to assert that the evolving script was incapable of committing, or the users unwilling to commit, complete propositions to writing before later in the Old Kingdom (J. Baines, "Literacy and Ancient Egyptian Society," 577; idem, "Literacy, Social Organization, and the Archaeological Record," 196; H. J. L. Vanstiphout, "Memory and Literacy in Ancient Western Asia," *CANE*, 2182). Continuous texts and letters were possible as early as the First Dynasty, and circumstantial evidence strongly suggests their presence. Many of the groups in the earliest annals resolve themselves into predicative statements; cf. the onomasticon (P. Lacau and J.-P. Lauer, *Fouilles à Saqqarah: La Pyramide à degrès, V: Inscriptions a l'encre sur les vases* [Cairo: Institut français d'archéologie orientale, 1965], passim), or sealings (T. E. Peet, *The Cemeteries of Abydos* [3 vols.; London: Egypt Exploration Fund, 1914], vol. 1, pl. 11). A consistent tradition of later times adamantly insists that medical works and the pharmacopoeia were products of the earliest kings, cf. U. Luft, "Zur Einleitung der Liebesgedichte auf Papyrus Chester Beatty I, ro XVI 9ff.," *ZÄS* 99 (1973): 108–16, esp. 110–11.

the realm of the activities of a civil service.[20] It was in the context of the
archive, and the prevailing atmosphere of the archivist, that the script came to
birth, underwent rapid development, and was fully used in the Late Predynastic
and Archaic periods. One can sense the overriding preoccupation of the state to
fix for all time in concrete, graphic form the memories of the present receding
into the past. The very invention brought with it the consciousness of a past in
contrast to the timeless present of a preliterate society.[21]

Failure to define what type of literacy is in question in ancient Near
Eastern societies has rendered a number of scholarly discussions virtually
worthless.[22] Since the use of writing was confined to the practical level of
recording facts, it was simply the "scribbling capacity" of the individual scribe
divided into the amount to be recorded that dictated how many people
thoroughly conversant with the script were required in any given situation.
Even as late as Ptolemaic times no stigma attached itself to total illiteracy
(being ἀγράμματος),[23] since intellectual stimulation, entertainment, and even
vital information were disseminated by oral transmission.[24] And the one aspect

---

[20] W. Helck, "Gedanken zum Ursprung der ägyptischen Schrift," in *Mélanges Gamal Eddin
Mokhtar* (ed. P. Posener-Krieger; Bibliothèque d'étude 97; Cairo: Institut français
d'archéologie orientale, 1985), 1:398.

[21] Cf. J. Assmann, "Nachwort," in *Schrift und Gedächtnis* (ed. A. Assmann et al.), 268.

[22] The most egregious offenders have been biblical scholars, for whom the mere existence
of a few seals and ostraca is evidence of an ancient Hebrew "reading public," fully literate
and creative (D. B. Redford, *Egypt, Canaan, and Israel in Ancient Times* [Princeton:
Princeton University Press, 1992], 304 n. 91). On the localization of scribal activity see
D. W. Jamieson-Drake, *Scribes and Schools in Monarchic Judah: A Socio-archaeological
Approach* (JSOTSup 109; Sheffield: Sheffield Academic Press, 1991), 151; also S. Niditch,
Oral World and Written Word: Ancient Israelite Literacy (LAI: Louisville, Ky.: Westminster
John Knox, 1996), 39–40.

[23] H. C. Youtie, "*Agrammatos*: An Aspect of Greek Society in Egypt," *Harvard Studies in
Classical Philology* 75 (1971): 161–76, esp. 168–71; idem, "P. Mich. inv. 855: Letter from
Heraklides to Nemesion," *ZPE* 27 (1977): 147–50.

[24] A similar situation obtained in Greece (R. Thomas, *Oral Tradition and Written Record in
Classical Athens* [Cambridge and New York: Cambridge University Press, 1989], 48, 54, 62;
M. V. Harris, *Ancient Literacy* [Cambridge, Mass.: Harvard University Press, 1989], 80, 86).
Even the Presocratics expected to be listened to, not read (E. A. Havelock, "The Linguistic
Task of the Presocratics," in *Language and Thought in Early Greek Philosophy* [ed. K.
Robb; Monist Library of Philosophy; La Salle, Ill.: Hegeler Institute, 1983], 7–82, esp. 9–10;
C. H. Kahn, "Philosophy and the Written Word: Some Thoughts on Herakleitos and the Early
Greek Use of Prose," in *Language and Thought in Early Greek Philosophy*, 115). The claims
made, with neither evidence nor demonstration, for the decisive role postulated for literacy in
the coming and enhancement of Greek civilization, are simply preposterous (cf. J. Goody and
I. Watt, "The Consequences of Literacy," in *Literacy in Traditional Societies* [ed. J. Goody;

of writing that might have enticed a broader public to learn to read, namely, magic, was the closely-guarded preserve of the lector priest.[25] The urge that every Egyptian felt to establish a "personal presence" in the form of a graphic image probably proved conducive to increasing "name literacy," i.e., the ability learned by rote to write one's own name.[26] Providing posterity with one's identity served one's own interests in the offering cult in terms of the all-important "pronouncement of the name."[27]

Cambridge and New York: Cambridge University Press, 1968), 27–68; J. Goody, *The Interface between the Written and the Oral*, 64ff.; idem, *The Logic of Writing and the Organization of Society* [Cambridge and New York: Cambridge University Press, 1986]; E. A. Havelock, *The Literate Revolution in Greece and Its Consequences* [Princeton: Princeton University Press, 1982]; idem, *The Muse Learns to Write: Reflections on Orality and Literacy from Antiquity to the Present* [New Haven: Yale University Press, 1986]; A. Burns, *The Power of the Written Word: The Role of Literacy in the History of Western Civilization* [Studia Classica 1; New York: P. Lang, 1989]). See the apposite remarks of Harris, *Ancient Literacy*, 41, and Vanstiphout, "Memory and Literacy," 2189. One wonders how much chagrin would be caused by facing up to the realization that one of the common texts attested in the Athenian agora, as late as the fourth century, is the crass and superstitious curse tablet! (J. M. Camp, *The Athenian Agora: Excavations in the Heart of Classical Athens* [London: Thames and Hudson, 1986], 140–41.) What a use for such a mind-liberating invention!

[25] For that "secret text of the lector's art" see *Urk.* 1:186.14–15; 187.13–14; 190.17; 202.2; J. S. F. Garnot, *L'Appel aux vivants dans les textes funéraires égyptiens des origines à la fin de l'ancien empire* (Cairo: Institut français d'archéologie orientale, 1938), 22, 32; P. Duell, *The Mastaba of Mereruka by the Sakkarah Expedition,* vol. 2 (Chicago: University of Chicago Press, 1938), pl. 130; H. Junker, ed., *Giza,* vol. 8 (Vienna and Leipzig: Holder-Pichler-Tempsky, 1947), Abb. 56.

[26] H. S. Smith, "The Rock Inscriptions of Buhen," *JEA* 58 (1972): 51; cf. the "slow-writers" of Graeco-Roman times (H. C. Youtie, "Between Literacy and Illiteracy," in *Akten des xiii. internationalen Papyrologenkongresses Marburg/Lahn, 2–6. August 1971* [ed. E. Kiessling and H.-A. Rupprecht; Munich: Beck, 1974], 481–83. The practice of ostracism at Athens is another example of the expected presence of name-literacy; yet even here it is clear that the vast majority of the population had recourse to a mere handful of scribes to inscribe their ballots! Cf. Harris, *Ancient Literacy*, 54–55.

[27] *Dm rn.f* (*WÄS* 5:449.8–13). Of course this expression could be a metonym for the survival of one's good reputation; cf. *Urk.* 4:131: "His name will be pronounced on account of his character"; *Urk.* 4:101: "Pronounce ye my name, recall ye my titulary . . . set my name in the mouths of your servants, and memory of me among your children"; *KRI* 5:41.3–4: "I have repulsed the lands at the (mere) mention of 'Egypt'; my name is pronounced in their land"; W. Wreszinski, *Ägyptische Inschriften aus dem K. K. Hofmuseum in Wien* (Leipzig, 1906), 63 (I, 21, lines 3–4): "May his name be pronounced from time to time and he will not drift into oblivion. He will survive from mouth to mouth and not cease for ever." The obverse, envisaged in curses, involved the complete annihilation of one's memory. E. Edel, *Die Inschriften der Grabfronten des Siut-Graber in Mittelägypten aus der Herakleopolitenzeit* (Opladen: Westdeutscher Verlag, 1984), 39: As for any rebel who will destroy this tomb, "he shall never find a place among the blessed dead in the necropolis, his children shall be

It has been assumed that "full literacy" was comparatively rare; that is to say, few had the training to read and compose a complex text. Formal schools, the institutions best suited to inculcate such literacy, date no earlier (on present evidence) than the early Middle Kingdom.[28] We have little idea, however, about the criteria of admission or the social classes catered to. The Satire of the Trades begins: "Here begins the instruction given by the man of *Tjaret* whose name was Duwa-khety for his son whose name was Pepy, as he was sailing southward to the Residence, to put him in the writing-school among the magistrates' children, the celebrities of the Residence."[29] If Helck is correct in thinking that *Tjaret* is the toponym *Ṯʒrw*, the fortress on the northeast edge of the Delta,[30] then the text is pointedly placing a "new boy" of rustic, frontier origin in the sophisticated capital city, enjoying the same access to scribal training as the sons of the nobility. The tomb of Akhtoy at Asyut (no. 4) contains another instructive reference: "Now as for any scribe or any intellectual, a real craftsman at his art, good at writing and well-learned—for a man's reputation bestows standing upon him—one who has gone through school, who may pass by this staircase and enter this tomb," etc.[31] The text seems to link "full literacy" with school training, but subtly counters aristocratic privilege: it is not illustrious pedigree that bestows rank, but a man's own intellectual achievement. Similarly, the fact that a bastard son of a mere doorkeeper could attend school and excel at his studies argues an openness to all classes.[32] The atmosphere surrounding other didactic pieces is

---

expelled from their tombs, he shall be deemed an enemy of the blessed dead, one unknown to the lord of the cemetery, [his name shall not be pronounced] among the blessed dead, he shall not be remembered by those on earth, his name shall not survive among his children . . . ." And again (ibid., 190): "As for him who does not intone these things (i.e., the offering formula), he is destined for the wrath of his town god and the king's slaughter; his name will not be pronounced upon earth forever, no invocation-offering shall go forth for him; his burial will not be in the Western Cemetery, he shall be burned as a criminal, Thoth shall make difficulties for him and he shall be spat upon." But the phrase conveyed the stronger notion of the piety of the living summoning the dead to the offering: "May my *bai* live and may it come out at the voice of him that pronounces its name" (*WÄS* 5:449.12 [Beleg-stellen]); ". . . coming quickly when his name is pronounced" (Berlin 2074 [ÄIKM]); "You shall give water to my statue, and my *bai* will hop forward when it is called" (*Urk.* 4: 440.14–15).

[28] E. Feucht, *Das Kind im alten Ägypten* (Frankfurt and New York: Campus, 1995), 225–36.

[29] W. Helck, *Die Lehre des Dwʒ-Ḥtjj* (2 vols.; Wiesbaden: Harrassowitz, 1970), 1:12–16.

[30] Ibid., 1:17–18.

[31] Edel, *Inschriften der Grabfronten*, 99 (cols. 66–67), partly restored.

[32] Cf. "Blinding of Truth," A. H. Gardiner, *Late Egyptian Stories* (Bibliotheca aegyptiaca l; Brussels: Éditions de la Fondation égyptologique Reine Élisabeth, 1932), 32–33 (4,7–5,8).

not at variance. The Satire of the Trades and the Miscellanies both urge insistently that the scribe enter the scribal profession, and both offer the enticement of parental satisfaction and approbation and the deterrent of the alternate prospect of a menial job. None of this bespeaks privilege. Uncertainty and bourgeois self-reliance imbue the entire genre.

And yet, while a scribal post might not, at least after the Old Kingdom, have been tied to birth, nonetheless the availability of an unrestricted (or largely so) access to school training did not issue in a literate community. The limits of practical need and the tendency to restrict membership both conspired to limit the number of the fully literate in ancient Egypt. While there was no reason to train more scribes than the civil service needed, there was every reason *not* to train an excess of lector priests, in view of the magical properties of the script.[33]

A rough but reliable gauge as to those who were capable of reading an extended text is provided in that genre of inscription known as the Call to the Living.[34] This, a subspecies of the autobiography, takes its rise from the identification of the deceased on a name-stone before the tomb. With the intent of signaling the identity of the occupant the better to focus cultic acts and offerings for his benefit alone, the tomb owner in the course of time added the offering-scene and offering formula, originally of separate purpose and origin. The whole underwent embellishment, the better to arrest posterity's attention: offering formula and titles before the name, then a marker indicating the owner's intent to speak, and finally his self-promoting statement.[35] Displayed prominently in a tomb setting, the Call to the Living constitutes a species of

---

[33] Magic was far too powerful to be allowed to drift into vulgar hands; moreover too many initiates would weaken the potency; cf. Ipuwer 6:6–7 (W. Helck, *Die 'Admonitions' Pap. Leiden I 344 recto* [Wiesbaden: Harrassowitz, 1995]).

[34] Garnot, *L'Appel aux vivants*; R. B. Parkinson, *Voices from Ancient Egypt* (London: British Museum Press, 1991), 136–42; M. Lichtheim, *Ancient Egyptian Autobiographies, Chiefly of the Middle Kingdom: A Study and an Anthology* (OBO 84; Freiburg: Universitätsverlag; Göttingen: Vandenhoeck & Ruprecht, 1988); a new comprehensive study is being planned by a student of mine, Dr. Steven Shubert.

[35] On the genre see J. Assmann, "Schrift, Tod, und Identität: Das Grab als Vorschule der Literatur im Alten Ägypten," in *Schrift und Gedächtnis* (ed. A. Assmann et al.), 71–79; Lichtheim, *Ancient Egyptian Autobiographies*; O. Perdu, "Ancient Egyptian Autobiographies," *CANE*, 2243–54; A. Gnirs, "Die ägyptische Autobiographie," *AELHF*, 191–241; idem, "(Auto)biographies," *OEAE*. The term itself, like all others applied to the genre (including "biographical statement"), is an unfortunate choice. The form and intent approximates most closely the self-promoting *curriculum vitae* (perhaps also the *cursus honorum*), that is, a set of credentials primarily designed to secure for the individual acceptance by both posterity and the gods into the hallowed company of the ancestors (H. Guksch, *Königsdienst: Zur Selbstdarstellung der Beamten in der 18. Dynastie* [Heidelberg: Heidelberger Orientverlag, 1994]).

long-distance communication in which a deceased individual addresses contemporaries or posterity wholly unknown to him. The deceased one has immediate and direct needs: food and drink, prayer-formulae, promises, and undertakings.[36] It would serve the dead man's purpose not at all to post such an inscription if no one could read it; and so he addresses first and foremost those who can.

The commonest formula, and also the oldest, is addressed to "all (ye) living upon earth"[37] and "everyman."[38] This use of generic terms suggests that the deceased hoped for the widest dissemination of his appeal, and the specific request does not seem to discriminate among "races" or social classes:[39] "You

---

[36] For the three desiderata, viz., offering formula, respect, and libations, see *Urk.* 4:2176.

[37] *Urk.* 1:122.9ff.; Garnot, *L'Appel aux vivants*, 50 (Xc), 56 (XIIa), 57 (XIIb), 60 (XIV), 75 (XIX); L. Habachi, *The Sanctuary of Heqaib* (Mainz am Rhein: P. von Zabern, 1985), pl. 57e; A. M. Blackman, *The Rock Tombs of Meir* (6 vols; Archaeological Survey of Egypt 22nd–25th, 28th–29th; London: Egypt Exploration Fund, 1914–53), vol. 4, pl. 4; H. G. Fischer, *Dendera in the Third Millennium B.C., Down to the Theban Domination of Upper Egypt* (Locust Valley, N.Y.: J. J. Augustin, 1968), 204 fig. 40, 206 fig. 42; D. Dunham, *Naga ed-Deir Stelae of the First Intermediate Period* (Boston: Published for the Museum of Fine Arts, Boston, by the Oxford University Press, H. Milford, 1937), pl. 15:2, pl. 31; J. J. Clère and J. Vandier, *Textes de la première periode intermédiaire et de la XIème dynastie* (Bibliotheca aegyptiaca 10; Brussels: Éditions de la Fondation égyptologique Reine Élisabeth, 1949), no. 17. This simple, unembellished formula is found in later periods as well (L. Speleers, ed., *Recueil des inscriptions égyptiens des Musées royaux du cinquantenaire à Bruxelles* (Brussels: Musées royaux d'art et d'histoire, 1923), no. 91; *Die Ägyptische Reliefs im Kestner-Museum Hannover: 100 Jahre Kestner-Museum Hannover, 1889–1989* (Hannover: Kestner-Museum, 1989), no. 21, p. 73; *ÄL* 70:6; G. Posener, "Une stèle de Hatnoub," *JEA* 54 (1968): 67–70, pl. IX, 6ff.; Bruxelles E 7429 (= L. Limme, *Stèles égyptiennes*, [Brussels: Musées royaux d'art et d'histoire, 1979], 46, col. 7–8); Leclant, *Montouemhât*, 18; *KRI* 5:670.

[38] A. M. Blackman, *Rock Tombs*, vol. 4, pl. 4; Garnot, *L'Appel aux vivants*, 1; *Urk.* 1:100.6–7; 49; 223.17–224.2; T. G. H. James, *The Mastaba of Khentika called Ikhekhi* (London: Egyptian Exploration Society, 1953), pl. 15; W. K. Simpson, *Mastabas of the Western Cemetery* (3 vols.; Boston: Department of Egyptian and Ancient Near Eastern Art, Museum of Fine Arts, 1980), vol. 1, pls. 5–6; for later examples, see *Urk.* 4:1632.6; *HTBM* 8 (1939), pl. 33 (1332).

[39] Cf. the specific reference of Mereruka: "I say this to all and sundry who may enter into (my) tomb" (H. Wild, "L'«Adresse aux visiteurs» du tombeaux de Ti," *BIFAO* 58 [1959]: 105). Moreover many Old Kingdom texts address the "80 men" who are to be lower the sarcophagus lid, and "all the craftsmen," i.e., both skilled and unskilled common laborers (Garnot, *L'Appel aux vivants*, 34, 41); cf. "all craftsmen and anybody" (W. M. F. Petrie, *Deshasheh* [London: Egypt Exploration Fund, 1898], pl. 7); "now as for any scribe, any wiseman, any commoner or dependent who may enter into this tomb and see what is in it" (F. Ll. Griffith, *The Inscriptions of Siût and Dêr Rîfeh* [London: Trübner, 1889], 226ff.); "O all ye living upon earth, all scribes, every lector-priest, and every foreigner . . . ," (*HTBM* 6 [1922], pl. 46 [488]).

shall offer to me of that which is in your hands. But if there is nothing in your hands, then you shall say orally: 'a thousand of bread, beer, beef, and fowl for the *ku* of . . .'"[40] The argument then proceeds, however, with a text that would demand full literacy: "(For the offering formula) is indeed no outlay of your (own) wealth, (but simply) breath of the mouth, of advantage to the noble; for a good deed is more advantageous to him who does it than for him for whom it is done."[41]

Already in the Old Kingdom, however, an element of specificity is sometimes added. While desirous that everyone, literate or not, should be prevailed upon to contribute to his otherworldly well-being, the deceased does not labor under a misapprehension. Realistically, in necropolis or on transit corridors the only people who are going to see his text are people with the wherewithal to travel, or whose business takes them on the road or to the cemetery. This for the most part will exclude the mass of the population, the menials of society, tied to the land, the workhouse, or the barracks, with movement strictly controlled if not forbidden. And so the tomb owner might gloss his call to the living or "everyman" by more specific terms such as "pensionnaires,"[42] "every bishop,"[43] "noma[rchs] of other townships,"[44] "*ku*-servants,"[45] "lector-priests,"[46] "*w'eb*-priests and deacons."[47] In fact, Old Kingdom texts in particular imply the colegiality of a class: the governing class serving the king, the *pʿt*, are expected to be literate. All "living upon earth"

---

[40] Cairo 20003 (H. O. Lange and H. Schäfer, *Grab- und Denksteine des mittleren Reiches im Museum von Kairo* [Berlin: Reichsdruckerei, 1902–25] = *CGC*, vols. 5, 7, 36, and 78).

[41] D. Dunham, *Semna-Kumma* (excavated by G. A. Reisner; published by D. Dunham and J. M. A. Janssen; Boston: Museum of Fine Arts, 1960), 61, pl. 91D; *ÄL* 89 (h and i); *Urk.* 4:1032.16–1033.1; P. Vernus, "La Formule 'souffle de la bouche' au Moyen Empire," *RdÉ* 28 (1976): 139–45; the argument can, in fact, achieve a high degree of complexity; cf. Habachi, *Sanctuary of Heqaib*, pl. 25 (fig. 4).

[42] *Imȝḫw* (M. W. F. Petrie, *Dendereh* [London: Egypt Exploration Society, 1900], pl. 7A; S. Hassan, *The Mastabas of Ny-ankh-pepy and Others* [Cairo: Institut français d'archéologie orientale, 1975], 10 fig. 5; N. Kanawati, "New Evidence on the Reign of Userkaf?" *GöM* 83 (1984): 38.

[43] Garnot, *L'Appel aux vivants*, 66 no. XVI.

[44] N. de G. Davies, *The Rock Tombs of Deir el-Gebrawi* (2 vols.; Archaeological Survey of Egypt, 11th–12th Memoir; London: Egypt Exploration Fund, 1902), vol. 2, pl. 24–25 (in contrast to "all you people of the *Dw-fy* township," i.e., the local population).

[45] Garnot, *L'Appel aux vivants*, 46 no. Xa.

[46] *Urk.* 1:187.4–6; 186.14–17; 202.15–203.3.

[47] E. Edel, "Zum Verständnis des Inschrift *Jzy* aus Saqqara," *ZÄS* 106 (1979): 107.

under Pharaoh are "servants, my peers" says the scribe;[48] and "I, Azy, am one of you (viz., the priests appealed to) . . . give me water, bread, and beer, to me, Azy, (for I am) one of you . . . !"[49]

Visits to stelae, graffiti, and tombs (apart from those entailed in mortuary service) are envisaged to be rather casual or fortuitous, often occasioned by curiosity. Visitors may be "going upstream or downstream," they may "pass by" the tomb and, attracted by its distinguished appearance, "enter to see what is in it . . . what I did upon earth." They may "see my offices from the king," or "read" them.[50] This introduces motivation beyond practical considerations. People are expected to be genuinely attracted by the aesthetics of the tomb or by an interest in the past. One recalls the passionate interest displayed in the story of Khamwese, which must be characteristic of all literati in all periods of Egyptian history: "Now N... [had nothing better] to do on earth but to go around the necropolis at Memphis reading the writings (*sḥw*) that were within the tombs of the Pharaohs and upon the stelae of the scribes of the House of Life."[51]

In texts subsequent to the fall of the Old Kingdom there is a tendency to focus the address more on a sacerdotal or scribal fraternity. Those addressed by the appeal include prophets, *w'eb*-priests, lector-priests and scribes,[52]

---

[48] *Urk.* 1:112.5–6; 147.9–12.

[49] Edel, "Zum Verständnis," 107; cf. W. Helck, "*Jnk wꜥ jm.tn,*" *ZÄS* 104 (1977): 89–93.

[50] *Urk.* 1:119.11; Petrie, *Dendereh,* pl. XIa.

[51] Khamois I, 3.9 (F. Ll. Griffith, *Stories of the High Priests of Memphis* [2 vols.; Oxford: Clarendon, 1900]).

[52] *WÄS* 4:478.3 (Belegstellen); *Urk.* 4:965–66, 1536, 1588, 1610; *KRI* 3:17.11–13, 7:24.14–15; P. Ramond, *Les stèles égyptiennes du Musée G. Labit à Toulouse* (Cairo: Institut français d'archéologie orientale, 1977), pl. II no. 2; pl. VI no. 6; H. M. Stewart, *Egyptian Stelae, Reliefs, and Paintings from the Petrie Collection* (3 vols.; Warminster: Aris & Phillips, 1976–1983), 2, pl. 29; A. Moret, *Galerie égyptienne: stéles, bas-reliefs, monuments divers* (Le Musée Guimet, Paris: E. Leroux, 1909), pl. 22 (C 24); *ÄIKM* 2:134 (7316); Louvre C.50 (UT); Leclant, *Montouemhât,* 60, 68; S. I. Hodachje and O. D. Berlev, "La père fondateur de la dynastie des princes de *Tjḥḥj* en Nubie," *Ägypten und Kusch: Fritz Hintze zum 60. Geburtstag* (ed. E. Endesfelder et al.; Berlin: Akademie-Verlag, 1977), pl. 2; K. Jansen-Winkeln, *Ägyptische Biographien der 22. und 23. Dynastie* (Ägypten und Altes Testament 8; 2 vols.; Wiesbaden: Harrassowitz, 1985); W. K. Simpson, *Inscribed Material from the Pennsylvania-Yale Excavations at Abydos* (New Haven: Peabody Museum of Natural History, Yale University; Philadelphia: University of Pennsylvania Museum of Archaeology and Anthropology, 1995), fig. 125 (NK 31); J. Vercoutter, *Textes biographiques du Serapéum de Memphis: Contribution à l'étude des stèles votives du Serapéum* (Paris: Librairie ancienne H. Champion, 1962), texts "O" and "T"; J. Leclant, *Enquêtes sur les sacerdoces et les sanctuaires égyptiens à l'époque dite 'éthiopienne' (25e dynastie)"*

acolytes, and god's-fathers;[53] rarely are secular offices included.[54] With the growth of large temple estates, especially those of Amun, the co-fraternity of the priestly community represents the sum total of the inscription's purview.[55] Sometimes even "support staff" is included.[56] In particular the appeal specifically begins to describe the scribe who will take note of the inscription in terms of his skill in reading or writing. Khaemhat addresses "every scribe who can interpret the script, who has facility in hieroglyphs, fluent and conversant in reading books."[57] Other descriptive epithets of the expected visitor include "one who knows how to read the hieroglyphs,"[58] "one good at writing and well-learned,"[59] "one skilled in hieroglyphs,"[60] "one skilled in

---

(Bibliothèque d'étude 17; Cairo: Institut français d'archéologie orientale, 1954), 48; G. Lefebvre, *Inscriptions conçernant les grands prêtres d'Amon, Rôm-Roy et Amenhotep* (Paris: P. Geuthner, 1929), 25; B. V. Bothmer, *Egyptian Sculpture of the Late Period, 700 B.C. to A.D. 100* (Brooklyn: Brooklyn Museum, 1969), pl. 49 no. 118, pl. 61 no. 153; S. Pernigotti, *La Statuaria egiziana nel museo civico archaeologico di Bologna* (Bologna: Istituto per la storia di Bologna, 1980), pl. IV, XXXIV; E. Doetsch-Amberger, *Die ägyptische Sammlung* (Cologne:J. P. Bachem, 1987), no. 34.

[53] *Urk.* 4:1495.14–16; A. P. Zivie, *Hermopolis et le nome de l'Ibis* (Cairo: Institut français d'archéologie orientale, 1975), 62; Musée Granet Aix-en-Provence, *Collection égyptienne* (Aix-en-provence, n.d.), 67 (12).

[54] Habachi, *Sanctuary of Heqaib*, pl. 183a; J. Tylor, *Wall Drawings and Monuments of El Kab: The Tomb of Sebeknekht* (London: B. Quaritch, 1896), pl. 2–3(1).

[55] Cairo 42227 (= Jansen-Winkeln, *Ägyptische Biographien*, A–12); 42214 (ibid., A–8); 42207 (ibid., A–3); Walters 167A (= G. Steindorff, *Catalogue of the Egyptian Sculpture in the Walters Art Gallery* [Baltimore: The Trustees, 1946], pl. 115); 177A (ibid., pl. 117); 227 (ibid., pl. 118; cf. the direct reference to "initiation"); R. el-Sayed, *Documents relatifs à Saïs et ses divinités* (Cairo: Institut français d'archéologie orientale, 1975), 85; Vienna AeS 34 (UT).

[56] "Ye who are people of the inventory of this house," Cairo 42210 (Jansen-Winkeln, *Ägyptische Biographien*, A–5); "the entire temple staff," Cairo 42207 (ibid., A–3), Cairo 42218 (ibid., A–9); Walters 167A; "people of Thebes, nobles and commoners alike," *HTBM* 5 (1914), pl. 40 (41645); Cairo 42232 (Jansen-Winkeln, *Ägyptische Biographien*, A–19); "people of Thebes, the congregation that sees Amun" (*Urk.* 4:1835.3).

[57] *Urk.* 4:1845.

[58] Leclant, *Montouemhât*, 68; Berlin 7316 (*ÄIKM*); A. Kamal, "Fouilles à Deir Dronka et à Assiout," *ASAÉ* 16 (1916): 65–114, esp. 88; *KRI* 1:353.10–11 ("who knows Thoth's script"); cf. Louvre 3023 (UT); Wenamun 2.54 ("a messenger from the land of Egypt . . . who knows writing"; Gardiner, *Late Egyptian Stories*); cf. Louvre C.14 ("difficult [passages] of the hieroglyphs"; UT).

[59] Edel, *Inschriften der Grabfronten*, 99.

[60] *Urk.* 4:121.1–2, 151.14–15, 1536; Leclant, *Montouemhât*, 17.

writing,"[61] ". . . who can interpret a text and is conversant with hieroglyphs,"[62] and "one who knows the hieroglyphs and is skilled in all types of script."[63] The genre of address to the living from the grave has thus undergone a modification, a restriction of sorts. From an initial breadth of appeal it has now come to reside within the bailiwick of the skilled scribe. One might suggest several explanations ranging from societal change through obsolescence of the formula in its original usage, but the evidential value of the change for Egyptian literacy is not immediately apparent.

Public Readings

It stands to reason that anyone who employs the written address to posterity in an exercise of genuine and vital self-interest will wish his appeal to be disseminated as widely as possible. And it makes no sense to commit the message to a form in which only the most learned will have access. A further dimension to the conventional practice of appealing to the living in writing awaits consideration.

The act of reading in ancient Egypt always involved vocalizing the text: there was no "silent reading."[64] The most common verb referring to this practice is best rendered "to recite aloud."[65] "And you are to set about reading the letter," says the scribe to the pupil, "the writing is in your hand, read (*šdi*) with your mouth."[66] The spoken word itself contained quasi-magical force, and

---

[61] *KRI* 1:331.1–2; 3:17.11–13; *Urk.* 2:62.10; 4:969.14, 1083.15–17; *HTBM* 6 (1922), pl. 49 (652); var. "skilled in knowledge," *Urk.* 4:1610; "skilled in his office," *KRI* 7:25.9.

[62] *HTBM* 9 (1970), pl. 21 (164); cf. M. Moursi, "Die Stele des Vezirs Re-hotep (Kairo JdE 48845)," *MDAI* 37 (1981): 324, Abb. 2.

[63] *WÄS* 5:477.15 (Belegstellen).

[64] T. G. Allen, "Some Egyptian Sun Hymns," *JNES* 8 (1949): 349–55, esp. 351–52 n. *h*; A. L. Oppenheim, "The Archives of the Palace of Mari," *JNES* 11 (1952): 129–39, esp. 133 n. 6.

[65] *šdi* (*WÄS* 4:563–564.16).

[66] P. Anastasi iii.3.10–11; v.23.3; P. Lansing i.4 (A. H. Gardiner, *Late Egyptian Miscellanies* [Bibliotheca aegyptiaca 7; Brussels: Édition de la Fondation égyptologique Reine Élisabeth, 1932]). Another verb, *nis*, "to call, invoke," is even more explicit of an audible performance (H. H. Nelson, "Certain Reliefs at Karnak and Medinet Habu and the Ritual of Amenophis I," *JNES* 8 (1949): 315 n. 92; M. Marciniak, *Les inscriptions hiératiques du temple de Thoutmosis III* (Deir el-Bahari 1; Warsaw: PWN- Éditions scientifiques de Pologne, 1974), pl. III–IIIA, 12–13; Musée Granet, *Collection égyptienne,* stela 12, p. 67; Leclant, *Montouemhât,* 60; P. Barguet, *Le papyrus N. 3176 (S) du Musée du Louvre* (Bibliothèque d'étude 37; Cairo: Institut français d'archéologie orientale, 1962) 6:l.

160   *Writings and Speech in Israelite and Ancient Near Eastern Prophecy*

its intonation liberated the power of the written text. The common scene of the lector priest on the day of the funeral represents him reading aloud from an unrolled papyrus.[67] A restoration text makes plain the distinction between what is written and what is read: "I restored the names of my fathers which I found obliterated on their gates, identified by text (*tit*), and correct in *reading* (*šdt*)."[68]

The deceased in his address to the living often envisages the passers-by, whom we have passed in review above, as he enters his tomb to view texts and reliefs. The former are expected to "recite" (*šdi*),[69] "to say with your

---

[67] Cf. "reading the many beatification spells" (*Urk.* 1:202.3); A. M. Blackman, *Rock Tombs*, vol. 2, pl. 10; vol. 3, pls. 22, 23; vol. 5, pl. 11; N. de G. Davies, *The Mastaba of Ptahhetep and Akhethetep at Saqqareh* (Archaeological Survey of Egypt; ed. F. Ll. Griffith; 8th–9th Memoir; London: Egypt Exploration Fund, 1898–99), vol. 2, pl. 31; M. A. Murray, *Saqqara Mastabas* (London: Egypt Exploration Society, 1904), vol. 1, pl. 23; P. E. Newberry, *Beni Hasan* (2 vols.; London: Egypt Exploration Society, K. Paul, 1890–92), vol. 1, pl. 17; N. de G. Davies and A. H. Gardiner, *The Tomb of Antefoker, Vizier of Sesostris I, and of His Wife, Senet (no. 60)* (London: G. Allen & Unwin, 1920), pl. 28, 32; idem, *The Tomb of Amenemhet (no. 82)* (Theban Tombs Series; London: Egypt Exploration Fund, 1915), pl. 11 ("start singing"), pl. 13, 21; H. E. Winlock, *Bas-Reliefs from the Temple of Ramesses I at Abydos* (New York [City] Metropolitan Museum of Art; Papers, vol. 1, pt. 1, no. 5; New York: Arno, 1973), pl. 9; W. M. F. Petrie, *Heliopolis* (London: School of Archaeology in Egypt, 1912), pl. 8:4; *LDÄÄ* 2:71b ("reciting the offering menu"); W. Fr. von Bissing, *Die Mastaba des Gem-ni-kai* (2 vols.; Berlin: A. Duncker, 1911), vol. 2, pl. 27–31; P. Duell, *The Mastaba of Mereruka* 2 pl. 130; *Medinet Habu IV: Festival Scenes of Ramses III* (Chicago: University of Chicago Oriental Institute, 1940), pl. 203 ("reciting the words to the master of singers"); S. Sauneron, "Les travaux de l'Institut français d'archéologie orientale en 1969–1970," *BIFAO* 69 (1971): 283–306, pl. 57 ("opening the mouth"); cf. E. Naville, *The Temple of Deir el-Bahari* (6 vols., London: Egypt Exploration Fund, 1905–08), vol. 4, pl. 110; A. H. Gardiner, "The Mansion of Life and the Master of the King's Largess," *JEA* 24 (1938): 83–91, pl. 5; H. Jacobsohn, *Die dogmatische Stellung des Königs in der Theologie der alten Ägypter* (Ägyptologische Forschungen 8; Glückstadt: J. J. Augustin 1939), 30–31, 34 ("reciting the dance-hymn"); cf. H. Goedicke, *Königliche Dokumente aus dem alten Reich* (Ägyptologische Abhandlungen 14; Wiesbaden: Harrassowitz, 1967), 80, text n. 7; A. H. Gardiner, *Ancient Egyptian Onomastica* (3 vols.; London: Oxford University Press, 1947), 1:55*–56*.

[68] Newberry, *Beni Hasan*, vol. 1, pl. 25–26 (lines 161–64).

[69] "This writing," *Urk.* 4:478.3 (Belegstellen); 1083:15–17, 1197, 1514:15–16, 1536, 1510; Florence 1551 (S. Bostico, *Museo archeologico di Firenze: Le stele egiziane* [Rome, 1959]); Cairo 20539 (Lange and Schäfer, *Grab- und Denksteine*); J. P. Corteggiani, "Une stèle héliopolitaine de l'époque Saïte," in *Hommages à Serge Sauneron* (ed. J. Vercoutter; Bibliothèque d'étude 81; Cairo: Institut français d'archéologie orientale, 1979), 1:115–54, pl. 24; Limme, *Stèles égyptiennes*, 46 col. 7–8; S. Sauneron, *Rituel de l'embaumement: pap. Boulaq III, pap. Louvre 5.158* (Cairo: Le Caire Imprimerie nationale, 1952), 5, 18. "This stela," *ÄL* 70:6, 80:3–4; *Urk.* 4:1610.4–8; *KRI* 1:331.1–2; Louvre C.50 (UT); K.-J. Seyfried, *Beiträge zu den Expeditionen des Mittleren Reiches in die Ost-Wüste* (Hildesheim: Pelizaeus-

mouths,"[70] and "to pronounce" (*dm*).[71] Such oral delivery, moreover, was not only intended for magical efficacy. The texts themselves envisage an audience: "O all ye living upon earth! All ye magistrates and pensionnaires, every scribe who will read and all ye people who will listen!"[72] "Beloved of the king and Osiris . . . shall he be, namely, any scribe who shall read, any person who may listen and any priest who may look on."[73] "O ye living upon earth . . . who may enter this tomb of the necropolis . . . and read your words on this stela, whether it be a scribe or (simply) one who listens . . ."[74] The audience, even though literate, is instructed to "listen,"[75] for the content of the text is to be made known by the "spoken word."[76] "Now as for any person who shall listen (to the contents of) this stela, they shall say: 'that's right!'"[77]

Here then is clear evidence of the life-situation, a formal reading, in which the content of a written text was disseminated among the illiterate population; but the mechanism was more broadly used than the private mortuary inscriptions suggest. The chancery often turned out numerous copies, in stela form, of government decrees and other officially authorized documents,[78] to ensure that their contents be known and widely disseminated: "Make copies of this decree

---

Museum, 1981), 27 (11); *HTBM* 6 (1922), pl. 49 (652); Wenamun, 2.54f. (Gardiner, *Late Egyptian Stories*); "who shall glance at my walls and read some of my phrases," *Urk.* 4:1845.

[70] Hassan, *Mastaba of Ny-ankh-pepy*, 10 fig. 5; Kanawati, "New Evidence," 38.

[71] *WÄS* 5:449.11–12; Urk. 4:440; Amarna I, pl. 39 recto 3 (N. de G. Davies, *The Rock Tombs of El-Amarna* [6 vols.; Archeological Survey of Egypt, 13th–18th and 35th Memoir; London: Egypt Exploration Fund, 1903–8], 1 [1906]); P. Berlin 2074 (*HPKM*); P. A. A. Boeser, *Beschreibung der ägyptischen Sammlung des Niederländischen Reichsmuseums der Altertümer in Leiden*, Vol. I, *Die Denkmäler der Zeit zwischen dem Alten und Mittleren Reich und des Mittleren Reiches*; Pt. 1: *Stelen*, Pt. 2: *Grabgegenstände, Statuen, Gefässe und verschiedenartige kleinere Gegenstände* (The Hague: Martinus Nijhoff, 1905–), pl. 19 no. 29; Wreszinski, *Ägyptische Inschriften*, 63(I).

[72] Tylor, *Tomb of Sebek-nekht*, pl. 2–3 line 1; W. Helck, *Historisch-biographische Texte der 2. Zwischenzeit und neue Texte der 18. Dynastie* (Wiesbaden: Harrassowitz, 1983), 42.

[73] Cairo 20017 (Lange and Schäfer, *Grab- und Denksteine*).

[74] *Urk.* 4:965–66.

[75] *HTBM* 9 (1970), pl. 21 (164); Wreszinski, *Ägyptische Inschriften*, no. 172:1–2; H. de Meulenaere, "La Stèle Louvre C 117," OLP 4 (1973): 77–84, pl. V (6–7). "Every wiseman is one who can listen (i.e., understand) what the early ancestors said" (*Urk.* 4:1084.8).

[76] *Urk.* 4:965.6, 1632.6; *HTBM* 5 (1914), pl. 40 ("my statement"); 8 (1939), pl. 33; 9 (1970), pl. 28.

[77] *ÄL* 80:1–2; cf. 3–4.

[78] Cf. Goedicke, *Königliche Dokumente*, Abb. 17: "You are to act in concert with N and fix this order, which has been made in many copies, in writing."

and have them taken to every nomarch of Upper Egypt, and have it set on a stone stela at the gate of [every temple] in which your monuments are (placed) so that the sons of the sons of the people may see it."[79] In a similar way, royal benefactions "are established in writing at the door of the upper gate of temple [X] before all the people of the land."[80] Awareness of the contents by as many people as possible was imperative, since such texts incorporated the letter of the law.[81] But the wide dissemination envisaged would have been impossible but for formal readings.[82] Publicly displayed royal inscriptions expect an *audience*, not a readership.[83] There is even evidence that the text of treaties was read out publicly from time to time;[84] and the reading aloud of a letter, or the verbal paraphrase based upon it, was the norm in Egypt.[85]

---

[79] Ibid., Abb. 28 (Coptos R, 5–7); cf. Abb. 8 (Coptos B, 48).

[80] J. D. Ray, *The Archive of Hor* (London: Egypt Exploration Society, 1976), text 3, recto 15–16.

[81] Cf. the phrase "to act in accordance with the wording of this decree," Goedicke, *Königliche Dokumente*, Coptos C and D; cf. *Urk.* 4:1261.2–4, 1270.9, 1271.19. The inscribing of a stela will be "for the sun-folk who pass by it, a great admonition when it becomes known" (*KRI* 6:5.6–7). Cf. S. Sauneron, "Le Dégagement du temple d'Esne: mur nord," *ASAÉ* 52 (1952): 37; idem, *Le Temple d'Esna* (5 vols.; Cairo: Institut français d'archéologie orientale, 1962–69), 3:287 (an offering list which "is in accordance with what is on the great stela of" Thutmose III).

[82] Cf. the similar situation in Greece, where stelae were read aloud (Thomas, *Oral Tradition and Written Record*, 64). On public display of texts, see Harris, *Ancient Literacy*, 50–51.

[83] *Urk.* 4:368.3 (Hatshepsut).

[84] Cf. *KBo* 2:11: "I am aware of the words of the oath, and I have caused the Egyptians to hear the words which are before the gods of Egypt . . ." (Ramesses II). The actual words then constituted the primary form of the treaty; cf. *LDÄÄ* 3:136.31 ("These words which are upon the tablet of silver").

[85] Cf. the formula "I have *heard* all the matters (literally, words) you sent me about by the hand of N" (J. Černý, *Late Ramesside Letters* [Bibliotheca aegyptiaca 9; Brussels: Éditions de la Fondation égyptologique Reine Élisabeth, 1939], 9:6–7, 27:11–12 and passim); sometimes the formula is expanded by the addition "by the mouth of N" (ibid., 32:1). Cf. "this writing of speaking" (R. A. Caminos, *Late Egyptian Miscellanies* [Oxford: Oxford University Press, 1954], 5). The setting is best conveyed in the story of the Contendings of Horus and Seth, where letters are both dictated and read aloud. The messenger could also report verbally to the recipient: "Make the message for him exactly as he said it" (*ÄL* 38:18; Černý, *Late Ramesside Letters*, 17:11–12). In this case the written text becomes nothing more than an *aide-mémoire*. In general see E. F. Wente, *Letters from Ancient Egypt* (Atlanta: Scholars Press, 1990), 6–9. If the letter were in a foreign language, the translation would be dynamic and idiomatic rather than literal (W. R. Bodine, "Linguistics and Philology in the Study of Ancient Near Eastern Languages," in *Working with No Data* [ed. D. M. Golomb; Winona Lake, Ind.: Eisenbrauns, 1987], 46), even though the interlanguage might have suffered fossilization (A.

The composition of triumph reliefs at Karnak, Luxor and Gurneh suggests an arrangement "user-friendly" to one who will read for the edification of others.[86] Specific captions identifying individuals gloss many figures in the ubiquitous Kadesh-reliefs, and in some cases (the Tunip relief-cum-text at Luxor and the Ramesseum in particular) the inscription pointedly aids in the interpretation of the scene for the general public. The labels are clear and obviously placed, and the "bloc-encomia" obviate the necessity to search for banalities. The ubiquitous phrase "the king himself speaks" (with variants)[87] introduces the hearer through the reader to the very utterances of Pharaoh himself. The experience of Germanicus at Thebes in 19 C.E. is a case in point.[88] The numerous instances of iconotrophy[89] attested by the sources show that, even when a reader was not present, the reliefs continued to be the object of folkloric interpretation.[90]

The Antiquity and Authorship of Written Material

If even limited literacy was unnecessary for the livelihood and edification of the masses of the population, those whose tasks exposed them to writing at all times often achieved a high degree of proficiency.[91] The iconic nature of the hieroglyphs fostered playfulness and cryptography: "There was no sign at all of which I did not know the workings; shapes which had no[t been drawn(?)], effective(?) and old, worn writings, I [was knowledgeable] about them."[92] The author of some new, rebus-like signs characterizes them as "signs which I made of my own design, playfully(?), not invented by the ancestors."[93] All scribes

---

Gianto, "Script and Word Order in EA 162: A Case Study of Egyptian Akkadian," *Or* 66 [1997]: 426–33). The resultant rendering would always be oral, and the writer sometimes enjoins the translating scribe to present the best paraphrase possible in the target language (cf. EA 286:61–4; 289:48–51).

[86] For the occasions of dissemination of information, see C. J. Eyre, "Is Egyptian Historical Literature 'Historical' or 'Literary'?" *AELHF*, 415–34, esp. 426–27.

[87] See below, p. 186.

[88] Tacitus, *Annali* 2.67.

[89] J. Vansina, *Oral Tradition as History* (Madison: University of Wisconsin Press, 1985), 10.

[90] Cf. Redford, *Pharaonic King-lists*, 254–59.

[91] Ibid., 166–67, 225 n. 84; cf. "priests who are familiar with the script of the 'House-of-Books,' who can interpret the 'Souls-of-Re'" (Louvre 229).

[92] *Urk.* 4:1082.2–5, cf. 1074.2–9.

[93] *Urk.* 4:406.10–11.

would pride themselves on their ability to "fill in lacunae"(*mḥ gm wš*)[94] and to be conversant with all "the difficult passages."[95]

Skepticism towards the postulate of royal literacy is misplaced, as there is abundant evidence that kings could read and write. We hear of the king "writing with his (own) fingers,"[96]and he calls for cases of books, reads letters and comments on the writing.[97] Thutmose III was a famous savant and author,[98] and both Neferhotpe and Ramesses II are recorded as themselves having consulted library books.[99] Among those monarchs who claimed to be able to read archaic texts, both Apophis[100] and Ramesses IV may be mentioned.[101]

The texts of the latter king are worth pursuing. Ramesses says: "I took thought in my heart on my father, my lord [Osiris and I consulted the books] of Thoth which are in the 'House-of-Life.' None of them at all did I leave unexamined, in order to search out the more important from the less important of the gods and goddesses—how difficult is their wording!" The same king, apparently, repeats his discovery in a papyrus in the Turin Museum:[102] "I neglected no ritual document since they came into being, nor (any) scroll of the most remote primordial times, in not perusing them to examine them and

---

[94] Redford, *Pharaonic King-lists,* 225 n. 84.

[95] *Itnw* (*Urk.* 4:1820.12–14); cf. P. Anastasi i.1.7, "able to decipher the difficult, recherché passages like him that composed them" (pace H.-W. Fischer-Elfert, *Die satirische Streitschrift des Papyrus Anastasi I* [Wiesbaden: Harrassowitz, 1986], 21 n. *v*—this is not a reference to *gnwt*). The term can also be applied to old toponyms (J. Vandier, *Le Papyrus Jumilhac* [Paris: Centre national de la recherche scientifique, 1953], 7:23) and prescriptive texts (PD 6321, x + 1.1; E. A. E. Reymond, *From Ancient Egyptian Hermetic Writings* [Vienna: Österreichische Nationalbibliothek, 1977], 34).

[96] *LDÄÄ* 2: pl. 76d.6. E. F. Wente, "The Scribes of Ancient Egypt," *CANE,* 2211–21, esp. 2214.

[97] *Urk.* 1:41; 60–63; 128–30; 179–80; *LDÄÄ* 2: pl. 76d.10; 76f.9; see also H. Goedicke, "Quotations in Old Kingdom Inscriptions," in *Ägyptologische Studien: Hermann Grapow zum 70. Geburtstag gewidmet* (ed. O. Firchow; Berlin: Akademie-Verlag, 1955), 93–106; idem, "Diplomatical Studies in the Old Kingdom," *JARCE* 3 (1964): 31–42; J. E. Quibell, *Excavations at Saqqara* (Cairo: Institut français d'archéologie orientale, 1908), 79.

[98] Redford, *Pharaonic King-lists,* 166–68.

[99] Helck, *Historisch-biographische Texte,* 21–22 (no. 32); M. Abdul-Razik, "The Dedicatory and Building Texts of Ramesses II in Luxor Temple: I, The Texts," *JEA* 60 (1974): 144.

[100] Helck, *Historisch-biographische Texte,* 57 (no. 85).

[101] *KRI* 6:22.4–7.

[102] A. H. Gardiner, "A Pharaonic Encomium," *JEA* 42 (1956): 9.

research them concerning thy (Amun's) form."[103] From these statements it appears that the king had gained access to an archaic document requiring a certain degree of erudition to read. That such texts should have been found in any archive in ancient times is remarkable.

In contrast to other collections of archives from the chequered histories of Mesopotamia, the Levant and Greece, the libraries of ancient Egypt reflect the continuum of three and one-half millennia of uninterrupted development. While on scores of occasions the collections of West Asian cities underwent fiery destruction through war and invasion, the "house of books" in Egypt enjoyed a charmed life, sharing with the state the benefits of secure geographical location and inviolate borders. As far as we know, the few invasions of Egyptian soil between the dawn of history and 671 B.C.E.—only four to be exact!—in no way resulted in the destruction of intellectual property. In fact, two of the invaders (the Hyksos and the Kushites) seem, if anything, to have valued writings, and to have taken steps to preserve and enlarge libraries. Under these considerations one cannot wonder at the ease with which Ramesses (or Shabaka) can access documents of hoary antiquity. Only with the disastrous invasion of Egypt by Artaxerxes III in 343 B.C.E. did document collections suffer major disruption.

The Egyptians regularly allude to "ancient writings," the mere mention of which is enough to endow a piece with authority.[104] They are cited as the source of land cadasters[105] and tax lists,[106] building plans[107] and calendars,[108] medical prescriptions[109] and mathematical texts.[110] As a stated *Vorlage*, "ancient texts" lend authority to regulations, laws[111] and social

---

[103] Ibid., *JEA* 41 (1955): 30, pl. VIII:7–8.

[104] *WÄS* 1:128.11, 13 (*iswt*); *gmyt m sš iswt*, "found in ancient writings," is the formula that is common.

[105] A. De Buck, *Egyptian Readingbook* (Leiden: Nederlands Instituut voor het Nabije Oosten, 1948), 68:11–12.

[106] *Urk.* 4:1111–12, 1120.5.

[107] *Dendera* 6:158f.

[108] A. M. Bakir, *The Cairo Calendar no. 86637* (Cairo: General Organisation for Government Printing Offices, 1966), recto 1, 1.

[109] P. Ebers xlvii.15–16 (G. M. Ebers, *Papyros Ebers* [Leipzig: W. Engelmann, 1875]); P. Berlin 3038.15.1ff. (UT); Luft, "Zur Einleitung der Liebesgedichte," 111.

[110] G. Robins and G. Shute, *The Rhind Mathematical Papyrus* (London: British Museum Publications, 1987), pl. I.

[111] A. H. Gardiner, "Inscriptions from the Tomb of Sarenput, Prince of Elephantine," *ZÄS* 45 (1908): pl. 7, l. 8; *Edfu* 5:126–7; J. Černý, *A Community of Workmen at Thebes in the*

mores,[112] and ensure that cultic performance and iconography conform to ancient and therefore acceptable prototypes.[113] Whatever the ancestors had said or written was *ipso facto* a precedent which under no circumstances could be ignored.

The backing of a written form for any human activity or speech assumed an importance in Egypt that it rarely enjoyed elsewhere. The phrase *mi nty r sš* and variants (literally, "in accordance with that which is in writing") glosses many a description of performances dependent for their efficacy (and legality) on adherence to a precise formula. Thus religious ritual (including daily service,[114] festival instructions,[115] and mortuary ritual[116]) is frequently stated to

---

Ramesside Period (Cairo: Institut français d'archéologie orientale, 1973), 18; cf. Cairo 42226 (UT) h.5 ("regulations of the ancestors"), h.9 ("that document of antiquity").

[112] P. Anastasi v.17.6 (Gardiner, *Late Egyptian Miscellanies*); W. Spiegelberg, "The Hieratic Text in Mariette KARNAK, pl. 46: A Contribution of [*sic*] the History of the Viziers of the New Empire," *Proceedings of the Society of Biblical Archaeology* 24 (1902): 320ff. (genealogy).

[113] *Urk.* 4:1867.15; cf. *Edfu* 7:27.9: "his sacred titulary before the gods in accordance with what is in ancient writings, his (present) temple being like his first temple"; *Dendera* 8:111: "his walls inscribed with his likeness in accordance with what is in ancient writings"; see *KRI* 1:293.12–13: (Paser praises a craftsman who is making a statue of the king) "This lordly statue (*twt n nb*) which you have produced, let it turn out like the old model; then Pharaoh l.p.h. will say: 'It gives satisfaction.'"

[114] *KRI* 5:116.12–13 ("I set down his offerings, his ritual and his procedure in accordance with what is in 'the Festival Book of Memphis'"); *Urk.* 2:37.13 (rites at Mendes "in conformity with what is in writing . . ."); ibid., 38.14–16 (". . . that which is found in the texts of Thoth"); ibid., 123 ("all rites performed in accordance with what is in [the book called] 'Festal Appearance of Khnum-re'"); cf. ibid., 167 (". . . [book called] 'Setting up the Offering-brazier'"); *Esna* 3:177 (offering performed "according to the divine offering-book of this god"); ibid., 3:287 (offering list "in accordance with what is on the great stela" of Thutmose III).

[115] P. Posener-Krieger and J. L. de Cenival, *The Abu Sir Papyri* (Hieratic Papyri in the British Museum; 5th ser.; London: Trustees of the British Museum, 1968), pl. 19 (what is in "the festival book of the time of king Kakai"); E. Chassinat, *Le Mystère d'Osiris au mois de Khoiâkh* (Cairo: Institut français d'archéologie orientale, 1966–68), 528 ("The chief lector priest is to recite the spells of 'Planting-the-Field' in accordance with what is in the festival book"); *Esna* 2:123 (55, 1: "every rite performed according to what is in the book"); ibid., 171:2; ibid., 3:288 (performance of a festival "in accordance with what is in the festival book"); cf. ibid., 3:8, 243 ("festival of rowing"), 291, etc. Cf. A. Grimm, *Die Altägyptischen Festkalender in den Tempeln der griechisch-römischen Epoche* (Wiesbaden: Harrassowitz, 1994), 142–46.

[116] Chassinat, *Le Mystère*, 799 col. 153 ("And they put on him his 14 amulets, according to what is in the 'Compendium' [*tmmt*]"); ibid., 358–59 (all the embalming instructions are to be accordance "with that which is in the 'Burial Rite'"); J. Vercoutter, "Une Épitaphe Royale

be "in conformance with what is in book X" or the like, and the texts are not
recited from memory, but from the book itself.[117] In particular, cult
paraphernalia and purifications are made strictly in accordance with written
prescriptions.[118] Even "secular" information could be sought in authoritative
written source books.[119]

What contributed greatly to the authority of texts was the authorship,
whether ancestral or divine. Oftentimes the specific ancestors were known, and
their names could be cited.[120] At times they rose to the status of natural

---

inédite du Serapéum," *MDAI* 16 (1958): 333–45, pl. 31,3 (Apis burial performed "in
conformity with what is in the compendium [*tmmt*] and every hieroglyphic writing").

[117] S. Schott, *Bücher und Bibliotheken im alten Ägypten: Verzeichnis der Buch- und Spruchtitel und der Termini technici* (Wiesbaden: Harrassowitz, 1990), 310–12; *Edfu* 6:88.2; R. O.
Faulkner, *The Papyrus Bremner-Rhind (British Museum no. 10188)* (Brussels: Éditions de la
Fondation égyptologique Reine Élisabeth, 1933), 1, 1–2; *Esna* 2:172 ("reading the text
[called] 'Dedication of the Field'").

[118] L. Habachi, "The Naos with the Decades (Louvre D 37) and the Discovery of Another
Fragment," *JNES* 11 (1952): 251–63, pl. 28 (over the image of a lion: "Shu, lord of the Perwer
. . . silver overlaid with gold in conformance with what is on the hieroglyphic scroll");
Leclant, *Montouemhât*, 25 line 18 (cult images "in accordance with what is in the 'Great
Inventory'"), sim. 213 line 10; cf. 217 line 33 (the Osirian barque "exactly according to its
customary form"); 197 line 3 ("I purified the temples of all the gods [and goddesses] of the
entire Southland in accordance with what was in (the book called) 'Purification-of-Temples'
. . ."); G. Lefebvre, "Textes du tombeaux de Petosiris," *ASAÉ* 22 (1922): 33–48, 139–56, esp.
34 ("All that I did [scil., in refurbishing the temple of Thoth] was in accord with what was in
the ritual book."); *Dendera* 8:85 (texts on temple walls inscribed with "spells from the god's
offering-book . . . in accordance with what is in the ritual book"); sim. IV, 170; V, 22; VII,
111–12; cf. C. Favard-Meeks, *Le Temple de Behbeit el-Hagara: essai de reconstitution et
d'interprétation* (Hamburg: H. Buske, 1991), 132; Chassinat, *Le Mystère*, 611 (unguent
manufacture "in accordance with what is in the chapter on unguents"); E. Naville, *The Shrine
of Saft el-Henneh and the Land of Goshen* (London: Trubner & Co., 1888), pl. 3
(representations of gods "[like] that which is on the scroll, (so) their images are made on the
naos"); ibid., pl. 4 ("[the divine forms] derived from another scroll of the temple, namely a
hieroglyphic book"); ibid., pl. 6 (1) (3) ("His Majesty himself gave the directive to set up
these images of the gods . . . every ennead being in its place—they were as that which is in
the scroll in their every detail").

[119] A. P. Zivie, "Un Fragment inédit de coudée votive," *BIFAO* 71 (1971): 187 fig. 3 (weights
and measures); K. Sethe, "Die ägyptische Bezeichnungen für die Oasen und ihre Bewohner,"
ZÄS 56 (1920): 51 (geographical information). In general, see Redford, *Pharaonic King-lists*,
215–23.

[120] Cf., e.g., P. Berlin 3057.xv.1ff., xxi.15, xxii.22 (*HPKM*); P. Ebers c.111.1f (Ebers,
Papyros Ebers); E. A. W. Budge, *Facsimiles of Egyptian Hieratic Papyri in the British
Museum* (London, 1910), pl. 41–42; see D. Wildung, *Die Role ägyptischer Könige im
Bewusstsein ihrer Nachwelt* (Berlin: B. Hessling, 1969); H. Grapow, *Grundriß der Medizin
der alten Ägypter* (Berlin: Akademie-Verlag, 1959), 274; T. G. Allen, *The Egyptian Book of*

celebrities: "Is there anybody here like Hordedef? Is there another like Imhotpe? No one has come along in our times like Neferty or Khety, the most outstanding of them. Let me acquaint you with the name of Ptah-em-djed-huty and Kha-kheperre-sonbu. Is there another like Ptahhotpe and Kairer too?"[121] Moreover the ancestral scribe did not have to enhance celebrity status through borrowing a "macho" image. As an intellectual he could glory, in the fashion of an antihero, in all the physical traits normally deemed detracting in a patriarchal society: "I know many people without strength and weak-armed, weaklings without muscle, and (yet) they are rich in houses and food! They don't have to say: 'Oh I wish I had . . . !' Come, let me tell you about the scribe Roy . . . he hasn't stirred nor moved quickly since he was born. He hated manual labor and never experienced it. (Yet now) he rests in the West, his body whole . . . I'll tell you of Pihripita who used to be in Heliopolis. [He was an old] boy of the king's-house l.p.h., he was small <like> a cat, (though) bigger than a monkey, (yet) he prospers in his house . . . Have you heard the name of Keykey, the 'dust-cloud'?[122] Undetected he moves over the ground in disarray, in tightly bound clothes. If you saw him at eventide in the dusk, you would think him a bird. . . ."[123] The intellectual has created his own stereotype without apology. Moreover it is a *living* stereotype; the aura of "authorship" need not await the passing of the "speaker."

There is a sense here of being in a long, unbroken line of scribes, as a candidate for "ancestral" status one day.[124] One who authored a text or stela seems more inclined than an artisan to claim and celebrate his creation. If it is a biographical statement, it will be presented as a truly *auto*biographical account

---

the Dead: Documents in the Oriental Institute Museum (Chicago: University of Chicago Press, 1974), pl. 37; W. Pleyte, *Chapitres supplémentaires du Livre des Morts 162 à 174, publiés d'après les monuments de Leide, du Louvre et du Musée Britannique* (2 vols.; Leiden: Brill, 1881), vol. 1, pl. 111 (L25b, 30, 31b).

[121] P. Chester Beatty IV verso 3.5; cf. verso 6.11ff. (A. H. Gardiner, *The Library of A. Chester Beatty: The Chester Beatty Papyri No. 1* [Oxford: Privately printed by J. Johnson at the Oxford University Press and published by E. Walker, 1931]). For a "scribal college" of literati producing a lot of classical Middle Kingdom "literature," see C. J. Eyre, "The Semna Stela: Quotation, Genre and Function of Literature," in *Studies in Egyptology Presented to Miriam Lichtheim* (2 vols.; ed. S. Israelit-Groll; Jerusalem: Magnes, 1990), 1:134–65; also Lesko, "Some Comments," 662–67.

[122] J. Hoch, *Semitic Words in Egyptian Texts of the New Kingdom and Third Intermediate Period* (Princeton: Princeton University Press, 1994), 287–88.

[123] P. Anastasi i.9.3–10.4 (Fischer-Elfert, *Die satirische Streitschrift*).

[124] Cairo 42230 (Jansen-Winkeln, *Ägyptische Biographien*): "It is one man that calls another to remembrance. I am one that makes offering to the ancestors, my brethren who came earlier . . . ."

of events, not simply as an ideal text.[125] Momentous events could call forth a rare though justifiable boast: "I was the one that set down (*smn*) the victories which (Thutmose III) achieved over every foreign land, put into writing just as they occurred."[126]

A scribe might boast of mere copying—penmanship and calligraphy were also marks of distinction—as much as authorship. A survivor will cite himself as the producer of a text on behalf of a deceased loved one (although he might have only authorized the text).[127] The act of writing is best attested in colophons. These range in size from extremely brief notices that the document is "finished,"[128] or "written,"[129] or "come to a conclusion,"[130] through extended forms naming the scribe,[131] to formal dedications to mentors and colleagues[132] and curses on adverse critics. But the use of the words "made (or written, or copied) by scribe N" does not guarantee that the named individual authored the

---

[125] Lichtheim, "Didactic Literature," *AELHF*, 254.

[126] *Urk.* 4:1004.9–10.

[127] E.g., *Urk.* 1:33.8, 12–13; 34.4–6, 12; 40.18; 65.4–6; 72–73; 119.17, etc. The verb *iri*, "to do or make," is ambiguous.

[128] *WÄS* 5:183 (*grḥ*?); cf. W. C. Hayes, *A Papyrus of the Late Middle Kingdom in the Brooklyn Museum (Papyrus Brooklyn 35.1446)* (Brooklyn: Brooklyn Museum, 1955), 60: "said by the scribe NN: 'it has been completed' (i.e., case closed)."

[129] Onkhsheshonqy 28, 11 (*sh*) (S. R. K. Glanville, *The Instructions of Onchsheshonqy*, vol. 2 of *Catalogue of Demotic Papyri in the British Museum* [London, 1956]).

[130] Contendings of Horus and Seth 16, 8 (Gardiner, *Library*); A. H. Gardiner and J. Černý, *Hieratic Ostraca* (Oxford: Griffith Institute, 1957), pl. 14, no. 1, line 8; P. Chester Beatty VIII recto 9.9 (Gardiner, *Library*); P. Berlin 3022.311 (= R. Koch, *Die Erzählung des Sinuhe* [Brussels: Éditions de la Fondation égyptologique Reine Élisabeth, 1990], 81: "finished from beginning to end as found in writing"); *ÄL* 42:11–12, 46:22–23.

[131] P. Anastasi iii.7, 10–11 (giving the date; Gardiner, *Late Egyptian Miscellanies*); The Taking of Joppa 3.13–14 (Gardiner, *Late Egyptian Stories*); P. Sallier IV verso 16.2 ("made by scribe N, the owner of this instruction"; Gardiner, *Late Egyptian Miscellanies*); P. Chester Beatty IX verso 3–4; Amenemope xxvii,18–xxviii,1 (E. A. W. Budge, *Facsimiles of Egyptian Hieratic Papyri in the British Museum, 2d series* [London, 1923]); Shipwrecked Sailor 187 ("finished from beginning to end, as found in writing, written by scribe N"; A. M. Blackman, *Middle Egyptian Stories* [Bibliotheca aegyptiaca 2; Brussels: Éditions de la Fondation égyptologique Reine Élisabeth, 1932]); Bakir, *Cairo Calendar*, pl. 49 (verso 19, 1: "book of the collection of the [. . .] by scribe N, their owner"); Barguet, *Le Papyrus N. 3176(S)*, iv, 27–28 ("finished, viz., the 'Festal Appearance of Sokar'; copied by scribe N"),

[132] Preceded by "for the *ku* of . . . ," P. Anastasi iii.4.11 and P. Bologna 1094.11.9 (Gardiner, *Late Egyptian Miscellanies*); *KRI* 2:101.11–14 (three dedicatees and date; "made by scribe N"); P. d'Orbiney 19.7–10 (three dedicatees; "made by scribe N, the owner of this writing"; Gardiner, *Late Egyptian Stories*).

work; in fact, in most cases the probability would be against such an assumption. Those texts we possess, if they do not originate in a classroom setting, fall into the category of "chance" copies of existing works, made by scribes for their private amusement.[133]

Archives

The most common and most ancient generic word for "library" (better "archive") in ancient Egyptian is *pr-mdȝt*, "house of documents."[134] *Mdȝt* originally referred to a rectangular piece of papyrus which, by being joined to others, could then form part of a roll.[135] Singly, such pieces offered themselves as suitable for letters[136] or compact decrees,[137] or even amuletic strips.[138] Later, the word was extended to cover any document, or even pericope, with single intent.[139] During the Old Kingdom the "house of the god's book(s)" and the "house of the records of the king's business" designated kinds of registries where decrees, work orders, conscription notices, inventories, "count" records, directives, and property transfers were kept.

---

[133] On the *ȝy-drf*, "(private) book-bag," i.e., a personal collection, see E. Iversen, "The Chester Beatty Papyrus No. 1, recto XVI, 9–XVII, 13," *JEA* 65 (1979): 78 n. 1; Schott, *Bücher und Bibliotheken*, 308 (1416); cf. R. Parkinson and S. Quirke, *Papyrus* (Austin: University of Texas Press, 1995), 61–65.

[134] *WÄS* 1:515.12. In the Old Kingdom the archives were in the main those of the royal administration (cf. Palermo Stone, verso 4, 2 "house of documents of the *snwt*-chamber of Memphis"), designated by the generic "god's-book": PT 267d; V. Wessetzky, "Anmerkungen über das Gottesbuch des Königs," in *Studien zu Sprache und Religion Ägyptens zu Ehren von Wolfhart Westendorf* (ed. F. Junge; Göttingen: F. Junge, 1984), 963–65.

[135] W. Helck, *Altägyptische Aktenkunde des 3. und 2. Jahrtausends v. Chr.* (Munich: Deutscher Kunstverlag, 1974), 3; Parkinson and Quirke, *Papyrus*, 16–19; cf. PT 954 (parallel to writing board and pen).

[136] *WÄS* 2:187.9; B. Gunn, "A Sixth Dynasty Letter from Saqqara," *ASAÉ* 25 (1925): 251 n. 2.

[137] Helck, *Altägyptische Aktenkunde*, 10–38.

[138] I. E. S. Edwards, *Hieratic Papyri in the British Museum*, 4th ser., *Oracular Amuletic Decrees of the Late New Kingdom* (London, 1960), pl. V, 55–56; p. 17 n. 54; *Urk.* 4:1364.17; Y. Koenig, "Les Effrois de Kenikerkhepeshef," *RdÉ* 33 (1981): 30 n. *a*.

[139] Religious document (very common), Schott, *Bücher und Bibliotheken*, 92–111; questions for an oracle: Černý, *Late Ramesside Letters*, 37:6–7; reports: P. Abbott 5.19 (T. E. Peet, *The Great Tomb Robberies of the Twentieth Egyptian Dynasty* [Oxford: Clarendon, 1930]); *KRI* 1:322.11; draft-lists: *KRI* 1:324.7; instructions: *KRI* 7:263.9; juridical documents: M. Malinine, *Choix de textes juridiques en hiératique anormal et en démotique* (Paris: H. Champion, 1953), 13 n. 17.

Oral Transmission and Tradition

The Scribal View

It is quite clear from the evidence passed in review above that the scribal tradition among the Egyptians constituted a strong mainstay of state organization and control, and an all-important cohesive element in Egyptian society. Scribal tradition took shape as a control regime for information selection and dispersal, didactic admonition and mind-shaping. Since oral tradition, by its very nature, resisted such control, state organs showed a subconscious urge to denigrate it.

Within the world of the scribe orality was suspect. The *sdd* of the people, the word in Egyptian which most closely approaches a genre term covering all aspects of popular orality,[140] could be regarded as liable to incorporate fantasy and therefore to be untrustworthy. In Hatshepsut's Pwenet text the imprecise knowledge of the "myrrh terraces, unknown to mankind and heard about (only) from mouth to mouth, in the oral tradition (*sdd*) of those of long ago" is contrasted with the accurate reports of the eyewitness accounts of the queen's men.[141] Often the uniqueness or incredible nature of an event will be expressed by a negative locution, in which oral tradition is cited: Sety I's prowess "had never been seen in the ancestors' writings, nor had oral accounts (*mdwt*) related it mouth-to-mouth."[142] The coming of the Hittite princess, as an event, "had not been heard of from mouth to mouth, had not been commemorated in the writings of the ancestors."[143]

No savant engaged in chronicling events, quantifying data, or writing up prescriptive texts would pay much attention to the oral culture around him.

---

[140] *WÄS* 4:394–95; cf. R. A. Caminos, "Review of *Eyptian Stelae, Reliefs, and Paintings from the Petrie Collection* by Harry Milne Stewart," *JEA* 64 (1978): 151–57, esp. 156; J. Assmann, "Eine Traumöffenbarung der Göttin Hathor," *RdÉ* 30 (1978): 33 n. 52; Schott, *Bücher und Bibliotheken*, 307–8, 365–66; W. Westendorf, "*ḥwj.t-sḏd*, das Schlagwort," *GöM* 72 (1984): 37–38. Erman's inclination to deny that *sdd* was a technical term (see H. Grapow, *Sprachliche und schriftliche Formung ägyptischer Texte* [Leipziger ägyptologische Studien 7; Glückstadt: J. J. Augustin, 1936], 59 n. 24) is, I believe, unjustified. The scribal stance represents the classical antithesis between *delectatio* and *veritas*; cf. G. M. Koch, *Zum Verhältnis von Dichtung und Geschichtsschreibung: Theorie und Analyse* (Frankfurt am Main: P. Lang, 1983), 14–31.

[141] *Urk.* 4:344.10; the ignorance of future generations in their oral discourse may be alleviated by a written record: *Urk.* 4:365.8–13.

[142] *KRI* 1:42.14–15; cf. *Urk.* 4:1281.2–3 ("a deed, in fact, never before done nor heard of in oral tradition," viz. Amenophis II's archery); P. Anastasi i.26.3 (rejection of oral tales); ibid., i.28.5 (confusing tales impossible to interpret; Fischer-Elfert, *Die satirische Streitschrift*).

[143] *KRI* 2:254.1–5.

Factual material transmitted mouth-to-mouth was almost by definition unreliable. When Ramesses IV consulted the books in the "house of life," and discovered there a description of Re and primeval times, he assures the reader "this is recounted in writing, not orally (literally, mouth-to-mouth)."[144] In her refurbishing of the temple of Thoth Hatshepsut says: "I [made the fes]tal appearance of this god at [his] festivals which I established for him again, since they had been (only) oral (*m r3*), and not (celebrated) at the proper time(s)."[145] A tax man might have received numerous *oral* reports on the tax status of a particular town, but invokes instead the "nome-archives of the comptrollers."[146] Oral communication might be overlong, embellished, and confusing. To the oral petition of a litigant, the presiding magistrate might say "these narratives (*sdyw*) you're telling me are multitudinous! . . . write everything that happened to your father . . . and write the narratives of what happened to you."[147] When reliable information was required about things that happened in the past, oral sources were not even considered. Instead, "search was made in the annals of the kings who lived aforetime."[148]

Terms for Oral Delivery

Egyptians were sensitive to *genre*, and generally operated and composed within generic parameters.[149] Occasionally genre terms will occur, often marginally, although formal pieces do not always begin with such a designation. Authors were free to modify and expand, and "interweaving and flexibility" strongly mark the final product.[150]

---

[144] *KRI* 6:22.11; cf. *LDÄÄ* 3:140.d.2 (information concerning desert wells passed on from mouth to mouth).

[145] *Urk.* 4:388.14–17.

[146] P. Rylands IX, 6/21–7/1; cf. 7/5 where tax overpayments are documented (F. Ll. Griffith, *Catalogue of the Demotic Papyri in the John Rylands Library, Manchester* [3 vols.; Manchester, 1909]).

[147] P. Rylands IX, 4/1– 4; sim. 5/13–14 (Griffith, *Catalogue*).

[148] Redford, *Pharaonic King-lists*, 83–84.

[149] Cf. J. Foster, "Literature," *OEAE*.

[150] R. B. Parkinson, "Teachings, Discourses, and Tales from the Middle Kingdom," in *Middle Kingdom Studies* (ed. S. Quirke et al.; New Malden, Surrey: SIA, 1991), 100; on the importance of structure and genre see also P. Thompson, *The Voice of the Past: Oral History* (Oxford: Oxford University Press, 1978), 109–10; Vansina, *Oral Tradition as History*, 79–81; P. Kaplony, "Die Definition der schönen Literatur im Alten Ägypten," in *Fragen an die altägyptische Literatur: Studien zum Gedenken an Eberhard Otto* (ed. J. Assmann, E. Feucht,

Most of the speeches our texts refer to fall broadly under the rubric of "audible statement" (*tpt-r3*), literally, "that which is on/in the mouth."[151] This term applies to a wide range of *paroles*, including divine utterance,[152] magical spells,[153] the *ḥtp-di-nsw* formula,[154] the address to the living,[155] wisdom discourse,[156] official statements by the king[157] or other high official,[158]or even the acclamation of the crowd.[159] All uses of the term, apart from the last, presuppose an irrevocable quality of commission or undertaking latent in the spoken word. The simplex *r3*, "spell, utterance," had a much wider range of meanings, from magical incantation to light verse.[160] A formal speech, usually metrically arranged and lyrical in character, may be termed a "declamation," *mdt* (literally, "word").[161] This may be a set piece of oratory, composed for entertainment or admonition.[162] Significantly, perhaps, it is used most often in a juridical context, where the formal speeches of litigants in a court of law are

---

and R. Grieshammer; Wiesbaden: Reichert, 1977), 289–314. All too often in Egyptological studies general content, inferred (or imputed!) motivation, and topoi are all lumped together under the genre rubric, with little attention paid to the ancient terminology and structure.

[151] For the genres herein summarized, see D. B. Redford, "Ancient Egyptian Literature: An Overview," *CANE*, 2225–39.

[152] *Urk.* 4:165.11–15, 322.10, 974.9; J. Barns, *Five Ramesseum Papyri* (Oxford: Griffith Institute at the University Press, 1956), pl. 1, A 16; the supposedly audible statements lent authority to a current situation.

[153] *KRI* 6:24.11; S. Sauneron, *Le Rituel d'embaumement*, 5, 11; P. Ram 7.A.5 etc. (Barns, *Five Ramesseum Papyri*).

[154] *ÄL* 70, 91.

[155] See above, pp. 154ff.

[156] P. BM 41541, 4, 8–9.

[157] Newberry, *Beni Hasan*, vol. 1, pl. 25, col. 26–7; P. Harris 79.10 (P. Grandet, *Le Papyrus Harris I, BM 9999* [Cairo: Institut français d'archéologie orientale, 1994]); *KRI* 4:3.5; 5:39.6–8, 66.6ff., 83.10–11.

[158] *KRI* 1:284.2: " . . . one for whom the Two Lands assembled, to hear his statement."

[159] P. E. Newberry, *El Bersheh* (2 vols.; London: Egypt Exploration Fund, 1892–94), vol. 1, pl. 14:8.

[160] Schott, *Bücher und Bibliotheken*, 127–275.

[161] G. Posener, "Les richesses inconnues de la littérature égyptienne," *RdÉ* 6 (1951): 27–48, esp. 46–47.

[162] Cf. G. Posener, "Fragment litteraire de Moscou," *MDAI* 25 (1969): 101–6, esp. 101ff.; P. Pushkin 4656 recto 1, verso 1 (UT); E. A. W. Budge, *Hieratic Papyri in the British Museum*, 2d ser. (London, 1928), pl. 45:6–8.

generically categorized.[163] A situation in which a speaker is defending himself inevitably calls forth all the skills and style of an orator. The plural of the term, *mdwt* ("words") can be used more generally of the contents of a speech,[164] whether royal,[165] divine,[166] or popular;[167] but it appears not to be a genre designation. Oral delivery of lighter vein may be identified as a *ḫn (n mdt),*[168] which, to judge from the cognate "rhythm-makers" (*ḫnwt*),[169] could sustain some such translation as "jingle."

A speech made by the king, especially one containing specific directives and having the force of law,[170] was consistently termed a "statement (literally, that which was said) from the Majesty of the Palace, l.p.h."[171] The fact that the king had *said* it (and not *written* it) lent the requisite weight.[172] Directives thus covered include construction projects,[173] disposition of booty,[174] the wording of

---

[163] Cf. e.g., Eloquent Peasant, 72 (F. Vogelsang, *Kommentar zu den Klagen des Bauern* [Untersuchungen zur Geschichte und Altertumskunde Ägyptens 6; Leipzig: Hinrichs, 1913]); Contendings of Horus and Seth 1, 10–11 (Gardiner, *Library*); P. Abbott 6.9 (Peet, *Great Tomb Robberies*); *ÅL* 39:1; Barns, *Five Ramesseum Papyri*, pl. 1, A,6,17.

[164] *LDÄÄ* 3: Blatt 136, 31 (treaty); P. Harris 47.8 (decree; Grandet, *Papyrus Harris*); P. Kahun 35.31 (F. Ll. Griffith, *Hieratic Papyri from Kahun and Gurob* [London: Bernard Quaritch, 1898]); *Urk.* 1:128 (letters).

[165] BM 1630, line 4 ("words of His Majesty"; UT); *Urk.* 4:242; Louvre C.1 (UT) etc.

[166] P. Berlin 3056.8.4 (*HPKM;* "the words of Heliopolis which are in front of the figure of Amun and the figure of Thoth which are on the wall," i.e., the *ḏd-mdw* formula used in the reliefs).

[167] BM 41541; *Urk.* 4:1185 (both wisdom texts); *KRI* 1:331.3–4 (offering formula).

[168] Eloquent Peasant B1, 19 (Vogelsang, *Kommentar*); 37; H. Goedicke and E. F. Wente, *Ostraka Michaelides* (Wiesbaden: Harrassowitz, 1962), pl. 24 no. 95; *Urk.* 4:1095.7; Neferty 49–50 (W. Helck, *Die Prophezeihung des Nfr.tj* [Wiesbaden: Harrassowitz, 1970]); BM 581; C. Ziegler, *Catalogue des instruments de musique égyptiens* (Musée du Louvre, Département des antiquités égyptiennes; Paris: Éditions de la Réunion des Musées Nationaux, 1979), 102.

[169] *Urk.* 4:1059; *KRI* 5:186.6–7.

[170] Cf. A. Nibbi, "Remarks on Two Stelae from the Wadi Basus," *JEA* 62 (1976): pl. 10 (parallel to *tp-rd,* "instruction," and *hpw,* "laws").

[171] *WÄS* 4:341.7.

[172] Cf. Old Kingdom *wḏ-nsw,* "king's command" (Goedicke, *Königliche Dokumente,* 10–12).

[173] *Urk.* 1:62.1, 62.16–17; 63.2–3; 4:194.1–2, 409.15; P. Tresson, *Mélanges Maspero IV* (Cairo: Institut français d'archéologie orientale, 1934), 817ff. line 7.

[174] *Urk.* 4:1021.

consultation,[175] appointments,[176] expeditions,[177] and other enactments of general legal force.[178] The purpose of the statement did not require the presence of a large audience, and consequently we are not dealing with a formal speech to be given before an assembly.[179]

Pharaoh's speech, or *obiter dicta*, could be termed "teaching" (*sbꜣyt*)[180] and encompassed specific commands, political agenda, and more abstruse instruction. Thus Horemheb's specific directives to his new boards of magistrates constituted "teaching,"[181] and the apodictic lesson of Amenemhet I for his son Senwosret could be included under the same rubric.[182] Royal instruction encompassing what moderns might call theology, metaphysics, and ethics qualified as "Pharaoh's teaching,"[183] and such Pharaonic instruction was delivered orally: "My lord promoted me and I performed what he taught, hearkening to his voice without ceasing";[184] "daily he used to rise early to teach me, inasmuch as I performed what he taught";[185] "how lucky he who hearkens to thy life-teaching!"[186]

---

[175] *Urk.* 4:651.

[176] G. Legrain, "Notes d'inspection XVI: Le protocole royal d'Osorkon II," *ASAÉ* 5 (1905): 282.

[177] *Urk.* 4:325.17.

[178] J. Harari,"Nature de la stèle de donation de fonction du roi Ahmôse à la reine Ahmôse Nofretari," *ASAÉ* 56 (1959): pl. facing p. 202, 2–3; *KRI* 1:50.12–13; 2:710.9.

[179] The authoritative nature of the "Statement from the Majesty of the Palace" is paralleled by the expression *ḥr.tw,* used of a divine utterance and tantamount to "oracle," literally, "one declares, dicitur" (Edwards, *Hieratic Papyri, Oracular Amuletic Decrees,* 4 n. 27; P. Klasens, "An Amuletic Papyrus of the Twenty-fifth Dynasty," *Oudheidkundige Mededelingen uit het Rijksmuseum van Oudheden te Leiden* 56 [1975]: 20–28, esp. 23; P. Turin 1882 recto 3.7–8; 4.8–9 (UT); KRI 5:243.12; 6:5.5, 22.11, 457.4; 7:100.15); the term also applies occasionally to royal pronouncements (P. Harris 79.10 [Grandet, *Papyrus Harris*]; *KRI* 1:293.12–13).

[180] Eyre, "Semna Stela," 144–45.

[181] J.-M. Kruchten, *Le Décret d'Horemheb* (Brussels: Éditions de l'Université de Bruxelles, 1981), 148, col. 5.

[182] P. Millingen 1.1 (W. Helck, *Der Text der Lehre Amenemhets I. für seinen Sohn,* 2d ed. [Wiesbaden: Harrassowitz, 1986]).

[183] N. de G. Davies, *Rock Tombs of El-Amarna,* 1 (1903), pl. 30.

[184] Ibid., 5 (1908), pl. 2:11.

[185] Ibid., 6 (1908), pl. 15 col. 10.

[186] Ibid., 6 (1908), pl. 25 col. 16.

The Contents of Oral Transmission

Yet at a level wholly different from that of the scribe a very lively oral tradition[187] thrived in Egypt among both the illiterate masses and the elite alike. Much that would pass as "belletristics" in our nomenclature is in actual fact the product of oral composition if not transmission. Author-function in an oral society is markedly different from writer-function. Cognitive preparation, split-second modification and immediate delivery contrast with and issue in a different product from the reasoned, laborious, studied, and doctrinaire work of the writer. Orality theory must, therefore, be a more useful tool in textual analysis. Of the six categories Vansina isolated in African oral tradition,[188] namely, formulae, poetry, epics, lists, stories, and legal texts, the first, second, and fifth are well represented by oral tradition in ancient Egypt. The authors of material within these categories, unlike the producers and keepers of the community traditions elsewhere in Africa, are for the most part marginalized, and their compositions relegated to the realm of *delectatio*. We have already seen how "the *sdd* of the people" stands in disrepute, as something promulgated without reference to a written authority. As indicated above, other operative terms include "utterance" (*tpt-r3*), "speech" (*mdt*), "calling to mind" (*sh3*), and "things spoken" (*r3.w*). The verbs that are used resonate with audible, not visible, tools of discourse: "to pronounce" (*dm*), "to say" (*dd*), "to speak" (*mdw*), "to repeat" (*whm*), "to intone" (*cš*), "to read aloud" (*šdi*), "to inform" (*rdi cm.tn*), "to sing" (*hsi*).

It is not surprising that, in a centralized state in which attention was focused on Pharaoh as the center of society, royal doings should have dominated the content of what was passed on orally. This oral material frequently derived from a speech delivered by the king to the people: "Hear what I have to say to you, all you people, magistrates who are responsible for the land, and you entire armed forces!"[189] "Set (the record of) my good reign in the mouth(s) of the young generations, in accordance with the magnitude of the benefactions I have done for them" (Merenptah).[190] "Pay attention to my utterances! Hear what I have to say to you, so that I might instruct you!" (Ramesses III to his court, introducing an encapsulated account of his reign and

---

[187] I use the word broadly here to signify the practice of oral composition and transmission as well as tradition (see Vansina, *Oral Tradition as History*, 13–20, 27–29 and passim).

[188] J. Vansina, "Once upon a Time: Oral Traditions as History in Africa," *Historical Studies Today* (ed. F. Gilbert and S. R. Graubard; New York: W. W. Norton, 1972), 422.

[189] *KRI* 2:320.9.

[190] *KRI* 4:11.3–5.

mighty acts).[191] People speak of and recount *(sḏd)* the king's victories: "Great joy has come over Egypt, cheering comes forth from the towns of To-mery! People speak about the mighty deeds" that Merenptah has performed.[192] "People talk of his victories in [all] lands";[193] "the Libyans tell of generation speaking to generation about his victories, and every old man tells his son";[194] "O ye who shall see my monument in future years and who shall speak of what I have done . . . !"[195] The formal *incipit* of a species of royal encomium takes the form "here begins the oral account *(sḏd)* of the victories of the lord of Egypt."[196] Such oral transmission can reach far afield: "Foreigners who see me shall relate my name to far-away and unknown lands!"[197] The chain of oral transmission can also be viewed as never-ending: "The lord of the gods . . . who magnified his mighty acts in order to cause that his victories be spoken of for millions of years coming."[198]

The fervent hope of all, king and commoner alike, was that their "name" should not perish in the memory and conversation of posterity. This hope often found its basis in the offering cult where the name of the deceased was invoked to provide a quasi-magical means to promote eternal survival of the person. "Pronounce ye my name, recall my titulary . . . put my name in the mouths of your servants, (leave) my memory with your children."[199] "His name shall be pronounced on account of his character!"[200] "My name shall flourish in the

---

[191] *Medinet Habu I: Earlier Historical Records of Ramesses III* (Chicago: University of Chicago Oriental Institute, 1930), pl. 83:56–7; sim. pl. 96; and ibid., IV, pl. 238; cf. *Urk.* 4:289 (Thoth announcing Hatshepsut's reign to the gods).

[192] *KRI* 4:18.1; cf. P. Anastasi ii.1.1 (Gardiner, *Late Egyptian Miscellanies*); cf. G. A. Gaballa, "Three Acephalous Stelae," *JEA* 63 (1977): 122–26, pl. 22 (where an encomium of the king followed by mortuary wishes in the first person seems to betray the oral practice of extemporizing paeons to the king).

[193] *KRI* 4:20.11; cf. 7.2; cf. *Urk.* 4:1281.2–3 (exploits in archery); cf. *KRI* 1:42.14–15 (Sety I's military prowess).

[194] *KRI* 4:15.7; cf. Belegstellen at *WÄS* 4:395.4 (prisoners to king, "grant us the breath which thou canst give so that we may live and recount thy power!").

[195] *Urk.* 4:365.8–9; cf. P. Millingen 3.1: "people sit working for me, and talking about me" *(sḏd im.i;* Helck, *Der Text)*.

[196] P. Anastasi ii.1.1 (Gardiner, *Late Egyptian Miscellanies*).

[197] *KRI* 2:64.

[198] *Urk.* 4:1244.17–18.

[199] *Urk.* 4:101 (Thutmose I to the priest of Abydos).

[200] *Urk.* 4:131.9; sim. 194:17.

mouths of people through the coming years, when they see the monuments I have created."[201] An official whose name is proverbial "abides (*ḏd*) in the mouths of the courtiers!"[202] Since N has been a righteous man, "so let my *bai* live, my spirit be divine, my name be wholly lasting in the mouth of the people."[203] Present fame also involved bruiting about one's reputation: "A son who listens to his father shall be remembered in the mouth of the living who are (now) on earth and those who shall be. . . ."[204] "His Majesty set me at his feet in my youth, and my name was pronounced among my peers."[205]

In a similar vein the fame and mighty acts of the gods often inform the oral discourse of the people: "I have collected thy greatness on display," says Nakhtefmut, "O thou lord of the gods! I relate thine excellence and thy goodness to the common folk."[206] A grateful sailor says "I shall relate thy power to the sovereign and acquaint him with thy greatness!"[207] "Mayest thou (Thoth) permit me to tell of thy victories when <I> am in any land; then the mass of humanity will say 'How great it is, what Thoth has done!'"[208] The penitent says: "Here begins the account (*sḏd*) of the might of Ptah, south-of-his-wall, the informing of men and mankind of the might of the power of this noble god."[209]

As these examples show, relating the might of god to the people *ipso facto* turns the piece of oral creation into a testimonial; and, as we shall see below, the very structure of the penitential psalm resonates with the traits of oral formulaic composition. "I will relate his power to him that sails downstream and upstream: 'Beware ye of him (viz., Amun)!' and I will repeat it to pious(?)

---

[201] *Urk.* 4:131.16–132.2.

[202] *Urk.* 4:1899.11; cf. 1063.3–4, "may your mummy abide in your chapel of the necropolis, [may your name] survive in the mouth of your children for ever!"; *KRI* 7:24.15, "your names shall abide from mouth to mouth"; *HTBM* 8 (1939), pl. 39 (155), "may your name abide from mouth to mouth of all the gods"; cf. Berlin 2293 (*ÄIKM*).

[203] *Urk.* 4:945.2–4; cf. Wreszinski, *Ägyptische Inschriften*, pl. 63 (I, 21, 3–4): "his name is pronounced from time to time and he shall not pass into oblivion, but exist from mouth to mouth without cessation forever!"; sim. Leclant, *Montouemhât*, pl. 6, p. 33.

[204] *ÄL* 41:9–10.

[205] *ÄL* 75:4.

[206] Cairo 42208 (Jansen-Winkeln, *Ägyptische Biographien*); Assmann, "Traumöffenbarung," Text 1, 15–16, p. 33 n. 52.

[207] Shipwrecked Sailor, 139–40 (Blackman, *Middle Egyptian Stories*).

[208] P. Anastasi v.9.8 (Gardiner, *Late Egyptian Miscellanies*).

[209] M. Sandman, *The God Ptah* (Lund: C. W. K. Gleerup, 1946), 51*, no. 263.

men and women, to great and small; I will relate it to generations yet unborn; I will relate it to the fish of the deep and the birds in the heavens; I shall repeat it to him that does not know it and him that does know it."[210] What a man has done or seen may be the subject of oral transmission. (Auto)biographical statements are to be subsumed under this rubric:[211] "Let me tell you the good things I have done!"[212] A man is commonly expected to relate his experiences: "Have they left a single survivor of the army of the northland or a fugitive to escape from them in order to tell about his escapade?"[213] "I tell you what I have seen."[214] "May you talk about your expedition to your wives!"[215] "How happy is he who relates what he has experienced after the painful affair is past! Now let me tell you something similar which happened on this island."[216] "I shall indeed relate what has happened to me and what I have seen!"[217] Such oral transmission often issues in wondertales of far-off places, "heard about from mouth to mouth in the oral tradition of the ancients."[218]

---

[210] A. Erman, "Denksteine aus der thebanischen Gräberstadt," *Sitzungsberichte der Bayerischen Akademie der Wissenschaften* 30 (1911): 1086–110, pl. 16:11ff.; cf. J. Vandier, *Tombes de Deir el-Médineh: La Tombe de Nefer-abou* (Mémoires publiés par les membres de l'Institut français d'archéologie orientale du Caire 69; Cairo: Institut français d'archéologie orientale, 1935), pl. 27:1; HTBM 7 (1934), pl. 29; 9 (1970), pl. 31, col. 3–4; Turin 284 (= R. V. Lanzone, *Dizionario di mitologia egiziana* [Turin: Litografia fratelli Doyen, 1881–86], pl. 27:4–6; Turin 279 (= Lanzone, *Dizionario* III, pl. 340:4); Stewart, *Egyptian Stelae* 1, pl. 40; cf. A. I. Sadek, *Popular Religion in Egypt during the New Kingdom* (Hildesheim: Gerstenberg, 1987), 234–40 (failing, however, to isolate taxonomically the genre of "penitential psalm").

[211] Gnirs, " Die ägyptische Autobiographie," 191–241.

[212] Davies, *Rock Tombs of El-Amarna,* 2 (1904), pl. 8:9; cf. Louvre C 117 (UT); de Meulenaere, "La Stèle Louvre C 117," 77–84, pl. V, 6–7.

[213] Piankhy, 24 (= N.-C. Grimal, *La Stèle triomphale de Pi(ankh)y au musée de Caire* [Cairo: Institut français d'archéologie orientale, 1981], 43).

[214] E. F. Wente, "Egyptian 'Make Merry' Songs Reconsidered," *JNES* 21 (1962): 127; cf. Khakheperrasoneb, recto 6.

[215] *ÄL* 88:23.

[216] Shipwrecked Sailor, 124–25 (Blackman, *Middle Egyptian Stories*).

[217] Ibid., 142–43.

[218] *Urk.* 4:344.10; cf. P. Anastasi i.20.7 (Fischer-Elfert, *Die satirische Streitschrift*), "let me tell you of another mysterious city!"

It is to be expected that aphorisms reside firmly within the realm of oral transmission.[219] "Is this the popular saying (*ḥn n mdt*): only on account of his master is a poor man's name pronounced?"[220] "Have you not heard it said: 'he who speaks in private is telling the truth'?"[221] Emotional outbursts might cause suspicion: "I am speaking truly! There's not a saying that has come forth from my mouth that is exaggerated!"[222] Court jargon is characterized by *bons mots*: "Come north that I may relate to you these sayings (*mdwt*) of friends and courtiers."[223] Happy sayings can dry tears.[224] They also carry an ancestral wisdom: "A son should respond with the phrases (*tsw*) of his father."[225] The defeated Meshwesh say: "We have heard for a long time(?) from the fathers of our fathers: 'she-who-breaks-our-back,' so they called Egypt."[226] However literate the ancestors, their sayings circulate orally: "I have heard what Hordedef and Imhotpe had to say, and how people (still) talk about what they talked about."[227]

Related to aphoristic material is a certain part of that broad didactic genre known as *sbȝyt*, "teaching."[228] The part in question encompasses collections of maxims designed to instruct the young in proper conduct and to shape behavior. When further qualified, the words "attestations" (and derivatives) and the "way of life" are used. Authorship is most often indicated by the pale "what *N* (the

---

[219] On the appropriateness of aphorism to oral delivery, see J. Barnes, "Aphorism and Argument," in *Language and Thought in Early Greek Philosophy* (ed. K. Robb; Monist Library of Philosophy; La Salle, Ill.: Hegeler Institute, 1983), 91–109.

[220] Peasant, B1, 19 (Vogelsang, *Kommentar*).

[221] Černý, *Late Ramesside Letters*, 41:15–16; cf. 67:13–16.

[222] *ÄL* 84:11–12.

[223] W. C. Hayes, "A Much-Copied Letter of the Early Middle Kingdom," *JNES* 7 (1948): 1–10, pl. 2:12.

[224] *ÄL* 80:19.

[225] P. Chester Beatty IV verso 6.8 (or "a son's responses should be in his father's phrases"; it is conceivable that something like "idiolect" is here intended; Gardiner, *Library*).

[226] *KRI* 5:65.1–2.

[227] Budge, *Hieratic Papyri*, pl. 45:6–8.

[228] For the enormous bibliography of this topic see in particular E. Hornung and O. Keel, eds., *Studien zu altägyptischen Lebenslehren* (OBO 28; Freiburg: Universitätsverlag; Göttingen: Vandenhoeck & Ruprecht, 1979); D. Römheld, *Wege der Weisheit: Die Lehren Amenemopes und Proverbien 22,17–24,22* (Berlin: de Gruyter, 1989); Lichtheim, "Didactic Literature."

father) made for" his son;[229] but amplifications of the introduction clearly indicate the oral nature of the delivery. The teaching of a man's father "he will similarly relate (*sḏd*) to his children . . . then they will tell it to their [*sic*] children."[230] Ptahhotpe's wisdom begins with "Here begin the fine phrases which *N* said to . . . ."[231] Amenemhet also "speaks by way of instruction to his children."[232] "How prosperous is he who hears thine instruction!"[233] "Come! Let me relate (*sḏd*) to you the condition of the soldier."[234] "You will realize that the statements I have made you are good. Don't neglect my words!"[235]

Falling broadly within the ambit of (popular) "wisdom" is the fable. The designation *sfḫt (n) mdt*, "narrated (?) fabula," militates strongly in favor of an oral setting and transmission.[236] The imperatives with which the genre is larded ("hear!" and "listen to . . . !" etc.) point unmistakably to a strong tradition of oral composition.[237]

Discourse about vaguely "religious" topics also fell within the repertoire of the raconteur. "Nobody comes (back) from over there (viz., the afterlife) that he might tell us their condition or tell us the state they're in."[238] Prayers were of

[229] Amenemope 1.13 (Budge, *Facsimiles*); Gardiner and Černý, *Hieratic Ostraca* 1, pl. 6,1.1; pl. 41, 1:1–5; Z. Žaba, *Les Maximes de Ptahhotep* (Prague: Éditions de l'Academie tchécoslovaque des sciences, 1956), 1; Luft, "Zur Einleitung der Liebesgedichte," 114; G. Posener, "Les richesses inconnues," 42; idem, "L'Exorde de l'instruction éducative d'Amennakhte," *RdÉ* 10 (1956), pl. 4:1; *ÄL* 68:11; W. Helck, *Die Lehre des Djedefhor und die Lehre eines Vaters an seinen Sohn* (Wiesbaden: Harrassowitz, 1984), 3, 29.

[230] *ÄL* 41:18–20.

[231] *ÄL* 37:6; Z. Žaba, *Les Maximes*, 1.

[232] A. H. Gardiner, "The Tomb of Amenemhet, High-Priest of Amon," *ZÄS* 47 (1910): 87–88; cf. G. Posener, *Catalogue des ostraca hiératiques littéraires de Déir el-Medina* (Cairo: Institut français d'archéologie orientale, 1972), vol. 2, pls. 62a (1248) and 74 (1266).

[233] Davies, *Rock Tombs of El-Amarna*, 6 (1908), pl. 25:16; cf. 4 (1906), pl. 2, 11.

[234] P. Anastasi iii.5.6 (Gardiner, *Late Egyptian Miscellanies*); P. Chester Beatty V recto 6:13 (Gardiner, *Library*); cf. P. Anastasi i.9.4 (of a scribe; Fischer-Elfert, *Die satirische Streitschrift*).

[235] Posener, "L'Exorde."

[236] W. Erichsen, *Demotisches Glossar* (Copenhagen: E. Munksgaard, 1954), 454; cf. *sfȝt*, p. 504; cf. W. Westendorf, *Koptisches Handwörterbuch: Bearbeitet auf Grund des Koptischen Handwörterbuchs von Wilhelm Spiegelberg* (Heidelberg: C. Winter Universitätsverlag, 1977), 339.

[237] E. Brunner-Traut, "Wechselbeziehungen zwischen schriftlicher und mündlicher Über-lieferung im Alten Ägypten," *Fabula* 20 (1979): 41.

[238] Budge, *Hieratic Papyri*, pl. 45.

course intoned, and would be *heard* by gods and deceased;[239] but they might also be passed on "from mouth to mouth."[240] Prophecies too issued (at least initially) in oral form.[241] The magic force of exact wording demanded that the "mysteries" (*sšt3*) be committed to writing; but oral transmission remained a distinct possibility,[242] and was sometimes interdicted.[243]

Other genre terms cover, broadly speaking, the area of entertainment. "Song" (*ḥst*) is a general category including love songs, drinking songs, encomia, etc., in fact anything that it was appropriate to sing to musical accompaniment.[244] Occasionally even magic spells might fall under this rubric, as some were intended to be sung[245] and may also have been treasured for their aesthetic qualities. Lyrics in general might qualify as "choice phrases of entertainment" (*tsw stpw <s>d3y-ḥr*).[246] The "Lament" (*nḥwt*), presumably the type of declamation to which Ipuwer and Khakheperrasoneb belong, may also be a genre term, but this remains controversial.[247]

---

[239] P. Harris 3.3–4 (Grandet, *Papyrus Harris*); cf. *Urk.* 4:509.16–17 (deceased to visitors) "call ye aloud (i.e., the offering formula). Look! With my two ears I can hear anyone who will speak!"

[240] C. E. Sander-Hansen, *Historische Inschriften der 19. Dynastie* (Brussels: Éditions de la Fondation égyptologique Reine Élisabeth, 1933), 27.

[241] Cf. H. S. Smith and W. J. Tait, *Saqqâra Demotic Papyri 1* (London: Egypt Exploration Society, 1983), no. 2, obv., 6/15 "prophetic utterances" (*sḏyw srw*); Barns, *Five Ramesseum Papyri*, pl. 1, A 16 "[. . .] for a period of up to 18 years, according to the snake's utterance." And of course it is a commonplace that Ram-gods speak their predictions: L. Kákosy, "Prophecies of Ram Gods," *Studia Aegyptiaca* 7 (Budapest, 1981): 139–54.

[242] Chassinat, *Le Mystère*, 779: "knowing the mystery without seeing or hearing (i.e., without text): (it is) what a father gave to his son."

[243] Merikare P vi.7–8 (W. Helck, *Die Lehre für König Merikare* [Wiesbaden: Harrassowitz, 1977]): "A man should do what is good for his *bai*: viz., monthly service as a priest, wearing white sandals, supporting the temple, *concealing the mysteries*, frequenting the shrine, eating bread in the temple."

[244] *WÄS* 3:165.2; M. V. Fox, *The Song of Songs and Ancient Egyptian Love Songs* (Madison: University of Wisconsin Press, 1985), 16.

[245] Ibid., 35.

[246] Neferty 7–8, 13–14 (Helck, *Prophezeihung*); Gardiner and Černý, *Hieratic Ostraca*, pl. 39, 1 recto, 1; P. Chester Beatty I, pl. 16.9 (Gardiner, *Library*).

[247] *WÄS* 2:305.17; Grapow, *Sprachliche und schriftliche Formung*, 60 n. 29; contrast H. Goedicke, *The Report about the Dispute of a Man with His Ba: Papyrus Berlin 3024* (Baltimore: Johns Hopkins Press, 1970), 183, 210 n. 307.

Narrative

Not all the genres that might be listed under *sḏꜣyt-ḥr* find a label-term in the surviving sources; but consistent characteristics based on form or content help to separate out various types. One clear category, attested during the second millennium B.C.E., might be characterized as "tales of droll." This category encorporates elements of Propp's "wondertale," but also the atmosphere of trickster-tales.[248] In fact it is the trick or magic act that often provides the sole focus of interest and usually prompts mild mirth. Always clearly pinpointed in time with no aversion to proper names, this type tells of magicians ingeniously entertaining a bored sovereign or cleverly exacting revenge; or of weak Till Eulenspiegels worsting the strong in a battle of wits.[249] They are set in the past and are often dated to a specific reign. A second story type is more closely akin to the true *Märchen*. Its plot is not tied to a specific time or place, and is therefore largely devoid of toponyms or personal names, preferring terms of relationship: father, son, older brother, younger brother, wife, sister, etc.[250] A third sub-genre could be dubbed "mythological stories." Like the approximant wondertales alluded to above, they abound in personal names and toponyms, but in all cases the setting and *dramatis personae* belong to the realm of the gods.[251] In some clear cases an iconotropic intent underlies a

[248] V. Propp, *Theory and History of Folklore* (Minneapolis: University of Minnesota Press, 1984), 67–123.

[249] Examples are to be found in the Westcar Papyrus, Neferkare and the General (see R. B. Parkinson, "Teachings, Discourses, and Tales"; idem, *Voices from Ancient Egypt*); Apophis and Sekenenre (H. Goedicke, *The Quarrel of Apophis and Seqnenre* [San Antonio, Tex.: Van Siclen, 1986]); The Taking of Joppa (Gardiner, *Late Egyptian Stories*, 82–85); The Turin Fragment (Thutmose III: G. Botti, "A Fragment of a Story of a Military Expedition of Tuthmosis III to Syria," *JEA* 41 [1955]: 64–71). Many of the tales hinted at in the Epitome of Manetho belong in this genre also: e.g., the Tale of King Hor (Redford, *Pharaonic King-lists*, 248–51).

[250] Cf. Shipwrecked Sailor (J. Baines, "Interpreting the Story of the Shipwrecked Sailor," *JEA* 76 [1990]: 55–72; Parkinson, "Teachings, Discourses and Tales," 115); the Herdsman (ibid., 116); the Doomed Prince (W. Helck, "Die Erzählung vom Verwunschenen Prinzen," in *Form und Mass: Beitrage zur Literatur, Sprache und Kunst Ägypten: Festschrift für Gerhard Fecht zum 65. Geburtstag* [ed. J. Osing and G. Dreyers; Ägypten und Altes Testament 12; Wisebaden: Harrassowitz, 1987], 218–25); The Two Brothers (Introductory Episode; S. T. Hollis, *The Ancient Egyptian 'Tale of Two Brothers': The Oldest Fairytale in the World* [Norman: University of Oklahoma Press, 1990]). For the characteristics of the class, see D. B. Redford, *A Study of the Biblical Joseph Story, Genesis 37–50* (Leiden: Brill, 1970), passim.

[251] Cf. Contendings of Horus and Seth (M. Broze, *Mythe et roman en Égypte ancienne: Les aventures d'Horus et Seth dans le Papyrus Chester Beatty I* [OLA 76; Louvain: Peeters, 1996]),

tale, in whole or in part;[252] and in many the magical efficacy of a protagonist's role provides the basic motivation for the narration.[253] In fact, in some cases it may have been solely the prospect of magical potency that prompted the creation of such pieces in their entirety. Some exemplars of this subgenre represent derivations from non-Egyptian mythology, whether loosely inspired native compositions or paraphrase-translations of Canaanite originals.[254]

It should be noted with respect to narrative that genre-diglossia, seen in the distinction between Middle Kingdom "classical" creations and New Kingdom "modernist" works, is largely illusory. The former constitute conscious creations by literati, undoubtedly for oral performance but nonetheless enjoying parallel existence in written form, under the aegis of the state regime. They survived, not because of any inherent excellence (although that was a later perception), but because a *later* regime fancied itself to be the "heir to the promises" of that earlier power bloc and wished to revive and prolong its cultural manifestations. Late Egyptian written "narrative" simply does not exist. It is the sporadic reflection of a vibrant oral tradition that had generic roots in the Middle Kingdom and that survived into the classical world and beyond.

Beginning in the Late Period,[255] a *topos* evolves out of the wondertale, largely dispenses with "droll," and becomes cynical and serious. It is a true

---

Seth and Apophis (Book of the Dead, ch. 39; E. Dondelinger, *Papyrus Ani: BM 10.470* [Graz: Akademische Druk- und Verlagsanstalt, 1979]); King Osiris and his Vizier Khentiamentiu (P. Chester Beatty V verso 1.1–2; Gardiner, *Library*).

[252] For example, the Book of the Cow of Heaven (E. Hornung, *Der ägyptische Mythos von der Himmelskuh: Eine Ätiologie des Unvollkommenen* (OBO 46; Freiburg: Universitätsverlag; Göttingen: Vandenhoeck & Ruprecht, 1982); the Myth of Anhur (F. de Cenival, *Le Mythe de l'oeil du soleil* [Sommerhausen: G. Zauzich, 1988]); Isis and the Name of Re (W. Pleyte and F. Rossi, *Papyrus de Turin* [Museo egizio di Torino; Wiesbaden: LTR-Verlag, 1981], pl. 131–33; P. Chester Beatty XI [Gardiner, *Library*]).

[253] This is especially true of the cycle of tales surrounding the birth and childhood of Horus; see A. Klasens, *A Magical Statue Base (Socle Behague) in the Museum of Antiquities at Leiden* (Leiden: Brill, 1952); Vandier, *Papyrus Jumilhac*; A. Massart, "The Egyptian Geneva Papyrus MAH 15274," *MDAI* 15 (1957): 172–85; CoffT 2, sp. 157 and passim. This list could easily be extended.

[254] Cf. Astarte and Yam (Gardiner, *Late Egyptian Stories*, 76–81; W. Helck, "Zur Herkunft der Erzählung des sog. 'Astartepapyrus,'" in *Fontes atque pontes: Eine Festgabe für Hellmut Brunner* [ed. M. Görg; Wiesbaden: Harrassowitz, 1983], 215–23); Seth and Astarte (A. Roccati, "Une Légende égyptienne d'Anat," *RdÉ* 24 [1972]: 152–59).

[255] The exact point in time and the attendant circumstances can only be guessed at; but the Herodotan folktales abundantly attest the presence of the *topos* no later than the mid-seventh century B.C.E. It may well prove correct that it was the perceived denigration of kingship as an institution, pursuant to the assumption of power by Libyan pharaohs with their proverbial "rages," that established a climate within which these tales flourished.

Volksmärchen, as it originates not at the level of the royal court entertainment but from below at the level of the street, whence the organs of power can be viewed only at a distance. The hero is a popular person, often a magician of low status and no longer necessarily enjoying royal patronage, who saves the day and rescues community or nation. His tricks may still astound the audience, but more shocking is the transformation of the royal persona. For the king now fulfils the role, not of an exalted and passive arbitor and guarantor of *ma'at,* but of a mere foil, and often a disreputable one, for the furtherance of the plot. He can be a miser,[256] an impious blasphemer,[257] a deceiver,[258] a naive medler,[259] or a helpless figurehead.[260] The king's lack of moral integrity serves only to enhance the figure of the "savior," the unknown magician, the mystical adept, the inspired wise man, above reproach and in touch directly with the Almighty.

The Setting of Oral Delivery

Apart from the vague, though nonetheless real, ambiance of the father-son chat which *s b3yt* invokes, there are other formal occasions in which oral delivery provides the focus. Perhaps, from the view of the ancients, the king's speech takes priority. A living being who could cause the mountains to disgorge their mineral wealth and by whose utterance a mountainous "horizon" could rise where none had before existed must in his very essence dispose of the power of the *logos.*[261]

What the king proclaimed by spoken word had a binding force, which made its inscripturation obligatory. Already we find in the Old Kingdom an epithet applied to chancery scribes that indicates their function as transcribers

---

[256] Cf. Rhampsinitus (Herodotus, *Historiae* 2.121).

[257] Cf. Pheron and Sethos (Herodotus, *Historiae* 2.112, 141).

[258] King Si-Sobek (G. Posener, *Le Papyrus Vandier* [Cairo: Institut français d'archéologie orientale, 1985]).

[259] The king in Onchsheshonqy (Glanville, *Catalogue of Demotic Papyri).*

[260] Cf. the Joseph Story, esp. Genesis 41, 46. Although too fragmentary for confident reconstruction, the Demotic tales from Saqqara seem to portray a helpless Pharaoh, caught up in events he cannot control (Smith and Tait, *Saqqâra Demotic Papyri I*); the kings of the Setna-cycle clearly fit this role (Griffith, *Stories*).

[261] *Ḥw* (*WÄS* 3:44.7–10); K. Sethe, *Dramatische Texte zu altägyptischen Mysterienspielen* (Leipzig: Hinrichs, 1928), 62–63; J. P. Allen, *Genesis in Egypt: The Philosophy of Ancient Egyptian Creation Accounts* (New Haven: Yale Egyptological Seminar, Deptartment of Near Eastern Languages and Civilizations, Graduate School, Yale University, 1988), 38; *Urk.* 1:108.10, 109.11; PT 153, 253.

of the *ipsissima verba* of the king, namely, (*n*) *ḫft-ḥr* 'of the presence.'²⁶²
Occasions of royal speeches, historically derived from the genre of biographical
statements,²⁶³ are termed "royal seances" (*ḥmst-nsw*)²⁶⁴ in the New Kingdom,
and involve a formal assembly addressed by Pharaoh. "His [*sic*] Majesty had
brought in the king's nobility, the dignitaries, the courtiers, the leaders of the
commons, to lay a command upon them . . . then occurred a sitting of the king
himself in the western hall of the palace, while these people were upon their
bellies . . . ."²⁶⁵ Also indicative of a *ḥmst-nsw* is the formula (with variants) "the
king himself speaks," glossing reliefs or a formal text.²⁶⁶ The prima facie
probability is that in all cases in which words are pointedly ascribed to the king
the alleged authorship must be taken seriously. There exists, after all, plenty of
evidence concerning the king's own writing ability,²⁶⁷ as well as scenes
showing scribes taking down his speeches and more casual *obiter dicta*.²⁶⁸
Close analysis of this style of royal inscription, where sufficient exemplars are
preserved from a particular reign, do indeed betray what may plausibly be taken
as evidence of individual idiolect.

   The king's court is the probable setting, and the king's presence the
justification, of another type of oral composition, namely, the royal panegyric
and derived forms. Though textual preservation is rather spotty—what evidence
is there for belletristics at the Old Kingdom court?—enough survives to discern

---

²⁶² W. Helck, *Untersuchungen zu den Beamtentiteln des ägyptischen Alten Reiches*
(Glückstadt : J. J. Augustin, 1954), 72; N. Strudwick, *The Administration of Egypt in the Old
Kingdom: The Highest Titles and Their Holders* (London: KPI, 1985), 211–13.123.

²⁶³ Redford, *Pharaonic King-lists*, 148–49.

²⁶⁴ *WÄS* 3:98.23; E. Blumenthal, "Die Koptosstele des Königs Rahotep (London U.C. 14327)"
in *Ägypten und Kusch: Fritz Hintze zum 60. Geburtstag* (ed. E. Endesfelder et al.; Berlin:
Akademie-Verlag, 1977), 75; Redford, *Pharaonic King-lists*, 149 n. 95.

²⁶⁵ *Urk.* 4:256.9–257.1; similarly *Urk.* 4:288, 349, 1252.12, 1380.11.

²⁶⁶ *Urk.* 4:257.5, 364.10, 2139.9–12, 2143.8–11.

²⁶⁷ *Urk.* 1:60.9–11 ("[His Majesty] himself wrote with his own fingers"); *Urk.* 4:166.10
("the king himself made it [the stela text] with his own hands"); 833.15–16 ("the king
himself commanded it, he put it in writing"); 1343 ("copy of the stela which his majesty
made with his own hands"). On royal literacy see the remarkable statement made about
Horemheb: "He is more knowledgable in arithmetic (*ḥsb*) than the master of writing (Thoth),
he is more skilled than the lord of Hermopolis (Thoth); he has recorded the captures of every
man by name, whether of the swordsmen, battalions, or marines" (*LDÄÄ* 3: pl. 120b). Cf.
also Apophis (Helck, *Historisch-biographische Texte*, 57); cf. in general Redford, *Pharaonic
King-lists*, 166–67.

²⁶⁸ Davies, *Rock Tombs of El-Amarna*, 1 (1903), pl. 8; 6 (1908), pls. 20, 29; *Urk.*
4:2125.11–14.

a *Sitz im Leben*. The king's person and actions at a given moment could provide the reason for an extemporized lyric by a high court official, sung out in the king's presence.[269] The intoning of hymns at times of arrival, departure, and morning toilet, and the adulation of the court as a "spontaneous" response to a speech, adopted formal characteristics but nonetheless arose within the oral atmosphere of courtly communication.[270] The artificial response of god to king derives from this setting.[271] One genre that betrays the type of "brittle" and artificial creation that a self-conscious court etiquette can produce is the "song-stela" (often called "rhetorical"). This may prove to be a later evolutionary stage in the development of court poetry, derived from the earlier harpers' songs and the genre known as the "collection of mighty deeds."[272] (While the former conjures up the ambiance of extemporized lyric at a banquet or other special occasion, sung to the accompaniment of the harp,[273] the latter seems related to prose composition lacking an early oral stage.)[274] The song-stela, as it appears in the Nineteenth and Twentieth Dynasties, is composed of strophes of

---

[269] Such seems to follow from the role played by Sehtepibre-onkh on the court excursion of Amenemhet II; see R. A. Caminos, *Literary Fragments in the Hieratic Script* (London: Griffith Institute at the University Press, 1956), pl. 8–16; cf. also A. Erman, *Hymnen an das Diadem des Pharaonen* (Berlin: Preussische Akademie der Wissenschaften, 1911).

[270] Cf. the hymn on the homecoming of Senwosret III (*ÄL* 65–67[12]); the charming piece of extemporized lyric by the royal family at the arrival of Sinuhe (R. Koch, *Erzählung des Sinuhe*, 76:13–79:3). Court responses are frequently encountered and become virtually a literary topos: *Urk.* 4:141.1–4, 838.6, 1242.15 (spontaneous rejoicing of the crowd); *Urk.* 4:165.7–166.5 (courtiers' compliments on the king's speech); *Urk.* 4:259–60 (wild rejoicing at the promotion of Hatshepsut; *Urk.* 4:354.7, 1241.10–19, 1345.12–13; *KRI* 2:329.3–331.2 (*tpt-r3*), 355–60 (formal response of the court); *Urk.* 4:1386 (court formally excuses itself); 1783.6–15 (paeon by individual courtier); *KRI* 1:10.5ff. (court greeting on a king's return).

[271] *Urk.* 4:1655–57, 1674–77, etc.

[272] E. Edel, "Bemerkungen zu den Schießsporttexten der Könige der 18. Dynastie," *SAK* 7 (1979): 23–40; W. Decker, "Das sogenannte Agonale und der altägyptische Sport," in *Festschrift Elmar Edel* (ed. M. Görg and E. Pusch; Bamberg: M. Görg, 1979), 90–104; idem, *Quellentexte zu Sport und Korperkultur im alten Ägypten* (St. Augustin: Richarz, 1975), texts 14, 15, 17; idem, *Sports and Games of Ancient Egypt* (trans. A. Guttmann; New Haven: Yale University Press, 1987), 36–59.

[273] The scene in a mortuary context is widespread and well-known; see, among other sources, Blackman, *Rock Tombs,* vol. 1, pl. 2–3; vol. 4, pl. 9–10; Peet, *Cemeteries of Abydos* III, pl. 23:5; W. Ward, "Neferhotep and his Friends," *JEA* 63 (1977): pl. 9. See L. Manniche, *Music and Musicians in Ancient Egypt* (London: British Museum Press, 1991), 24–35.

[274] On the other hand, a certain "chatty" conversational style is to be noted: "I speak accurately of what he did . . ." (*Urk.* 4:1245.9); "now after these things I have just told you about . . ." (*Urk.* 4:1280.11).

widely varying lengths, each ending in the "Great Name" (the double cartouche) of the king. An example from the reign of Merenptah describes it as a song, probably to be sung to harp accompaniment.[275] Singers and musicians regularly attended upon the royal court.[276]

Royal or private prayers and supplications recall a temple setting, and are to be spoken. "I speak blessed supplications, hymns, and earnest prayers . . . ,"[277] says Ramesses III.[278] "Come to me, O Preharakhte!" says the devotee, "hear my prayers and my daily supplications and my nighttime hymns!"[279] "O thou that hearest prayer, hear the supplication of him that calls to thee!"[280] Penitential prayers generally mention temple courts[281] and an audience of multitudes. It is unclear whether royal encomia and god's response have roots in oral practice.

The social setting in which stories were narrated can be elicited partly from context. The court, royal or provincial, is specifically indicated in some pieces, and the purpose is said to be the diversion of the royal or aristocratic occupant. "Then Bauefre (son of Khufu) got up to speak (as participating entertainer before his father), and he said: 'I shall let [your] majesty hear of a marvel that occurred in the time of your father Snofru.'"[282] The audience craves "one who can say . . . good words and choice phrases diverting . . . to listen to."[283] A scribe may "direct his speech towards what has happened and make it public for men."[284] The speaker may model his tale so as to admonish an audience on a casual occasion: "Let me relate (*sḏd*) to you something similar that happened to

---

[275] G. Roeder, "Zwei hieroglyphische Inschriften aus Hermopolis (Oberägypten)" *ASAÉ* (1954): 315–442, pl. 3–4.

[276] Cf. G. Posener, "Le Conte de Néferkarê et du général Siséné (Recherches Littéraires 6)" *RdÉ* 11 (1957): 119–37, esp. 126; Barns, *Five Ramesseum Papyri*, pl. I; Manniche, *Music and Musicians*, ch. 6.

[277] *Snsw*, which can also mean a hymn of adoration (G. Vittmann, "Die Hymne des Ostrakons Wein 6155 und Kairo CG 25214," *Wiener Zeitschrift für die Kunde des Morgenlandes* [1980]: pl. 1 line 1).

[278] P. Harris 2.24, 57.1; cf. 1.3 (Grandet, *Papyrus Harris*).

[279] P. Anastasi ii.10.4 (Gardiner, *Late Egyptian Miscellanies*).

[280] Erman, "Denksteine," 1105–7.

[281] Ibid., pl. 16, lines 7–8; B. Bruyère, *Mert seger à Deir el-Médine* (Cairo: Institut français d'archéologie orientale, 1929–30), 25 fig. 16.

[282] P. Westcar (*ÄL* 26:3–5).

[283] Neferty 7 (Helck, *Prophezeihung*, 7).

[284] Barns, *Five Ramesseum Papyri*, pl. 1:17.

me too."[285] A social setting for storytelling may be alluded to in a passage from Ipuwer, but the rendering is difficult. "Lady musicians (once) in chambers, are (now) in weaving mills. . . . Storytellers [(once) in . . .] are (now) at the grindstones."[286] If correctly understood, the passage would link storytelling with singing as courtly entertainment. It has even been suggested that particularly gifted raconteurs functioned in this profession for remuneration.

Little can be deduced on the basis of direct indication from the written copies of Egyptian *Märchen* to prove the existence of an oral stage of transmission—or to reveal the social setting—lying at the roots of these creations. Numerous colophons in fact refer to written *Vorlagen*, so that oral composition, if posited, must be set at several removes. Yet some pieces indirectly imply the setting in which their telling would have been appropriate. The final lines of the Two Brothers require Bata, now king, to recapitulate the entire tale to the court to set them straight on what had brought events to this pass.[287] The Contendings of Horus and Seth resolves itself into declamations to an assembled court in which, partly by narrating events, arguments are presented. Similarly the extensive speeches in the Eloquent Peasant in fact constitute on one plane the "case for the plaintiff" presented before the magistrates orally, and later with the "frame-story" (in writing) before the king in a court setting.[288] Again, the king and his entourage provide the setting in which the ecstatic potter utters his (prophetic) narrative,[289] while Si-osir narrated his account of events before Pharaoh, nobles, and commons.[290] While this evidence points to the concourse of elite circles, fables are among the things to be repeated "in the street."[291]

---

[285] Shipwrecked Sailor 21–22; cf. 142–43 (Blackman, *Middle Egyptian Stories*); sim. perhaps P. Berlin 3024.67ff. (*HPKM*): "Listen to me, look, listening is good for people" as introduction to an embedded narrative in a debate.

[286] Ipuwer 4:12–13. Helck's restoration [ṯsw], i.e., "those who narrate [phrases]," (*Die 'Admonitions' Pap. Leiden I, 344 recto* [Wiesbaden: Harrassowitz, 1995], 20) is not only anomalous but also unlikely; the contrast lies in the identity of the establishments in which these entertainers *once* plied their trade.

[287] P. d'Orbiney 19.4 (Gardiner, *Late Egyptian Stories*).

[288] R. B. Parkinson, *The Tale of the Eloquent Peasant* (Oxford: Griffith Institute, Ashmolean Museum, 1991).

[289] L. Koenen, "Prophezeiungen des 'Topfers,'" *ZPE* 2 (1968): 178–209.

[290] Griffith, *Stories* 2:5, 24–25.

[291] W. Spiegelberg, *Demotische Texte auf Krügen* (Leipzig: Hinrichs, 1912), 16–17.

The Author

In many preserved examples of oral discourse, interestingly enough mostly in instructional (wisdom) literature,[292] the identity of the speaker is clearly indicated, whether historical or not. The source of the *bon mot* excites interest, and its reputed author is held in awe. This was true whether the individual in question is king, wise man, or commoner.[293] When the author's identity was unclear or a piece was clearly anonymous, it could always become pseudepigraphic and be ascribed to an illustrious celebrity of the remote past or to "the ancestors," "those who lived long ago."[294] But a formal identification of these worthies *as authors* nowhere appears. In the famous pictorial list of ancestors from the Ramesside period ("Daressy" fragment)[295] the individuals are remembered as bygone celebrities, and their titles—vizier, high-priest of Ptah, king's-scribe, embalming master—do not include anything noting their creative accomplishments. Authorship per se never crystallized as an independent function to be celebrated in isolation.

An accomplished speaker[296] rising to the standard of a persuasive orator fills the texts that have survived, and clearly fulfilled a prominent societal role. Wholly committed to language, the orator abjures doctrine and evidence in favor of spectacle.[297] In contrast to the mere writer, his art reaches a metaphrastic height of persuasion that sets him apart from other literati.[298] Wisdom texts stress the premium placed on skilled oratory: "Become a craftsman in speech," counsels Merikare's father, "that you may be strong. The sword of the king is his tongue, (for) speech is more powerful than any

---

[292] Foster, "Literature"; Parkinson, "Teachings, Discourses, and Tales," 96.

[293] Cf. Parkinson, *Eloquent Peasant*, 72.

[294] *Urk.* 4:344.10 (wondrous tales of distant lands); Merikare 34–35 ("Maat comes to him 'strained,' in the manner of speaking of the ancients"; Helck, *Die Lehre für König Merikare*); *ÄL* 36:21–37:1 ("So I shall tell him the speech of those who listen, the style of those who were aforetime, who of old listened to the gods"); *Esna* 2:123 (". . . the scroll of the gods and what the ancestors said").

[295] D. Wildung, *Sesostris und Amenemhet: Ägypten im Mittleren Reich* (Munich: Hirmer, 1984), 14 fig. 4.

[296] *Mdw.ty* (*WÄS* 2:182.6); cf. Redford, "Ancient Egyptian Literature," 2223–24.

[297] He therefore roughly approximates Barthes's *author* in contrast to the *writer* (R. Barthes, *Critical Essays* [trans. R. Howard; Evanston, Ill.: Northwestern University Press, 1981], 145–46).

[298] Cf. P. de Man, *Resistence to Theory* (Minneapolis: University of Minnesota Press, 1986), 15.

weapon."[299] Skill in speech outweighs the martial arts: "Speech never 'bails out' before weaponry. There is no mighty man who comes up in [. . .], and he who is conversant with speech is privy to the (judicial) hearing. There is no *qmȝ*-soldier with whom people take counsel! Get facility in speech—there's no pain in that!"[300] Since all speech acts in the Egyptian speaker's repertoire, even those within the realm of entertainment, were perlocutionary in nature,[301] the speaker frequently found himself within the eye of controversy. A good speaker was a rabble-rouser and therefore a threat: "The (professional) speaker is the scum of the city!" rages one self-consciously apprehensive king, "Put him down! Slay his children, wipe out his name! He is a disturber of the city!"[302] "Drastic measures will be used," Neferty predicts, "in order to silence the mouth that speaks: a phrase is answered by the blow of a stick, and one speaks (in return[?]) with 'Slay him!'. . . a verbal statement is like fire in the heart. People have no patience with the utterance of the mouth."[303] If violence was somehow precluded, the resultant frustration could issue in derision: "'Informer' is what they call a wiseman, 'Chatterer' is what they call an orator."[304] *Mdw,* "to speak" often bears the overtones of a wrangle. "Do not keep silent when you answer an argument heatedly."[305]

But a speaker could exercise his talent with compassion and sensitivity. He might become a "speaker (i.e., spokesman) for every neglected one."[306] "I am one . . . who knows the (appropriate) word for the frustrating situation . . . who silences weeping with a happy saying. . . . I am a good person, not irascible, who does not seize a man for saying something. . . . I am one who speaks honestly in any office, [an] incisive speaker in situations of meanness."[307]

---

[299] Helck, *Die Lehre,* 17; P. Derchain, "Éloquence et politique. L'Opinion d'Akhtoy," *RdÉ* 40 (1989): 37–47.

[300] Helck, *Lehre des Djedefhor,* 32–34.

[301] T. Eagleton, *Literary Theory: An Introduction* (Minneapolis: University of Minnesota Press, 1996), 102–3.

[302] Helck, *Lehre für König Merikare,* 10.

[303] Helck, *Prophezeihung,* 39, 42; similarly "words are like fire, they ignite useless(?) debate"; idem, *Lehre des Djedefhor,* 62.

[304] Barns, *Five Ramesseum Papyri,* pl. 9, verso ii.4.

[305] P. Devaud, *Ptahhotep,* 37:376; cf. the idiom *mdw m,* "to speak against, criticize, verbally abuse" (*WÄS* 2:179.17).

[306] *Urk.* 4:2090.7.

[307] *ÄL* 80–81; D. M. Doxey, *Egyptian Non-royal Epithets in the Middle Kingdom* (Leiden: Brill, 1998), 56.

In most *Märchen* and adventure tales it is an E(xternal) N(arrator) that tells the story.[308] He is at most the implied author; his relationship to the material attached to his name is fictive. The oral nature of folklore, and its durability in contrast to a written creation, automatically commit the author to oblivion.[309] This is true even in heavily embedded texts,[310] such as Shipwrecked Sailor, Prophecies of Neferty, King Si-Sobek, Eloquent Peasant, or Khamois, or in cases in which frame narratives encase a much different genre. "Wisdom texts" frequently favored an EN to establish the setting within a frame story in which the body of the embedded text could be delivered by a protagonist named within the frame.[311] In autobiographical creations, real or imagined, the narrator must be identified—the genre demands it—though he is not necessarily "character-bound" (except perhaps in fictitious biographies).

Much of what Egyptians meant by "fine speech" is to be viewed against the backdrop of the moot, the council discussion, or the parley; the speaker in fact becomes consultant and debater. "Fine speech" anticipated by centuries the liberalizing tendencies of Greek rhetoric.[312] The key word in this regard is *ndt-r3* (and derivatives),[313] meaning "to ask (or give) advice, counsel; to consult." One strove to be an "able counselor,"[314] "one with whose counsel people are

---

[308] M. Bal, *Narratology: Introduction to the Theory of Narration* (trans. C. van Boheemen; Toronto: University of Toronto Press 1985), 122–23.

[309] Cf. J. Assmann, "Schriftliche Folklore: Zur Entstehung und Funktion eines Überlieferungstyps," in *Schrift und Gedächtnis* (ed. A. Assmann, J. Assmann, and C. Hardemeir; Beiträge zur Archäologie der literarischen Kommunikation 1; Munich: W. Fink, 1983), 175–93, esp. 180.

[310] Ibid., 142–43; Quirke, "Narrative Literature," *AELHF*, 268–70.

[311] In the case of pre-New Kingdom Wisdom, e.g. Ptahhotpe, Hordedef, and Kagemni in particular (but not Merikare or Amenemhet), the attribution of material to ideal figures of remote antiquity must be false; and to that extent these specimens of *sb3yt* must be classified as pseudepigraphic. Cf. J. H. Charlesworth, *The Old Testament Pseudepigrapha* (2 vols.; Garden City, N.Y.: Doubleday, 1983–1985), 1:xxv.

[312] G. Kennedy, *The Art of Persuasion in Greece* (Princeton: Princeton University Press), 23. In terms of Eagleton's idyllic society "before the Fall," belletrics as part of the libidinal-aesthetic were still intertwined with the cognitive and ethico-political (T. Eagleton, *The Ideology of the Aesthetic* [Oxford: Blackwell, 1990], 366).

[313] *WÄS* 2:371.22–372.6.

[314] *Iqr ndt-r3*: BM 572; cf. *Urk.* 4:127.15 ("polished speaker, able counselor"); T. Säve-Söderbergh, "The Paintings in the Tomb of Djehuty-hetep at Debeira," *Kush* 8 (1960): 24–44, fig. 1; Doxey, *Egyptian Non-royal Epithets*, 53–54.

content,"[315] "counseling with statement(s) of goodness."[316] Counsel was closely tied to administration: "one true of counsel, who enforces the laws of Him-that-is-in-the-palace."[317] This type of discourse had graduated to an art form for which strategies designed to facilitate success had been devised.[318]

Audience Reception

It is not always easy to identify the audience in any Egyptian narrative creation that has come down to us in writing. Within the fictionality of frame narratives, an audience will sometimes be indicated: a man's children, the king and his court, the courtiers, an individual commander, and so forth. In the so-called autobiographical narrative the speaker envisages a much broader audience; in narratives arising within the context of magic spells even the local female population of the lowest rank can be targeted. The New Kingdom penitential psalms are addressed to illiterate workers as well as the animal population. In entertainment narrative the *dramatis personae* as well as the setting incorporate every social level, making it rather difficult to concur with the conclusion that such narrative was *written* in its original form *by* an elite and *for* an elite.

Within the realm of information transfer and/or dissemination,[319] oral composition had to ensure reception. The criteria marking the "reader-canon," in the sense of those pieces which spontaneously capture the audience's imagination,[320] could not be ignored by the speaker-performer. Both information giver (= speaker) and information receiver (= audient populace/ interpretive community) were locked into a limited but dominant series of genre expectations, deviation from which might excite suspicion or a perception of

---

[315] Cairo 42185 (Jansen-Winkeln, *Ägyptische Biographien*).

[316] P. Turin 154 (UT).

[317] Cairo 583 (UT).

[318] See further below.

[319] J. H. Shea and D. B. Cleveland, "History and Foundations of Information Science," *Annual Review of Information Science and Technology* 12 (1977): 249–75.

[320] Cf. G. Steiner, "Critic/Reader," *New Literary History* 10 (1979): 423–52, esp. 445–47. If the term *canon* is to be used at all in Egyptology, it can only be as a "phenomenon of reception," a literary corpus of great works decided upon by the interpretive community (N. Veldhuis, "Tin.tir = Babylon, the Question of Canonization and the Production of Meaning," *JCS* 50 [1998]: 77–85).

incompetence or disfavor.[321] Historical narration might involve a certain "midrashic" evaluation,[322] but such commentary remained narrowly fixed within tight parameters.[323] Only an undisputed success, such as for example a Thutmose III or an Amenophis III, could permit himself the luxury of tampering with or modifying these expectations and the formulaic verbiage in which they were couched.

The intellectual and aesthetic creations of oral culture require rules of analysis different from those applicable to literature and belletristics.[324] Central to the mechanisms of oral creation and transmission is memory activation, or *aide-mémoire*. The exercise is not intended to promote memorization per se but, since the message must be transmitted within an illiterate society, to ensure the adoption of an oral mechanism optimal to its successful dissemination. Since the average size of a language unit accessible for processing by a listener comprises six words, and never exceeds ten, overall *placement* of words takes on absolute priority in importance, both in oral formulation and transmission.[325] The words themselves do not constitute the meaningful acoustical chunks of data to be processed and transmitted, and purely lexical analysis yields only limited results.[326] An auditor builds up a "mental thesaurus" of oral formulae,

---

[321] Each audience was socially conditioned and their reception historically fixed and uncompromising (R. M. Fowler, "Who is the 'Reader' in Reader Response Criticism?" *Semeia* 31 (1985): 5–23, esp. 14; Eagleton, *Literary Theory*, 72–73). Cf. the self-conscious attention to the interplay between orator, host, and critical audience in the *Odyssey* (L. E. Doherty, "The Internal and Implied Audience of *Odyssey* 11," *Arethusa* 24 [1991]: 145–76; B. Louden, "Eumaios and Alkinoos: The Audience and the *Odyssey*," *Phoenix* 51 [1997]: 95–114). This would seem to constitute a disincentive to the introduction of the personal into oral communication (cf. B. Allen, "The Personal Point of View in Orally Communicated History," *Western Folklore* 38 [1979]: 110–18).

[322] A. Burns, "Spoken History in an Oral Community," *International Journal of Oral History* 9 (1988): 99–113; cf. J. Cruikshank, "Myth and Tradition as Narrative Framework: Oral Histories from Northern Canada," *International Journal of Oral History* 9 (1988): 198–214.

[323] Redford, *Pharaonic King-lists*, 259–75.

[324] M. Nasta, "Principes d'analyse d'une versification orale," *Les Études classiques* 62 (1994): 101–29; 63 (1995): 197–224.

[325] Z. Zevit, "Cognitive Theory and Memorability in Biblical Poetry," *Ma'ariv* 8 (1992): 202–3. Cf. the common use of subject-fronting in Egyptian narration to maintain topic continuity (G. Brown and G. Yule, *Discourse Analysis* [Cambridge and New York: Cambridge University Press, 1983], 134–38).

[326] Several works unwittingly highlight the limitations of this sort of analysis: cf. A. J. Spalinger, *Aspects of the Military Documents of the Ancient Egyptians* (New Haven: Yale

not words; and, to be easily recalled, the contents of this thesaurus must be immediately satisfying to the *Id*'s appetite for synesthetic rhythm. And as soon as rhythm is introduced into the equation, the oral formulation becomes ipso facto quantifiable metrically. In short, oral formulaic discourse constitutes the metric framework within which the hegemonic message is delivered.[327] Under these conditions oral delivery could easily expand into lengthy orations.[328]

At one level in the interplay between speaker and audience the former has a distinct and immediate advantage. The speaker—his royal or common origin is immaterial in this regard—automatically occupies the prestigious role of authority; his discourse has the advantage of being hegemonic.[329] And at one level no distinction is to be made between a discourse that is fictional and one that is factual. Pharaoh's audience and a street-corner orator's audience share this in common, namely, that whatever the speaker says must be regarded as corresponding to reality.[330] This does not mean that skepticism does not influence the degree of the audience's receptivity, but it does so only to the degree that persuasion and aesthetic quality are lacking. Aesthetics here encompass both plausibility and outstanding oratory. Preposterous and incredible tales, produced anonymously rather than by a named authority, constitute the "*sdd* of the people," to be treated with contempt and disbelief.[331]

A speaker takes pains constantly to assure his listeners that he is not exaggerating. "I speak truly of what he did!" protests the narrator of Thutmose III's fantastic exploits, "there is no falsification nor distortion—after all, it was in the presence of his entire army!—there is not a phrase of exaggeration

---

University Press, 1982), passim; B. Cifola, "The Terminology of Ramses III's Historical Records with a Formal Analysis of the War Scenes," *Or* 60 (1991): 9–57.

[327] Metre is a "transparent signifier of order" (Hodge, *Literature as Discourse,* 84); on Egyptian metre, see H. Brunner, "Metrik," *LÄ* 4:120–22; G. Fecht, "Prosodie," *LÄ* 4:1127–54.

[328] M. Clark "Did Thucydides Invent the Battle Exhortation?" *Historia* 44 (1995): 375–76.

[329] S. R. Slings, "Orality and the Poet's Profession," *Acta Antiqua* 33 (1990–92): 9–14; M. Foucault "The Discourse on Language," in *Critical Theory since 1965* (ed. H. Adams and L. Searle; Tallahassee: University Presses of Florida, 1990), 142–58.

[330] P. J. Rabinowitz, "Truth in Fiction: A Re-examination of Audiences," *Critical Inquiry* 4 (1977): 121–41; S. Richardson, "Truth in the Tales of the Odyssey," *Mnemosyne* 49 (1996): 393–402; Eyre, "Is Historical Literature 'Political' or 'Literary'?" 416.

[331] See above, pp. 171ff. Herodotus's sources, clearly oral, doubtless were mainly Memphite and priestly in nature (A. B. Lloyd, *Herodotus Book II. Commentary* III [Leiden: Brill, 1988], 1, 5, 115); but it remains an index of how priestly archives of the Late Period tended to incorporate anything that had achieved inscripturation, that much of this oral tradition derived from the "*sdd* of the people" (Redford, *Pharaonic King-lists,* 227).

therein!"[332] Thus one appeals to eyewitnesses for corroboration: "My Majesty has seen them (scil., the Nubians). It is no false statement!"[333] Audiences were skeptical of "wonders that had happened in the time of" the ancestors, and survived only in "the knowledge of them that had passed away." Under these conditions "truth can never be distinguished from falsehood."[334]

But the undoubted character and/or skill of the speaker may dispel skepticism and ensure favorable reception. "My Majesty has said this in truth so that everybody may know: my great aversion is speaking falsely. There is not a statement of distortion therein!"[335] Even the villain can force the audience to accept the lie. Intriguingly, Falsehood (presumably by the force of his declamation and rhetorical skill) wins the court's acceptance of his cock-and-bull description of his gargantuan knife, while his young nephew, Son-of-Truth, as yet lacking a reputation, is scoffed at by the same court for attempting to use the same trope in describing his "Babe"-like bull. The boy wins out only by trumping his dastardly uncle in the game, skillfully bringing to the court's consciousness the absurdity of this very rhetorical figure.[336] Less commonly, a written source may be cited in support of an incredible statement: "They (the supplies brought into the staging areas) were more plentiful than anything, more than anything His Majesty's army had (ever) seen—and that's no mistatement!—they are set down in the daybook of the king's house."[337]

The Modalities of Oral Delivery

Many of the markers that fall under the rubric of strategies bearing upon the relationship of discourse and reality are lost to us forever. Prosody, which occupied a prominent place in the ancient Egyptian language, can be detected

---

[332] *Urk.* 4:1245.9–11.

[333] *ÄL* 84:8–9; cf. Khakheperrasonbu, recto 6 (A. H. Gardiner, *Admonitions of an Egyptian Sage* [Leipzig: Hinrichs, 1909]).

[334] *ÄL* 26:3–5; cf. 28:17–19.

[335] *Urk.* 4:835.11–14; cf. 101.12–13.

[336] P. Chester Beatty II 1.8–2.3; 9.1–10.4 (Gardiner, *Library*). The Blinding of Truth is a folkloric exemplar of the triangular focalization violator-violated-avenger, common in the east Mediterranean and northeast Africa, and often couched in a family setting. While the pattern informs origin stories and iconotrophies—in Egypt the Osiris story is most famous—there is no reason to derive the Blinding of Truth from any of these. It simply uses a common topos. See Bal, *Narratology*, 104ff.; Vansina, *Oral Tradition as History*, 71–74 (for a similar tale).

[337] *Urk.* 4:693.8–11.

only where syntactic patterns demand its sometime presence. The "language acts" (the "metasigns")[338] of speakers and the modalities of gesture ("body language") and tone can only be guessed at nowadays;[339] and metalinguistic evidence of "direct phonetic description," which Indo-European studies sometimes enjoy,[340] is also largely lacking. Only occasionally are we favored with graphic depictions of gestures used in singing.[341] And we are too far removed in time and too starved for evidence to comment on a speaker's use of lexicon, dialect, or idiolect as tools of modality. It is probable—indeed we have evidence of it—that an "official language" was striven for, in contradistinction to the argot of the masses;[342] but such social diglossia do not form a significant background to belletristic creations.

We are thrown back, therefore, on the descriptive profile of what "fine speech" (*mdwt nfrt*)[343] meant to the ancients. The qualifier indicates clearly the status of an art or craft. This aspect of skill was understood as involving not only psychological effect, accoustical enhancements, and expressive fluency, but also manipulation of content and form. In fact it was the masterful melding of the expected with the unexpected that produced the great practitioner in *mdwt nfrt.*

Genre Manipulation

In order to provide both formal concealment and strength for his message an ideologue might make novel use of a genre.[344] A song-type used for popular titillation is jarringly transmogrified into a vehicle for irreverent debunking, and the singer/harpist therewith marginalizes himself as a mocker of ancestral

---

[338] Hodge, *Literature as Discourse*, 78; Vansina, *Oral Tradition as History*, 83.

[339] H. Penzl, "Did Henrik van Veldeken (1145–ca. 1200) Write in a 'German Dialekt'?" in *The Berkeley Conference on Dutch Linguistics, 1989: Issues and Controversies, Old and New* (ed. T. F. Shannon and J. P. Snapper; Lanham, Md.: University Press of America, 1991), 62.

[340] R. Lass, *Historical Linguistics and Language Change* (Cambridge and New York: Cambridge University Press, 1997), 78.

[341] A. Schlott, "Einige Beobachtungen zu Mimik und Gestik von Singenden," *GöM* 152 (1996): 55–70

[342] Cf. A. Loprieno, "Linguistic Variety and Egyptian Literature," *AELHF*, 519–20.

[343] Essentially "Belles-lettres" (P. Vernus, "Langue littéraire et diglossie," *AELHF*, 558).

[344] On the importance of genre to Egyptian textual studies, see the salutary remarks of R. B. Parkinson, "Types of Literature in the Middle Kingdom," *AELHF*, 311. On genre manipulation, see idem, "Teachings, Discourses and Tales," 99–100.

wisdom and the ancestors themselves.[345] In more serious vein, a species of wondertale presents the audience with a well-known human type, worthy indeed of emulation, a priest in fact, only to dash the entire basis for such religiosity by revealing the stark "reality" of the afterlife.[346] A species of a "call to the living" similarly turns into a *Jenseitsklage* of utter despair and hopelessness at the dark reality of nothingness beyond the grave.[347] A speech-form (*mdt*) that promises routine entertainment appalls the listener by a prophecy of horrors to come.[348] An epistle, ostensibly giving information, reveals itself to be a lament over injustice and calamity and a cry for redress.[349] The dispassionate recording of verbatim depositions in a court case (usually tedious in substance) suddenly is found to be the encasement for that fundamental dispute which stands at the foundation of the Egyptian state: the conflict of Horus and Seth and the criterion for cosmic authority. Yet even with this realization the author has not released the listener. The boring formulae of the court recorder contrast with the amusing, picaresque treatment of the subject matter, and the whole degenerates into one loud guffaw.[350] The gods, in

---

[345] On "Harpers' Songs" see J. Assmann, "Fest des Augenblicks—Verheissung der Dauer: Die Kontroverse der ägyptischen Harfnerlieder," in *Fragen an die altägyptische Literatur: Studien zum Gedenken an Eberhard Otto* (ed. J. Assmann, E. Feucht, and R. Grieshammer; Wiesbaden: Reichert, 1977), 55–84; Fox, *Song of Songs,* 244–45. L. Kákosy and Z. I. Fabian, "Harper's Song in the Tomb of Djehutimes (TT 32)," *SAK* 22 (1993): 211–225, esp. 214. While sometimes called "Make Merry Songs," these products of a sort of "Black Comedy" basically cock a snook at accepted, mainstream morality. Their call to present enjoyment and self-indulgence is an intentionally deceptive codicil. See also M. Patane, "Existe-t-il dans l'Égypte ancienne une littérature licentieuse?" *BSÉG* 15 (1991): 91–93.

[346] Cf. the wrongly-named "ghost-story" (J. von Beckerath, "Zur Geschichte von Chonsuem-hab und dem Geist," *ZÄS* 119 [1992]: 90–107). This sort of counterblast is common within the context of the mortuary appeal to posterity from the end of the New Kingdom.

[347] Cf. K. Jansen-Winkeln, "Zwei Jenseitsklagen," *BSÉG* 17 (1993): 41–47 and the literature there cited.

[348] Prophecies of Neferty (Helck, *Prophezeihung*) and King Si-Sobek (Posener, *Papyrus Vandier*): see above, pp. 176.

[349] R. A. Caminos, *A Tale of Woe: From the Hieratic Papyrus in the A. S. Pushkin Museum of Fine Arts in Moscow* (Oxford: Griffith Institute, Ashmolean Museum, 1977); idem, "The Moscow Literary Letter," in *Fragen an die altägyptische Literatur: Studien zum Gedenken an Eberhard Otto* (ed. J. Assmann, E. Feucht, and R. Grieshammer; Wiesbaden: Reichert, 1977), 147–53.

[350] Gardiner, *Library.* While the material that constitutes the seventeen individual episodes of this piece is generally not new—seven of the episodes find parallels in Old and Middle Kingdom sources—the *Contendings* represents a stage in a transmission history of some

short, are brought down to earth, and the normal distancing of audience and protagonists disappears. The polymath couches his didactic description of the educational standard of the accomplished king's-scribe in epistolary format, but enlivens a dull message by imaging an *incompetent* king's-scribe, an "anticelebrity," deserving of derision.[351] The same letter exchange is used in a similarly eccentric fashion, not for information transfer, but for the "black" humor of insult. Crotchety Neith blasts Re and the Ennead, Re and Osiris hurl invectives at each other,[352] the childless miser is exposed for what he is[353]—all in a successful amalgam of the didactic and the comic.

Psychological Factors

The good orator must be "controlled of speech with his wits about him."[354] He should deliver his message "without confusion (ʿm-ib)"[355] and should think before he does so, "speaking according to the consideration of his heart."[356] "You must be patient the moment when you speak; you must speak with distinction, and then the magistrates who are listening will say, 'How fine is the issuance of his mouth!'"[357] The same patience should be exhibited to listening to what is said in response.[358] A good disposition (mnḫ-ib)[359] is advisable, and one must also be "calm and speak to the point(?)."[360] Specific situations may involve problem-solving in council, or even danger to the speaker, but the very attempt to speak under such conditions called forth admiration. "Patient of

---

complexity. (The contention that it was composed for some specific Twentieth Dynasty festivities misses this essential point.) See the author's forthcoming monograph on this story.

[351] Fischer-Elfert, *Die satirische Streitschrift*.

[352] Contendings of Horus and Seth 3,2–5; 14,6–15,8 (Gardiner, *Library*).

[353] Berlin P. 10627 (*HPKM*).

[354] J. Janssen, *De traditioneele Egyptische Autobiographie voor het Nieuwe Rijk* (Leiden: Brill, 1946), 9–10, 94; Mo'alla, Inscription no. 3 (J. Vandier, *Mo'alla: La Tombe d'Ankhtifi et la tombe de Sébekhotep* [Bibliothèque d'étude 18; Cairo: Institut français d'archéologie orientale, 1950], 171); *ÄL* 40:7.

[355] BM 569 (UT).

[356] *Urk.* 4:971.2.

[357] *ÄL* 42:1–2.

[358] Cairo 20539 I.b.5–6 (UT).

[359] BM 100, recto 5 (UT); Doxey, *Egyptian Non-royal Epithets*, 44.

[360] Ḥr-ib mdw r sp ḫpr: Cairo 1409b (UT); Doxey, *Egyptian Non-royal Epithets*, 60–61.

speech in situations where silence (is desirable),"[361] "speaking deliberately (literally, loud of voice) with respect to situations where one ought to be silent"[362] were good and laudible epithets. Such a one feared not to "speak aloud when the gentry is silent on the day when fear is spread and Upper Egypt is in silence,"[363] or to "speak in situations of provocation (*ḏnd*)."[364] It is a mark of distinction to be "a unique mouth which speaks while (other) mouths are silent (i.e., either through apprehension or reticence)."[365] "I am one," says Antef, "who knows the appropriate word for the frustrating occasion (*qndt ḥr.s*) . . . who silences the weeper with a happy saying . . . incisive speaker in situations of meanness (*ḥns-ib*)."[366] The intent in such cases must be "to quench the heat in words" and to be fearless in speech whether or not one's peers appear to be sycophants.[367]

Craft Skill

In fulfilment of its primary functions of informing and persuading, oral delivery in ancient Egypt had become a sophisticated art form in which the scribal schools presumably gave training.[368] From the earliest period of their history the Egyptians had elicited a standard of excellence from the varieties of the spoken word. The intonation of magic spells belonged to "the art of the utterance"[369] or "the craft (of the lector-priest)," the word *ḥmw* clearly recalling the skills of an artisan.[370] Dire consequences could result from the incompetent

---

[361] Helck, *Historisch-biographische Texte*, no. 49, line 7.

[362] Ibid., no. 24 line 2; cf. Janssen, *De traditioneele Egyptische Autobiographie*, 70, Bb, 10–14.

[363] Mo'alla Inscr. 3 (Vandier, *Mo'alla*, 177); Petrie, *Dendereh*, pl. 8.

[364] BM 581 (UT); Doxey, *Egyptian Non-royal Epithets*, 57.

[365] Jansen-Winkeln, *Ägyptische Biographien*, 3.6.13.

[366] BM 581 (UT).

[367] Jansen-Winkeln, *Ägyptische Biographien*, 1.8.5 and 1.8.8.

[368] N. Shupak, *Where Can Wisdom be Found? The Sage's Language in the Bible and Ancient Egyptian Literature* (OBO 130; Fribourg: University Press; Göttingen: Vandenhoeck & Ruprecht, 1993), 226–29.

[369] *WÄS* 3:85.1–2.

[370] Garnot, *L'Appel aux vivants*, 22 (text V), p. 32 (text VIb); *Urk.* 1:186.14–15, 187.13–14; 190.17; Junker, *Giza,* Abb. 56; Duell, *Mastaba of Mereruka* 2, pl. 130. Admittedly the "craft" in this case pertained more to esoteric and magical abilities to ensure a transfiguration, than to lyrical or oratorical skill.

botching of a spell: "'Look!' says the widower, praying to his deceased wife, 'I am the one you loved on earth, (so) fight for me and care for my name. I have not garbled a phrase before you when I "made your name to live upon earth." So take away the sickness of my body and act effectively on my behalf!'"[371]

Oratory too was a skilled craft: "I was a craftsman in speech, an assessor of hearts";[372] "I regulated my speech, I was a craftsman in response."[373] Carrying the metaphor to a florid extension, one worthy claims himself to be "a construction-master of monuments of speech."[374] More common are references to being "effective (*mnḫ*) at speaking,"[375] "effective in phrasing,"[376] "effective in consultation (*nḏt-rꜣ*),"[377] "competent (*iqr*) in speech, speaking, phrasing,"[378] or simply "good (*nfr*) at speaking" (and knowing when to keep silent).[379]

Skill in speaking was a distinguishing feature on a social level. It was possible to "discern a man according to his utterance,"[380] and one strove to be "in good voice in the house of his lord."[381] This was not easy, as "it is a real craftsman that speaks in council, for speech is more difficult than any work."[382]

---

[371] E. F. Wente, "A Misplaced Letter to the Dead," OLP 6/7 (1976): 595.

[372] Jansen-Winkeln, *Ägyptische Biographien*, 3.6.4.

[373] Ibid., 3.6.5.

[374] Ibid., 3.6.18.

[375] Cairo 20539 II.b.5 (UT). Cf. Doxey, *Egyptian Non-royal Epithets*, 44–46.

[376] Hammamat 48, line 11 (J. Couyat and P. Montet, *Les Inscriptions hiéroglyphiques et hiératiques du Ouâdi Hammamat* [Mémoires publiés par les membres de l'Institut français d'archéologie orientale du Caire 34; Cairo: Institut français d'archéologie orientale, 1912]).

[377] Cairo 20538 I.c.6 (UT); BM 572:10 (UT); *Urk.* 4:1476.

[378] Doxey, *Egyptian Non-royal Epithets*, 53–54; Jansen-Winkeln, *Ägyptische Biographien*, 3.6.14; Cairo 20538, I.c.7; Helck, *Historisch-biographische Texte*, no. 57, line 9.

[379] Jansen-Winkeln, *Ägyptische Biographien*, 3.6.2. On the use of language in "emplotment" in narrative, see M. Collier, "The Language of Literature: On Grammar and Texture," *AELHF*, 531–54.

[380] Griffith, *Inscriptions,* 182.

[381] Munich GL WAF 35 (UT).

[382] *ÄL* 40:9–10; cf. 37:12–13.

Style[383]

Above all, the good speaker had to be "incisive" (*spd-r3* or *spd-ns*)[384] and "precise" (*ʿq3*),[385] without exaggeration.[386] He should strive for originality and new ways of saying things: "Oh would that I had unknown locutions (*ḫnw ḫmmw*), strange phrases (*tsw ḫppyw*), in fact new ways of speaking not used before!"[387] Repetition (i.e., of what had been said before), and use of the clichéd phrases of the ancestors[388] were frowned upon.[389] Equally objectionable were flippancy,[390] loquacity,[391] pretentiousness,[392] and even (upon occasion)

---

[383] Cf. esp. W. Guglielmi, "Der Gebrauch rhetorischer Stilmittel in der ägyptischen Literatur," *AELHF*, 465–97.

[384] "Incisive speaker in situations of meanness," BM 581 (UT); "incisive speaker with pleasant phrases," *Urk.* 4:1816.17, *Urk.* 7:65.16; "incisive speaker within the council house," Cairo 20765 a.10 (UT); cf. Newberry, *El Bersheh* 2, pl. 13:5; "incisive speaker in the conclave of the magistrates," *Urk.* 7:59.11; Blackman, *Rock Tombs,* vol. 3, pl. 12; Berlin 1204 (UT); "speaker with incisive words in camera," Jansen-Winkeln, *Ägyptische Biographien*, 3.6.11; Doxey, *Egyptian Non-royal Epithets*, 54.

[385] "Precise speaker," *Urk.* 4:507.6–7; "precise of speech," *Urk.* 4:993.6; "with precise words," Hammamat 114 (Couyat and Montet, *Inscriptions*).

[386] "Knowing how to speak free of exaggeration," P. Montet, "Les Tombeux de Siout et Deir Rifeh," *Kêmi* 6 (1936), 133(11); *Urk.* 7:43.17; "without the ancestors' exaggeration of speech," Khakheperrasonbu, recto 4 (Gardiner, *Admonitions*); cf. Hammamat 47:11 (Couyat and Montet, *Inscriptions*); "without a phrase of exaggeration," *Urk.* 4:430.1; cf. *KRI* 7:230.7; "others who will hear (my biographical statement) will not say: 'False! He never did it!'" *Urk.* 4:1199.15; see also above.

[387] Khakheperrasonbu, recto 2–3 (G. E. Kadish, "British Museum Writing Board 5645: The Complaints of Kha-kheper-Rēʿ-Senebu," *JEA* 59 [1973]: 77–90).

[388] Khakheperasonbu, recto 3 (Kadish, "British Museum Writing Board 5645").

[389] *KRI* 7:230.7. "I am a trusty official, free of repetetiveness (*r wḥm*)"; Khakheperrasonbu, recto 3: "free of repetition (*wḥmyt*)" (Kadish, "British Museum Writing Board 5645"); R. O. Faulkner, *Concise Dictionary of Middle Egyptian* (Oxford: Printed for The Griffith Institute at the University Press by V. Ridler, 1962), 67.

[390] Hammamat 199, "free of flippancy" (*is n ns*, literally, "lightness of tongue"; Couyat and Montet, *Inscriptions*).

[391] Literally, "moving of mouth," i.e. a babbler (*šm-r3*): *Urk.* 4:971.8. Cf. Posener, "L'Exorde," pl. 4:10, "a long speech is inappropriate."

[392] Literally, "greatness of mouth" (*ʿ3 r3*): "who makes a true statement without saying it pretentiously": *Urk.* 1:224.18; cf. *Urk.* 4:1531.1–5 (among the nobles).

loudness.[393] To be "accomplished"[394] at speaking involved a smoothness of tone,[395] a confidence in one's ability,[396] and an agreeableness and earnestness resulting in persuasion.[397] The result could be that a good speaker elicited "reliance" (*rhn*) on his words from his audience;[398] the king himself might be quite captivated.[399]

Speechifying

While oral interchange is often envisaged as taking place in the privacy of a "one-on-one" conversation—the life situation of much wisdom composition points to precisely such—oratorical delivery often presupposes the presence of a large audience.[400] Examples quoted above lay stress on the self-confident assertion and skill in discourse and argument that were required when one spoke before the body of magistrates. Ptahhotpe even lays down rules governing controlled debate with a "disputant in his element (*ȝt.f*)."[401] A

---

[393] *KRI* 1:361.7.

[394] *Skm-ns*, "perfected of tongue like the god himself" (Copenhagen 1241g [UT]); "perfected of tongue in the council of the magistrates" (A. H. Gardiner, "The Tomb of a Much-Travelled Theban Official," *JEA* 4 [1918]: 28–38, see pl. 8:7—not "hoary-tongued"); cf. *Urk.* 4:1476.

[395] "Cf. "unique voice when speaking, 'flowing with poured milk'" (Jansen-Winkeln, *Ägyptische Biographien*, 3.6.15); "my mouth was 'natron,' afflictions were purified upon my lips" (*Urk.* 4:1076.12–13).

[396] "Able-voiced speaker" (Wady el-Hudi 4); "one who knows his utterance when speaking in the palace" (Jansen-Winkeln, *Ägyptische Biographien*, 3.6.12; Cairo 20539).

[397] "Convincing with fine speech" (*hnn mdwt iqr*) (*Urk.* 4:1816.5); "convincing of speech (*hnn mdwt*) to those who know their oratory" (BM 572, 10 [UT]); "one with whose statements the king is content (*hrr*)," (*Urk.* 4:959.5, 993.8, 1452.4, 1465.12); "one with agreeable phrases (*hr tsw*)" (*Urk.* 4:435.2, 1816.17); cf. also the common epithet of viziers "speaker who satisfies (*shrr*) the entire land" (*Urk.* 4:1412.18, 1576.10, 1777.9, 1794.6, 1821.17, 1915.9, 1928.20, etc.); cf. "satisfying the commons" (*Urk.* 4:1813.12, 1408.11 [temple context]; Jansen-Winkeln, *Ägyptische Biographien*, 2.1.21–22); "with whose utterances people are at ease" (*Urk.* 4:546.8–9; 1011.7 [*hrr*]).

[398] *Urk.* 4:473.7.

[399] Jansen-Winkeln, *Ägyptische Biographien*, 1.8.11.

[400] Cf. the expression *ȝ r ḏr.f dmḏ m bw wꜥ*, "the entire country, gathered together in one place," *KRI* 5:39.6; sim. P. Harris 75.10–76.1 (Grandet, *Papyrus Harris*); *KRI* 2:332.12–13.

[401] *ÄL* 37:18–38:7; cf. G. Fecht, "Ptahhotep und die Disputierer (Lehre des Ptahhotep nach Pap. Prisee. Max. 2–4, Dev. 60–83)," *MDAI* 37 (1981): 143–50.

successful speaker in such a context might be deemed "a unique mouth which destroys (other) mouths," i.e., in the cut and thrust of argument.[402]

In the context of hortatory speeches the audience would be of a more heterogenous nature than the council of the magistrates, and perhaps required a different approach. Even so, the audience in the context of a royal speech would have comprised the extended royal family, support staff, religious and civil officials and the military;[403] one doubts that any of the mass of the population would have heard the enunciation of Pharaoh, except through repetition.[404] No matter what the composition of the assembled listeners, however, one had still to be "articulate of speech in the midst of the multitude."[405] One had also to arrest the attention of the crowd, and imperative forms often begin a speech. Subject matter, if overdrawn, could also rivet the audience's attention; although, as we have seen, exaggeration was a plausible and frequent complaint. More serious were the occasions on which the audience responded to the speaker with violence. Words that were "unseemly" (*bn r st.w*, literally, "not appropriate") and "not fit to be heard" (*bn š3w sḏm.w*) brought howls of rage from the audience along with demands that the speaker be removed.[406]

The interplay between audient assembly and speaker was complex and subtle, but never static. The listeners unconsciously espoused a standard, namely, that which the texts adduced above attest to, and were quick to react to speechifying which failed to meet it. Consequently speakers strove to "say what is good and repeat what is desired," a phrase that encompasses not only *ma'at*

---

[402] *Urk.* 7:32.14.

[403] Cf. *KRI* 5:14.15ff., 17.4–5 (overseers, royal offspring, butlers, courtiers, and all army officers); 28.9 (magistrates, courtiers, and all army officers); 33.3 (king's children, butlers, and charioteers); 66.6ff. (royal children, great magistrates, army officers, and charioteers); 83.10–11 (king's offspring, magnates of the Council of Thirty, retainers); 191.6ff. (magistrates, priests, army and chariotry officers); occasionally the speech is directed to "all men, the magistrates who are on earth, and the whole army" (*KRI* 2:320.9) and might include "every citizen of Egypt . . . and the youths of this land" (*KRI* 5:39.6ff.), but the language sounds formulaic.

[404] Thutmose I's speech anouncing Hatshepsut's promotion was directed at "the king's nobles, the dignitaries, the courtiers, the entourage of the residence, and the leaders of the commons (*rḫyt*)," (*Urk.* 4:256), but the latter heard only indirectly: "they came forth to them rejoicing, they danced, they exulted; and when all the common people heard (in) all the hamlets of the residence, they came out to them rejoicing, they exulted exuberantly, hamlet upon hamlet therein . . ." (*Urk.* 4:259).

[405] Literally, "finding his mouth . . .", Janssen, *Traditioneele Egyptische Autobiographie*, 114 (Gb, 15); Helck, *Historisch-biographische Texte*, no. 24 line 3; no. 57, line 9.

[406] Cf. the reaction of the Ennead in the Contendings of Horus and Seth to the insults of Baba (P. Chester Beatty I 3.11–12; cf. 4.8–9; Gardiner, *Library*).

but also genre expectations associated with a particular aesthetic.[407] As we have seen, verbosity, repetition, clichéd delivery, and irresolute delivery, would all invoke an adverse response. Of course the speaker's identity might place him in a privileged position with respect to the audience. Only he, as actor, victim, visionary, autobiographer, or messenger, was in possession of information the audience presumably was waiting for; and his hearers would have at least to suspend judgment on style if they wished to acquire the facts in a connected and uninterrupted manner.

The Mechanics of Oral Composition and Transmission

Whether written in advance or extemporized, the dissemination of information by the state or of admonitory or diverting material by a private speaker was thought of essentially in terms of oral promulgation and performance.[408] Even if a written form of the words issued simultaneously, an author literally conceived and created his work *orally*, with *oral* modalities in mind. An amanuensis or even the original author copied *by ear*, repeating phrases audibly in the manner they would be presented to the audience; there was no "silent reading."[409] Even in the case of an authoritative *Vorlage* a text is apt to become little more than an *aide-mémoire*.[410]

---

[407] Doxey, *Egyptian Non-royal Epithets*, 52–53.

[408] S. T. Hollis, "Tales of Magic and Wonder from Ancient Egypt," *CANE*, 2255–64, esp. 2256. Even the Presocratics intended "publication" as "recital" (cf. J. P. Hershbell, "The Oral-Poetic Religion of Xenophanes," in *Language and Thought in Early Greek Philosophy* [ed. K. Robb; Monist Library of Philosophy; La Salle, Ill.: Hegeler Institute, 1983], 128). Nor does complexity of composition (cf. W. Barta, "Ein metrisch geformter Stelentext des Mittleren Reiches," in *Form und Mass: Beiträge zur Literatur, Sprache und Kunst Ägypten: Festschrift für Gerhard Fecht zum 65. Geburtstag* [ed. J. Osing and G. Dreyers; Ägypten und Altes Testament 12; Wiesbaden: Harrassowitz, 1987], 63–77) preclude the basic intent to deliver orally. It is oversimplified and misleading to claim that "oral literature" is restricted to a limited number of types of discourse and lacks originality in the creation of "original" works (Vanstiphout, "Memory and Literacy," 2193).

[409] Cf. Oppenheim, "Archives of the Palace," 133 n.6. *Hörfehler*, which abound in schoolboy texts, all point to the vocalization of the text by the copyist; there is no distinction to be expected between mistakes from dictation and those from copying. Cf. B. van de Walle, *La transmission des textes littéraires égyptiens* (Brussels: Fondation égyptologique Reine Élisabeth, 1948), 62–3; J. M. Sasson, "Literary Criticism, Folklore Scholarship, and Ugaritic Literature," in *Ugarit in Retrospect: Fifty Years of Ugarit and Ugaritic* (ed. G. D. Young; Winona Lake, Ind.: Eisenbrauns, 1981), 81–98; Harris, *Ancient Literacy*, 36 n. 37.

[410] Cf. M. L. West, *Early Greek Philosophy and the Orient* (Oxford: Clarendon, 1971), 5. Prior to the Hellenistic Period, caution should be exercised in postulating any "oral register," i.e., a calculated style in contrast to extemporized creation (J. Foley, *The Singer of Tales in*

Oral composition has left numerous signs of its presence. We have reviewed above the circumstantial evidence of terms describing style, content, and delivery. There remain several other items of evidence.

Dicitur

Two *Märchen* are glossed in their *incipits* by the term *ḫr.tw*, "it is said."[411] Normally *ḫr*, when in the mouth of the king (or said of him), indicates an authoritative utterance;[412] when in the mouth of the gods, an oracle.[413] But in everyday speech it had simply the force of oral discourse, corresponding roughly to *dicitur* in mediaeval lives, and *tote* in fables.[414] The force of the expression not only alleges an oral root to the tale herein transcribed, but also distances the transcriber from the piece. The text becomes thereby tagged as an "unauthorized" account to which a certain degree of skepticism attaches itself. This is, in fact, none other than the *sḏd* of the people.

Mnemonics

Mnemonic devices abound in narrative texts of various genres and intents. Some works hang together and show plot sequences dependent largely on word plays and homonymous passages that could be appreciated only when vocalized. For example, the schoolboy model letter of Middle Kingdom date[415] leaps inexplicably from a lengthy epistolary salutation to the first person

---

Performance [Bloomington: Indiana University Press, 1995], 15–17). In either case the final product will have to be presented to the audience; and they, by their implicit response, will help to decide its shape. The result will be no different than the creations of Walter von Stolzing and Beckmesser; both worked from a prepared piece already in written form, yet both extemporized. The Egyptians themselves were aware of the role a written piece played in the transmission of a tradition: "I (a royal person is implied) have come today along with Ptah, and I sit among the Ennead. The Magnates of the Horizen have been brought to them, and a document conveying what I said, given to them as their *aide-mémoire* (*sḫȝ*)" (CoffT VII 231:m–q).

[411] P. Harris 500.4.1 (Grandet, *Papyrus Harris*); P. d'Orbiney 1.1 (Gardiner, *Late Egyptian Stories*); *WÄS* 3:317–18; Meeks, *Année lexicographique* 2:286; 3:222.

[412] Cf. P. Harris 79.10 (Grandet, *Papyrus Harris*, 44–45).

[413] Edwards, *Hieratic Papyri*, 4 n. 27; I. Shirun-Grumach, *Offenbarung, Orakel, und Königs-novelle* (Wiesbaden: Harassowitz, 1993), 148 n. 34; cf. *KRI* 5:5.5; 243.12; 6:457.4; 7:100.15.

[414] Assmann, "Schriftliche Folklore," 179; cf. Coptic "inquit," see Westendorf, *Koptisches Handwörterbuch*, 348.

[415] Hayes, "A Much-Copied Letter," 9–10.

account of Au who, decked out in his finery, meets a harim-inmate who tells him to go to his wife who weeps because of his fishing and fowling. The speaker (Au?) then requests the woman to go north that he might address a fine speech to her. He is next found by an unspecified group of people, then tells us he found his father, and finally launches into a stereotypical set of epithets that convey the love and respect in which he is held by his relatives. The piece concludes with a brief eulogy of scribes and writing, and a statement that the speaker was taught by his father. This disjointed and rambling patchwork has little sense and less "literary" merit (in spite of the overly charitable opinion of some scholars). If the "plot" sequence is not entirely explained by homonymy, the latter certainly provides a mnemonic device to help the schoolboy remember the curious subject matter. Thus the unusual personal name, Au,[416] is anticipated by (m) ꜣwt-ḏt in line 1 and iꜣwt (nfrt) in line 4; by ꜣw mꜣ.n.i in line 7 and ꜣw mꜣ.n.k in line 10. The rare iꜣdw of line 9 was used because of dꜣiw in the same line. Lines 10–12 provide plays using the consonants m, r, and t/t (vowel) in iw rmm.s tw ḥr rmw.k, (ḥmt.k im) mr.ti and mi r.t. St wꜣt of line 13 is to be compared with mꜣst of line 14, mi nmḥw of line 14 with (i.n.i) min m niwt of the same line, kt niwt of line 14 with kꜣt n it.i of line 18, wbꜣ n wnwt.f (line 22) with sbꜣ.n wi it.i.

Similarly Ipuwer displays paranomasia in the use of homophonic "tags" as mnemonic links to assist, presumably, in the recitation of this large assemblage of *antitheta* in an accepted order. For in the kind of description Ipuwer indulges in there is no obvious sequence involving causation, and the order is for the most part arbitrary.[417] One might, for example, compare the following: cḏꜣ m st nbt (A10[a]) anticipating [ḥcḏꜣ] m st nbt (A10[b]), wsr (B2) recalled by šwꜣw of B3, iwty nb (B25) by iwty n.f (B26), and wsr (B26) by šri (B28). Sometimes verses appear to be grouped together by use of the same key word. Thus sḥꜣ is found successively in B 47, 48 and 49; B 50 and 51 share šd; 51 and 52 share ssw; C 16 and 17 share sḏr; C4, 5, and 7 share forms of the idiom wꜣy r; B29 and 30 share qꜣnr; (Note: B 29 is reduplicated at B 41, but now because of imt shared with B 40). Š dt of B33 is resumed by šdw in the next couplet, cwꜣyt (B39) by cwt (B40), cnd (B42) by ind (in interpolation IV), nf (B44) by nfꜣ (B45), iwty-ḥt (C24) by iwty n.f (C25). This list could easily be lengthened, but the evident sensitivity towards various kinds of memory aids shows clearly the priority assigned to oral delivery.

---

[416] H. Ranke, *Die ägyptischen Personennamen* (2 vols.; Glückstadt: J. J. Augustin, 1935–1977), 1:1.

[417] The numbering is taken from Helck, *'Admonitions.'*

The Oral Formula

Like extemporized poetry in the ancient Near East, pre-Islamic Arabia, and Africa, the lyrical output of ancient Egypt was distinguished by a prosody governed by the distribution of accentuated syllables within a stich (intonational phrase).[418] In contrast to the precisely measured European lyric, in which accented and unaccented syllables follow a numbered sequence (irrespective of meaning), the Egyptian lyric derives from the balancing of stresses in individual hemistichs without regard for the number or position of unaccented syllables which are governed solely by phonotactic constraints.

This type of prosodic patterning lends itself to, indeed at times requires, an accompaniment of percussion instruments supplying a complexity of rhythms and counterrythyms; and, while speechifying did not need such an orchestral setting, the delivery must have been mesmerically rhythmic. A hemistich of two to four "beats" dominated every piece, balanced by its partner of equal or reduced beat-content.[419] Bound constructions counted a single beat, and vocatives are sometimes outside the metric structure; rarely a tristich will appear. Couplets of distich lines often organized the thought of the speaker,[420] but the hemistich constituted the irreducible unit or building block. As pointed out above, the maximum number of words a listener is able to handle is six—ten is the limit of recall[421]—and it is therefore incumbent on the speaker to treat hemistichs themselves as the units the audience will recognize. A speaker will use a stock of set phrases, some well known, some novel, distributed in

---

[418] Cf. G. Fecht, "Prosodie," *LÄ* 4:1127–54. A superficial resemblance to Greek "prose-rhythm" is becoming increasingly difficult to maintain. Not only is there a chronological problem—quantitative prose appears only in the late fifth century—but the *clausulae* are significantly absent from Egyptian metric structure. Whether the *sense* of the passage and its consistency ought to be the point of departure for studies in metrics (G. Burkhard, "Der formale Aufbau altägyptischer Literaturwerke: Zur Problematik der Erschliessung seiner Grundstrukturen," *SAK* 10 [1983]: 78–118) remains moot; certainly it can be a check on results. For rhythm in extended oratorical forms, see N. Frye, *The Anatomy of Criticism: Four Essays* (Princeton: Princeton University Press, 1971), 251 ff.

[419] B. Mathieu, "Études de métrique égyptienne I: Le distique heptamétrique dans les chants d'amour," *RdÉ* 39 (1989): 63–82; idem, "Études de métrique égyptienne II: Contraintes métriques et production textuelle dans l'*Hymne à la crue du Nil*," *RdÉ* 41 (1990): 127–41. I have preferred to use "stich," as it seems in its metric application in Greek (a line of ca. 15 syllables) to approximate Egyptian usage.

[420] Cf. J. Foster, "Thought Couplets in Khety's Hymn to the Inundation," *JNES* 34 (1975): 1–29; idem, *Thought Couplets and Clause Sequences in a Literary Text: The Maxims of Ptah-hotep* (Toronto: Society for the Study of Egyptian Antiquities, 1977).

[421] Zevit, "Cognitive Theory and Memorability," 202–3.

sequences that will be meaningful and arresting for the hearers. It is these "oral formulae"[422] that, in the aggregate, identify the idiolect of the speaker; his word choice counts for far less. Thus, in analyzing a piece of clearly oral formulaic composition, a simple listing of lexical items will prove nothing. It is only in the choice of formulae and the use of prosodic patterns that the author's particular "signature" can be detected.

The Egyptian term that approaches most closely the notion of the oral formula of hemistich length is *ṯsw*, normally translated "phrase."[423] The root means "to tie up, to knot," and then "to fabricate, create."[424] So closely is *ṯsw* associated with oral, metrical composition that it is used metonymously for aphoristic wisdom,[425] addresses to the living (biographical statements),[426] fatherly advice,[427] manuals,[428] and prophecy.[429] In specifying the scope of oratorical skill, epithets often use a qualifier involving *ṯsw*.[430] Thus an orator is "adept at phrasing" (*iqr ṯsw*),[431] or uses "choice phrases."[432] The latter may be

---

[422] Cf. the standard work of A. B. Lord, *The Singer of Tales* (Harvard Studies in Comparative Literature 24; Cambridge, Mass.: Harvard University Press, 1960); also R. C. Culley, *Oral Formulaic Language in the Biblical Psalms*, (Near and Middle East Series, 4; Toronto: University of Toronto Press, 1967); Vansina, *Oral Tradition as History*, 52–53; Niditch, *Oral World*, 4–9. That such formulae correspond to reality cannot now be doubted, although a definition as well as what may be called "the coefficient of elasticity" remain problematical (cf. S. Vanseveren, "La Formule homérique: problèmes de définition," *Les Études classiques* 66 [1998]: 225–36).

[423] Cf. Luft, "Zur Einleitung der Liebesgedichte," 108: "eine kleine Sprucheinheit"; E. Blumenthal, "Die literarische Verarbeitung der Übergangszeit zwischen Alten und Mittleren Reich," *AELHF*, 125 (a "stilistische und metrische Einheit"). The concept overlaps significantly with the notion of "phonological word" (R. F. Person Jr., "The Ancient Israelite Scribe as Performer," *JBL* 117 [1998]: 601–9, esp. 603–4).

[424] *WÄS* 5:396–99.

[425] P. Anastasi i.11.1, 3 (Fischer-Elfert, *Die satirische Streitschrift*); G. Posener, "Les richesses inconnues," 42.

[426] *Urk.* 4:1845.14.

[427] P. Chester Beatty IV verso 6.8 (Gardiner, *Library*); *ÄL* 37:6.

[428] *Urk.* 4:1089.7ff.; P. Sallier III.iv.3 (G. Möller, *Hieratische Lesestücke* [Leipzig: Hinrichs, 1927–35]).

[429] P. Chester Beatty IV 3.7ff. (Gardiner, *Library*).

[430] Doxey, *Egyptian Non-royal Epithets*, 62.

[431] BM 100, recto 5 (UT); *Urk.* 4:419.8; 7:57.21; Louvre C 127:8 (UT).

[432] Neferty 7–8 (paralleling "fine words"; Helck, *Prophezeihung*); MMA 57.95 (UT); Helck, *Historisch-biographische Texte*, no. 49:5; Jansen-Winkeln, *Ägyptische Biographien*, 3.6.8;

"sweet(-sounding)"[433] and soothing.[434] The aptly chosen one, the *mot juste* as it were, can even contribute to furthering discussion and solving problems: a speaker takes pride in "finding the (appropriate) phrase when it is lacking"[435] or "finding the phrase that settles difficulties."[436] Appreciation of the prosodic suitability of a phrase combined with an intuitive sense of its impact must underlie such boasts as "putting a phrase in its (proper) place," or "speaking a phrase at its (appropriate) times."[437] In the cult, lack of skill could be disastrous; it was unthinkable that one should "botch up a phrase when 'making-(one's)-name-to-live-upon-earth.'"[438] Proper use of the oral formula could be a man's salvation.[439]

Word Play

Word plays are ubiquitous in a wide variety of genres we would otherwise single out as the product of oral composition and destined for oral transmission. Some are intended as mnemonic helps.[440] Love poems, for example, might display word plays keyed into the numbering of stanzas.[441] Subtle plays are

Leclant, *Montouemhât*, 68, 70 n. *d.*

[433] P. Chester Beatty I, pl. 16:9 (Gardiner, *Library*).

[434] *KRI* 1:48.6 (*shry* + the heart of a god as object).

[435] Janssen, *Traditioneele Egyptische Autobiographie*, 9–10, 114; Cairo 20502, 1 (UT); Fischer, *Dendera in the Third Millennium B.C.*, 141; E. Brovarski renders *tsw* by "solution" in "Ahanakht of Bersheh and the Hare Nome in the First Intermediate Period," in *Studies in Ancient Egypt, the Aegean, and the Sudan: Essays in Honor of Dows Dunham on the Occasion of his 90th Birthday* (ed. W. K. Simpson and W. Davis; Boston: Department of Egyptian and Ancient Near Eastern Art, Museum of Fine Arts, 1981), 14–30, see p. 18; var. "finding the (appropriate) phrase when it is in 'lacuna'" (*Urk.* 4:1817.9).

[436] Cairo 20538 I.c.10–11 (UT); 20539 II.b.5 (UT).

[437] Hammamat 114 (Couyat and Montet, *Inscriptions*).

[438] Wente, "A Misplaced Letter," 595ff.

[439] Jansen-Winkeln, *Ägyptische Biographien*, 3.6.7.

[440] This is not to make light of the mechanism. Some wordplays have serious intent (cf. J. Foster, "Wordplay in the *Eloquent Peasant*. The Eighth Complaint," *Bulletin of the Egyptological Seminar* 10 [1989–90]: 61–76; Eyre, "Is Egyptian Historical Literature 'Historical' or 'Literary'?" 420–21.

[441] Gardiner, *Library*, pl. XX–XXVII: "<first stanza> unique (*w*ˤ) is my sister … second (*mḥ-sn*) stanza: my brother (*sn.i*) draws forth my heart … Third (*mḥ-ḥmt*) stanza: my heart intends (*ḥmt*) to see her beauty …" and so forth. See Fox, *Song of Songs*, 60, 65, 210, and passim.

strewn throughout narrative, serving not only as aids to recitation but also indicating a sort of deeper unity of essence to the piece. In the Doomed Prince the lad mounts (*tsy*) to his roof and spies a dog (*tsm*); he is taken to the eastern (*ȝbtt*) frontier and told, "go where you please" (*ȝb.k*); he passes by (*sni*) the sons of the Syrian princes who welcome him and kiss (*sni*) him, and later he makes himself out to be a chariot-warrior's son (*snni*).[442] In the Two Brothers, Bata cares for (*nwy*) the cattle, and later Anpu cares for (*nwy*) Bata.[443] The monster Sea calls to (ʿš) the Cedar (ʿš) to seize the woman.[444] The Contendings of Horus and Seth turn upon word plays on the root *ȝȝw*, sometimes in *ȝ(w)t* ("office"), sometimes in *ȝwt* ("cattle"), sometimes in *ȝwt* ("old").

Some narratives, especially iconotropic stories, take their rise from single words or short phrases, which can generate wholly new variants on the same theme. An apparent "mistake" lies at the root of the process, but always in a way that depends upon a vocalized *Hörfehler* rather than a written one. Thus the words *ḏȝi* ("to ferry over"), *ȝs* ("bald"), *ȝwt* ("herds"), *ḥȝt* ("forefront"), and *nbw* ("gold") are the ingredients in two tales told of Nemty the boatman (*mḫnty*), god of the twelfth Upper Egyptian township.[445] In the Contendings of Horus and Seth, the Ennead, with Isis in mind, warns Nemty not to ferry over (*ḏȝi*) any woman to the island on which the gods are taking a recess. Isis disguises herself into a lame old woman (*ȝwt*) and inveigles him into ferrying her across for the fare of a gold ring (*ḥtm n nbw*). In punishment the gods remove the forefront (*ḥȝt*) of Nemty's feet,[446] and he swears off gold, declaring "gold has, for me, been turned into the abomination of my city."[447] In a snippet of myth in a New Kingdom hemerology[448] Nemty appears in a similar role: "[. . .] the procession (*ḫntyw*) upon the river for preventing the crossing (*ḏȝy*) of [any] male snakes [. . . or anything] that flies with hostile intent against that *Neshmet*-barque of Osiris which was proceeding upstream to Abydos. . . . Now

442 P. Harris 500 recto 4.7; 5.1–2; 5.7; 5.13 etc. (Gardiner, *Late Egyptian Stories*).

443 P. d'Orbiney 8.3 (Gardiner, *Late Egyptian Stories*).

444 P. d'Orbiney 10.7 (Gardiner, *Late Egyptian Stories*).

445 F. Gomaa, *Die Besiedlung Ägyptens während des Mittleren Reiches* (2 vols., Beihefte zum Tübinger Atlas des Vorderen Orients, Reihe B, Geisteswissenschaften, 66; Wiesbaden: L. Reichert, 1986–87) 1:258.

446 Thus turning him into the type of clawless cult-statue known as *cḥm* (*WÄS* 1:225.15–226.5; Meeks, *Anneée lexicographique* 2:78; W. Helck, "Kultstatue," *LÄ* 3:859–65 [generic for any thereomorphic statue]).

447 P. Chester Beatty I 5.4–8.1 (Gardiner, *Library*).

448 Bakir, *Cairo Calendar*, pl. XIII–XIV.

<he> (Seth?) had turned himself into a hairless (?) tot (*iȝs šry*)[449] in the arms of [his] nurse. Gold (*nbw*) was given to Nemty by way of reward[450] as the fare, with the words, 'So cross over (*ḏȝi*) to the west.' Then he accepted it [but to the (ultimate)] damage of the divine limbs, while a gang followed him like an army of snakes." These hostile cohorts of Seth turned themselves into "flocks of goats" (*ꜥwt nḏ st*), and the gods "made a great slaughter <of them> . . . . Then a sacrifice was made of the forefront (*ḥȝt*)[451] in the presence of (?) Nemty; so you should not bring gold (*nbw*) anywhere near the House of Nemty down to this (very) day."

Sometimes a traditional trait of a protagonist or a basic plot pattern will be variously shaped by a word or phrase. Baba is traditionally a terrifying monkey-god "with red ear(s) and ruddy bottom (*ṯsm ꜥrt.f*)"[452] who tends to speak calumny (*ḏd bin/btȝw*) and is sexually overpowering (*nḫt ḥnn*).[453] An early hypostasis of kingship and connected with Upper Egypt,[454] Baba is spoken of in the PT and CoffT as "bull (*kȝ*, probably pronounced **ko*)[455] of the baboons,"[456] son of "her that knew not (*iḫmt*),"[457] and "one in whose absence

---

[449] Possible "little old thing," if *isw* is to be read instead of *iȝsw*. Note that the pustule (Gardiner, *Sign List*, Aa 2) is used both in the Contendings of Horus and Seth and the Hemerology.

[450] *Fqȝw*; an homonym means "cake" (Faulkner, *Concise Dictionary*, 98). Note that in the Contendings of Horus and Seth Isis had originally offered a cake (*wḫȝt*) as fare (P. Chester Beatty I 5.13 [Gardiner, *Library*]).

[451] By a copying error the text reads *ns*, "tongue" (recto XIV, 2); the correct reading could also yield *ḥȝty*, "heart."

[452] PT 1349b.

[453] See P. Derchain, "Bebon: le dieu et les mythes," *RdÉ* 9 (1952): 23–47; J. Vandier, "La Légende de Baba (Bebon) dans le Papyrus Jumilhac," *RdÉ* 9 (1952): 121–23; P.-P. Koemoth, "La plante m3tt, le feu et la puissance virile," *BSÉG* 17 (1993): 57–62.

[454] Derchain, "Bebon," 24–25, 30.

[455] Westendorf, *Koptisches Handwörterbuch*, 55.

[456] PT Spruch 320; CoffT VI, spell 668. Later he was to be closely associated with dogs (cf. Massart, "The Egyptian Geneva Papyrus") and even turtles (F. Labrique, "Rapiecage ou reécriture? La porte d'Évergète, le temple d'Esna," in *Egyptian Religion: The Last Thousand Years: Studies Dedicated to the Memory of Jan Quaegebeur* [ed. W. Clarysse, A. Schoors, and H. Willems; Leuven: Peeters, 1998], 897–901).

[457] PT 515c.

people (remain) alive (*ꜥnḫ m ḥm.f*)."[458] In the Contendings of Horus and Seth[459] Baba insults Re by declaring his shrine (*k3ry*, pronounced **ko* at this period)[460] to be empty. Re thereupon goes into a sulk and lies down (*nmꜥ*) on his bed. He is only revived when his daughter Hathor comes to him and playfully uncovers her vulva (*k3t*) before his eyes. In a tale from P. Jumilhac[461] Baba again hurls his verbal abuse, this time against Thoth, accusing him among other things of having eaten Re's offerings, an "abomination." While Baba is lying (*nmꜥ*) upon his bed, Thoth "stuffed his (Baba's) penis deep inside his (Baba's) bottom (*ꜥrt.f*) and brought forth his 'Power' against him, (for) it seized upon his penis inside the orifice (*k3t*) of his bottom, and he did not know (*n rḫ.f*) . . . ."[462] In a more favorable context a coffin text had long since made Baba's privates and their potential known to mankind: "Provide yourself with that penis of Baba which makes children and sires beasts. And in what shall it be put? In the thighs where the legs split."[463] Again: the consonantal combination *d + b* generates widely differing versions of a myth. In a well-known combat episode, Horus and Seth submerge themselves as two hippopotami (*db.w*).[464] In the mythology of the eighteenth township of Upper Egypt Horus's plucked-out eyes are buried in two boxes (*db.w*) on the mountain.[465] In the mythology surrounding Bata the "back" (*s3/psḏ*) provides a focus for story production. The bull Bata is an avatar of Seth, the quintessential sacrificial victim (*sm3*): lassoed, castrated, and doomed to carry Osiris on his back.[466] In the Two Brothers, Bata castrates himself, changes into a bull and carries his brother Anpu on his back.[467] In the story he expresses revulsion at the sexual advances of his sister-in-law; in the myth the sight of man and woman coupling (*sm3*) is anathema to him.

---

[458] PT 516c.

[459] P. Chester Beatty I 3.9–4.3 (Gardiner, *Library*).

[460] Westendorf, *Koptisches Handwörterbuch*, 56.

[461] Vandier, *Papyrus Jumilhac*, 16.10–16; additional material in D. Kurth, "Bebon und Thoth," *Studien zur altägyptischen Literatur* 19 (1992): 225–30.

[462] I believe this translation of a rather difficult passage brings out the inherent insult of the bizarre self-copulation.

[463] CoffT V, 92c–g.

[464] P. Sallier IV.2, 6ff. (Gardiner, *Late Egyptian Miscellanies*); P. Chester Beatty I 8.3ff. (Gardiner, *Library*).

[465] P. Jumilhac 14.4ff. (Vandier, *Papyrus Jumilhac*).

[466] P. Jumilhac 20.14–21 (Vandier, *Papyrus Jumilhac*).

[467] P. d'Orbiney 14.5–15.2 (Gardiner, *Late Egyptian Stories*).

Repetition and Multiforms

The repetition of blocks of narration is a mainstay in the speaker's art. These are inevitably not repeated verbatim from the initial occurrence of the words but, depending upon the audience, reception may be embellished and expanded. The narrator may thereby heighten suspense, draw out the story, slow the plot, or emphasize character. Such a practice is ubiquitous in Egyptian *Märchen*.[468] Similarly "multiforms," different instantiations of a character or theme with the same function or purpose, point clearly to the oral origins of a narrative. The Contendings of Horus and Seth offers persuasive examples in the roles assigned to Neith, Baba, and Osiris and in the repetition of the themes of the worsting of the slow-witted vilain.[469]

Structure

Structure of narrative often betrays the oral nature of its composition. For one thing, the author is usually heterodiegetic (not a protagonist in his own story)[470] and narrates without personal involvement. The speaker employs devices to focus the listeners' attention: repetition of blocks of narrative material;[471] the second version always "padded out" and longer than the first; subject fronting to mark the transition to a new topic;[472] predictability in character (though not necessarily in plot) consonant with the limitations oral composition imposes on description; furtherance of narrative sequence through the employment of syntagmatic elements;[473] and maintaining single linearity in the storytelling (so that text and *fabula* become identical).

The connecting formulae between incidents are links that make sense in oral discourse. (In Egyptian the phrase *m-ḫt hrw qnw sw3 ḥr-s3 nn* ["Now after many days had passed after this . . ."]), with variants, is the favored formula.) Formulae are metonymic signifiers within the discourse code of a particular

---

[468] Cf. Redford, *Study of the Biblical Joseph Story*, 153–56.

[469] J. M. Foley, *The Theory of Oral Composition: History and Methodology* (Bloomington: Indiana University Press, 1988), 10, 12, and passim.

[470] G. Genette, *Narrative Discourse: An Essay in Method* (trans. J. E. Lewin; Ithaca, N.Y.: Cornell University Press, 1980).

[471] Bal, *Narratology*, 61.

[472] Brown and Yule, *Discourse Analysis*, 134–36.

[473] Cf. the use of *ꜥḥꜥ.n* in the Shipwrecked Sailor and Sinuhe (Collier, "Language of Literature," 533–35).

community.[474] They are constructed on metric lines for the convenience of oral delivery, but they trigger in the ear of the auditor a complex of meaning. The relationship between formula and culture component arises over time within and out of a climate of oral, not written, discourse; for such "tags" are tested in a medium where immediate reception and response can be gauged.

The Judgment of the Scribe and "Inscripturation"

Even from the ubiquity of such formulae as "to repeat," "to relate," "to cause (others) to relate," "from mouth to mouth," and so forth, a society is mirrored in which the essential means of spreading the word was oral communication. Most of the population, at least before the end of the fourth century B.C.E., knew only this mechanism for narrative, poetry, and civic pronouncements. For them the sight of a man reading from a scroll immediately signified ritual, beatification, and magic.

But out of sight, as it were, a preservation strategy was being employed that involved something more than collective or individual memory. In spite of their apparent contempt for what was conceived and passed on orally, scribes labored under an archival penchant to record; and what was deemed of aesthetic merit and practical value must be fixed to avoid possible loss. The scribe, unconsciously, thus becomes an evaluator of an oral product.

The widespread wisdom (i.e., instructional material) genre is firmly rooted on the one hand in an oral culture of aphorism. We have noted above how often a man *speaks* to his son.[475] *Sb3yt* is sometimes paralleled by *tsw*,[476] the term that indicates metrically patterned stichoi.[477] On the other hand, however, "teaching" enjoys more perhaps than any other belletristic category a transmission history within the realm of scribal tradition. In fact, wise men of the past are said to have *written* their books. "As for those wise scribes from the period that came after the gods, they who prophesied what would come to pass—and it did!—their names abide forever (even though) they are gone, they have finished their lives, and all their generation is forgotten. They did not make tombs of copper or stelae of bronze; they were not able to leave behind heirs in the form of children [. . .] pronouncing their names. (But) they made themselves heirs of the writings and teachings that they made. They set

---

[474] J. M. Foley, *Immanent Art: From Structure to Meaning in Traditional Oral Epic* (Bloomington: Indiana University Press, 1991), 11.

[475] Above, pp. 179–81.

[476] Posener, "Les richesses inconnues," 42; idem, "L'Exorde," pl. 4:1.

[477] See above, pp. 206–10.

themselves [the book(?) as lector-]priest, the writing-tablet as 'Son-whom-he-loves,' the teaching being their tombs, the pen their child, and the face of the stone the[ir] wife. . . . Doors and chapels were made, (but) they have gone to ruin, their mortuary priests are gone, their stelae are covered with earth and their tombs forgotten. But their names are still pronounced on account of their books, which they made, since they were good."[478]

An apt demonstration of this assertion of the primacy of written tradition emerges from the story-frame within which the teaching for Kagemni is set.[479] The sage has delivered himself *orally* to his children, and his words have been recorded. Then "the vizier made his children read it (back) after he had completed the 'Condition of Men.'[480] . . . Finally he said to them: 'as for everything that is in writing on this scroll, listen to it just as I said it. Do not go beyond what is authorized.' Then they prostrated themselves, and then they read it in accordance with what was in writing." The same sense of a "received text" emerges from a passage in Anastasi I (11, 1–3): "You have quoted me a phrase (*tsw*) of Hordedef, (but) you do not know whether it is the best (reading) or an inferior one:[481] which stanza comes before it and which [after] it?"[482] Precision in transcribing is also the burden of the Eloquent Peasant (B 1, 126–29): "Then the chief steward . . . said: 'now stay here that you may listen to your petitions'; and he had every petition read out to the letter(?) from a new papyrus." Neferty's wisdom is taken down immediately by the king himself;[483] and the ancestors' speeches "remain in written form" and can be easily consulted.[484]

The evidence above reveals a scribal standard, a set of criteria employed in selection. The words of the ancestors were deemed worthy of inscripturation under the following circumstances: (1) The content displayed foresight and perspicacity. (2) The ancestor in question was not anonymous but known by

---

[478] P. Chester Beatty IV verso 2.5–13 (Gardiner, *Library*).

[479] *ÄL* 43:8; A. H. Gardiner, "The Instruction Addressed to Kagemni and His Brethren," *JEA* 32 (1946): 71–74.

[480] Apparently the title of the Wisdom in question.

[481] Literally, "good or bad."

[482] On the transmission of *sb3yt* see A. Volten, *Studien zur Weisheitsbuch des Anii* (Copenhagen: Levin & Munksgaard, Ejnar Munksgaard, 1937), 49–50. (The present haphazard arrangement of pericopes conceals an original logical order; years of schoolhouse dictation are responsible.)

[483] Neferty 16–17 (Helck, *Prophezeihung*).

[484] Merikare 35–36 (Helck, *Die Lehre für König Merikare*).

name; his name continued to be pronounced on account of his works. (3) His words were "good," that is to say, they met standards of genre expectation, numinosity,[485] style, and aesthetics (as adumbrated above). Behind these standards lurks a need to ascribe and authenticate authorship, which in any other society might have fostered the growth of a canon.[486] In Egypt, however, "canonicity" was a small part of the intellectual baggage. In the sense of a *rule* or *model* to copy, the works of the wisemen of the past could have been characterized as *kanones*, as the old Greek authors were; but the notion of an external, graded scale against which a writing was to be measured for spiritual content is not reflected in ancient Egyptian thought.[487] Texts might be copied and embellished, but they were not interpreted and made coherent.[488] It is even a question to what extent scribal activity was influenced by the notion of "received text." The Egyptians knew what an "interpolation" was,[489] as well as a "variant."[490] But interpolations and variants were neither always nor necessarily measured against a gauge of pristine wording.

A second scribal strategy leading inevitably towards inscripturation of oral production is to be found in pieces used, in a loose sense, for "religious" purposes. Sacred creations, both iconographic and oral, might reveal something of what the gods wished humanity to know, but they never at any moment constituted the unalterable and complete revelation that required precise, written reproduction. For the words of the ancestors were valued, not only for

---

[485] Cf. Barthes, *Critical Essays*, 10–11. This quality, evidenced principally in art (where it has been misunderstood as "decorum"), belongs to the *master*, the *elite*; "numen" is the ultimate signifier.

[486] Stabilizing a tradition "once for all delivered to the saints" because it embodied the whole truth did not constitute a motive in the development of a canon (A. Assmann and J. Assmann, *Kanon und Zensur* [Beiträge zur Archäologie der literarischen Kommunikation 2; Munich: W. Fink, 1987], 7). Therefore those who looked for meaning outside the bounds of codification and canon did not experience suspicion and hostility (R. C. Poulsen, *Misbegotten Muses: History and Anti-history* [New York: P. Lang, 1988], 40). Momentary "effectiveness" in fact resisted canon.

[487] Parkinson ("Teachings, Discourses, and Tales," 94) refers aptly to "general codification of earlier 'classical' compositions"; see also J. Assmann, "Gibt es eine 'Klassik' in der ägyptischen Literaturgeschichte?" *ZDMG* Supplement 6 (1985): 35–52.

[488] Assmann, *Das kulturelle Gedächtnis*, 174–75.

[489] Cf. the gloss to a textual expansion of *BD* 163–65 (Grapow, *Sprachliche und schriftliche Formung*, 58 n. 9): "spells taken from another scroll over and above the (standard) 'Going-forth-by-Day.'" Cf. E. Naville, *The Funeral Papyrus of Iouya* (Cairo: Institut français d'archéologie orientale, 1908), text appended to spell 149.

[490] Cf. the ubiquitous *ky r3, ky zp, kt md3t* (*WÄS* 5:111–12).

their aesthetic and practical worth, but equally because they could be "effective" (*mnḫ*) and "beatify"(*s3ḫ*); and when these considerations spill over, as they inevitably do, into the realm of "magic" (*ḥq3*), it becomes absolutely incumbent on the scribe to write down the speaker's words. It is beyond our present knowledge why particular pieces should have suggested themselves as powerful incantations to effect specific goals; but it is a fact that writings as disparate as hymns, poems, declarations, and mythological stories could be used as potent magic if pronounced correctly and accompanied by specific ritual.

And here the mere writer-scribe loses his control as an arbiter. For magical potency is never fixed, but undergoes constant expansion and change. The magician adds, modifies, and discards as he senses the substance *ḥq3* constantly redistributing itself throughout the cosmos. The whole thrust of the spell aims at the release of power through decoding, and thereby appropriating some part of a thing's essence; and such decoding never ceases, as the essence belongs properly to the realm of "becoming" (*ḫpr*) and is forever eluding attempts finally to fix its form. All that the writer-scribe can do is to try to keep abreast of a genuinely oral tradition that enjoys its own vibrant life, and record its momentary stages.

From the Oral to the Written: The Case of Old Babylonian Prophecy[1]

Karel van der Toorn
Amsterdam University

Introduction

The study of ancient history is a study of silent witnesses. The ancients have become mute. Words they once spoke either have been lost forever or reach us through the echo of written records. However, words written can never replace words spoken. The very fact of fixation in writing affects the nature and content of the communication. It is up to the historian to determine how the two different modes of communication are related. That question is especially relevant when the communication, reflected in writing, is by nature a speech act. Prophecy is a case in point. Prophets are speakers. And yet their message can only be reconstructed on the basis of written words. This essay will deal with the relationship between the oral and the written, focusing on Old Babylonian prophecy.

The phenomenon of prophecy can be approached from various angles. I will here analyze it as a particular form of communication. Prophecy is the transmission of a message, from a god, through a prophet, to its destination. In the Old Babylonian records of prophecy this destination is usually the king. In addition to the god, the prophet, and the king, the prophetic communication usually involves other parties as well. The prophet rarely speaks to the king in person. In the majority of documented cases, he delivers his message to a deputy of the king, who then transmits it to its destination. Other people are

[1] An earlier version of this essay was published in *JNSL* 24/1 (1998): 55–70. Permission to reprint the article in revised form is gratefully acknowledged.

implicated, accidentally or on purpose, when they witness the one or the other phase of this process of communication.

We owe our knowledge of Old Babylonian prophecy to the fact that somewhere along the lines of communication, writing was used as a medium. These records of prophecy are known by Assyriologists and biblical scholars as "prophetic" letters or documents—"prophetic" because they refer to or cite prophecies. After the first publication of a prophetic letter from Mari in 1950,[2] their number has been steadily increasing, and now totals some forty published texts (revelatory dreams excluded).[3] Most of them can be found in Durand's edition of the prophetic texts from Mari,[4] but some must be looked for in other places.[5] Mostly it is the king's deputy who has the message put in writing,[6] and

---

[2] A. Lods, with G. Dossin, "Une tablette inédite de Mari, intéressante pour l'histoire ancienne du prophétisme sémitique," in *Studies in Old Testament Prophecy Presented to Professor Theodore H. Robinson by the Society for Old Testament Study on His Sixty-fifth Birthday* (ed. H. H. Rowley; Edinburgh: T&T Clark, 1950), 103–10.

·[3] The first to advocate explicitly a clear separation between prophecies and dreams is I. Nakata, "Two Remarks on the So-called Prophetic Texts from Mari," *Acta Sumerologica* 4 (1982): 143–48, esp. 143. He has been followed by J.-M. Durand (*Archives épistolaires de Mari I/1* [ARM 26; Paris: Éditions Recherche sur les civilisations, 1988], 377–452 [prophecies], 455–482 [dreams]); D. Charpin ("Le Contexte historique et géographique des prophéties dans les textes retrouvés à Mari," *Bulletin of the Canadian Society for Mesopotamian Studies* 23 [1992]: 21); and, on their authority, by most other recent writers on Mari prophecy. (Particular texts from *Archives épistolaires* will be cited below with the designation ARM 26 plus the numbers assigned them by Durand.) Though this separation is methodologically sound, it should not lead to a neglect of the relationship, from a point of view of both psychology of religion and institutional kinship, between prophetic oracles and prophetic dreams. According to various biblical texts the dream is one of the usual ways in which prophets received their messages (see, e.g., Num 12:6; Jer 23:25). According to some of the Mari texts, gods could appear in dreams and pronounce a rather clear oracle (see, e.g., ARM 26 nos. 233 and 238).

[4] Durand, *Archives épistolaires*, 377–452.

[5] L. Cagni (*Le profezie di Mari* [Testi del Vicino Oriente antico 2/2; Brescia: Paideia, 1995]) based his work almost entirely on the edition of the prophetic texts and the dream reports by Durand in ARM 26. He thus failed to include ARM 26 no. 371 and A.1968 (published in J.-M. Durand, "Le Mythologème du combat entre le Dieu de l'Orage et la Mer en Mésopotamie," *MARI* 7 [1993]: 43–45, but known before from D. Charpin and J.-M. Durand, "La Prise du pouvoir par Zimri-Lim," *MARI* 4 [1985]: 297 nn. 20–21).

[6] ARM 26 nos. 195, 196, 197, 198, 199, 200, 201, 202, 203, 204, 205, 206, 207, 208, 209, 210, 211, 212, 213, 214, 215, 216, 217, 218, 219, 220, 221, 221bis, 222, 223, 237, 243, 371, A.1121+A.2731 (B. Lafont, "Le Roi de Mari et les prophètes du dieu Adad," *RA* 78 [1984]: 7–18), A.1968 (Durand, "Mythologème du combat," 43–45).

on occasion it is the prophet himself.[7] In addition there are the references to prophets in dream reports,[8] in letters to the king,[9] and in lists of expenditures.[10] The written document is the sole means by which we can hope to reconstruct the phenomenon of Old Babylonian prophecy—and for that reason we must be glad to have it. At the same time, however, the written report is just one link in the chain of transmission; it is, in a sense, accidental to the whole process. Even though the documents are contemporary with the prophecies, they must be used with caution and discrimination if we wish to obtain a complete picture of the prophetic communication. The first delivery of the message must be distinguished from its transmission, the reception being yet another phase of the process of communication.

The Place and Mode of Revelation

The prophetic message originates with the god; such, at any rate, is the conviction of the prophet and his audience. Most modern Assyriologists would take a different view, but it is useful, for the time being, to adopt the perspective of the ancients. Before any message can be transmitted, then, it must be revealed by the god.

In the communication with their prophets, the Old Babylonian gods tend to follow the rule that revelations occur in the sanctuary. This is an important point that has not received the attention it deserves. The servant who is to keep the king informed about the prophecies from Terqa, a famous religious center, hears the oracles as they happen "in the temple of the god."[11] When a god speaks directly through the mouth of a prophet, the latter utters the prophecy first in the temple. The *āpilum* or *āpiltum* "rises" (*itbi*) or "stands" (*izziz*), normally in front of the god (i.e., the divine image) on whose behalf he is speaking, and delivers the divine message in the temple.[12] The ecstatic, too,

---

[7] ARM 26 nos. 192, 193, and 194; FLP 1674 and FLP 2064, both published in M de J. Ellis, "The Goddess Kitītum Speaks to King Ibalpiel: Oracle Texts from Ishchali," *MARI* 5 (1987): 235–66.

[8] Most notably ARM 26 no. 227.

[9] E.g., ARM 26 no. 414.

[10] See Durand, *Archives épistolaires*, 380–81, 396–99.

[11] ARM 26 no. 196: [8]*ig[e]rrûm ša ina bīt ilim* [9] *i[ba]ššû tešemmû* [10]*a[n]a ṣēr[iy]a šupram.*

[12] A.1121+2731 (= Lafont, "Le Roi de Mari," 7–18): 29–30 (Addu temple at Aleppo); ARM 26 nos. 195:5–7 (temple of Ḫišamitum); 204:4–5 (Bēlet-ekallim temple); 209:4–7 (during sacrifices for Dagan); 211:5–9 (Bēlet-ekallim temple); 219:4'–6' (Ninḫursagga temple).

receives the revelation in a sanctuary; this is the place where he or she gets into a frenzy (*immaḫi, immaḫu*),[13] utters loud cries (*šitassû*),[14] and gives the oracle.[15] When a prophet delivers an oracle outside the sanctuary, at the residence of the royal deputy for instance, it must be assumed that he repeats an oracle revealed to him in the sanctuary.[16] For that reason the prophet presents himself as a messenger of the god (DN *išpuranni*):[17] he transmits the message (*ṭēmum*) which he received at an earlier stage.[18]

The notion of the temple as a place of revelation comes to the fore in several dream reports as well. The dream of one Malik-Dagan offers a fine illustration. This is what the man says:

> In my dream I was going, together with a companion, from the district of Saggarātum, through the upper district, to Mari. Before I got to my destination, I entered Terqa. As soon as I came into Terqa, I visited the temple of Dagan, and did obeisance to Dagan. As I did obeisance, Dagan opened his mouth and spoke to me in these terms: Have the Yaminite rulers and their armies made peace with Zimrilim's army that has come up? I said: They did not make peace. Just before I left he spoke to me: Why is it that Zimrilim's messengers are not steadily present before me? And why doesn't he put a complete report before me? Had he done so, I would have delivered the Yaminites into Zimrilim's hand a long time ago. Go now, I send you. You shall say to Zimrilim: Send me your messengers and put a complete report before me. Then I will make the Yaminites crawl in a fisherman's box and put them at your disposal.[19]

There is nothing in this account to suggest that Malik-Dagan was in the temple when he received the dream; this is not a case of incubation or temple sleep.[20]

---

[13] ARM 26 no. 213:4–7; 214:5–7.

[14] ARM 26 no. 202:15–16, cf. 7–8.

[15] ARM 26 no. 200:3–6 (Annunītum temple); 215:9–16 (Dagan temple at Tuttul); 227:6–20 (Abba temple, dream report); 237:22–23 (Annunītum temple).

[16] Cf. ARM 26 no. 212:5–12, cf. rev. 10'–11', where the *assinnum* (transvestite) of Annunītum comes to the palace and delivers an oracle received in the temple of Annunītum.

[17] ARM 26 no. 210:11 (a woman married to a free citizen, on behalf of Dagan); 220:19 (*muḫḫûm* of Dagan); 221:15 (*muḫḫûm* of Dagan). Note that the *āpilum* never refers to himself as a messenger of the god, even when he gives his oracle outside the temple (ARM 26 no. 371; A.1121+2731:46–47; A.1968:3–4). This fact suggests that the *āpilum* was known to be an interpreter of the god and did not need to explain the capacity in which he spoke.

[18] ARM 26 no. 212 rev. 10'–11'; cf. no. 414:32–33.

[19] ARM 26 no. 233:9–39.

[20] For a likely case of incubation see ARM 26 no. 232:7–9: "Dagan, your lord, put me to sleep and no one dared to touch me. Dagan spoke to me as follows . . ."; cf. no. 235, possibly

And yet his dream was clearly a revelation, culminating in his being commissioned to deliver a message to the king. Not only does this account show the close links that exist between messenger prophecies and certain dream experiences; it also reflects the fact that prophets normally receive their revelations in the temple. When they were not in the temple in person, they visited the temple in their dreams.[21]

The dream report of Malik-Dagan puts into relief yet another aspect of Old Babylonian prophecy. It is clear from the description that Dagan is supposed to speak from within his image. In fact, the author of the letter makes no distinction between the god and his image. It is evident from other texts that the prophet who makes himself the mouthpiece of the god rises and stands before the god, that is, the image of the god, in whose name he delivers an oracle. Note the following description.

> And the ecstatic (*muḫḫûm*) rose before (igi) Dagan and spoke as follows: Shall I never drink clean water? Write to Your Lord that he should let me drink clean water![22]

This text renders explicit a procedure that remains implicit in most other texts, where it is simply said that the prophet "rises" or "stands" in the temple. In all cases, however, the prophet puts himself in front of the god in whose name he speaks and thus makes himself an extension of that god. There is no room for misunderstanding as to who is speaking. That is why we never find, in any of the reports describing a prophecy delivered in the temple, a phrase identifying the divine speaker.[23] The expression *umma DN-ma* ("thus god So-and-so") is restricted to letters from gods or their *āpilum*.[24] The only time when the prophet finds it necessary to say that god So-and-so has sent him (DN *išpuranni*) is

---

a dream received in the temple of Annunītum, and no. 238, a dream by the temple supervisor of Itūr-mēr that was presumably received in the temple precinct of the goddess. ARM 26 no. 236 reports a vision (dream?) received in the temple of Itūr-mēr.

[21] See also ARM 26 nos. 227:6–20 (dream about two *muḫḫû* in the temple of the god Abba); 230 (dialogue between an old man and Itūr-mēr in the stelae-temple of Dagan); 237:8–21 (events in the temple of Bēlet-ekallim); 240 (temple of Bēlet-ekallim?).

[22] ARM 26 no. 215:15–21. See also ARM 26 no. 227:6ff. "In my dream Ḫadnu-El and Iddin-Kubi, the ecstatics, were alive and went before Abba. They spoke as follows . . ." (an oracle from the god Abba continues here).

[23] Compare the texts mentioned in n. 12. ARM 26 no. 213:7 is no exception because the phrase *umma Annunītumma* is not a quotation from the prophecy but an explanation by Queen Šibtu, who sent the letter. The one time where one does encounter a self-introduction is A.1121+2731:14–15, 49–50 (Lafont, "Roi de Mari," 7–18), but there it serves not to reveal the identity of the divine speaker, but to underline the favors formerly bestowed by the god.

[24] See ARM 26 nos. 192; 193; 194; and FLP 1674 (= Ellis, "Goddess Kitītum," 235–66).

when the prophecy is transmitted to someone outside the sanctuary.[25] The *Botenformel*, then, does not belong to the prophecy properly speaking, but to the introduction to the secondarily transmitted prophecy.

Inspiration is the usual channel through which the god spoke to the ecstatic. The Babylonian term for ecstatic, *muḫḫûm*, derives from a verb *maḫû*, occurring mostly in the N-stem with the meaning "to rave, to go mad, to get a fit, to fall into a trance, to go into a frenzy." Formally, *muḫḫûm* belongs to a class of words denoting physical or mental disabilities:[26] it might be translated as "madman,"[27] and corresponds to Greek μάντις"—which, presumably, is etymologically connected with μαίνομαι, "to act madly, to rave, to be delirious." When the god seized the ecstatic, the latter went into a frenzy and started to utter words that were really words of the god. Being possessed, the prophet appeared to lose his self-control; his behavior bordered on the compulsory. He had no command over his speech, and the words he uttered were not always intelligible and coherent.

Prophecies based on the interpretation of signs were the domain of the *āpilum*. The term *āpilum* derives from the verb *apālu*, "to answer, to pay a claim, to correspond to," and occurs already in third-millennium Ebla texts in the sense of "interpreter."[28] Also in a religious context, the *āpilum* is best understood as an "interpreter";[29] the term corresponds to Greek προφήτης.[30] The case of the prophets of Adad in Aleppo offers an illustration of the

---

[25] See n. 17.

[26] *GAG*, § 55n.

[27] Note the association with the *lillatum*, "crazy woman." See G. Bardet et al., *Archives administratives de Mari* (ARM 23; Paris: Éditions Recherche sur les civilisations, 1984), 1:354 and n. 67.

[28] See W. von Soden, "Dolmetscher und Dolmetschen im alten Orient," in *Aus Sprache, Geschichte und Religion Babyloniens* (ed. L. Cagni and H.-P. Müller; Naples: Istituto universitario orientale, Dipartimento di studi asiatici, 1989), 351–57, esp. 351–52. It is likely that the functionary known as *āpilu* at Nuzi was likewise an interpreter (W. Mayer, *Nuzi-Studien I: Die Archive des Palastes und die Prosopographie der Berufe* [AOAT 205/1; Kevelaer : Butzon & Bercker; Neukirchen-Vluyn : Neukirchener Verlag, 1978], 140–41.

[29] The more usual translation, "answerer," is less attractive because it implies "that the person provides an answer to an explicit or implicit inquiry"; see H. B. Huffmon, "Ancient Near Eastern Prophecy," *ABD* 5:478. The fact of the matter is that an *āpilum* delivers oracles without being solicited; to say that there has been an "implicit inquiry" goes well beyond the available evidence.

[30] Note that the Greek term also means "interprète d'un dieu, d'où celui qui transmet ou explique la volonté des dieux" (A. Bailly, *Dictionnaire Grec-Français* [Paris: Hachette, 1950], s.v. προφήτης).

procedure by which the *āpilum* might obtain his oracle.[31] During the extispicy performed on the occasion of the sacrifices (*ina têrētim*), the god Adad "is present" (*izzaz*). This observation corresponds with the traditional apodosis *manzāz* (or *mazzāz*) ^d*Adad*, "presence of Adad," in the omen literature.[32] The diagnosis, established by the diviner *bārûm*, is then elaborated by the prophets (lú.meš *a-pí-lu*) of Adad in a message to Zimrilim reminding him of Adad's help and the king's duty to give something in return. Their prophecy has been confirmed by the repeated presence of Adad during the extispicy. The prophets of Adad interpret the will of their god on the basis of the result of an extispicy; there is no hint of a trance or a sudden illumination.

The Transmission of the Message

Once the revelation has taken place, the oracle must be transmitted to its final destination. In the Old Babylonian prophecies for which we have written evidence, this is usually the king. In none of the documented cases has the king himself been present in the temple when the revelation occurred. Often, however, there is a royal deputy who has heard the prophecy. It is then his responsibility to relay the oracle to his master; the prophet's task is finished.[33]

Often enough the prophet bears the responsibility for the transmission of the message, because neither the king nor his deputy was present in the temple. The prophet has basically two ways to go about this: he can either go and see the royal deputy, deliver his message, and enjoin upon him to relay the message to the king, or he can write to the king himself, give the letter to the royal deputy, and have him forward it. On occasion there are attendant intermediaries: the temple supervisor (*šangû*) may inform the royal deputy of a prophecy that occurred in the temple, expecting the deputy to inform the king,[34] or the prophet may deliver his message to a courtier, who relays it to his superior, who in turn relays it to the king.[35] In the majority of cases, however,

---

[31] A.1121+A.2731, published in Lafont, "Le Roi de Mari," 7–18.

[32] See, for instance, A. Goetze, *Old Babylonian Omen Texts* (YOS 10; New Haven: Yale University Press, 1947), 10 52 iii 10 *mazzāz* ^dim, and other references given in *CAD* M/1 238, s.v. *manzāzu* 7.

[33] See ARM 26 nos. 195; 196; 200; 202; 204; 209; 211; 215; 219; A.1121+A.2731:13–33.

[34] See ARM 26 nos. 200 and 201; 216:19–24; other prophecies from the temple of Annunītum (see nos. 198; 213; 214; 237:22–33) may have come to the notice of the palace likewise through the agency of Aḫum, the temple supervisor.

[35] See ARM 26 no. 208 obv. The *āpilum* does not get beyond the gate of the palace at Mari. A courtier relays his message to Queen Šibtu, who informs King Zimrilim in a letter.

there are two intermediaries between the god and the king: first the prophet, and then the deputy. The royal deputy is accountable to the king. If he does not inform his master of the oracle that has come to his knowledge, he sins against the king. The deputies, governors, and ambassadors of Zimrilim are well aware of this duty. Thus the ambassador Nūr-Sîn writes from Aleppo:

> Formerly, when I was stationed in Mari I passed on to My Lord every word that a prophet or prophetess would say. Now that I am stationed in another country wouldn't I send word to My Lord of what I hear them say? If sooner or later some accident should happen, wouldn't My Lord say: "Why didn't you write me the message the prophet spoke to you?"[36]

Embarrassed by the demands of the prophets of Aleppo, Nūr-Sîn defends himself by saying that it would be a dereliction of duty if he concealed a prophecy from the king. The administration did indeed require its servants to be on the alert for any oracle that might come to their notice.[37] Temple supervisors, too, were expected to report prophecies to the king.[38]

The prophet is accountable to his god. If he does not transmit the message he received, he fails to fulfil his duty as a messenger. As long as the oracle does eventually reach the king, the prophet's sense of duty cannot be questioned. The attitude of the deputy who has to convey the message to the king is an uncertain factor, however. To increase the chances of the message being passed on to the king, the prophet may inform two representatives of the king.[39] The same purpose is served when the prophet delivers his oracle in the presence of a witness.[40] Witnesses were not necessarily aware of the contents of the

---

[36] A.1121+A.2731: ³⁴*panānum inūma ina Mari wašbāku* ³⁵*lú āpilum u āpiltum mimma awatam* ³⁶*ša iqa[bb]ûnim ana bēlīya utâr* ³⁷ *inanna i[n]a mātim šanītim wašbāku* ³⁸ *ša ešemmû u iqabbûnim* ³⁹ *ana bēlīya ul ašappar* ⁴⁰ *šumma urram šēram mimma ḫiṭ[ītu]m ittabši* ⁴¹ *bēlī kiam ul iqabbi ummāmi* ⁴² *awatam ša lú āpilum iqbikum . . .*⁴³ *. . . ammīnim ana ṣēriya* ⁴⁴ *lā tašpuranni.*

[37] See also ARM 26 nos. 196:7–10.

[38] ARM 26 no. 200:1–6. A biblical parallel is found in Amos 7:10–13, where Amaziah, the priest of Bethel, reports to the king an oracle pronounced by Amos in the temple of Bethel.

[39] ARM 26 no. 199:41–54.

[40] A.1121+A.2731:46–47.60–61. Nūr-Sîn's letter mentions other witnesses, in line 7, in connection with a prophetic order by one Alpân. In this case the initiative to have witnesses seems to lie with the king's official. This is how I translate lines 6–12: "[On] account of the *zukrum* to be given to Adad, Alpân spoke to me before Zu-ḫatnim, Abi-šadî, and PN3: 'Give the *zukrum* . . . and the cows. My Lord (i.e., Adad), in the presence of . . . men, ordered me to give the *zukrum*, saying: In the future, let him (i.e., Zimrilim) not come back upon his

prophecy. After the *āpilum* Atamrum dictated a letter containing a message from the sun-god Šamaš, he brought it to the king's deputy and urged him, in the presence of witnesses, to forward the letter to the king, and to recommend to him to act in accordance with its contents.[41] Atamrum used witnesses to put pressure on the royal deputy, hoping thus to ensure that his letter would reach the king. It is the equivalent of our certified mail.[42]

On occasion the role of witnesses is transferred to an audience. They did not ask to get involved in the transmission of the prophecy, but once they have heard it they become partners of the prophet. In many a report, the audience goes unmentioned. When the deputy has heard the prophecy in the temple, however, it is fairly sure that other visitors have been present at the scene.[43] At times, it is clear that the prophet seeks the presence of an audience. According to one report,[44] an ecstatic from the Dagan temple in Terqa assembled the elders of the city in the Saggaratum gate,[45] devoured a living lamb before their eyes,[46] and then announced that there would be an epidemic among the cattle (*ukultum*, literally a "devouring") unless the sacred property (*asakkum*) of the god be returned and an anonymous evil-doer be banned from the city.[47] The

---

promise to me!' I secured witnesses for him (lú.meš *šībī aškunšum*). My Lord should be aware of it."

[41] ARM 26 no. 414:35–42 "That man made witnesses take their stand (lú.meš *šībī ušzizamma*) and said to me: Have this tablet brought quickly (to the king) and let him act in accordance with the content of the tablet. This is what he said. Now I have sent that tablet to My Lord."

[42] *Pace* Durand, *Archives épistolaires*, 383.

[43] See ARM 26 nos. 195; 204; 209; 215; 219:4'–6', 17'–22'.

[44] ARM 26 no. 206.

[45] Durand interprets this detail to mean that the event took place in the city of Saggaratum, which leads him to the identification of Zimrilim's official as Yaqqim-Addu. No other text from Mari mentions a *muḫḫûm* from the Dagan temple from Saggaratum, however, whereas Terqa is the home of various other ecstatics and kindred folk. Since Saggaratum lies north of Terqa upstream along the Ḫabur, the Saggaratum gate must have been the name of the northern gate of Terqa.

[46] I assume that the report mentions the consumption of the lamb before the gathering of the elders on account of the impact this act of savagery made on the writer. The actual order of events should be reversed.

[47] It is possible that this unidentified evildoer should be identified with Sammêtar, majordomo of the palace in Mari, but once governor at Terqa. According to another prophecy, Dagan had cursed the bricks of the house of Sammêtar — for which reason it was never to be rebuilt (ARM 26 no. 243:9–12). Sammêtar was not popular with the inhabitants of Terqa (cf. ARM 26 no. 232:14–21). The very idea of his house being restored made them physically sick (ARM 26 no. 234 rev. 16'–18').

deputy who informed the king about this event did not fail to point out that the prophet did not speak in secret (*ina simištim*) but in the presence of the elders.[48] Their involvement made it nearly impossible for the authorities to act as if nothing had happened.

The role of the audience raises the question of the true destination of the prophecy. In some cases there is an obvious distinction between the apparent addressee and the intended audience. From Babylon, there is a report of a prophecy by the *āpilum* of Marduk directed at Išme-Dagan, the king of Ekallātum, as he lies bed-ridden in Babylon.[49] The prophet first goes to the palace gate of King Hammurabi to announce in a loud voice (*ištanassi*) that Išme-Dagan will not escape from the hand of Marduk. As nobody replies, the *āpilum* goes to the lodging of Išme-Dagan himself and there, "in the midst of the entire population" (*ina puḫur mātim kališa*), accuses the diseased king of having appropriated the temple treasures of Marduk to buy peace with Elam. No one dares to say a thing. For whom is the prophecy intended? Not Išme-Dagan, to be sure. The prophet vents his indignation first at King Hammurabi, who extends hospitality to Išme-Dagan. When the palace fails to react, he cries out an indictment of Išme-Dagan before a crowd of citizens. Although the prophecy is apparently directed at Išme-Dagan, these citizens are the actual audience of the prophet. Their silent approval of his critique increases the pressure on Hammurabi to dissociate himself from Išme-Dagan.

From the Oral to the Written

As the prophecy finally reaches its destination, it has passed several intermediaries, and we cannot be sure that the words reported to the king are a faithful reproduction of the message the prophet received from the god. Is there any way to assess the effects of the way in which the prophecy was transmitted upon its written form?

To answer this question, it is necessary to distinguish between reports of prophecy written by royal deputies and members of the court, on the one hand, and letters from prophets themselves, on the other. When prophets are themselves responsible for the written fixation of their messages, they may choose to couch their letters either as letters from the gods or as letters dictated by themselves. This is merely a matter of form: it is optional to add "Thus says

---

[48] ARM 26 no. 206:32–34.

[49] ARM 26 no. 371:9–33. For an earlier commentary see M. Anbar, "Mari and the Origin of Prophecy," in Kinattūtu ša dārâti: *Raphael Kutscher Memorial Volume* (ed. A. F. Rainey; Tel Aviv: Journal of the Institute of Archaeology of Tel Aviv University, Occasional Publications 1, 1993), 1–5, esp. 3–5.

So-and-so, the prophet" before the mandatory sentence "Thus says god So-and-so."[50] From the one reference to a prophet asking for a scribe to write down a divine message,[51] it may be inferred that the Babylonian prophets, quite like the biblical Jeremiah (chap. 36), did not write themselves but made use of a scribe. Since a scribe in antiquity is also an editor, the letters by prophets cannot be regarded, without qualification, as the transcript of the *ipsissima verba* of the prophet. Nor do the revelation of the message and its dictation coincide; the few days that lay between them may have erased or added certain details in the memory of the prophet.[52]

We must be aware, moreover, of the fact that the Babylonian prophets did not use the epistolary medium because they wanted their very words to be preserved for posterity but on account of the confidentiality of their message. They knew that they were transmitting "the secrets of the gods" (*niṣrētum ša* dingir.meš, *niṣrēt* dingir.meš) to quote a letter from the goddess Kitītum.[53] For that reason the scribe at the service of the prophet had to be "discreet" (*naṣrum*).[54] The letter was dispatched, through the agency of a royal deputy, in a sealed envelope so that, besides the prophet and his scribe, nobody but the king (and his secretary) would learn its contents.

The fact that prophets would themselves write to the king (that is, with the help of a scribe) suggests that they realized that their message could be altered if they left its transmission to someone else. The occasional use of witnesses points in the same direction. Officials reporting a prophecy to the king would summarize the prophetic message; they often wrote, as one of them says, "the tenor of the words (the prophet) spoke" (*ṭē[m awātim ša] idbubunimma*).[55] In the exceptional case where they tried to reproduce the words of a prophet in a

---

[50] Compare ARM 26 no. 194:2–3 with nos. 192:2, 16, 26; 193:3–4; FLP 2064:2 (see Ellis, "Goddess Kitītum," 239); FLP 1674:2 (see Ellis, "Goddess Kitītum," 240 n. 25).

[51] ARM 26 no. 414:29–33.

[52] Note the formulation in ARM 26 no. 414:29–35 "Atamrum the *āpilum* of Šamaš came to me and said: Send me a discreet scribe, that I may have him write down the message which Šamaš sent me for the king." The verbal form (*ṭēmam ša Šamaš ana šarrim*) *išpuranni* may be an Assyriasm (*-anni* < *-am-ni*, see *GAG*³, § 83b), or it could be interpreted in analogy with ARM 26 no. 212 recto 10'–11' *ṭēm* PN *ša Annunītum išpuraš[š]u*, translated by Durand "La nouvelle d'Ilî-haznaya qu'Annunîtum m'a envoyée par son intermédiaire."

[53] FLP 1674:3.7 (see Ellis, "Goddess Kitītum," 240 n. 25).

[54] ARM 26 no. 414:31. For *mār bīt ṭuppī naṣram* as "discreet scribe," see D. Charpin, "Contexte historique," 25. Contrast Durand, *Archives épistolaires*, 391 n. 80, who interprets the adjective in the sense of "competent."

[55] ARM 26 no. 199:54–56.

literal manner, they chose a formulation that emphasized that the king was given a verbatim report. When she quotes the rather crude terms which the transvestite Šēlebum used in his message, Inibšina (the presumed writer of the letter) stresses that she herself writes "in the terms in which Šēlebum spoke" (*[an]a pî Šēlebum i[qbêm]*).[56] A similar significance must also be given to the expression "I wrote my lord the very words of her mouth" (*[aw]āt pîša ana bēliya ašpuram*).[57]

In most, if not all, cases, the *ipsissima verba* of the prophet will probably elude us forever: the original voice has been modified through the intervention of scribes and informers, none of whom regarded verbal accuracy as an imperative in communicating the message to the king. Whether their version of a given prophecy was in conformity with its original formulation is usually impossible to say, not only because the oral original is irretrievable, but also because we possess but one version of the event. Were we to have two versions of one prophecy, it might be possible to reconstruct the original by means of text-critical study. Several authors have claimed that, in fact, there is one instance where this is possible; they refer to "one prophecy, delivered by a single divine messenger but communicated to the king by at least three different Mari personalities."[58] The letters are written by Sammêtar, majordomo of Zimrilim at Mari; Inibšina, priestess at Mari and daughter of the king; and by Kanisân, an official at Mari. They all report on a prophecy that goes back, ultimately, to Dagan of Terqa. The case merits a reassessment.

The various reports date from the time when Zimrilim was planning to conclude a treaty with King Ibal-pi-El from Ešnunna. For one year there had been armed hostilities between them, but now, in the sixth year of Zimrilim's reign, the king of Ešnunna was offering peace. Zimrilim was inclined to accept, but before committing himself to the treaty he consulted the gods of the principal cult centers of his kingdom. Lupaḫum, an *āpilum* of Dagan, received orders to solicit an oracle from Dagan of Terqa. He was to report to Sammêtar at Mari.

From the letter Sammêtar sent to Zimrilim it is clear that the prophets of Terqa were not in favor of the treaty. Their god Dagan promises peace through conquest, which is not the same as peace through alliance. In a private

---

[56] ARM 26 no. 198:1".

[57] ARM 26 no. 217:28.

[58] J. M. Sasson, "Water beneath Straw: Adventures of a Prophetic Phrase in the Mari Archives," in *Solving Riddles and Untying Knots: Biblical, Epigraphic, and Semitic Studies in Honor of Jonas C. Greenfield* (ed. Z. Zevit, S. Gitin, and M. Sokoloff; Winona Lake, Ind.: Eisenbrauns, 1995), 600. See also Charpin, "Contexte historique," 23–25; S. B. Parker, "Official Attitudes Toward Prophecy at Mari and in Israel," *VT* 43 (1993): 57–60.

communication to Sammêtar, the *āpilum* who transmitted the words of the prophets ("Siege Tower and Battering Ram have been given to you: they go at your side, they come to your aid") intimates that the oracle of victory should be interpreted as advice against the treaty:

> I am afraid the king will commit himself (lit.: touch his throat) to (the peace proposal of) the man of Ešnunna without asking the god. (. . .) Now, when he has not asked the god, he must not commit himself (lit.: touch his throat).[59]

Shortly after Lupaḫum left, Sammêtar received the visit of a *qammātum* of Dagan, also from Terqa:

> The next day a *qammātum* of Dagan of Terqa came to me and spoke to me in the following terms: "Beneath the straw the water is running. They keep sending messages proposing peace, and they even send their gods, but it is a very different wind they are planning in their hearts. The king must not commit himself (lit. touch his throat) without (first) asking the god." She asked for an ordinary *laharûm*-garment and a bracelet, which I gave her. She also gave her oracle in the chapel of Bēlet-ekallim to the priestess Inibšina.[60]

The Mari archives also contain a letter by Inibšina in which she reports her version of the oracle the *qammātum* gave to her in the Bēlet-ekallim temple:

> Now a *qammātum* of Dagan of Terqa came to me and spoke to me in the following terms: "The friendship of the Man of Ešnunna is a fraud: beneath the straw the water is running (*šapal tibnim mû illakū*). In the very net which he knots I will collect him, and his possession from of old I will put to utter waste." This is what she said to me. Now take care of yourself. Do not enter the treaty without an oracle (*balum têrtim*).[61]

From these two passages it would seem that Dagan's *qammātum* acted at her own initiative, and that the oracle she gave had been communicated to her personally by the god. A letter by Kanisân, also residing in Mari, shows that the woman was in fact relaying an oracle that resounded like a refrain in the Dagan temple at Terqa:

> My father Kibri-Dagan wrote to me in Mari saying: "[I heard] the words that are being said [in the temple of Dagan]. Thus they say: Beneath the

---

[59] ARM 26 no. 199: [30] *as[s]uri šarrum balum ilim šâlim* [31] *ana* lú-[èš]-nun-na[ki] *napištašu* [32] *ilappat* (...) [38] *[in]anna balum i[la]m iš[a]llu* [39] *n[apiš]tašu lā ilappat.*

[60] ARM 26 no. 199:41–54.

[61] ARM 26 no. 197:6–24. I take lines 22–24 to read: *. . .ba-lum te-er-tim, a-na li-ib-bi a-d[e-e], la te-er-ru-u[b]* For the expression see *ABL* no. 386:19 and cf. *ABL* no. 472:1–2. The reading *a-na- li-ib-bi a-lim* [ki] by Durand makes little sense, unless one understands that entering the city (Mari, presumably) is tantamount to entering the treaty.

straw the water is running. The god of my lord will come and deliver his enemies into his hand. Now the ecstatic (*muḫḫûm*) has again begun to vociferate as before." This is what Kibri-Dagan wrote to me. For his own good My Lord must not be negligent about making oracular inquiries. . . .[62]

A comparison of the relevant passages allows us to reconstruct the events. Alarmed by the prospect of an alliance with Ešnunna, the Dagan prophets at Terqa experience an outburst of frenzied activity. The one phrase that keeps cropping up in the reports, "beneath the straw the water is running" (*šapal tibnim mû illakū*), is the core of their oracles. Its origin is most likely traced to the one *muḫḫum* who does not stop vociferating. The striking phrase is elaborated by the other prophets in promises of victory of Zimrilim over the ruler of Ešnunna.

When the anonymous *qammātum* from Terqa comes to report the prophecy at the palace of Mari, she quotes the saying about the straw, which she then proceeds to interpret. Applying it to the peace proposals of Ešnunna, she explains that the ruler of Ešnunna harbors hostile intentions,[63] and that his friendship is a feint.[64] Her exegesis leads to the advice to the king not to commit himself to the treaty against the will of the god.[65] Since Lupaḫum volunteered exactly the same advice in a private conversation with Sammêtar, the majordomo of the palace,[66] it is uncertain whether this conclusion was actually drawn by the *qammātum* or by the person she reported to.[67]

From the one instance where we can check the various reports of a prophetic oracle against one another, it is clear that the Babylonians attached no particular importance to the *ipsissima verba* of the prophets. Since they did not adhere to a doctrine of literal inspiration, they made no special effort to preserve the exact formulation in which prophets couched their message. In Babylonia, as elsewhere in the ancient Near East, "people who recorded an orally delivered statement did not feel obligated to register it in the precise form

---

[62] ARM 26 no. 202:5–20.

[63] ARM 26 no. 199:45–48.

[64] ARM 26 no. 197:11–12.

[65] The advice is formulated euphemistically by saying that the king must not commit himself to the treaty "without asking the god." But this is precisely what Zimrilim has done by sending Lupaḫum to inquire after the opinion of the god. Neither Lupaḫum nor the *qammātum* from Terqa has any doubt that Dagan is opposed to the treaty.

[66] ARM 26 no. 199:29–40.

[67] In ARM 26 no. 197:22–24 it is Inibšina who ventures the advice; in no. 199:49–50 the words are put in the mouth of the *qammātum*.

in which they heard it. As it reached different ears, the statement was shaped to suit the perspective of the hearer."[68] To say that the "Mari prophetic texts . . . have preserved the original texts of the prophecies"[69] is to presume an attitude of the Old Babylonian officials and scribes toward spoken prophecies that is anachronistic. The notion of a literal dictation by a god occurs for the first time around 1200 B.C.E. in the Catalogue of Texts and Authors, where certain literary works are attributed to legendary sages who wrote "at the dictation of" (ša pî) the god Ea.[70] The Old Babylonian prophecies make no clear distinction between the words of the god and the interpretation by the prophet; nor does the interpretation stop once the prophet has delivered his message. The king's informant, the scribe, and the messenger transmit their understanding of the prophecy. The hermeneutical process that accompanies the transmission of the oracle shapes its written form.

Conclusion

The study of Old Babylonian prophecy as a particular form of communication opens up intriguing perspectives on the relationship between the oral message and its transmission in writing. The ease with which writers move from citation to paraphrase and interpretation should caution us against the quest for the *ipsissima verba* of the prophets. As long as the tradition reflected the spirit of the prophetic revelation it was considered to be truthful. The notion of a literal inspiration (and the views on inerrancy it eventually entailed) was first applied to texts that existed in written form only. Since the Babylonian prophets, much like their biblical counterparts, were primarily speakers,[71] their oracles were meant for an oral performance. Inasmuch as writing was used, it was not as a means of preservation, but as an aid in the process of communication. The prophecy, written by the prophet or reported by an informer, would eventually be read aloud to the king, and thus reenter the oral

---

[68] Sasson, "Water beneath Straw," 607.

[69] So Anbar, "Mari and the Origin of Prophecy," 5.

[70] Dictation by a deity serves as a model for later compositions, such as the Erra Epic. See L. Cagni, *L'epopea di Erra* (Studi semitici 34; Rome: Istituto di studi del Vicino Oriente dell'Universita, 1969), 126, V 42–44; see also the commentary, ibid., 254. The lines are presumably a secondary intercalation in the text from the mid-first millennium.

[71] "Die Propheten sind ursprünglich nicht Schriftsteller, sondern Redner gewesen" (H. Gunkel, "Die Propheten als Schriftsteller und Dichter," in *Die großen Propheten* [ed. H. Schmidt; Göttingen: Vandenhoeck & Ruprecht, 1915], xxxviii). "The preexilic prophets themselves did not write down the words they spoke. Prophets are speakers" (J. J. Schmitt, "Preexilic Hebrew Prophecy," *ABD* 5:483).

register—with all the possibilities of paraphrase and interpretation this mode of delivery entailed.[72]

---

[72] Note that the messenger who brought the tablet could, after being interrogated, supply further details and interpretations. See S. A. Meier, *The Messenger in the Ancient Semitic World* (HSM 45; Atlanta: Scholars Press, 1989), 203–8.

Spoken, Written, Quoted, and Invented: Orality and Writtenness in Ancient Near Eastern Prophecy

Martti Nissinen
University of Helsinki

Sources for Ancient Near Eastern Prophecy

Apart from the Hebrew Bible, the ancient Near Eastern documentation of prophecy—the transmission of divine messages to human addressees by human transmitters[1]—consists basically of two kinds of sources: oracles of deities in written form and references in documents of different kinds—letters, inscriptions, administrative records, and religious texts—that mention prophets, quote their sayings, or speak of their activities. The majority of the sources fall into two major corpora of texts, the first coming from eighteenth-century Mari and the second from seventh-century Nineveh. The updated list of pertinent documents from Mari consists of forty-nine letters with prophetic quotations to

---

[1] Even though there is no perfect unanimity about what the concept of "prophecy" includes or excludes, the aspect of transmission is the common denominator of the majority of currently used definitions of prophecy. Cf., among others, T. W. Overholt, *Channels of Prophecy: The Social Dynamics of Prophetic Activity* (Minneapolis: Fortress, 1989), 17–25; H. B. Huffmon, "Ancient Near Eastern Prophecy," *ABD* 5:477–82, esp. 477; H. M. Barstad, "No Prophets? Recent Developments in Biblical Prophetic Research and Ancient Near Eastern Prophecy," *JSOT* 57 (1993): 39–60, esp. 46–47; L. L. Grabbe, *Priests, Prophets, Diviners, Sages: A Socio-Historical Study of Religious Specialists in Ancient Israel* (Valley Forge, Pa.: Trinity Press International, 1995), 107; M. Weippert, "Prophetie im Alten Orient," *Neues Bibel-Lexikon* 3 (1997): 196–200, esp. 197; K. van der Toorn, "Old Babylonian Prophecy between the Oral and the Written," *JNSL* 24 (1998): 55–70, esp. 55 (a revised version of this article is included in this volume); and (with further qualifications) M. Nissinen, *References to Prophecy in Neo-Assyrian Sources* (SAAS 7; Helsinki: Neo-Assyrian Text Corpus Project, 1998), 4–9.

the king, Zimri-Lim,[2] as well as a literary text ("Epic of Zimri-Lim"),[3] two cultic texts,[4] and fourteen administrative documents[5] that mention prophets (*āpilum/āpiltum, muhhûm/muhhūtum*).[6] The Neo-Assyrian corpus includes twenty-nine individual oracles of Assyrian prophets addressed to the kings Esarhaddon and Assurbanipal[7] and twenty other texts—inscriptions, letters, administrative documents, cultic texts, and a treaty—alluding in some way to prophets (*raggimu/raggintu, mahhû/mahhūtu*)[8] or their sayings.[9]

---

[2] According to the list in J.-G. Heintz ("La 'fin' des prophètes bibliques? Nouvelles théories et documents sémitiques anciens," in *Oracles et prophéties dans l'antiquité: Actes du Colloque de Strasbourg, 15–17 Juin 1995* [ed. J.-G. Heinz; Université des sciences humaines de Strasbourg, Travaux du Centre de recherche sur le Proche-Orient et la Grèce antiques 15; Paris: De Boccard, 1997], 195–214, esp. 214), the following texts are included in this group: ARM 26/1 nos. 194–223, 229, 232–240 (J.-M. Durand, *Archives épistolaires de Mari I/1* [Paris: Éditions Recherche sur les civilisations, 1988], 417–52, 468–69, 471–82); ARM 26/2 no. 371 (D. Charpin et al., *Archives épistolaires de Mari I/2* [Paris: Éditions Recherche sur les civilisations, 1988], 177–79); A 1121 + A 2731 (B. Lafont, "Le Roi de Mari et les prophètes du dieu Adad," *RA* 78 [1984]: 7–18; to be included in ARM 26/3); A 1968 (J.-M. Durand, "Le Mythologème du combat entre le Dieu de l'Orage et la Mer en Mésopotamie," *MARI* 7 [1993]: 41–61). This list is now supplemented by the following texts: ARM 26/1 nos. 227, 243 (Durand, *Archives épistolaires*, 467, 499–500); ARM 26/2 no. 414 (Charpin et al., *Archives épistolaires*, 294–95) and ARM 27 no. 32 (M. Birot, *Correspondance des gouverneurs de Qaṭṭunân* [Paris: Éditions Recherche sur les civilisations, 1993], 88–90).

[3] An edition of this text is announced by M. Guichard (*NABU* 1994/105); for the time being it is only possible to consult the passages presented by D. Charpin and J.-M. Durand, "La Prise du pouvoir par Zimri-Lim," *MARI* 4 (1985): 297–343, esp. 325, 328, 332; and Durand, *Archives épistolaires*, 393.

[4] A 3165 (Ritual of Ištar, Text 2); A 1249b+ (Ritual of Ištar, Text 3); see J.-M. Durand and M. Guichard, "Les Rituels de Mari," in *Florilegium marianum III: Recueil d'études à la mémoire de Marie-Thérèse Barrelet* (ed. D. Charpin and J.-M. Durand; MNABU 4; Paris: Société pour l'étude du Proche-Orient ancien, 1997), 19–78.

[5] ARM 9 no. 22; ARM 21 no. 333; ARM 22 nos. 167, 326; ARM 23 no. 446; ARM 25 no. 15, 142; A 3796; A 4676; M 5529+; M 9921; M 11299; M 11436; T 82; see Durand, *Archives épistolaires*, 380–81, 396–99.

[6] For designations of prophets in the documents from Mari, see Durand, *Archives épistolaires*, 386–99 (*āpilum/āpiltum, muhhûm/muhhūtum, assinnum, qammatum*), and Heintz, "La 'fin,'" 198–202 (*nabûm*).

[7] These texts are now all published in S. Parpola, *Assyrian Prophecies* (SAA 9; Helsinki: Helsinki University Press, 1997).

[8] For Neo-Assyrian prophetic designations, see Parpola, *Assyrian Prophecies*, xlv–xlvii; Nissinen, *References*, 9–10.

[9] Most of these (Esarhaddon Nin. A i 84–ii 11; Ass. A i 31–ii 26; Assurbanipal A ii 126–

In addition, a variety of texts from different times and places have been interpreted as evidence of ancient Near Eastern prophecy. These include two oracles of the goddess Kititum from eighteenth-century Eshnunna,[10] two Hittite fourteenth-century prayers with a possible reference to prophets among other practitioners of divination,[11] a fourteenth-century letter of King Tušratta of Mitanni to Amenophis III of Egypt containing a quotation of an oracle of Ištar/Šauška of Nineveh,[12] four references to persons called *munabbiʾātu* in administrative lists from thirteenth-century Emar,[13] lexical lists and omen texts from different periods,[14] a Middle-Assyrian administrative text from the thirteenth century mentioning "prophets and prophetesses" (*mahhû, mahhūtu*) in Kar-Tukulti-Ninurta,[15] the Egyptian report of Wenamon referring to a prophetic appearance in Byblos in the eleventh century,[16] the inscription of

---

iii 26; B v 46–vi 16; T ii 7–24; SAA 2 no. 6 § 10; SAA 7 no. 9; SAA 10 nos. 109, 111, 284, 294, 352; SAA 13 no. 37 [= S. Parpola, *Letters from Assyrian Scholars to the Kings Esarhaddon and Assurbanipal* (Kevelaer: Butzon & Bercker, 1983), 317]; *ABL* 1217+; *CT* 53 17+; 938) are analyzed in Nissinen, *References*; to these should be added SAA 12 no. 69 (decree of expenditures from the time of Adad-nerari III), SAA 13 no. 144 (a letter of Nabû-reši-išši); the "Marduk ordeal" (SAA 3 no. 34; dupl. SAA 3 no. 35); and the Tammuz and Ištar ritual in W. Farber, *Beschwörungsrituale an Ištar und Dumuzi: Attī Ištar ša ḫarmaša Dumuzi* (Akademie der Wissenschaften und der Literatur, Veröffentlichungen der orientalischen Kommission 30; Wiesbaden: Franz Steiner, 1977), 140–42 (A IIa:31, 59 *mahhê u mahhūti*).

[10] FLP 1674; 2064; see M. de J. Ellis, "The Goddess Kitītum Speaks to King Ibalpiel: Oracle Texts from Ishchali," *MARI* 5 (1987): 235–66.

[11] *ANET*, 396.

[12] EA 23; see W. L. Moran, *The Amarna Letters* (Baltimore and London: Johns Hopkins Press, 1992), 61–62. The prophetic nature of this oracle has been recognized by Parpola, *Assyrian Prophecies*, xlviii.

[13] Emar 373; 379; 383; 406; see D. Arnaud, *Recherches au Pays d'Aštata 6* (3 vols.; Paris: Éditions Recherche sur les civilisations, 1985–87), 353, 360, 375–77, 403; and cf. D. E. Fleming, "The Etymological Origins of the Hebrew *nābîʾ:* The One Who Invokes God," *CBQ* 55 (1993): 217–24; ibid., "*nābû* and *munabbiātu:* Two New Syrian Religious Personnel," *JAOS* 113 (1993): 175–83.

[14] Lexical lists: MSL 12:102, 213, 132, 158, and 238; omen texts: *CT* 38:4; Tablets in the Collections of the British Museum 332; R. Labat, *Traité akkadien de diagnostics et prognostics médicaux* (Leiden: Brill, 1951), 4; and C. Boissier, *Documents assyriens relatifs aux présages* (Paris: Emile Bouillon, 1894–99), 211; see Parpola, *Assyrian Prophecies*, ciii n. 222; civ n. 232.

[15] VAT 17999 (*mahhuʾā mahhuʾāte*); see H. Freydank, "Zwei Verpflegungstexte aus Kār-Tukultī-Ninurta," *Altorientalische Forschungen* 1 (1974): 55–89; and cf. Parpola, *Assyrian Prophecies*, xlvii, cv n. 244.

[16] *ANET*, 25–29.

Zakkur, king of Hamath (ca. 800 B.C.E.), who in his distress receives an encouraging oracle from Baal-Shamayin through prophets ([*b*]*yd ḥzyn w byd ʿddn*),[17] the inscription of Deir ʿAlla from ca. 700 B.C.E. reporting a vision of Balaam, the "visionary of the gods" (*ḥzh ʾlhn*),[18] the roughly contemporary Ammonite Citadel inscription with an oracle of the god Milkom[19] and, finally, two ostraca from Lachish (ca. 600 B.C.E.) which seem to refer to prophets (*nbʾ*),[20] thus being the only extrabiblical extant sources for prophecy in preexilic Judah.

Despite the surprisingly high number—139—of individual extrabiblical texts listed above, that with more or less probability are taken as evidence for prophecy in the ancient Near East, it must be admitted that the source material as a whole is haphazard and uneven, the share of the texts from elsewhere than Mari or (Neo-)Assyria being about one-eighth at best. The vast chronological and geographical distribution of the bits and pieces supplementing the source material from Mari and Assyria is nevertheless impressive, documenting prophetic activity of some kind in different parts of the ancient Near East through the centuries and thus witnessing to an established tradition.

As regards the topic of this article, the issue of orality and writtenness of prophecy, the restricted quantity and random nature of the source material constitute problems; all conclusions regarding orality must be made on the basis of written and, as such, secondary documents, as the oral presentation is not within our reach. Even the conclusions drawn from the written records can often be founded on only a very limited set of sources. However, the existing material, consisting of various text types and different ways of documenting prophetic words, is comprehensive enough to give at least a partial insight into the transmission process from oral to written. For its proper assessment, it is necessary first to take a look at prophecy from the point of view of transmission

---

[17] *KAI* 202; see the translation and discussion in H. Donner and W. Röllig, *Kanaanäische und aramäische Inschriften,* Band II: *Kommentar* (3d ed.; Wiesbaden: Harrassowitz, 1973), 204–11.

[18] J. Hoftijzer and G. van der Kooij, *Aramaic Texts from Deir ʿAllā* (Documenta et Monumenta Orientis Antiqui 19; Leiden: Brill, 1976).

[19] The prophetic nature of this inscription is emphasized by B. Margalit, "Ninth-Century Israelite Prophecy in the Light of Contemporary NWSemitic Epigraphs," in *"Und Mose schrieb dieses Lied auf": Studien zum Alten Testament und zum Alten Orient: Festschrift für Oswald Loretz* (ed. M. Dietrich and I. Kottsieper; AOAT 250; Münster: Ugarit-Verlag, 1998), 515–32.

[20] Lachish 3:20 and 16:5; see J. Renz, *Die althebräischen Inschriften, Teil 1: Text und Kommentar, Handbuch der althebräischen Epigraphik* (ed. J. Renz and W. Röllig; Darmstadt: Wissenschaftliche Buchgesellschaft, 1995), 1:412–19, 433–34.

and then see to what extent the sources reveal the different channels used in the chain of communication.

Prophecy as a Process of Communication

If prophecy is perceived as the transmission of divine messages to human recipients, messages also called (prophetic) oracles and prophecies, the question of the means of that transmission immediately rises. This question inevitably includes the issue of the role of orality and writtenness in the process of alleged divine-human communication which necessarily consists of at least three components, and usually includes one additional component. There must be a *message* to be delivered. A message needs a *sender,* which in the case of prophecy is believed to be a divine one, as well as an *addressee* who is supposed to take notice of the message. Furthermore, as transmission and not just any revelation of the divine to a human recipient, the prophetic process of communication must involve one additional element: the transmitter, the *prophet.* In an ideal case, then, prophecy is a two-phase process, consisting of the divine revelation to the prophet and its transmission by him or her to a third party. The prophet, however, is not always directly linked with the destination of the message. When it comes to the different channels of transmitting the message from the prophet to the addressee, the process shows itself as much more complicated, and here the role of oral performance, the written record, and the difference between these two becomes significant.

A prophetic message is claimed to be of divine origin, which, of course, cannot be verified by any human means and can only be believed by the recipient or addressee. The first phase of the prophetic process of communi-cation, the revelation of the divine sender of the message, is neither oral nor written but relies solely upon the experience of the prophet, presented as a vision, a dream, an audio-visual appearance or the like. The revelation can be experienced by a variety of means. So-called ecstasy, a god-possessed state usually combined with frantic behavior, is well documented as a condition of receiving and transmitting divine revelations and is implied by such verbs as *mahû* in Akkadian[21] and *nibbāʾ/hitnabbēʾ* in Hebrew.[22] The state of frenzy as such is no prerequisite of prophecy (dreams, for instance, do not presuppose it); nevertheless, divine revelations are a matter of subjective experience beyond

---

[21] The noun *muhhûm/mahhû* is derived from this verb used for prophetic frenzy, e.g., in ARM 26 nos. 213:7; 214:7; and 222:6, 13.

[22] This denominal verb (< *nābîʾ*) is the terminus technicus for acting as a prophet in the Hebrew Bible, often implying ecstasy or an altered state of consciousness caused by the spirit of God (Num 11:24–30; 1 Sam 10:10–13; 19:20, 24; 1 Kgs 18:29; 22:10; Joel 3:1).

everyday perception and unattainable to other persons without any share in the same experience. Hence, the very existence of the first and decisive phase of the prophetic communication is entirely dependent on the credibility of the prophet—which is impossible to control in the actual situation by any rational means. Even though it was firmly believed in the ancient Near East that gods did speak and send messages through human mediators, the impossible authentication of the origin of the message caused problems concerning the reliability of the prophet—problems that could be solved only by waiting for the proclaimed word to become true (e.g., Deut 18:21–22), with the help of some divinatory means (e.g., ARM 26 no. 239:10–11), or by confessional criteria beyond the actual process of communication (e.g., Deut 13:2–6).

Since the actual addressee of the prophetic message is normally a different person from the one who receives the revelation, the message needs to be transmitted to whom it concerns. This brings forth the second, human and controllable part of the process, the delivery of the actual prophetic message by communicable means. If the message is performed orally (and/or by means of an action[23]) in the absence of the addressee, as is demonstrably often the case, its delivery to the addressee is up to the judgment of those who hear or see the performance. If they, for one reason or another, do not consider the message worth conveying to the actual destination, the addressee may never receive it. Even though the prophets certainly attempted to perform in the presence of people whom they believed to be in a position to make a personal contact with the addressee, and even though these may have been responsible for reporting the message, it was by no means sure that they would actually do so.[24] This reveals a further hindrance to the prophetic process of communication: the eventual spatial distance between the prophet and the addressee, which leaves even the second phase of the process exposed to many factors of uncertainty

---

[23] Cf. the "symbolic acts" of the prophets, familiar not only from the Hebrew Bible, but also from Mari (ARM 26 no. 206; see Heintz, "La 'fin,'" 202–12).

[24] This responsibility is acknowledged by Nur-Sîn in the letter A 1121+:34–39: "Previously, when I was still residing in Mari, I would convey every word spoken by *āpilum* or *āpiltum* to my lord. Now, living in another land, would I not communicate to my lord (everything) what I hear and they tell me?" This may be compared to the responsibility of reporting all astrological observations, even the untoward ones, to the king. Bel-ušezib, Esarhaddon's Babylonian astrologer, writes that, during the reign of Sennacherib, some scholars deliberately shirked this task (SAA 10 no. 109 recto 1–13), and Marduk-zapik-šeri confesses that he, during his confinement, did not dare to report his observations to the king (SAA 10 no. 160:6–8). On the other hand, Balasî, one of the most famous scholars, reports to Esarhaddon dutifully, and yet with deep anxiety, that he has nothing to report (SAA 10 no. 45).

concerning the memory, honesty, logistic resources, and personal interests of those involved in the conveyance of the message.

As a rule, a prophecy is a meaningful message that is meant to be understandable to the addressee who is supposed to be affected—encouraged, warned, or commanded to act—by it. Although the words used by the prophets are usually quite intelligible,[25] even a clear and understandable message always undergoes changes, even substantial ones, in the course of the communication process. Writing down the contents of the message does not necessarily "save" it in its orally performed form. Not only is the message adjusted to scribal conventions and phraseology, it may also be misunderstood or deliberately reformulated by intermediaries who may not aim at the literal preservation of the wording of the message but rely consciously on their own interpretations, not forgetting the supposed perspective of the one to whom the prophetic message is to be transmitted.[26] Even the person who reads the written tablet out to an illiterate addressee may contribute strongly to his or her understanding of the message.

From the point of view of the communication process, prophecy does not necessarily presuppose any literary activity at all. Every phase of the communication from the prophet to the addressee is possible without scribal involvement, even though the use of scribal assistance evidently facilitates the process and is urgently needed in some cases. However, the process can never be purely literal unless all the persons involved are fully literate, which would rarely have been the case in the ancient Near East.

The further sections of this essay attempt to demonstrate the different phases of the prophetic process with the help of the fragmentary collection of the written sources at our disposal. All the information we have is based on the interpretation of prophecy by other people in a variety of ways and for a variety of purposes. This inevitably raises questions concerning the reliability and viability of these documents when it comes to their use as sources of information regarding the phenomenon of prophecy in the ancient Near East.

---

[25] However, the mysterious words *hallalatti enguratti* in SAA 9 no. 7 recto 3–5 are virtually inexplicable for a modern scholar, and it is quite possible that they are intentionally obscure. See Parpola (*Assyrian Prophecies*, 39) for the possible philological explanations. Another famous example of an ambiguous message is the proverbial utterance *šapal tibnim mû illakū* ("beneath the straw runs water") quoted and interpreted in three Mari letters (ARM 26 nos. 197, 199, and 202), for which see below.

[26] Cf. the deliberations to this effect by J. M. Sasson, "Water beneath Straw: Adventures of a Prophetic Phrase in the Mari Archives," in *Solving Riddles and Untying Knots: Biblical, Epigraphic, and Semitic Studies in Honor of Jonas C. Greenfield* (ed. Z. Zevit, S. Gitin, and M. Sokoloff; Winona Lake, Ind.: Eisenbrauns, 1995), 599–608, esp. 607; see also van der Toorn, "Old Babylonian Prophecy," 68.

Does the available set of sources sufficiently and reliably represent the different forms and manifestations of ancient Near Eastern prophecy? Why are some aspects of this phenomenon so well documented while others remain obscure? Why have so few prophecies been deposited in archives, and whose interests have thereby been served? Are the prophetic utterances transmitted so that they reflect the actual proclamations in concrete situations? If not, what is the role of the transmitters, interpreters, and editors of the prophetic words? Are prophecies believed to have a substance independent from their interpretation? Could it be that in some cases written prophecies are not based on actual prophetic performances at all? Is it possible to reconstruct the very words of the prophets themselves, or is the whole concept of the prophet's *ipsissima verba* an anachronistic application of later notions of originality and literal inspiration?

These questions, familiar from the study of prophecy in the Hebrew Bible, show that the problems concerning the relationship of the written record and the spoken word transmitted by it and interpreted in it are typical of prophetic sources in general.

Oracular Reports

The most immediate written record of a prophetic appearance is a report containing the oracle proper and identifying at least the names of the deity speaking and the addressee. This kind of documentation of prophecy is represented by the two oracles of the goddess Kititum to King Ibalpiel II of Eshnunna (FLP 1674 and 2064) and the seven Neo-Assyrian tablets with oracles to the kings Esarhaddon and Assurbanipal (SAA 9 nos. 5–11). The better-preserved oracle from Eshnunna (FLP 1674) provides a good example of what such a report looks like:

> O King Ibalpiel, thus says Kititum:
> The secrets of the gods are placed before me. Because you pronounce my name with your mouth, I constantly disclose the secrets of the gods for you. On the advice of the gods and by the command of Anu, the country is given you to rule. You will ransom the upper and lower country, you will redeem the upper and lower country. Your commerce will not diminish, there will be a perm[anent] food of peace [for] any country that your hand keeps hold of. I, Kititum, will strengthen the foundations of your throne, I have established the protective spirit for you. May your [e]ar be attentive to me!

The Eshnunna oracle does not name the transmitter of the divine message; it is conceivable that we have to do here with prophetic transmission because of the close parallel between this text and the Mari documents[27] as well as the Neo-Assyrian prophecies.[28]

In the Neo-Assyrian reports, the name of the prophet is usually indicated,[29] for example, at the beginning of SAA 9 no. 7, which is particularly interesting since it presents all four components of the prophetic process of communication—the message, the sender, the addressee, and the prophet—in a nutshell (lines 1–2):

> Thus the prophetess Mullissu-kabtat:
> This is the word of Queen Mullissu:
> Fear not, Assurbanipal!

This is the only available report that begins with the prophet's name.[30] Otherwise there is no customary way to begin the report. The name of the prophet may be indicated in a colophon at the end (SAA 9 nos. 6 recto 11–12 and 9 recto 4–7) or on the side (SAA 9 no. 10 side 1–2) of the tablet, sometimes together with the place of origin (SAA 9 nos. 6 recto 12 and 9 recto 5) and, once, even with the date of the oracle (SAA 9 no. 9 recto 4–7: Nisan 18, 650). The proclaimer is explicitly called a prophet in SAA 9 no. 7:1 (Mullissu-kabtat *raggintu*), 10 side 2 (Dunnaša-amur MÍ.GUB.BA[31]) and, probably, in SAA 9 no. 6 recto 11 (Tašmetu-ereš [*raggimu*]).[32] One report, SAA 9 no. 8, is void of any

---

[27] For comparison of FLP 1674 with Mari documents, see Ellis, "Goddess Kitītum," 251–56.

[28] A thorough comparison with the Eshnunna prophecy and Neo-Assyrian prophecies is yet to be accomplished; cf., for the time being, M. Nissinen, "Die Relevanz der neuassyrischen Prophetie für die alttestamentliche Forschung," in *Mesopotamica – Ugaritica – Biblica: Festschrift für Kurt Bergerhof* (ed. M. Dietrich and O. Loretz; AOAT 232; Kevelaer: Butzon & Bercker; Neukirchen-Vluyn: Neukirchener Verlag, 1993), 217–58, esp. 223–24 n. 25.

[29] It is certainly missing in SAA 9 no. 8 and possibly also in SAA 9 no. 5, unless indicated at the destroyed end of the last line (recto 7). If this is the case, the notice must have been very short indeed. The writing is big and, according to the average script density, only about seven signs are missing from that line. Note, however, that in SAA 9 no. 6 the colophon is written in smaller script (cf. the photograph of SAA 9 nos. 5 and 6 in Parpola, *Assyrian Prophecies*, pl. VIII).

[30] Note, however, the beginning of the Deir ʿAlla inscription, for which see below.

[31] This prophetess is the proclaimer of SAA 9 no. 9 as well (there without the title) and may be identical with Sinqiša-amur, the prophetess of SAA 9 nos. 1.2 and [2.5]; see Parpola, *Assyrian Prophecies*, il–l. For the reading of MÍ.GUB.BA (SAA 9 no. 10 side 2) as *raggintu* instead of *mahhūtu*, see ibid., xlvi.

[32] Parpola, *Assyrian Prophecies*, 35: "Tašmetu-ereš, a [prophet *of* . . .] pro[phesied] (this) in the city of Arbela" ([ᵐ]ᵈ LÁL—KAM-*eš* LÚ.[*ra-gi-mu x x x x ina* š]À URU.*arba-ìl ir-t*[*u-gu-*

information regarding the prophet. All this variability suggests that the reports were not composed according to a strict formula or standard.

In every report in which the divine name is intact, the deity speaking is Ištar or one of her manifestations: Kititum in Eshnunna and Mullissu in Assyria.[33] All extant reports are addressed to a king or a crown prince—Ibalpiel, Esarhaddon, or Assurbanipal—or, in the case of SAA 9 no. 5 (cf. SAA 9 nos. 1.7, 1.8), to Esarhaddon's mother, Naqia. As the recipient of the oracle, she actually represents her son, the crown prince, who is the ultimate addressee; but, since he was at that time fighting for his kingship against his brothers, he was not within the reach of the prophet.[34]

The reports are firsthand written documents of prophetic performances; there is no way to get closer to the actual utterances of ancient Near Eastern prophets than the wording of these reports. However, the few extant examples cannot possibly cover the whole range of socioreligious aspects of prophecy. Furthermore, at the very moment the prophetic message is written down it becomes a more or less refined literary form, adjusted to necessary scribal conventions and stylized according to the prevailing customs. Hence, unless the oral utterances were actually performed in a "ready-for-press" manner, they are hardly identical with the verbatim text of the actually promulgated divine messages.[35] This is not to say that the prophets could not in any circumstances have used sophisticated language, nor that the intermediaries would be anything other than faithful in copying their words. As stressed above, it belongs to the dynamics of communication that the message never remains exactly the same when it proceeds from one phase to the next in the course of communication. The shift from spoken to written language especially requires, and also produces, an opening for interpretation, not to mention eventual translation into

---

um]). This restoration makes sense, not only by comparison with SAA 9 no. 3 iv 31, but also with regard to the remains of the concluding verb in perfect form, most probably *ragāmu*.

[33] Both Eshnunna oracles, even the poorly preserved FLP 2064, are represented as words of Kititum. SAA 9 nos. 5 and 6 are words of Ištar of Arbela, whereas Mullissu speaks in SAA 9 no. 7, and Mullissu and Ištar of Arbela together in SAA 9 no. 9. In SAA 9 nos. 10 and 11 the name of the deity speaking has not been preserved; note, however, that SAA 9 no. 10 is proclaimed by the same prophetess (Dunnaša-amur) as SAA 9 no. 9. A more problematic case is SAA 9 no. 8, in which the name of the deity is broken away. Since the lacuna on line 2 is too small to include the divine determinative and another sign, the sign DINGIR alone suggests itself (Parpola, *Assyrian Prophecies*, 40 ad loc.); alternatively, the divine name is exceptionally written without the determinative (cf. the pure EN for Marduk in SAA 13 no. 139:1, recto 1).

[34] For the historical circumstances, see Nissinen, *References*, 23–24.

[35] On the Eshnunna oracles cf. Ellis, "Goddess Kitītum," 256.

another language, which may sometimes have occurred at Mari where at least part of the population spoke Amorite.

The role of the scribe, then, remains decisive regardless of his memory and meticulousness or the quality of the language actually spoken by the prophet. Besides literary stylization, it is possible that the scribe does not repeat every word uttered by the prophet in the report but gives a summary of what he judges to be the essential substance of the message. The material restrictions alone set strict bounds on the length of the report. Above all, the work of the scribe requires an understanding of the text to be written, an understanding corresponding not only to the intellectual world and professional skill of the scribe but also to the requirements of those to whom the written product is to be delivered. All this means that even the firsthand written documents of prophecy, however faithfully they may aim to preserve the message delivered in the oral performance, make the prophetic words accessible only through a scribal filter.

The above deliberations are based on the assumption that the reports of prophecies were written by people other than the prophets. But what if the prophets wrote the reports themselves? While this cannot be categorically excluded, the available sources make it less than probable for various reasons. The colophons, together with the very common quotation particles (*mā*),[36] alone suggest a hand different from that of the speaker. A prophet's use of a scribe is well known from the biblical narrative of Jeremiah, who summons Baruch son of Neriah to write down the words spoken by him (Jeremiah 36).[37]

Moreover, a letter from Mari proves that a prophet could ask for a scribe to write divine words on a tablet then to be forwarded to its destination by another person. Yasim-El, an official of the king Zimri-Lim, writes to the king from Andarig in the northeastern part of the kingdom of Mari (ARM 26 no. 414:29–42) as follows:

> Moreover, Atamrum, prophet (*āpilum*) of Šamaš, came to me and spoke to me as follows: "Send me a discreet[38] scribe (*mār bīt tuppi naṣram*)! I will have him write down the message which Šamaš has sent me for the king." This is what he said to me; I sent Utu-kam and he wrote this tablet. This man (= Atamrum/Utu-kam) appointed witnesses and said to [me a]s

---

[36] SAA 9 no. 6 (3x); SAA 9 no. 7 (12x + restorations); SAA 9 no. 8 (6x); SAA 9 no. 10 (2x); SAA 9 no. 11 (3x).

[37] Whether or not the narrative of Jeremiah 36 is historical, it is certainly designed to present a chain of events plausible to the implied readers; cf. Barstad, "No Prophets?" 59.

[38] For this translation, see D. Charpin, "Le Contexte historique et géographique de prophéties dans les textes retrouvés à Mari," *Bulletin of the Canadian Society for Mesopotamian Studies* 23 (1992): 31 n. 18.

follows: "Send this tablet quic[kly] and let him (the king) act according to its words." This is what he said to me. Now I have sent this tablet to my lord. [39]

This letter not only presents an interesting example of the process of communication—a kind of "certified mail"[40] involving the prophet, scribe, witnesses (who may or may not be aware of the contents of the message written on the tablet),[41] and the intermediary who takes care of its transportation to the king—but also raises the question as to why the prophet needed a scribe. The possible explanations[42] include the "top secret" nature of the message, thus preventing its oral performance (the letter does not indicate whether the prophet actually spoke the message in public), the prophet's imperfect knowledge of Akkadian, and his possible illiteracy. Even without assuming the total illiteracy of the prophet, everything points to the conclusion that the scribe was needed because his professional skill exceeded the prophet's ability to produce a written document of sufficiently high standard.

Literacy in Mesopotamia may have been generally more common than has been presumed hitherto;[43] nevertheless, only professional scribes could fully master the complexity of the cuneiform script and the subtleties of the courtly language required by royal correspondence, whereas people who were slightly familiar with the difficult script would only have managed simple writing, perhaps liable to clumsy orthography and less refined idiolect.[44] The prophetic

---

[39] Transliteration and translation by J.-M. Durand in Charpin et al., *Archives épistolaires*, 294–95; cf. Charpin, "Contexte," 21–31, esp. 24–25; H. B. Huffmon, "The Expansion of Prophecy in the Mari Archives: New Texts, New Readings, New Information," in *Prophecy and Prophets: The Diversity of Contemporary Issues in Scholarship* (ed. J. Gitay; SBLSS; Atlanta: Scholars Press, 1997), 7–22, esp. 11–12; A. Malamat, *Mari and the Bible* (Studies in the History and Culture of the Ancient Near East 12; Leiden: Brill, 1998), 127–30.

[40] This is how van der Toorn ("Old Babylonian Prophecy," 62) describes the procedure conceivable from this letter.

[41] Cf. the two mentions of the use of witnesses in the letter of Nur-Sîn from Aleppo (A 1121+: 46–47, 60–61).

[42] Cf. Malamat, *Mari and the Bible*, 130.

[43] See the arguments to this effect in F. H. Cryer, *Divination in Ancient Israel and Its Near Eastern Environment: A Socio-Historical Investigation* (JSOTSup 142; Sheffield: Sheffield Academic Press, 1994), 138–41; S. Parpola, "The Man without a Scribe and the Question of Literacy in the Assyrian Empire," in *Ana šadî Labnāni lū allik: Beiträge zu altorientalischen und mittelmeerischen Kulturen: Festschrift für Wolfgang Röllig* (ed. B. Pongratz-Leisten, H. Kühne, and P. Xella; Kevelaer: Butzon & Bercker; Neukirchen-Vluyn: Neukirchener Verlag, 1997), 315–24.

[44] See the analysis by Parpola ("Man without a Scribe") of the letter *ABL* 151, written by an official who wrote the letter himself because he did not have a scribe; the very message of

reports available to us (e.g., FLP 1674; SAA 9 nos. 7 and 9) are written in highly polished style by an experienced scribal hand,[45] which makes the involvement of professional scribes probable indeed. This fact, without proving the illiteracy of the prophets as such, corresponds to the different professional training of prophets and scholars. Astrology and extispicy applied traditional omen literature, and thus their practitioners had to be highly literate. This was hardly necessary in the education of prophets, whose expertise did not include copying and interpreting canonical literature and who received divine messages by techniques other than scribal skills. This, admittedly, does not exclude the prophets' knowledge of literature. As devotees of Ištar they were certainly familiar with myths, hymns, and prayers recited in the cult of the goddess. So the question remains as to what extent the obvious allusions to literary works in the Neo-Assyrian prophecies[46] and their unmistakable linguistic affinity with contemporary religious literature—such as the hymns and prayers of Assurbanipal (e.g., SAA 3 nos. 1–3, 7, 12–13) and letters from gods (e.g., SAA 3 nos. 44–46)—go back to the prophets themselves or to the stylistic virtuosity of the scribes.

The reports do not disclose how they are related to actual prophetic performances. Some of them are certainly written with the purpose of relaying the information to the king, who at the time of the oracle is far away.[47] In such cases the writing is motivated by the geographical distance between the prophet and the addressee. However, it is also imaginable that the reports are written in order to document an oral performance in front of the king, for example, while he is visiting the temple of the oracular deity, in order to make the message known among those not attending the actual event. In both cases the writing may serve archival purposes as well.

Two basic formats are used in the design of the prophetic reports: the vertical format (*tuppu*) designed for letters (*egirtu*) and documents like treaties, lists, royal decrees, etc. (FLP 1674; 206; SAA 9 nos. 9–11), and the horizontal format (*u'iltu*) used for notes, reports, receipts, etc. (SAA 9 nos. 5–8).[48] This

---

the letter is that he needed one.

[45] For these qualities of the Eshnunna oracle and Neo-Assyrian prophecy reports, see Ellis, "Goddess Kitītum," 256, and Parpola, *Assyrian Prophecies*, lx–lxi, respectively.

[46] E.g., the allusion to Gilgamesh in SAA 9 no. 9, already identified by H. Zimmern, "Gilgameš-Omina und Gilgameš-Orakel," *ZA* 24 (1910): 166–71.

[47] This is certainly the case in SAA 9 no. 5.

[48] For the difference and purpose of these formats, cf. K. Radner, "The Relation between Format and Content of Neo-Assyrian Texts," in *Nineveh, 612 BC: The Glory and Fall of the Assyrian Empire* (ed. R. Mattila; Catalogue of the 10th Anniversary Exhibition of the Neo-

difference is significant insofar as it informs us about the purpose of the writing. The *uʾiltu* format is used for disposable documents that are not necessarily meant for long-term preservation, even though they may be neatly written and are well represented in the archives. The *ṭuppu* format, in contrast, is intentionally designed for archival storage. With regard to the small number of preserved documents, one is tempted to assume that the basic form of a written prophetic document was a report of *uʾiltu* type, which in the normal case was thrown away and only sometimes ended up in the archives, maybe because of the special importance of the message in question. This assumption is corroborated, in a way, by the fact that some of the reports are designed in *ṭuppu* format, the masterpiece being the especially beautifully written tablet, SAA 9 no. 9.[49] This suggests that library copies were occasionally prepared of some reports that were found to be of extraordinary significance. Such copying implies more than a mere act of filing. By being reproduced in a library copy the oracle is intentionally made part of the corpus of literature to be learned by posterity, thus the process of communication is intended to proceed on a literary level.

If the number of extant reports of prophecy from Eshnunna and Assyria is small, the Mari archives leave us entirely in the dark; not a single document of this kind has been preserved. There are at least two explanations for this fact, neither of which can be really proved: either such reports were never made at Mari or they were systematically disposed of after they were read to the addressee. In any case, the epistolary medium was more important at Mari for presenting prophecies than in Assyria (see below).

Collections of Oracles

From a tidy library copy of a single oracle, it is not a long way to a collection of several prophecies. As a matter of fact, some reports give the impression of being combinations of more than one oracle. In SAA 9 no. 7.14 the word *šanītu* ("secondly") may suggest that the present unity is a secondary

---

Assyrian Text Corpus Project; Helsinki: Helsinki University Press, 1995), 63–78; Parpola, *Assyrian Prophecies*, liii.

[49] The highly qualified design of this tablet is visible from the photograph in Parpola, *Assyrian Prophecies*, pls. XI–XII. It deserves attention that the prophecy is written by the same scribe who also wrote tablet SAA 3 no. 13, a dialogue of Assurbanipal with the god Nabû, which, without itself being a prophecy, has many affinities with the actual prophetic oracles showing that the language and metaphors used in prophecies are not typical to them only, but in all likelihood draw from a common repertoire.

composition,[50] and SAA 9 no. 8 certainly gives account of two or more separate oracles:

> Words [concerning the Elam]ites:
> Thus says [the God[51]]: "I have go[ne, I ha]ve come!"
> Five, six times he s[ai]d this. Then (he said): "I have come from the
> [m]ace. The snake in it I have hauled and cut in pieces." And (he said): "I
> have crushed the mace."
> And (he said): "I will crush Elam! Its army shall be levelled to the ground.
> This is how I will finish off Elam."

This report dates from one of the Elamite campaigns of Assurbanipal, most probably that of 653, providing a good example of the encouraging prophetic messages (*šipir mahhê*) Assurbanipal claims to have received while attacking Teumman, the king of Elam.[52] The oracles belong together, the curious mace and snake metaphor being explained by the promise of vanquishing Elam. The tablet, thus, reports a series of prophetic performances, possibly in answer to an inquiry, or inquiries, concerning Assurbanipal's Elamite war.

Combining prophetic and other divinatory messages from one or several sources is well represented in documents of different kinds. Not only does the narrative of Jeremiah 36 presuppose, if not necessarily document, such a practice;[53] there are also many Mari letters in which the writer gives an account of several prophecies and/or dreams at once.[54] The plaster inscription of Deir ʿAlla, consisting of a heading (line 1; written in red ink) and a narrative in third person (lines 2–5), followed by a series of visions (lines 5 ff.), clearly consti-

---

[50] M. Weippert ("'Das Frühere, siehe, ist eingetroffen . . .': Über Selbstzitate im Prophetenspruch," in *Oracles et prophéties dans l'antiquité: Actes du Colloque de Strasbourg, 15–17 Juin 1995* [ed. J.-G. Heinz; Université des sciences humaines de Strasbourg, Travaux du Centre de recherche sur le Proche-Orient et la Grèce antiques 15; Paris: De Boccard, 1997], 147–69, esp. 153–57) explains lines 3–13 as a quotation from an older oracle.

[51] Cf. above, n. 32.

[52] In Prism B v 93–96 (R. Borger, *Beiträge zum Inschriftenwerk Assurbanipals: Die Prismenklassen A, B, C = K, D, E, F, H, J, und T sowie andere Inschriften* [Wiesbaden: Harrassowitz, 1996], 104), Assurbanipal tells how Aššur and Marduk had encouraged him with "good omens, dreams, speech omens and prophetic messages" (*ina ittāti damqāti šutti egerrê šipir mahhê*).

[53] On different views regarding the relationship of storytelling and historicity in Jeremiah 36, see W. McKane, *Jeremiah 2: Commentary on Jeremiah xxvi–lii* (ICC; Edinburgh: T&T Clark 1996), 910–21.

[54] A 1121+; ARM 26 nos. 199, 237 (for these, cf. A. Schart, "Combining Prophetic Oracles in Mari Letters and Jeremiah 36," *JANESCU* 23 [1995]: 77–88); also ARM 26 nos. 194, 200, 209, 223, 371.

tutes a scribal compilation, possibly copied on the wall from a "book" (*spr*) of Balaam son of Beor.[55]

Archival copies of texts intentionally designed as collections of prophetic oracles have only been preserved from the time of Esarhaddon on three multicolumn *ṭuppu* tablets, which include ten (SAA 9 no. 1), six (SAA 9 no. 2), and three (SAA 9 no. 3) individual oracles, respectively. In addition, the tiny fragment SAA 9 no. 4 probably preserves a remnant of a multicolumn tablet, originally about the size of other collections.[56] All tablets refer to historical circumstances surrounding Esarhaddon's ascent to the throne of his father: the victorious civil war of 681 B.C.E. (SAA 9 no. 1), the enthronement (SAA 9 no. 3), and the beginning of his reign (SAA 9 no. 2).[57] All four were probably written by the same scribe.[58]

It is beyond doubt that the collections, all beautifully written with skillful layout, are prepared for archival purposes. The individual oracles included in them are probably selected and copied from written prophecy reports which were no longer saved after the compilation of the collections. The editorial activity is visible in the standardized design of the collections, all of which follow roughly the same format. In SAA 9 nos. 1 and 2, each individual oracle is followed by an indication of the name of the prophet and place of origin, separated by a dividing line from the following oracle, in SAA 9 no. 1 also from the oracle to which it belongs, e.g., SAA 9 no. 1.2 ii 9–10:

---

[55] Even though the text is poorly preserved and its structure is difficult to reconstruct from the extant fragments, this can be concluded on the basis of the better-preserved combination 1 (lines 1–16) alone, and becomes all the more probable if the combinations 1 and 2 originally belong together. For recent analyses of this text, see, e.g., M. Weippert, "The Balaam Text from Deir ʿAllā and the Study of the Old Testament," in *The Balaam Text from Deir ʿAlla Re-evaluated: Proceedings of the International Symposium Held at Leiden, 21–24 August 1989* (ed. J. Hoftijzer and G. van der Kooij; Leiden: Brill, 1991), 151–84; M. Dijkstra, "Is Balaam Also among the Prophets?" *JBL* 114 (1995): 43–64; A. Lemaire, "La disposition originelle des inscriptions sur plâtre de Deir ʿAlla," *SEL* 3 (1986): 79–93; idem, "Oracles, politique et littérature dans les royaumes araméens et transjordaniens (IXᵉ–VIIIᵉ s. av. n.è.)," in *Oracles et prophéties dans l'antiquité: Actes du Colloque de Strasbourg, 15–17 Juin 1995* (ed. J.-G. Heinz; Université des sciences humaines de Strasbourg, Travaux du Centre de recherche sur le Proche-Orient et la Grèce antiques 15; Paris: De Boccard, 1997), 188–93. Dijkstra ("Is Balaam Also?" 60) defends the unity of the fragments while Lemaire ("Disposition") keeps combinations 1 and 2 apart. As Weippert notes (pp. 177–78), the very fact that the texts are written on the same wall speaks for the intentional compilation of texts, even if the combinations originally stemmed from different sources.

[56] Parpola, *Assyrian Prophecies*, lix.

[57] For the dates, see ibid., lxviii–lxx.

[58] Ibid., lv.

By the mouth of Sinqiša-amur, a woman from Arbela.[59]

On the other hand, SAA 9 no. 3 has rulings between the oracles, with a concluding authorship indication after a blank space (lines iv 31–35), probably referring to the prophet [La-dagil-i]li as the proclaimer of all five prophecies included in the collection. The collections are likely to have had headings and colophons including other information (e.g., date), although there is no absolute proof for this since the beginning is destroyed in every one of them and the end is extant only in SAA 9 no. 3.[60] In view of the unsystematic design of the extant reports, it is clear that the editor of the collections has attempted a standardized manner of representation, which has required at least a slight stylization of the reports.

The collection of SAA 9 no. 3 differs from the others in that it contains cultic instructions embedded between prophetic oracles, following a sequence of rituals on the occasion of the enthronement of Esarhaddon, each accompanied by a prophetic proclamation. The well edited structure of the tablet can be outlined as follows (rulings as in the original):[61]

3.1

i 1–13	[heading?] + introductory oracle (*šulmu*)
	— theme: cosmic well-being
i 14–26	description of a ritual procession to Ešarra

---

[59] *ša pi-i* Mí.*si-in-qi-šá—a-mur* DUMU.Mí URU.*arba-ìl*. For variants, see ibid., lxiii.

[60] Cf. ibid., lxiii, where it is pointed out that the breaks leave enough room for such notes and that SAA 9 no. 9, possibly using SAA 9 no. 1 as a model, has a date at the end of the text.

[61] Cf. the outline of E. Otto, "Die Ursprünge der Bundestheologie im Alten Testament und im Alten Orient," *Zeitschrift für altorientalische und biblische Rechtsgeschichte* 4 (1998): 1–84, esp. 58–59; idem, *Das Deuteronomium: Politische Theologie und Rechtsreform in Juda und Assyrien* (BZAW 284; Berlin and New York: de Gruyter, 1999), 80–84. For SAA 9 no. 3, which belongs to the most discussed documents of Neo-Assyrian prophecy, see also Parpola, *Assyrian Prophecies*, l, lviii–lix, lxx; T. J. Lewis, "The Identity and Function of El/Baal Berith," *JBL* 115 (1996): 401–23, esp. 406–8; A. Laato, "The Royal Covenant Ideology in Judah," in *"Laßet uns Brücken bauen . . ."*: *Collected Communications to the XVth Congress of the International Organization for the Study of the Old Testament, Cambridge, 1995* (ed. K.-D. Schunck and M. Augustin; BEATAJ 42; Frankfurt am Main: P. Lang, 1998), 95–99; Weippert, "Das Frühere," 157–60; and Nissinen, *References*, 26–28, 76–77.

3.2

i 27–ii 7   oracle (*šulmu*) of Aššur to the Assyrians
— theme: victory and global rule of Esarhaddon

ii 8–9   placing of the *šulmu* before the courtyard gods

3.3

ii 10–25   oracle (*šulmu*) of Aššur
— theme: historical flashback of preceding events; a
demand for praise

ii 26   placing of the *šulmu* before the statue Aššur in the temple

ii 27–32   reading the covenant tablet (*ṭuppi adê*) before Esarhaddon

---

3.4

ii 33–iii 15   oracle (*abutu*) of Ištar
— theme: meal of covenant
ii 33–34 introductory formula
ii 35 ff. oracle
iii 2–6 cultic instructions
iii 7–15 oracle

3.5

iii 16–iv 30 oracle (*abutu*) of Ištar
— theme: Esarhaddon's responsibilities to Ištar
iii 16–17 introductory formula
iii 18–iv 30 oracle with cultic demands (iii 32–37)

iv 31–35   colophon (authorship indication)

The texts included in this collection fall into two categories, which are divided from each other by a double ruling. The first part consists of oracles of salvation and the well-being (*šulmu*) of Aššur.[62] They are presented without introductory formulae and are followed by cultic instructions, whereas the words (*abutu*) of Ištar in the second part are introduced by the formula, *abat Issār ša Arbail ana Aššūr-ahu-iddina šar māt Aššūr*, "The word of Ištar of Arbela to Esarhaddon, king of Assyria," and the cultic instructions are embedded in the wording of the oracles. This bisection probably reflects different

---

[62] Even though only 3.3 is expressly an oracle of Aššur, it is feasible to conclude that the two preceding oracles which mention only this god are also presented as his words. That Aššur is referred to in the third person in these oracles does not necessarily prevent them from being his words (cf. SAA 9 no. 9:3–7, recto 1–3).

phases of the enthronement ritual, the first three oracles and accompanying instructions following the cultic procession directed towards the statue of Aššur and the throne room in the temple of Ešarra, the following two attaching to the subsequent meal of covenant on the temple terrace (*ina muhhi [taml]ê*, line iii 2).

As in the collections SAA 9 nos. 1 and 2, the oracles in SAA 9 no. 3 were most likely copied from individual reports of oracles proclaimed by the prophet during the enthronement rituals and joined together by the editor, who also provided the collection with brief descriptions of the cultic maneuvers at respective stages of the ritual.[63] All that was said hitherto concerning the role of the scribe in editing and stylizing the oracles is certainly true here as well; but there is no reason to doubt the actual appearance of the prophet in the ritual.[64]

The fact that all collections of prophecies available to us derive from the reign of Esarhaddon may not necessarily be a pure coincidence. Until proved otherwise, it may be assumed that Esarhaddon, whose predilection for prophecy is best documented, was the first king to let individual prophecies be compiled in archival collections. He emphasized more than any other king of Assyria, except his son Assurbanipal, that he was a protégé of Ištar, the goddess whose devotees the prophets were and who, according to their words, had made, raised, and chosen the king.[65] Furthermore, against the background of the turbulence preceding Esarhaddon's ascent to power, it is clear that any suspicions of the legitimacy of his reign had to be removed and the potential usurpers reminded of the fate of those who contradict the divine ordinance concerning his kingship.[66] The use of prophecy for this purpose is conceivable even from the inscriptions of Esarhaddon and Assurbanipal, as shown below.

As much as the motivation for the compiling of Neo-Assyrian prophecies arises from the contemporary ideological background and political needs, the significance of this procedure exceeds historical actualities. The very process of

---

[63] Weippert ("Das Frühere," 159–160) suggests that the first part of the oracle proper in SAA 9 no. 3.3 (lines ii 10–18) is a quotation from an earlier oracle.

[64] Cf. the prophetic performances during the substitute king ritual in the year 671 B.C.E., reported by Mar-Issar in SAA 10 no. 352.

[65] See Parpola, *Assyrian Prophecies*, xxxvi–xliv; and cf. SAA 9 nos. 1.4 ii 32; 1.6 iii 15–18; 2.5 iii 26–28; 7:12–13, recto 6–11; 9:3–6, recto 1–3; also SAA 3 no. 3.

[66] Parpola (ibid., xxxix) justly stresses that Esarhaddon and Assurbanipal by no means needed to sanction their rule and assert their kingship by prophecies, since they were not usurpers but properly invested as crown princes. On the other hand, the population was divided into supporters and opponents of Esarhaddon during the civil war in 681, which in the beginning of his reign undoubtedly necessitated an ideological campaign against those who were not convinced of the divine approval of Esarhaddon's rule.

writing, collecting, selecting, compiling, and filing prophetic oracles is scribal activity, that is, intellectual work, as the result of which the texts in question become part of the tradition that the coming generations learn and interpret. Since the prophecies are composed in language that is not only generally understandable but mostly even of a high literary standard, using devices common to literary works and poetry in general, they are all the more convenient to be used repeatedly for different people and for various purposes. The very act of collecting individual oracles enables them to transcend specific historical situations and gives them a generally applicable meaning.[67]Under Esarhaddon and Assurbanipal, Assyrian prophecy apparently developed from spoken performance into an established written tradition that became a source of intellectual inspiration and scholarly interpretation. However, this development seems not to have survived the fall of Assyria in 612 B.C.E. The process was too short to bear fruit comparable to the blossoming of the prophetic literature in the Hebrew Bible; nevertheless, this development already demonstrates the initial phases of the emergence of prophetic books.

Letters with Prophetic Quotations

Letters reporting prophetic performances are best preserved in the royal correspondence of Mari. The relatively high number of letters points towards the conclusion that this was the primary means of recording prophecies at Mari, unless all other reports were instantly thrown away or entirely escaped the spade of the archaeologist. Thanks to the previous studies of the transmission of prophetic messages in Mari letters,[68] a brief summary of the most important patterns will suffice in this article.

Most commonly, the sender of the letter has been informed of a prophecy or of a dream[69] by the prophet or dreamer him/herself and writes to the king

---

[67] Cf. Schart, "Combining Prophetic Oracles," 92.

[68] See F. Ellermeier, *Prophetie in Mari und Israel* (Theologische und orientalistische Arbeiten 1; Herzberg: Erwin Jungfer, 1968), 76–164; and cf. the more recent contributions of S. B. Parker, "Official Attitudes toward Prophecy at Mari and in Israel," *VT* 43 (1993): 50–68; J. M. Sasson, "The Posting of Letters with Divine Messages," in *Florilegium marianum II: Recueil d'études à la mémoire de Maurice Birot* (ed. D. Charpin and J.-M. Durand; MNABU 3; Paris: Société pour l'étude du Proche-Orient ancien, 1994), 299–316; idem, "Water beneath Straw"; and van der Toorn, "Old Babylonian Prophecy."

[69] Since the distinction between prophecies and dreams is not significant in respect of the process of communication, no difference is made in this article between the letters that expressly present the divine messages as delivered by a prophet (*āpilum, muhhûm*, etc.) and those that report dreams of persons who do not necessarily qualify as prophets. As regards the definition of the relationship of prophecy with other forms of divination, however, the

Zimri-Lim about it. In many cases the sender mentions expressly that the prophet or dreamer came to the person in question to tell the message—for example, in ARM 26 no. 233:5–8:

> On the day I sent this tablet to my lord, Malik-Dagan, a man from Šakkâ came to me and spoke to me as follows.[70]

In other letters prophets are said to "arise" (*tebûm*) or "stand up" (*izuzzum*) to deliver the message,[71] while some letters just quote the sayings of the prophets or dreamers without any further indications of how they came to the knowledge of the sender.[72] A few letters present the prophets or dreamers themselves as senders,[73] while some are dispatched on the express request of the prophet.[74] On the other hand, the sender of the letter may have inquired about the oracles on his or her own initiative.[75]

It is not unusual to find several oracles of one or more prophets combined in a single letter,[76] and in one letter the sender reports on a dream of his own

---

distinction is relevant, since not all dreamers are prophets, and some Mari dreams, conventionally included in the "prophetic" corpus, may actually turn out to be experienced by people other than prophets. For the difference between prophecies and dreams at Mari, see I. Nakata, "Two Remarks on the So-called Prophetic Texts from Mari," *Acta Sumerologica* 4 (1982): 143–48; and note the classification of the "prophetic" texts into three categories by Durand, *Archives épistolaires* ("Exchange of letters with gods": ARM 26 nos. 191–94; "Prophetic texts": 195–223; and "Dreams": 224–40).

[70] *ūm ṭuppi annêm ana [s]ēr bēlīja ušābilam Malik-Dagan awīl Šakkâ il <li> kamma kī'am iqbêm.* Cf. A 1121+; A 1968; ARM 26 nos. 196 (?), 197, 198, 199, 206, 210, 217 (?), 220, 221, 221bis, 233, 234 (?), 243, 414. In ARM no. 218 Queen Šibtu says that the prophet had brought the message to the gate of the palace to be forwarded to her.

[71] A 1121+; ARM 26 nos. 195, 204, 209, 211, 219.

[72] ARM 26 nos. 200, 203(?), 213, 215, 227, 236, 238.

[73] ARM 26 nos. 194 (an anonymous *āpilum* of Šamaš), 232 (Zunana), and 239 (Šimatum); possibly also ARM 26 nos, 205 and 218 (the names of the senders destroyed).

[74] ARM 26 no. 210 (an anonymous *aššat awīlim,* "wife of a free man"); ARM 26 no. 414 (Atamrum).

[75] As in ARM 26 no. 207, according to which Queen Šibtu had "given drink to male and female 'signs'" inquiring about the campaign of Zimri-Lim against Išme-Dagan, king of Assyria. The curious expression *ittātim zikāram u sinništam ašqi aštālma* may refer to a practice of giving drink to male and female persons—prophets?—who themselves (whether or not in the state of intoxication) act as "signs"; see J.-M. Durand, "In vino veritas," *RA* 76 (1982): 43–50. Another case of inquiry is presented by Tebi-gerišu (ARM 26 no. 216), who assembled the *nabûm*s of the Haneans in order to make them deliver an oracle for the sake of the well-being of Zimri-Lim (see Heintz, "La 'fin,'" 198–202).

[76] Cf. above, n. 53.

together with an oracle of a *muhhūtum*.[77] Many letters do not just concentrate on prophecies, but give information about other matters as well.[78] Some oracles are said to have been delivered in public; in these cases the sender of the letter is not the only person to have experienced the prophetic performance.[79]

The vague statements about prophets "arising" with their messages do not necessarily always imply that the senders of the letters are really eyewitnesses of the oral performances. Some letters indeed reveal more complicated chains of communication. Bahdi-Lim delivers to the king a tablet with words of a *muhhūtum*, given to him by the priest Ahum; his own writing is a cover letter void of any reference to the contents of the tablet (ARM 26 no. 201). The priest Ahum, himself the sender of one letter (ARM 26 no. 200), acts as an intermediary in two further dispatches. He reports a prophecy of Ahatum, "a slave girl of Dagan-Malik," to Queen Šibtu, who writes about it to the king (ARM 26 no. 214) and reports a dream of an anonymous man to the official Kibri-Dagan, who writes:

> A man [has se]en a dre[am and] Ahum told (it) [to me]: "The army [of the enemy has entered] the fortif[ied] cities, [Ma]ri, Terqa [and Sa]ggaratum. (If) they (manage to) plun[der an]ything, they will [stay in] the fortifications of [my] lord." [Ahum told] me this dream of his and [sh]ifted the responsibility on me (*arnam elīja [u]tērma*),[80] saying: "Write to the ki[ng]!" Therefore, I have written to my l[or]d. (ARM 26 no. 235:7–20)

In an even more tangled case (ARM 26 no. 202), Kibri-Dagan informs his son Kanisan about oracles he knows to have been spoken in the temple of Dagan, and Kanisan, in turn, repeats the message written by his father in the letter he sends to the king. Finally, Ušareš-hetil writes to his father or superior Dariš-libur about the death of a royal child predicted by the prophet Irra-gamil, and he asks Dariš-libur to bring this tragedy and the accompanying prophetic word to the king's knowledge (ARM 26 no. 222).

The conveyance of a prophecy to its destination in letters may, as we see, constitute a complicated process. The Mari letters present a full range of participants in the chain of communication from the prophet through one or more go-betweens—eyewitnesses and their confidants, scribes and conveyers,

---

[77] ARM 26 no. 237 (Addu-duri).

[78] A 1121+; ARM 26 nos. 196, 215, 217, 414.

[79] ARM 26 no. 206, delivered before the eyes of the elders at the city gate and accompanied by a "symbolic act" of eating a lamb (see Heintz, "La 'fin,'" 202–8); and ARM 26 no. 371 on prophetic oracles spoken at the city gate and "in the assembly of the [whole] cou[ntry]" (*ina puhur m[ātim kalîša]*; cf. SAA 10 no. 352 recto 1–2).

[80] For the expression *arnam turrum*, see Durand, *Archives épistolaires*, 477.

etc.—to King Zimri-Lim. The one who informs the addressee of the divine message is neither necessarily identical with the person who actually heard and memorized the message nor with the one who writes the tablet.

The quotations of prophetic utterances in Mari letters, like the ones in Assyrian reports, may be taken as firsthand written records of prophecy. However, reports and letters differ from each other in that the role of the author of the letter is not similar to that of a scribe. Important as the personal contribution of the scribe is to the formulation of the written prophecy, it is more limited than that of the sender of the letter who usually provides the addressee with his or her own opinion and interpretation of the prophecy, often placing it in a wider context and making suggestions as to how it should be heeded. The subjective emphasis of the letter-writers is often recognizable, especially when several letters from a single person can be compared.[81] Prophecies attaching to specific political situations, like Zimri-Lim's diplomacy with Eshnunna,[82] appear in letters intertwined with personal views of the writer, the prime example of which is provided by the threefold interpretation of the saying *šapal tibnim mû illakū* ("beneath straw runs water") by Inib-šina, the king's sister (ARM 26 no. 197), the majordomo Sammetar (ARM 26 no. 199) and the above-mentioned Kanisan (ARM 26 no. 202), who each give their own version of the prophetic word proclaimed by a prophetess (*qammatum*) in the temple of Dagan at Terqa.[83] Without being substantially opposed to each other—all are ill-disposed towards a peaceable policy with Eshnunna—the part of the quotation following the uniformly repeated saying is different and obviously freely formulated in all three cases.

---

[81] Sasson, "Posting of Letters," 305: "Thus, no matter which divinity is at stake, no matter what prophecy is being communicated, no matter which prophet is chosen as conduit, when transmitted through Aunt Addu-duri, the message will caution the king about treachery or danger (XXVI: 195, 238); via Sister Inibšina, it will warn him about letting down his guard (XXVI: 197, 204); through the Wife Šiptu, it will comfort and cheer him (XXVI: 211, 213, 236)."

[82] Cf. Charpin, "Contexte," 22–25.

[83] See Parker, "Official Attitudes," 57–60; Sasson, "Water beneath Straw"; and also van der Toorn, "Old Babylonian Prophecy," 65–68. To be sure, the letter of Kanisan, after referring to the oracle, continues: "Now, as before, the *muhhûm* has broken out into constant declamation" (ARM 26 no. 202:14–16). At least according to the idea of Kanisan, then, it is the *muhhûm* and not the *qammatum* that delivered the oracle. Whoever the original proclaimer may have been, the fact that two different persons are credited as the source for the saying speaks for itself.

These observations not only caution us against reconstructing the precise wording of orally delivered prophecies[84] but also make fully understandable the usual practice of attaching the prophet's hair and garment thread (*šārtum u sissiktum*) to the letter, probably for the purpose of authenticating the message by means of extispicy.[85] The need for a "countersignature" of another diviner reflects the nonempirical nature of the prophetic method of divination on one hand, and the vulnerability of the chain of communication on the other.

Outside the corpus of Mari, letters with quotations of prophecy are less numerous; however, they provide evidence of some aspects of the use of prophecy not represented in Mari letters. Situated chronologically between the two main corpora of ancient Near Eastern prophecy, the Amarna correspondence includes a letter with an oracle that is possibly of prophetic origin. King Tušratta of Mitanni writes to his son-in-law, the pharaoh Amenophis III of Egypt (EA 23:13–25):

> Thus (says) Šauška (Ištar)[86] of Nineveh, the Lady of all countries: "I want to go to Egypt, the country that I love, and (then) return." Now I have sent her and she is on her way.

> Now, during the reign of my father (Šuttarna II), . . .[87] went to that country. Just as she was honored when she dwelt there earlier, let my brother now honor her ten times more than earlier. Let my brother honor her and (then) joyfully let her go so that she may return.[88]

The letter is written just before the death of Amenophis III, to whom the statue of Ištar of Nineveh, believed to have curative power, had been sent even earlier during his illness. Renewed travel to Egypt, presumably for a similar purpose, is presented as the will of the goddess herself. The means by which the oracle is

---

[84] See esp. van der Toorn, "Old Babylonian Prophecy," 68.

[85] A 1968:14'–15'; ARM 26 nos. 198:2"–3", 200:22–23, 201:15, 203:11, 204:16–20, 214:21–25, 217:29, 229:17–18, 233:53, 237:29–30. These objects may serve as an "identity card" (Malamat, *Mari and the Bible*, 78–79), representing in the extispicy ritual the personality of the prophet (cf. Durand, *Archives épistolaires*, 40).

[86] For the Hurrian main goddess, Šauška, who is habitually identified with Ištar, see G. Wilhelm, *Grundzüge der Geschichte und Kultur der Hurriter* (Darmstadt: Wissenschaftliche Buchgesellschaft, 1982), 71–73.

[87] An untranslatable word; cf. Moran, *Amarna Letters*, 62 (ad loc.).

[88] Cf. the translations of Moran, *Amarna Letters*, 61–62, and H.-P. Adler, *Das Akkadische des Königs Tušratta von Mitanni* (AOAT 201; Kevelaer: Butzon & Bercker; Neukirchen-Vluyn: Neukirchener Verlag, 1976), 170–73; for the letter, see also Wilhelm, *Grundzüge*, 41.

received is not indicated, but being the goddess of prophecy above all others, Ištar of Nineveh is likely to have been thought to express her will by the mouth of a prophet. If this is true, prophecy serves here as an instrument of diplomacy and sign of the goodwill of the Hurrian king, who certainly does not refer to the word of a foreign goddess, but of the one worshipped in his own capital. Compared with the Mari letters, this reference to a divine word is different, not only in advocating peaceful relations towards a foreign nation, which is unheard of in the pertinent letters from Mari, but first and foremost as a statement justifying the action that has already been accomplished by the sender of the letter. There is neither warning nor promise, just a friendly wish that the token of goodwill would be accepted by the pharaoh and that the goddess would meet with all the respect and veneration she deserves during her visit in Egypt.

The Assyrian royal correspondence includes six letters in which prophetic words are quoted or paraphrased.[89] Four writers report a prophetic (oral) performance, while the remaining two underpin their own opinions with a reference to prophetic oracles. A case comparable to the prophetic appearances in the letters from Mari is reported by Nabû-reši-išši in SAA 13 no. 144.10 side 1:

> The sacrifices of the king [. . .] have been performed on the [14]th [day], the 16th, [the 18th], the 20th [. . . . . .] (Break of 7 lines)
>
> [. . .] she prophesied (*tarrugu[m]*[90]): "Why did you give the [. . .]-wood, the grove, and the . . . to the Egyptians? Say in the king's presence that they should be given back to me. I will (then) give total abundance [to] his [. . .]."[91]

If the letter is sent from Arbela, as it seems,[92] it is likely to relate to rituals of the temple of Ištar of Arbela, during which the goddess had made a demand by the mouth of a prophetess concerning some property of hers that has unduly been given to Egyptians. Such a performance is imaginable in the temple to

---

[89] In addition, there are three letters, the prophetic nature of which is still at issue (SAA 13 nos. 43, 139, 148); cf. provisionally Parpola, *Assyrian Prophecies*, lxxvii, and R. M. Whiting in *Letters from Priests to the Kings Esarhaddon and Assurbanipal* (ed. S. W. Cole and P. Machinist; SAA 13; Helsinki: Helsinki University Press, 1998), xvii.

[90] Pf. sg. 3. fem. of *ragāmu;* the assimilation r + t is rare but not impossible in Neo-Assyrian, see SAA 5 no. 164:15 KUR.*zi-ki-ti-a* (< Zikirtu); SAA 10 no. 69 recto 5 *tak-pi-ti* (< *takpirtu*) and cf. S. Parpola, "*likalka ittatakku*: Two Notes on the Morphology of the Verb *alāku* in Neo-Assyrian," *StudOr* 55 (1984): 183–209, esp. 206 n. 39.

[91] See Whiting in Cole and Machinist, *Letters*, xvii. I failed to analyze this letter in my *References*.

[92] See the note of K. Radner in Cole and Machinist, *Letters*, 116.

which the Assyrian prophets had a special attachment—seven out of fifteen prophets known by name come from Arbela,[93] and even a prophetess from Calah, Urkittu-šarrat, proclaims the word of Ištar of Arbela (SAA 9 no. 2.4). The scene is also reminiscent of Mari letters that include similar demands (e.g., ARM 26 no. 215). By quoting the oracle, or summarizing its actual message, the writer, who probably is a temple official, discreetly looks after the interests of the temple, presenting the return of the temple property as divine will.

Prophecies are not always referred to in a positive tone, however. Another temple official, Adad-ahu-iddina, tells about a prophetess who prophesied in Ešarra, the Aššur temple of Assur (SAA 13 no. 37:7 recto 14):

> The prophetess (*raggintu*) Mullissu-abu-uṣri, who took the king's clothes to the land of Akkad, has prophesied (*tartugum*) [in the] temple: "[The t]hrone from the te[mp]le [. . .] (Break of 5 lines) [L]et the throne go! I shall overcome my king's enemies with it." I said: "I will not turn over the throne without the permission of the king, my lord." Whatever the king, my lord, commands, we will act accordingly. [94]

Since the prophetess is demanding something that the writer is reluctant to deliver, he shifts the responsibility of the interpretation of the divine message onto the king himself. The letter is probably connected with a substitute king ritual in which the throne is needed, perhaps the one reported by Mar-Issar in SAA 10 no. 352, during which a prophetess—possibly the same one—appeared twice, assuring the kingship of the substitute and proclaiming to him an oracle of victory[95] in the "assembly of the country" (*ina puhur ša māti*; cf. ARM 26 no. 371:31–32). Mar-Issar, who in this letter gives an account of the successfully performed substitute king ritual in the year 671, leans on the divine word as the legitimization of the unusual choice of the substitute, who this time was the son of a high Babylonian temple official.[96]

---

[93] I.e., Ahat-abiša (SAA 9 no. 1.8), Bayâ (SAA 9 no. 1.4, [2.2]), Dunnaša-amur (SAA 9 nos. 9 and 10), Issar-la-tašiyaṭ (SAA 9 no. 1.1), La-dagil-ili (SAA 9 nos. 1.10, 2.3, and 3), Sinqiša-amur (SAA 9 no. 1.2, [2.5]) and Tašmetu-ereš (SAA 9 no. 6).

[94] For this letter, see S. Parpola, *Letters from Assyrian Scholars to the Kings Esarhaddon and Assurbanipal. Part 2: Commentary and Appendices* (AOAT 5/2; Kevelaer: Butzon & Bercker; Neukirchen-Vluyn: Neukirchener Verlag, 1983), 329; Nissinen, *References*, 78–81; and Whiting in Cole and Machinist, *Letters*, xvii.

[95] Cf. K. van der Toorn, "L'Oracle de victoire comme expression prophétique au Proche-Orient ancien," *RB* 94 (1987): 63–97, esp. 93.

[96] For this letter, see B. Landsberger, *Brief des Bischofs von Esagila an König Asarhaddon* (Mededelingen der Koninklijke Nederlandse Akademie van Wetenschappen, afd. Letterkunde. Nieuwe Reeks 28/6; Amsterdam: Noord-Hollandsche Uitgevers Maatschappij, 1965), 46–51; Parpola, *Letters*, 270–72; and Nissinen, *References*, 68–77.

Nabû-reši-išši and Adad-ahu-iddina present the prophetic oracles as clear instructions concerning individual cases and may have heard the message from the mouth of the prophetesses. Their point of view is practical; the messages transmitted by them, without necessarily being verbatim quotations, probably repeat their substance correctly. In the case of Adad-ahu-iddina, who reports a message unpleasant from his point of view, this is all the more probable. Mar-Issar, on the other hand, does not present himself as an eyewitness; he tells that he has "heard" about the first appearance of the prophetess (SAA 10 no. 352:22). The formulaic saying "You will take over the kingship" (*šarrūti tanašši,* line 25) may be Mar-Issar's own two-word summary of the divine message to the substitute. Whether or not he had been present in the "assembly of the country" is not indicated; at least the peculiar metaphor of the oracle is less likely to have been invented by him: "I have revealed the 'thieving polecat'[97] of my lord and placed it in your hands" (lines recto 2–4). In all three cases the chain of communication is close to Mari models.

A more complicated case is at hand in *ABL* 1217, where Nabû-rehtu-uṣur tries his best to convince King Esarhaddon of a conspiracy against him. Nabû-rehtu-uṣur exposes a word of the god Nusku proclaimed by a woman in the vicinity of Harran—probably in the cedar temple erected by Esarhaddon on his way to Egypt less than a year earlier (SAA 10 no. 174:10–16)—according to which the kingship will be taken away from the Sargonid dynasty (*ABL* 1217 recto 4–5):

> This is the word of Nusku: The kingship is for Sasî! I will destroy the name and seed of Sennacherib!

This (pseudo-)prophecy is but one piece of information among others that Nabû-rehtu-uṣur announces in this and two further letters (*CT* 53 17+ and 938). However, he has not heard the alleged Nusku oracle with his own ears. Compared with other available data concerning the conspiracy in question, which indeed was discovered and quelled in good time at the beginning of the year 670, he turns out to be dependent on partially fallacious sources. He is right about the crucial role of the eunuchs in the conspiracy, but he is not aware of the true role of Sasî. In reality, the man who was proclaimed king by the woman in Harran was probably an undercover agent who kept the king well informed of the moves of the insurrectionists.[98] Nabû-rehtu-uṣur quotes the words of the Harranean woman in good faith, showing himself a victim of intentionally misleading propaganda.

---

[97] Reading *kakkišu šarriqtu*; see Nissinen, *References,* 74–75.

[98] For arguments supporting this theory, and for the correspondence of Nabû-rehtu-uṣur in general, see Nissinen, *References,* 108–53.

A different type of prophetic quotation is represented in letters by two Assyrian scholars who belonged to the inner circle of Esarhaddon. Nabû-nadin-šumi uses, in his letter to Esarhaddon, the word of Ištar of Arbela and Ištar of Nineveh straightforwardly as an argument for banishing a person from Assyria (SAA 10 no. 284 recto 4–9):

> According to what Ištar of N[ineveh] and Ištar of Arbela have said: "Those who are disloyal (*ša . . . lā kēnūni*) to the king our lord, we shall extinguish from Assyria," he should indeed be banished from Assyria! [99]

That the writer really quotes prophecy is conceivable from his own formulation alone, but becomes all the more probable by comparison with the prophecy of Urkittu-šarrat in which Ištar of Arbela and Mullissu promise to search out the disloyal ones (*lā kēnūti*) and deliver them into the hands of the king, though not mentioning banishment (SAA 9 no. 2.4 ii 29–33). If this is the very source referred to by Nabû-nadin-šumi, it is easy to note how freely he reiterates the oracle, adapting the message for his own purposes.

A second reference of similar kind can be found in a letter of Bel-ušezib, the famous Babylonian astrologer who in an earlier letter complained about the favor the prophets and prophetesses had found in the king's eyes while he felt himself deserted (SAA 10 no. 109). However, in his letter about Esarhaddon's campaign in Mannea, he quotes divine words, to all appearances of prophetic origin (SAA 10 no. 111 recto 23–26):

> Bel has said: "May Esarhaddon, king of Assyria, be seated on his throne like Marduk-šapik-zeri, and I will deliver all the countries into his hands."[100]

The divine statement, the origin of which cannot be demonstrated by any extant source, is situated at the end of the letter which begins with quotations from astrological omen collections. Obviously, Bel-ušezib attempts a scriptural confirmation of the contents of the letter. In addition, there is a pro-Babylonian message embedded in the name of Marduk-šapik-zeri,[101] who once rebuilt and

---

[99] For this letter, see Parpola, *Letters*, 208, and Nissinen, *References*, 102–5.

[100] Cf. the argumentation in Nissinen, *References*, 99–101. For this letter, see also F. M. Fales and G. B. Lanfranchi, "ABL 1237: The Role of Cimmerians in a Letter to Esarhaddon," *East and West* 31 (1981): 9–33.

[101] King of Babylon in 1081–1069, known also from a Neo-Assyrian inscription copy concerning the restoration of Ezida, the temple of Nabû, in Borsippa; see G. Frame, *Rulers of Babylonia from the Second Dynasty of Isin to the End of Assyrian Domination (1157–612 BC)* (Royal Inscriptions of Mesopotamia, Babylonian Periods 2; Toronto: University of Toronto Press, 1995), 45–49.

fortified the city of Babylon—an effort to which Esarhaddon, too, encouraged even by prophets (e.g., SAA 9 no. 2.3), committed himself throughout his reign. Both scholars quote prophecy without any allusion to actual prophetic appearances. The divine words are not attached to any concrete situations but are used as generally applicable sentences, the prophetic origin of which is not specifically indicated. This makes it probable that the quotations are drawn from written sources rather than oral performances; if this is true, the letters of Nabû-nadin-šumi and Bel-ušezib illustrate how archival copies of prophecies were used by contemporaries. One may assume that the medium through which the divine words once had been uttered was immaterial to the writers, who used them as scriptural references belonging to their learned tradition. Their concern, instead of "original" contexts or *ipsissima verba,* was the viability of the tradition in the contemporary situation.

Literary Quotations of Prophetic Words

An important group of sources for prophecy in the ancient Near East is formed by inscriptions, literary texts, and administrative records that in one way or another document prophetic activity. While a great number of them just mention prophets as cultic functionaries[102] or recipients of royal grants or food rations,[103] some of these sources indeed quote or paraphrase divine messages delivered by them.

The Mari documents include one literary reference to prophecy in the so-called Epic of Zimri-Lim (lines 137–142):

> Zimri-Lim—his name is heroic to Dagan.
> His protection is Itur-Mer, the warrior.
> The prince of the land saw his sign, the *āpilum*:
> "The king goes forth with forceful heart!
> Adad shall go at his left side,
> Erra, the mighty one, at his right side." [104]

The highly poetical text calls the prophet himself the "sign."[105] What follows seems like a divine word to Zimri-Lim, spoken by the *āpilum,* which shares

---

[102] See above, nn. 4 and 9.

[103] See above, nn. 5 and 14.

[104] Translated from Durand, *Archives épistolaires,* 393; cf. above, n. 3.

[105] The passage uses an inverted word order: *īmurma ittašu āpilam eṭel māti*[*m*], literally, "He saw his sign, the prophet (he saw), the prince of the land." For other examples of calling people "signs" (ARM 26 no. 207 [cf. above n. 74]; Isa 8:18), see Durand, *Archives épistolaires,* 392–93.

many features with Neo-Assyrian oracles.[106]

A further literary work in which divine messages are quoted as deriving from the mouth of a prophetic intermediary is the report of Wenamon, the Egyptian who tells about his visit to Byblos in the eleventh century, quoting a "great seer" (*ꜥdd ꜥꜣ*)[107] who, in an ecstatic state, uttered words presented as a message of Amon (lines 1:39–40):

> Bring the god up! Bring the envoy who is carrying him!
> It is Amon who sent him. It is he who made him come! [108]

These words, directed to the prince of Byblos, who had ordered Wenamon to get out of his harbor, succeeded in making the prince change his mind. Provided that Wenamon is reporting a real case and that the quotation at least remotely resembles words really spoken, the situation (i.e., prophetic authentication of a private person's credentials) is interesting and not quite typical of ancient Near Eastern prophecy as we know it in general. However, it must not be forgotten that the Egyptian author, drawing on his own memory and literary skills, is reporting or inventing events foreign to his own country and culture.

Neither of these cases can be valued as a precise or even authentic report of a prophetic performance. Even if the Epic of Zimri-Lim may celebrate events that actually happened[109] and the poetic paraphrase of prophecy is quite plausibly formulated, it is literature in the first place. The report of Wenamon, as it may be to a great extent fictitious, can hardly be taken as an accurate account of factual events. Both texts, then, rather than giving access to actual prophetic utterances, provide an example of how nonprophetical authors, according to their own idea of prophecy, paraphrase prophetic oracles.

The same may be said of the inscription of Zakkur, the king of Hamat and Luʿaš, but not without qualifications. Some two centuries later than Wenamon, this king gives an account of a prophetic word delivered to him while he was besieged by his enemies (*KAI* 202 A 11–15):

---

[106] Cf. especially SAA 9 no. 1.4, in which the "beams of your heart" (*gešūrē ša libbīka* line 19) render a similar idea (cf. SAA 9 no. 9:7 [*uša*]*škanāšu libbu* "[They g]ive him heart," i.e., the goddesses) and where the gods at the right and the left side of the king can also be found (line 24; cf. SAA 9 nos. 1.6 iv 26–32, 2.2 i 21, 5.6).

[107] For discussion on the Egyptian *ꜥdd*, the normal meaning of which is "child," but which in this case may be related to the Aramaic *ꜥddn,* "seer, messenger," see J. E. Hoch, *Semitic Words in Egyptian Texts of the New Kingdom and Third Intermediate Period* (Princeton: Princeton University Press 1994), 86–87.

[108] Translation from M. Lichtheim, *Ancient Egyptian Literature. Vol. 2: The New Kingdom* (Berkeley: University of California Press, 1975), 225.

[109] See Charpin and Durand, "La Prise," 326–28.

I lifted up my hands to Baal-Sha[may]in, and Baal-Shamayi[n] answered me. Baal-Shamayin [spoke] to me [by] means of seers (*ḥzyn*) and messengers (*ʿddn*). Baal-Shamayin [spoke to me]: "Fear not! For I have made [you] ki[ng. I will sta]nd by you and I will rescue you from all [these kings who] have laid a siege against you."

The divine words, the source of which is not indicated, may well be formulated by the scribe who composed the inscription. In all likelihood, however, they are closer to actual prophetic performances than either of the preceding cases. Not only does the inscription indicate the Old Aramaic designations for prophets (*ḥzyn*, *ʿddn*), it also repeats the famous "fear not" formula (*ʾl tzḥl*; cf. Akkadian *lā tapallah*, Hebrew *ʾal tîrāʾ*), describes a situation closely akin to the one referred to in SAA 9 no. 3.3 ii 10–13,[110] and presents an oracle that is in every respect parallel to Mesopotamian and biblical prophecy. The author of the inscription must have had a good grasp of the language and repertoire of the "seers" and "messengers." In view of the reference to a "book" of Balaam in the temporally, geographically, and linguistically not-so-distant Deir ʿAlla inscription,[111] it is not impossible to assume a written source here.

The inscription of Zakkur is the only royal inscription outside Assyria in which prophecy is cited, and even in the inscriptions of the Assyrian kings such quotations are uncommon. As a matter of fact, there are only two cases classifiable as prophetic examples. The first, the affinity of which to the divine message in the Zakkur inscription is palpable, belongs to Assurbanipal's account of his Elamite campaign in 653 B.C.E. (Prism B v 46–49):

Ištar heard my desperate sighs and said to me: "Fear not!" She made my heart confident (saying): "Because of the 'hand-lifting' prayer you said, your eyes being filled with tears, I have mercy upon you."[112]

The second quotation is to be found in the account of Assurbanipal's war against Ahšeri, the king of Mannea (Prism A iii 4–7):

---

[110] "Now these traitors conspired against you, expelled you and surrounded you. You, however, opened your mouth (crying): 'Hear me, O Aššur!'" Cf. Esarhaddon's own account of the same situation in Nin A i 53–62 (R. Borger, *Die Inschriften Asarhaddons, Königs von Assyrien* [AfO Beiheft 9; Graz: Selbstverlag, 1956], 43).

[111] The language of the Deir ʿAlla inscription is "auf dem Weg (. . .), Aramäisch zu werden, ohne es schon ganz geworden zu sein" (E. A. Knauf, *Midian: Untersuchungen zur Geschichte Palästinas und Nordarabiens am Ende des 2. Jahrtausends v. Chr.* [Abhandlungen des Deutschen Palästina-Vereins 101; Wiesbaden: Harrassowitz, 1988], 64–65 n. 313; cf. the analysis of Weippert, "Is Balaam Also?" 159–64). There is one remarkable linguistic feature it shares with the Zakkur inscription: the consecutive imperfect.

[112] Borger, *Beiträge*, 100.

Ištar, who dwells in Arbela, delivered Ahšeri, who did not fear my lordship, up to his servants, according to the word (*amātu*) that she had said in the very beginning: "I will, as I have said, take care of the execution of Ahšeri, the king of Mannea." [113]

The fact that quasi-verbatim quotations of prophecies can be found only twice does not, however, tell the whole truth about the significance of prophecy in the inscriptions of Esarhaddon and Assurbanipal. Contrary to their predecessors, both kings repeatedly claim to have received prophetic messages (*šipir mahhê*) that support their rule or give them confidence in war, mostly mentioned along with other means of divination like dreams and omens of different kinds.[114] Prophecy thus forms just one, yet a very distinctive, part of the divinatory apparatus the kings needed to be able to say that they have acted upon the command (*ina qibīt*) or with the help (*ina tukulti*) of the Great Gods.[115] When paraphrasing divine messages, the inscriptions do not necessarily specify the source of the message. For this reason, it is sometimes difficult indeed to distinguish between prophecy and other divinatory messages cited or reported in the inscriptions. The prisms of Assurbanipal, for example, describe dreams seen by a *šabrû* ("visionary, dreamer"),[116] by Gyges, king of Lydia,[117] and even by the whole army,[118] all of which bear a close resemblance to the language of contemporary prophecies. All this indicates that it was the message rather than the method that was important for the authors of the inscriptions who demonstrated divine determination for royal deeds.

In any case, the very mention of prophecy in the inscriptions proves indisputably the established role of prophecy among other forms of divination in the time of Esarhaddon and Assurbanipal. It is clear that, when commenting on prophecy, they document the view of the king and his scholarly entourage, according to which the wars of the Assyrian king were waged upon the

---

[113] Ibid., 35.

[114] Esarhaddon: Nin A ii 5–8 (Borger, *Inschriften*, 45); Ass A i 31 – ii 26 (ibid., 2). Assurbanipal: Prism B v 93–96 (Borger, *Beiträge*, 104); Prism T ii 16–17 (ibid., 141).

[115] For these and related expressions indicating divine justification of the kings' actions, see F. M. Fales and G. B. Lanfranchi, "The Impact of Oracular Material on the Political Utterances and Political Action of the Sargonid Dynasty," in *Oracles et prophéties dans l'antiquité: Actes du Colloque de Strasbourg, 15–17 Juin 1995* (ed. J.-G. Heinz; Université des sciences humaines de Strasbourg, Travaux du Centre de recherche sur le Proche-Orient et la Grèce antiques 15; Paris: De Boccard, 1997), 99–114, esp. 104–6.

[116] Prism A iii 118–127; B v 49–76 (Borger, *Beiträge*, 40–41, 100–101).

[117] Prism A ii 95–110parr; E-prisms (ibid., 30–31, 181–183).

[118] Prism A v 95–103 (ibid., 50).

command of the gods. Fully corresponding to this imperial ideology, the wording of the prophetic oracles and other divine messages cited in the inscriptions may be freely formulated paraphrases invented by the scribes, who certainly mastered the appropriate style and language. The complicated redaction history of the annals of Assurbanipal, in the prisms dating from 666 to 639 B.C.E., clearly demonstrates the creativity of the scribes.[119]

On the other hand, attention should be paid to the fact that Esarhaddon and Assurbanipal are the only kings to mention prophecies in their inscriptions, which corresponds to the fact that the practice of filing the very copies of prophetic reports and collections in royal archives is likewise documented only from the time of these two kings. The royal archives were certainly utilized by the authors of the inscriptions, hence the references to prophecy—whether accurate quotations or free inventions—may also go back to written reports to which the scribes had easy access.

It is important to note that the scribes of Esarhaddon, and probably also those of Assurbanipal, obviously used the archival copies of prophecy. This is conceivable from the inscriptions of Esarhaddon, which not only refer to prophecies but evidently presuppose knowledge of the prophetic oracles collected in SAA 9 nos. 1, 2, and 3.[120] Esarhaddon's account of his rise to power (Nin A), written in 673, can be followed almost step-by-step with SAA 9 no. 1 in hand; in fact, it is feasible to conclude that the collection in SAA 9 no. 1, the oracles of which were delivered eight years earlier, was prepared at the same time and for the same purpose as the inscription: to justify the investiture of Assurbanipal as crown prince and warn the eventual dissidents against any thoughts of insurrection. Moreover, the account of the beginning of his reign (Ass A) from year 679, corresponds to the oracles in SAA 9 no. 2 from the same year, and the surprising affinity of the pertinent section of the Nin A inscription with the oracle SAA 9 no. 3.3 evidently suggests that the prophecy has served as a source for the account in the inscription.[121] This means that the

---

[119] Cf. the dates of the prisms in A. K. Grayson, "The Chronology of the Reign of Assurbanipal, " ZA 70 (1980): 227–45, esp. 245; and the case studies by M. Cogan and H. Tadmor, "Gyges and Assurbanipal: A Study in Literal Transmission," Or 46 (1977): 65–85; and P. Gerardi, "The Arab Campaigns of Aššurbanipal: Scribal Reconstruction of the Past," SAAB 6 (1992): 67–103.

[120] On the relationship of the inscriptions and prophecies, see Parpola, Assyrian Prophecies, lxviii–lxxv; Nissinen, References, 14–34.

[121] For the commonalities of these texts, see M. Weippert, "Assyrische Prophetien der Zeit Asarhaddons und Assurbanipals," in Assyrian Royal Inscriptions: New Horizons in Literary, Ideological, and Historical Analysis (ed. F. M. Fales; Orientis Antiqui Collectio 17; Rome: Istituto per l'Oriente, 1981), 71–115, esp. 94–95; Nissinen, References, 26–28.

historical narrative of the inscriptions partially depends on prophecies; hence the view of the prophets, ideologically well in line with that of the scribes, is indirectly represented in the work of the scholars.

The references to prophets and their words in the sources discussed above no longer belong to concrete contexts in time and place; instead, they have become part of textual contexts created by the craftsmen of the literary works and inscriptions. Even in cases that may originate from actually spoken words in concrete situations, it is the historical and ideological paradigm of the textual world that serves as the interpretative framework for prophecy. Hence, the literary references to prophecy should first and foremost be taken as evidence for the use and interpretation of prophecy by contemporary or succeeding generations. To some extent this is true for all written documents of prophecy; however, the evidence for prophecy in literary works and inscriptions belongs to a more advanced phase in the communication process, and thus is further away from actual prophetic performance.

Conclusion

From the source material discussed in this article, the general conclusion may be drawn that ancient Near Eastern prophecy was basically oral performance, that is, delivery of verbal messages spoken by a prophet. The message could be transmitted orally by one or several go-betweens all the way through, from prophet to destination. Occasionally, but never quite systematically, the spoken word ended up in written form, for different purposes and under varying circumstances. Writing was used, not only as an aid for memory, but also either (a) to make the divine message communicable if the addressee was not reachable by means of oral communication, or (b) to preserve the oracle for posterity, thus enabling its subsequent quotation and interpretation.

Based on observations made above, the prophetic process of communication can be outlined by the following two models (excluding the simplest case of a direct encounter between the prophet and the addressee), one being purely oral and the other involving scribal activity:

1. *Spoken message*:
    a. A prophet, on his/her own initiative or in answer to an inquiry, claims to have experienced a divine revelation and performs the divine message orally and/or by other means to be transmitted to the addressee.
    b. Another person attends the prophetic performance, memorizes the message and assumes the task of its transmission.

(c_{1+n}). If person b is unable to deliver the message directly to the addressee, other intermediaries participate in its transmission.

d. The addressee receives the spoken message from person b or from another intermediary (c_{1+n}).

2. *Written message*:

a, b, and c_{1+n} as in the spoken message.

d. Person b or another intermediary employs a scribe to write the prophetic message down; the scribe prepares a tablet, possibly in several phases from the first draft to the final, polished, and well written form.

e_{1+n}. The tablet is given to a person who transports it to the destination; several conveyers may be necessary.

f. Someone (e.g., a court officer) receives the tablet at the final destination and, if the addressee is illiterate, reads it out in his or her presence.

g. The addressee hears and interprets the message.

If the written message, for one reason or the other, is found to be worth preserving, the process may continue even after the message has reached the addressee:

h. The written record containing the prophetic message or a stylized copy of it is stored in an archive or reinscribed on another object, on a wall, or on a monument.

i. Individual documents may be copied and compiled into collections of prophetic oracles; the selection, copying, compiling, and eventual standardization of form and content requires redactional activity.

j. The individual records and/or collections of oracles, now being a part of the scribal tradition rather than words meant for a particular situation, are used as reference works and quoted, paraphrased, and reinterpreted in various phases, according to the needs of the interpreters.

These are not the only possible models for the prophetic process of communication, just the most plausible ones that can be reconstructed from the available sources. The process could certainly take alternative routes. In theory, if there are literate persons among the prophets, they may formulate the written form of the message themselves; the Hebrew Bible, unlike the remaining documentation from the ancient Near East, seems to take this possibility into account (Isa 30:8; Hab 2:2). On the other hand, the prophet him- or herself may use a scribe and dispatch the message to the destination without speaking to an audience (cf. ARM 26 no. 414; see above).

Contrary to the prophetical books of the Hebrew Bible, which are at our disposal only in their final form, having been edited and augmented over and over again during the centuries, the ancient Near Eastern evidence for prophecy makes it possible to observe earlier phases of the prophetic process of communication. The reports, collections, letters, and even the inscriptions are substantially closer in time to the spoken words, which makes their dating and sociohistorical context considerably easier to determine. The student of prophecy in the societies of Assyria and Mari, hence, is better off than one who attempts to reconstruct the role of prophecy in preexilic Israel and Judah with the help of the prophetic books and narratives of the Hebrew Bible, the dating and historical background of which is virtually always debatable. But even the ancient Near Eastern documents are no punctilious memoranda of "original" prophecies, but secondary records liable to the whole dynamics of human communication. When it comes to the very utterances of the prophets, the source-critical problems concerning the transmission and interpretation of the prophecies immediately emerge, and the student of the Bible and the ancient Near Eastern sources, often one and the same person, finds him- or herself in a similar situation.

The search for *ipsissima verba*, declared invalid for quite some time in the study of biblical and extrabiblical prophecy but still looming between the lines, implies the idea of a pristine condition of prophecy in the actual performance situation, often elevating the primary formulation of the divine message above all phases of the subsequent process of transmission. However, the evidence from Mari and Assyria shows that, while the faithful transmission of the divine message was doubtless regarded as essentially important, it was not motivated by the idea of literal inspiration, but rather by the pursuit of appropriate interpretation and application. In this respect, prophecies can be compared with omens and the results of other divinatory processes.

The very writtenness of biblical and ancient Near Eastern prophecy shows that prophecy is more than the prophets, their words, and personalities. Considered from the point of view of communication, prophecy covers a wide range of components, human and divine, reflecting not just the spirituality and expressive power of the prophet, but the whole network of social, political, and religious perspectives represented by the participants in the communication process and the communities around them. The openness to interpretation belongs to the very nature of a process which can proceed only if the message is meaningful. Since meanings of words emerge within a sociolinguistic context, there is no repetition of a message without an interpretative adaptation corresponding to the perception of the ones who are supposed to hear it. The intermediaries, addressees, and interpreters of the prophetic messages, hence, are not mere instruments and objects of the divine word, but active participants whose needs and preferences keep the process advancing. Without their participation there is no meaningful message to be heard and heeded, no communication, no prophecy.

Bibliography

Abdul-Razik, M. "The Dedicatory and Building Texts of Ramesses II in Luxor Temple: I, The Texts." *JEA* 60 (1974): 142–60.

Achtemeier, P. J. "*Omne verbum sonat:* The New Testament and the Oral Environment of Late Western Antiquity." *JBL* 109 (1990): 3–27.

Adler, H.-P. *Das Akkadische des Königs Tušratta von Mitanni.* AOAT 201. Kevelaer: Butzon & Bercker; Neukirchen-Vluyn: Neukirchener Verlag, 1976.

Allen, B. "The Personal Point of View in Orally Communicated History." *Western Folklore* 38 (1979): 110–18.

Allen, J. P. *Genesis in Egypt: The Philosophy of Ancient Egyptian Creation Accounts.* New Haven: Yale Egyptological Seminar, Department of Near Eastern Languages and Civilizations, Graduate School, Yale University, 1988.

Allen, T. G. "Some Egyptian Sun Hymns." *JNES* 8 (1949): 349–55.

—————. *The Egyptian Book of the Dead: Documents in the Oriental Institute Museum.* Chicago: University of Chicago Press, 1974.

Alonso Schökel, L. "Jeremías como anti-Moisés." Pp. 245–54 in *De la Torah au Messie: Mélanges Henri Cazelles.* Edited by M. Carrez, J. Doré, and P. Grelot. Paris: Desclée, 1981.

Alster, B. "Interaction of Oral and Written Poetry in Early Mesopotamian Literature." Pp. 23–69 in *Mesopotamian Epic Literature: Oral or Aural?* Edited by M. E. Vogelzang and H. L. J. Vanstiphout. Lewiston, N.Y.: Mellen, 1992.

Anbar, M. "Mari and the Origin of Prophecy." Pp. 1–5 in Kinattūtu ša dārâti: *Raphael Kutscher Memorial Volume.* Edited by A. F. Rainey. Tel Aviv: Journal of the Institute of Archaeology, Tel Aviv University, 1993.

Arnaud, D. *Recherches au Pays d'Aštata 6.* 3 vols. Paris: Éditions Recherche sur le civilisations, 1985–87.

Arnett, W. S. *The Predynastic Origin of the Egyptian Hieroglyphs: Evidence for the Development of Rudimentary Forms of Hieroglyphs in Upper*

Egypt in the Fourth Millennium B.C. Washington, D.C.: University Press of America, 1982.

Assmann, A., and J. Assmann. *Kanon und Zensur.* Beiträge zur Archäologie der literarischen Kommunikation 2. Munich: W. Fink, 1987.

Assmann, J. *Ägypten: Eine Sinngeschichte.* Munich: Hanser, 1996.

————. "Fest des Augenblicks—Verheissung der Dauer: Die Kontroverse der ägyptischen Harfnerlieder." Pp. 55–84 in *Fragen an die altägyptische Literatur: Studien zum Gedenken an Eberhard Otto.* Edited by J. Assmann, E. Feucht, and R. Grieshammer. Wiesbaden: Reichert, 1977.

————. "Gibt es eine 'Klassik' in der ägyptischen Literaturgeschichte?" *ZDMG* Supplement 6 (1985): 35–52.

————. *Das kulturelle Gedächtnis: Schrift, Erinnerung und politische Identität in frühen Hochkulturen.* Munich: C. H. Beck, 1992.

————. "Nachwort." Pp. 265–84 in *Schrift und Gedächtnis.* Edited by A. Assmann, J. Assmann, and C. Hardemeir. Beiträge zur Archäologie der literarischen Kommunikation 1. Munich: W. Fink, 1983.

————. "Schrift, Tod, und Identität: Das Grab als Vorschule der Literatur im Alten Ägypten." Pp. 64–93 in *Schrift und Gedächtnis.* Edited by A. Assmann, J. Assmann, and C. Hardemeir. Beiträge zur Archäologie der literarischen Kommunikation 1. Munich: W. Fink, 1983.

————. "Schriftliche Folklore: Zur Entstehung und Funktion eines Überlieferungstyps." Pp. 175–93 in *Schrift und Gedächtnis.* Edited by A. Assmann, J. Assmann, and C. Hardemeir. Beiträge zur Archäologie der literarischen Kommunikation 1. Munich: W. Fink, 1983.

————. "Eine Traumöffenbarung der Göttin Hathor." *RdÉ* 30 (1978): 22–50.

Bailly, A. *Dictionnaire Grec-Français.* Paris: Hachette, 1950. S.v. προφήτης.

Baines, J. "Interpreting the Story of the Shipwrecked Sailor." *JEA* 76 (1990): 55–72.

————. "Literacy and Ancient Egyptian Society." *Man,* NS, 18 (1983): 572–99.

————. "Literacy, Social Organization and the Archaeological Record: The Case of Early Egypt." Pp. 192–214 in *State and Society: The Emergence and Development of Social Hierarchy and Political Centralization.* Edited by J. Gledhill, B. Bender, and M. T. Larsen. London and Boston: Unwin Hyman, 1998.

Baines, J., and C. J. Eyre. "Four Notes on Literacy." *GöM* 61 (1983): 65–96.

Bakir, A. M. *The Cairo Calendar no. 86637.* Cairo: General Organisation for Government Printing Offices, 1996.

Bakker, E. *Poetry in Speech: Orality and Homeric Discourse.* Ithaca, N.Y.: Cornell University Press, 1997.

Bal, M. *Narratology: Introduction to the Theory of Narration.* Translated by C. van Boheemen. Toronto: University of Toronto Press, 1985.

Bardet, G., et al. *Archives administratives de Mari 1.* ARM 23. Paris: Éditions Recherche sur les civilisations, 1984.

Barguet, P. *Le Papyrus N. 3176 (S) du Musée du Louvre.* Bibliothèque d'étude 37. Cairo: Institut français d'archéologie orientale, 1962.

Barnes, J. "Aphorism and Argument." Pp. 91–109 in *Language and Thought in Early Greek Philosophy.* Edited by K. Robb. Monist Library of Philosophy. La Salle, Ill.: Hegeler Institute, 1983.

Barns, J. *Five Ramesseum Papyri.* Oxford: Griffith Institute at the University Press, 1956.

Barstad, H. M. "No Prophets? Recent Developments in Biblical Prophetic Research and Ancient Near Eastern Prophecy." *JSOT* 57 (1993): 39–60.

Barta, W. "Ein metrisch geformter Stelentext des Mittleren Reiches." Pp. 63–77 in *Form und Mass: Beiträge zur Literatur, Sprache und Kunst Ägypten: Festschrift für Gerhard Fecht zum 65. Geburtstag.* Edited by J. Osing and G. Dreyers, Ägypten und Altes Testament 12. Wiesbaden: Harrassowitz, 1987.

Barthes, R. *Critical Essays.* Translated by R. Howard. Evanston, Ill.: Northwestern University Press, 1981.

Barton, J. *Oracles of God: Perceptions of Ancient Prophecy in Israel after the Exile.* New York and Oxford: Oxford University Press, 1986.

Beard, M., et al., eds. *Literacy in the Roman World.* Journal of Roman Archaeology Supplement Series 3. Ann Arbor, Mich.: Journal of Roman Archaeology, 1991.

Becker, U. *Jesaja—von der Botschaft zum Buch.* FRLANT 178. Göttingen: Vandenhoeck & Ruprecht, 1997.

Beckerath, J. von. "Zur Geschichte von Consuemhab und dem Geist." *ZÄS* 119 (1992): 90–107.

Ben Zvi, E. "Atypical Features, the Meta-prophetic Character of the Book of Jonah, and Other Communicative Messages." Unpublished paper presented at the annual meeting of the Pacific Northwest Society of Biblical Literature, Tacoma, Wash., 1999.

———. *A Historical-Critical Study of the Book of Zephaniah.* BZAW 198. Berlin and New York: de Gruyter, 1998.

———. *A Historical-Critical Study of the Book of Obadiah.* BZAW 242. Berlin and New York: de Gruyter, 1996.

———. "Looking at the Primary (Hi)story and the Prophetic Books as Literary/Theological Units within the Frame of the Early Second Temple Period: Some Considerations." *SJOT* 12 (1998): 26–43.

———. *Micah.* FOTL. Grand Rapids, Mich.: Eerdmans, 2000.

————. "Twelve Prophetic Books or 'The Twelve': A Few Preliminary Considerations." Pp. 125–56 in *Forming Prophetic Literature: Essays on Isaiah and the Twelve in Honor of John D. W. Watts*. Edited by J. W. Watts and P. R. House, JSOTSup 235. Sheffield: Sheffield Academic Press, 1997.

————. "The Urban Center of Jerusalem and the Development of the Literature of the Hebrew Bible." Pp. 194–209 in *Aspects of Urbanism in Antiquity: From Mesopotamia to Crete*. Edited by W. G. Aufrecht, N. A. Mirau and S. W. Gauley, JSOTSup 244. Sheffield: Sheffield Academic Press, 1997.

Benson, L. D. "The Literary Character of Anglo-Saxon Formulaic Poetry." *Publications of the Modern Language Association* 81 (1966): 334–41.

Bieber, M. *The History of the Greek and Roman Theater*. Princeton: Princeton University Press, 1961.

Birot, M. *Correspondance des gouverneurs de Qaṭṭunân*. ARM 27. Paris: Éditions Recherche sur les civilisations, 1993.

Bissing, W. F. von. *Die Mastaba des Gem-ni-kai*. 2 vols. Berlin: A. Duncker, 1911.

Black, J. A., and W. J. Tait, "Archives and Libraries in the Ancient Near East." Pp. 2197–2201 in *Civilizations of the Ancient Near East*. Edited by J. M. Sasson. 4 vols. New York: Scribner, 1995.

Blackman, A. M. *Middle Egyptian Stories*. Bibliotheca aegyptiaca 2. Brussels: Éditions de la Fondation égyptologique Reine Élisabeth, 1932.

————. *The Rock Tombs of Meir*. 6 vols. Archaeological Survey of Egypt 22nd–25th, 28th–29th Memoir. London: Egypt Exploration Fund, 1914–53.

Blackwell, T. *An Enquiry into the Life and Writings of Homer*. London, 1735.

Blair, H. *Lectures on Rhetoric and Belles Lettres*. 2 vols. London, 1783.

Blenkinsopp, J. *Prophecy and Canon: A Contribution to the Study of Jewish Origins*. Notre Dame, Ind.: University of Notre Dame Press, 1977.

————. *Sage, Priest, Prophet: Religious and Intellectual Leadership in Ancient Israel*. LAI. Louisville, Ky.: Westminster John Knox, 1995.

Blumenthal, E. "Die Koptosstele des Königs Rahotep (London U.C. 14327)." Pp. 63–80 in *Ägypten und Kusch: Fritz Hintze zum 60. Geburtstag*. Edited by E. Endesfelder et al. Berlin: Akademie-Verlag, 1977.

————. "Die literarische Verarbeitung der Übergangszeit zwischen Alten und Mittleren Reich." Pp. 105–36 in *Ancient Egyptian Literature: History and Forms*. Edited by A. Loprieno. Probleme der Ägyptologie 10. Leiden: Brill, 1996.

Bodine, W. R. "Linguistics and Philology in the Study of Ancient Near Eastern Languages." Pp. 39–54 in *Working with No Data*. Edited by D. M. Golomb. Winona Lake, Ind.: Eisenbrauns, 1987.

Boeser, P. A. A. *Beschreibung der ägyptischen Sammlung des Niederländischen Reichsmuseums der Altertümer in Leiden*. The Hague: Martinus Nijhoff, 1910–20. Vol. III, *Die Denkmäler der Zeit zwischen dem Alten und Mittleren Reich und des Mittleren Reiches*. Pt. 2, *Grabgegenstände, Statuen, Gefässe und Verschiedenartige kleinere Gegenstände*. III, *Stelen*. Milan, 1913.

Boissier, C. *Documents assyriens relatifs aux présages*. 1 vol. in 3 parts. Paris: Emile Bouillon, 1894–99.

Borger, R. *Beiträge zum Inschriftenwerk Asssurbanipals: Die Prismenklassen A, B, C=K, D, E, F, H, J, und T sowie andere Inschriften*. Wiesbaden: Harrassowitz, 1996.

———. *Die Inschriften Asarhaddons, Königs von Assyrien*. AfO Beiheft 9. Graz: Selbstverlag, 1956.

Bostico, S. *Museo archeologico di Firenze: Le stele egiziane*. Rome, 1959.

Bothmer, B. V. *Egyptian Sculpture of the Late Period: 700 B.C. to A.D. 100*. Brooklyn: Brooklyn Museum, 1969.

Botti, G. "A Fragment of a Story of a Military Expedition of Tuthmosis III to Syria." *JEA* 41 (1955): 64–71.

Brovarski, E. "Ahanakht of Bersheh and the Hare Home in the First Intermediate Period." Pp. 14–30 in *Studies in Ancient Egypt, the Aegean, and the Sudan: Essays in Honor of Dows Dunham on the Occasion of His 90th Birthday*. Edited by W. K. Simpson and W. Davis. Boston: Department of Egyptian and Ancient Near Eastern Art, Museum of Fine Arts, 1981.

Brown, G., and G. Yule. *Discourse Analysis*. Cambridge and New York: Cambridge University Press, 1983.

Brown, J. *A Dissertation on the Rise, Union and Powers, the Progressions, Separations, and Corruptions, of Poetry and Music*. 2d ed. London, 1773.

Brown, W. P. *Character in Crisis: A Fresh Approach to the Wisdom Literature of the Old Testament*. Grand Rapids, Mich.: Eerdmans, 1996.

Broze, M. *Mythe et roman en Égypte ancienne: Les aventures d'Horus et Seth dans le Papyrus Chester Beatty I*. OLA 76. Louvain: Peeters, 1996.

Brunner, H. "Metrik." Pp. 120–22 in vol. 4 of *Lexikon der Ägyptologie*. Edited by W. Helck, E. Otto, and W. Westendorf. Wiesbaden: Harrassowitz.

Brunner-Traut, E. "Wechselbeziehungen zwischen schriftlicher und mündlicher Überlieferung im Alten Ägypten." *Fabula* 20 (1979): 34–46.

Bruyère, B. *Mert seger à Deir el-Medine.* Cairo: Institut français d'archéologie orientale, 1929–30.

Bryan, B. "Evidence for Female Literacy from Theban Tombs of the New Kingdom." *Bulletin of the Egyptological Seminar* 6 (1984): 17–32.

Budde, K. *Das Buch der Richter.* KHC 7. Tübingen: Mohr, 1897.

————. *Jesajas Erleben: Eine gemeinverständliche Auslegung der Denkschrift des Propheten (Kap. 6,1–9,6).* Gotha: Leopold Klotz Verlag, 1928.

Budge, E. A. W. *Facsimiles of Egyptian Hieratic Papyri in the British Museum.* London, 1910.

————. *Hieratic Papyri in the British Museum, 2nd Series.* London, 1923.

Burkhard, G. "Der formale Aufbau altägyptischer Literaturwerke: Zur Problematik der Erschliessung seiner Grundstrukturen." *SAK* 10 (1983): 78–118.

Burns, A. *The Power of the Written Word: The Role of Literacy in the History of Western Civilization.* Studia Classica 1. New York: P. Lang, 1989.

————. "Spoken History in an Oral Community." *International Journal of Oral History* 9 (1988): 99–113.

Cagni, L. *L'epopea di Erra.* Studi semitici 34. Rome: Istituto de studi del Vicino Oriente dell'Universita, 1969.

————. *Le profezie di Mari.* Testi del Vicinio Oriente antico 2/2. Brescia: Paideia, 1995.

Caminos, R. A. *Late Egyptian Miscellanies.* Oxford: Oxford University Press, 1954.

————. *Literary Fragments in the Hieratic Script.* London: Griffith Institute at the University Press, 1956.

————. "The Moscow Literary Letter." Pp. 147–53 in *Fragen an die altägyptische Literatur: Studien zum Gedenken an Eberhard Otto.* Edited by J. Assmann, E. Feucht, and R. Grieshammer. Wiesbaden: Reichert, 1977.

————. "Review of *Egyptian Stelae, Reliefs and Paintings from the Petrie Collection* by Harry Milne Stewart." *JEA* 64 (1978): 151–57.

————. *A Tale of Woe: From a Hieratic Papyrus in the A. S. Pushkin Museum of Fine Arts in Moscow.* Oxford: Griffith Institute, Ashmolean Museum, 1977.

Camp, J. M. *The Athenian Agora: Excavations in the Heart of Classical Athens.* London: Thames and Hudson, 1986.

Cannuyer, C. "Brelan de 'Pharaons' Ramses XI, Thoutmosis III et Hatschepsout." Pp. 98–115 in vol. 1 of *Studies in Egyptology Presented to Miriam Lichtheim.* Edited by S. Israelit-Groll. Jerusalem: Magnes, 1990.

Carasic, M. "Who Were the Men of Hezekiah (Proverbs XXV:1)?" *VT* 44 (1994): 291–300.

Caravelli, A. "The Song Beyond the Song: Aesthetics and Social Interaction in Greek Folksong." *JAF* 95 (1982): 129–58.

Caroll, R. P. *When Prophecy Failed.* London: SCM, 1979.

Carter, C. E. "The Province of Yehud in the Post-Exilic Period: Sounding in Site Distribution and Demography." Pp. 106–45 in *Second Temple Studies 2: Temple Community in the Persian Period.* Edited by T. C. Eskenazi and K. H. Richards. JSOTSup 175. Sheffield: JSOT Press, 1994.

Cenival, F. de. *Le Mythe de l'oeil du soleil.* Sommerhausen: G. Zauzich, 1988.

Černý, J. *A Community of Workmen at Thebes in the Ramesside Period.* Cairo: Institut français d'archéologie orientale, 1973.

———. *Late Ramesside Letters.* Bibliotheca aegyptiaca 9. Brussels: Éditions de la Fondation égyptologique Reine Élisabeth, 1939.

Champion, T. C., ed. *Centre and Periphery: Comparative Studies in Archaeology.* London and Boston: Unwin Hyman, 1989.

Charlesworth, J. H. *The Old Testament Pseudepigrapha.* 2 vols. Garden City, N.Y.: Doubleday, 1983.

Charpin, D. "Le Contexte historique et géographique des prophéties dans les textes retrouvés á Mari." *Bulletin of the Canadian Society for Mesopotamian Studies* 23 (1992): 21–31.

Charpin, D., and J.-M. Durand. "La Prise du pouvoir par Zimri-Lim." *MARI* 4 (1985): 297–343.

Charpin, D., et al. *Archives épistolaires de Mari I/2.* ARM 26/2. Paris: Éditions Recherche sur les civilisations, 1988.

Chassinat, E. *Le Mystère d'Osiris au mois de Khoiâkh.* Cairo: Institut français d'archéologie orientale, 1968.

Childs, B. S. "The Enemy from the North and the Chaos Tradition." *JBL* 78 (1959): 187–98.

Cifola, B. "Ramses III and the Sea Peoples: A Structural Analysis of the Medinet Habu Inscriptions." *Or* 57 (1988): 275–306.

———. "The Terminology of Ramses III's Historical Records with a Formal Analysis of the War Scenes." *Or* 60 (1991): 9–57.

Clark, M. "Did Thucydides Invent the Battle Exhortation?" *Historia* 44 (1995): 375–76.

Clements, R. E. "The Immanuel Prophecy of Isa 7.10–17 and Its Messianic Interpretation." Pp. 225–40 in *Die Hebräische Bible und ihre zweifache Nachgeschichte: Festschrift R. Rendtorff.* Edited by E. Blum, C. Macholz, and E. E. Stegemann. Neukirchen-Vluyn: Neukirchener Verlag, 1990 (repr. in *Old Testament Prophecy: From Oracles to Canon,* by R. E. Clements [Louisville, Ky.: Westminster John Knox, 1996] 65–77).

———. *Isaiah 1–39.* NCB. London: Marshall, Morgan, & Scott, 1980.

Clère, J. J. and J. Vandier. *Textes de la première période intermédiaire et de la XIème dynastie.* Bibliotheca aegyptiaca 10. Brussels: Éditions de la Fondation égyptologique Reine Élisabeth, 1949.

Cogan, M., and H. Tadmor. "Gyges and Assurbanipal: A Study in Literal Transmission." *Or* 46 (1977): 65–85.

Coggins, R. "An Alternative Prophetic Tradition?" Pp. 77–94 in *Israel's Prophetic Heritage: Essays in Honour of Peter R. Ackroyd.* Edited by R. Coggins, A. Philips, and M. Knibb. Cambridge: Cambridge University Press, 1982.

Cohen, N. G. "From *Nabi* to *Mal'ak* to 'Ancient Figure.'" *JSS* 36 (1985): 12–24.

Cole, S. W., and P. Machinist, eds. *Letters from Priests to the Kings Esarhaddon and Assurbanipal.* SAA 13. Helsinki: Helsinki University Press, 1998.

Collier, M. "The Language of Literature: On Grammar and Texture." Pp. 532–54 in *Ancient Egyptian Literature: History and Forms.* Edited by A. Loprieno. Probleme der Ägyptologie 10. Leiden: Brill, 1996.

Collins, J. "Literacy and Literacies." *Annual Review of Anthropology* 24 (1995): 75–93.

Conrad, E. W. "Heard But Not Seen: The Representation of 'Books' in the Old Testament." *JSOT* 54 (1992): 45–59.

Cooper, J. S. "Babbling on Recovering Mesopotamian Orality." Pp. 103–22 in *Mesopotamian Epic Literature: Oral or Aural?* ed. M. E. Vogelzang and H. L. J. Vanstiphout. Lewiston, N.Y.: Mellen, 1992.

Corteggiani, J. P. "Une stèle héliopolitaine de l'époque Saite." Pp. 115–54 in *Hommages à Serge Sauneron*, 1. Edited by J. Vercoutter. Bibliotheque d'étude 81. Cairo: Institut français d'archéologie orientale, 1979.

Couyat, J., and P. Montet. *Les Inscriptions hiéroglyphiques et hiératiques du Ouâdi Hammamat.* Mémoires publiés par les membres de l'Institut français d'archéologie orientale du Caire 69. Cairo: Institut français d'archéologie orientale, 1912.

Crenshaw, J. L. "The Deuteronomist and the Writings." Pp. 145–58 in *Those Elusive Deuteronomists: The Phenomenon of Pan-Deuteronomism.* Edited by L. S. Schearing and S. L. McKenzie. JSOTSup 268. Sheffield: Sheffield Academic Press, 1999.

———. *Education in Ancient Israel: Across the Deadening Silence.* ABRL. New York: Doubleday, 1998.

———. "Freeing the Imagination: The Conclusion to the Book of Joel." Pp 129–47 in *Prophecy and Prophets: The Diversity of Contemporary Issues in Scholarship.* Edited by Y. Gitay. SBLSS. Atlanta: Scholars Press, 1997.

————. *Joel.* AB 24C. New York: Doubleday, 1995.

————. *Old Testament Wisdom.* Rev. and enl. ed. Louisville, Ky.: Westminster John Knox, 1998.

————. "The Primacy of Listening in Ben Sira's Pedagogy." Pp. 172–87 in *Wisdom, You Are My Sister: Studies in Honor of Roland E. Murphy, O.Carm., on the Occasion of His Eightieth Birthday.* Edited by M. L. Barré. CBQMS 29. Washington, D.C.: Catholic Biblical Association of America, 1997.

————. *Prophetic Conflict: Its Effect upon Israelite Religion.* BZAW 124. Berlin and New York: de Gruyter, 1971.

————. "Sirach." *NIB* 5:601–867.

————. *Urgent Advice and Probing Questions: Collected Writings on Old Testament Wisdom.* Macon, Georgia: Mercer University Press, 1995.

————. "Who Knows What YHWH Will Do? The Character of God in the Book of Joel." Pp. 185–96 in *Fortunate the Eyes That See: Essays in Honor of David Noel Freedman in Celebration of His Seventieth Birthday.* Edited by A. Beck et al. Grand Rapids, Mich.: Eerdmans, 1994.

Cribiore, R. *Writing, Teachers, and Students in Graeco-Roman Egypt.* ASP 36. Atlanta: Scholars Press, 1996.

Cruikshank, J. "Myth and Tradition as Narrative Framework: Oral Histories from Northern Canada." *International Journal of Oral History* 9 (1988): 198–214.

Cryer, F. H. *Divination in Ancient Israel and Its Near Eastern Environment: A Socio-Historical Investigation.* JSOTSup 142. Sheffield: Sheffield Academic Press, 1994.

Culley, R. C. "An Approach to the Problem of Oral Tradition." *VT* 13 (1963): 113–25.

————. *Oral Formulaic Language in the Biblical Psalms.* Near and Middle East Series 4. Toronto: University of Toronto Press, 1967.

————. "Oral Tradition and Biblical Studies." *Oral Tradition* 1 (1986): 30–65.

————. *Themes and Variations: A Study of Action in Biblical Narrative.* SBLSS. Atlanta: Scholars Press, 1992.

Davies, G. *Ancient Hebrew Inscriptions.* Cambridge: Cambridge University Press, 1991.

Davies, N. de G. *The Mastaba of Ptahhetep and Akhethetep at Saqqareh.* Archeological Survey of Egypt. Edited by F. Ll. Griffith. 8th–9th Memoir. London: Egypt Exploration Fund, 1898–99.

————. *The Rock Tombs of Deir e-Gebrawi.* 2 vols. Archeological Survey of Egypt, 11th–12th Memoir. London: Egypt Exploration Fund, 1902.

————. *The Rock Tombs of El-Amarna.* 6 vols. Archeological Survey of Egypt, 13th–18th and 35th Memoir. London: Egypt Exploration Fund, 1903–08.

Davies, N. de G., and A. H. Gardiner. *The Tomb of Amenemhet (no. 82).* Theban Tombs Series. London: Egypt Exploration Fund, 1915.

————. *The Tomb of Antefoker, Vizier of Sesostris I, and of His Wife, Senet (no. 60).* London: G. Allen & Unwin, 1920.

Davies, P. R. "The Audiences of Prophetic Scrolls: Some Suggestions." Pp. 48–62 in *Prophets and Paradigms: Essays in Honor of Gene M. Tucker.* Edited by S. B. Reid. JSOTSup 229. Sheffield: Sheffield Academic Press, 1996.

————. *In Search of Ancient Israel.* JSOTSup 148. Sheffield: JSOT Press, 1992.

————. *Scribes and Schools: The Canonization of the Hebrew Scriptures.* LAI. Louisville, Ky.: Westminster John Knox, 1998.

Davis, E. F. *Swallowing the Scroll: Textuality and the Dynamics of Discourse in Ezekiel's Prophecy.* JSOTSup 78. Sheffield: Almond, 1989.

De Buck, A. *Egyptian Readingbook.* Leiden: Nederlands Instituut voor het Nabije Oosten, 1948.

De Saussure, F. "The Object of Study." Pp. 1–9 in *Modern Criticism and Theory.* Edited by D. Lodge. London and New York: Longman, 1988.

Decker, W. *Quellentexte zu Sport und Korperkultur im alten Ägypten.* St. Augustin: Richarz, 1975.

————. "Das sogenannte Agonale und der altägyptische Sport." Pp. 90–104 in *Festschrift Elmar Edel.* Edited by M. Görg and E. Pusch. Bamberg: M. Görg, 1979.

————. *Sports and Games of Ancient Egypt.* Translated by A. Guttmann. New Haven: Yale University Press, 1987.

Derchain, P. "Bebon: le dieu et les mythes." *RdÉ* 9 (1952): 23–47.

————. "Éloquence et politique. L'Opinion d'Akhtoy." *RdÉ* 40 (1989): 37–47.

Dijkstra, M. "Is Balaam Also among the Prophets?" *JBL* 114 (1991): 43–64.

Doane, A. "The Ethnography of Scribal Writing and Anglo-Saxon Poetry: Scribe as Performer." *Oral Tradition* 9 (1994): 420–39.

Doetsch-Amberger, E. *Die ägyptische Sammlung Köln.* Cologne: Bachem, 1987.

Doherty, L. E. "The Internal and Implied Audience of *Odyssey* 11." *Arethusa* 24 (1991): 145–76.

Donaldson, L. E., and R. S. Sugirtharajah, eds. *Postcolonialism and Scriptural Reading.* Semeia 75. Atlanta: Scholars Press, 1996.

Dondelinger, E. *Papyrus Ani: BM 10.470.* Graz: Akademische Druk- und Verlagsanstalt, 1979.

Donner, H., and W. Röllig. *Kanaanäische und aramäische Inschriften, Band II: Kommentar.* 3d ed. Wiesbaden: Harrassowitz, 1973.

Doxey, D. M. *Egyptian Non-royal Epithets in the Middle Kingdom.* Leiden: Brill, 1998.

Duell, P. *The Mastaba of Mereruka by the Sakkarah Expedition.* Vol. 2. Chicago: University of Chicago Press, 1938.

Dunham, D. *Naga ed-Deir Stelae of the First Intermediate Period.* Boston: Published for the Museum of Fine Arts, Boston, by the Oxford University Press, H. Milford, 1937.

———. *Semna-Kumma.* Excavated by G. A. Reisner and published by D. Dunham and J. M. A. Janssen. Boston: Museum of Fine Arts, 1960.

Durand, J.-M. *Archives épistolaires de Mari I/1.* ARM 26/1. Paris: Éditions Recherche sur les civilisations, 1988.

———. "In vino veritas." *RA* 76 (1982): 43–50.

———. "Le Mythologème du combat entre le Dieu de l'Orage et la Mer en Mésopotamie." *MARI* 7 (1993): 41–61.

Durand, J.-M., and M. Guichard. "Les rituels de Mari." Pp. 19–78 in *Florilegium marianum III: Recueil d'études á la mémoire de Marie-Thérèse Barrelet.* Edited by D. Charpin and J.-M. Durand. MNABU 4. Paris: Société pour l'étude du Proche-Orient ancien, 1997.

Eagleton, T. *The Ideology of the Aesthetic.* Oxford: Blackwell, 1990.

———. *Literary Theory: An Introduction.* Minneapolis: University of Minnesota Press, 1996.

Ebers, G. M. *Papyros Ebers.* Leipzig: W. Engelmann, 1875.

Edel, E. "Zum Verständnis der Inschrift des *Jzy* aus Saqqara." *ZÄS* 106 (1979): 105–16.

———. "Bemurkungen zu den Schießsporttexten der Könige der 18. Dynastie." *SAK* 7 (1979): 23–40.

———. *Die Inschriften der Grabfronten des Siut-Graber in Mittelägypten aus der Herakleopolitenzeit.* Opladen: Westdeutscher Verlag, 1984.

Edwards, I. E. S. *Hieratic Papyri in the British Museum,* 4th ser. *Oracular Amuletic Decrees of the Late New Kingdom.* London, 1960.

Eliot, T. S. *What Is a Classic? An Address Delivered before the Virgil Society on the 16th of October, 1944.* London: Faber & Faber, 1945.

Ellermeier, F. *Prophetie in Mari und Israel.* Theologische und orientalistische Arbeiten 1. Herzberg: Erwin Jungfer, 1968.

Ellis, M. de J. "The Goddess Kitītum Speaks to King Ibalpiel: Oracle Texts from Ishchali." *MARI* 5 (1987): 235–66.

Erichsen, W. *Demotisches Glossar.* Copenhagen: E. Munksgaard, 1954.

Erman, A. "Denksteine aus der thebanischen Gräberstadt." *Sitzungsberichte der Bayerischen Akademie der Wissenschaften* 30 (1911): 1086–10.

———. *Hymnen an das Diadem der Pharaonen.* Berlin: Preussische Akademie der Wissenschaften, 1911.

Eyre, C. J. "Is Egyptian Historical Literature 'Historical' or 'Literary'?" Pp. 415–34 in *Ancient Egyptian Literature: History and Forms.* Edited by A. Loprieno. Probleme der Ägyptologie 10. Leiden: Brill, 1996.

———. "The Semna Stela: Quotation, Genre, and Function of Literature." Pp. 134–65 in vol. 1 of *Studies in Egyptology Presented to Miriam Lichtheim.* Edited by S. Israelit-Groll. Jerusalem: Magnes, 1990.

Eyre, C. J., and J. Baines, "Interactions between Orality and Literacy in Ancient Egypt." Pp. 91–120 in *Literacy and Society.* Edited by K. Shousboe and M. T. Larsen. Copenhagen: Akademisk Forlag, 1989.

Fairchild, H. N. *The Noble Savage.* New York: Columbia University Press, 1928.

Falck, C. *Myth, Truth, and Literature: Towards a True Post-Modernism.* 2d ed. Cambridge and New York: Cambridge University Press, 1994.

Fales, F. M., and G. B. Lanfranchi. "ABL 1237: The Role of Cimmerians in a Letter to Esarhaddon." *East and West* 31 (1981): 9–33.

———. "The Impact of Oracular Material on the Political Utterances and Political Action of the Sargonid Dynasty." Pp. 99–114 in *Oracles et prophéties dans l'antiquité: Actes du Colloque de Strasbourg, 15–17 Juin 1995.* Edited by J.-G. Heinz. Université des sciences humaines de Strasbourg, Travaux du Centre de recherche sur le Proche-Orient et la Grèce antiques 15. Paris: De Boccard, 1997.

Farber, W. *Beschwörungsrituale an Ištar und Dumuzi: Attī Ištar ša ḫarmaša Dumuzi.* Akademie der Wissenschaften und der Literatur, Veröffentlichungen der orientalischen Kommission 30. Wiesbaden: Franz Steiner, 1977.

Faulkner, R. O. *Concise Dictionary of Middle Egyptian.* Oxford: Printed for The Griffith Institute at the University Press by V. Ridler, 1962.

———. *The Papyrus Gremner-Rhind (British Museum no. 10188).* Brussels: Éditions de la Fondation égyptologique Reine Élisabeth, 1933.

Favard-Meeks, C. *Le Temple de Behbeit el-Hagara: essai de reconstitution et d'interprétation.* Hamburg: H. Buske, 1991.

Fecht, G. "Ptahhotep und die Disputierer (Lehre des Ptahhotep nach Pap. Prisse. Max. 2–4, Dev. 60–83)." *MDAI* 37 (1981): 143–50.

———. "Prosodie." Pp. 1127–54 in vol. 4 of *Lexikon der Ägyptologie.* Edited by W. Helck, E. Otto, and W. Westendorf. Wiesbaden: Harrassowitz.

Feucht, E. *Das Kind im alten Ägypten.* Frankfurt and New York: Campus, 1995.

Ferguson, A. *An Essay on the History of Civil Society.* 4th ed. London, 1773.

Finnegan, R. H. *Oral Poetry: Its Nature, Significance, and Social Context.* Cambridge: Cambridge University Press, 1977. Repr., Bloomington: Indiana University Press, 1992.

———. "What is Orality—If Anything?" *Byzantine and Modern Greek Studies* 14 (1990): 130–49.

Fischer, H. G. *Dendera in the Third Millennium B.C. Down to the Theban Domination of Upper Egypt.* Locust Valley, N.Y.: J. J. Augustin, 1968.

———. "*s ḫȝ.sn* (Florence, 1774)." *RdÉ* 24 (1972): 64–71.

Fischer-Elfert, H.-W. *Die satirische Streitschrift des Papyrus Anastasi I.* Wiesbaden: Harrassowitz, 1986.

Fishbane, M. *Biblical Interpretation in Ancient Israel.* Oxford: Clarendon, 1985.

Fleming, D. E. "The Etymological Origins of the Hebrew *nābî'*: The One Who Invokes God." *CBQ* 55 (1993): 217–24.

———. "*nābû* and *munabbiātu:* Two New Syrian Religious Personnel." *JAOS* 113 (1993): 175–83.

Floyd, M. H. "Falling Flat on Our Ars Poetica, or, Some Problems in Recent Studies of Biblical Poetry." Pp. 118–31 in *The Psalms and Other Studies on the Old Testament Presented to Joseph I. Hunt.* Edited by J. C. Knight and L. A. Sinclair. Cincinnati, Ohio: Forward Movement Publications for Nashotah House Seminary, 1990.

———. "The Nature of the Narrative and the Evidence of Redaction in Haggai." *VT* 45 (1995): 470–90.

———. "Prophecy and Writing in Habakkuk 2,1–5." *ZAW* 105 (1993): 462–81.

———. "Zechariah and Changing Views of Second Temple Judaism in Recent Commentaries." *RelSRev* 25 (1999): 257–63.

Foley, J. M. *Immanent Art: From Structure to Meaning in Oral Traditional Epic.* Bloomington: Indiana University Press, 1991.

———. "The Implications of Oral Tradition." Pp. 31–57 in *Oral Tradition in the Middle Ages.* Edited by W. F. H. Nicolaisen. Medieval and Renaissance Texts and Studies 112. Binghamton, N.Y.: Center for Medieval and Early Renaissance Studies, State University of New York at Binghamton, 1995.

———. *The Singer of Tales in Performance.* Bloomington: Indiana University Press, 1995.

———. *The Theory of Oral Composition: History and Methodology.* Bloomington: Indiana University Press, 1988.

———. "Traditional Signs and Homeric Art." Pp. 56–82 in *Written Voices, Spoken Signs: Tradition, Performance, and the Epic Text.* Edited by E.

Bakker and A. Kahane. Cambridge, Mass.: Harvard University Press, 1997.

Foster, J. "Literature." In *Oxford Encyclopedia of Ancient Egypt*. Edited by D. B. Redford. New York: Oxford University Press, forthcoming.

———. *Thought Couplets and Clause Sequences in a Literary Text: The Maxims of Ptah-hotep*. Toronto: Society for the Study of Egyptian Antiquities, 1977.

Foucault, M. "The Discourse on Language." Pp. 142–58 in *Critical Theory since 1965*. Edited by H. Adams and L. Searle. Tallahassee: University Presses of Florida, 1990.

Fowler, R. M. "Who is the 'Reader' in Reader Response Criticism?" *Semeia* 31 (1985): 5–23.

Fox, M. V. *The Redaction of the Books of Esther: On Reading Composite Texts*. SBLMS. Atlanta: Scholars Press, 1991.

———. *The Song of Songs and Ancient Egyptian Love Songs*. Madison: University of Wisconsin Press, 1985.

———. "Thought Couplets in Khety's *Hymn to the Inundation*." *JNES* 34 (1975): 1–29.

———. "Wordplay in the *Eloquent Peasant*. The Eighth Complaint." *Bulletin of the Egyptological Seminar* 10 (1989–90): 61–76.

Frame, G. *Rulers of Babylonia from the Second Dynasty of Isin to the End of Assyrian Domination (1157–612 BC)*. Royal Inscriptions of Mesopotamia, Babylonian Periods 2. Toronto: University of Toronto Press, 1995.

Freimarck, V. "The Bible and Neo-Classical Views of Style." *Journal of English and German Philology* 51 (1952): 507–26.

Freydank, H. "Zwei Verpflegungstexte aus Kār-Tukultī-Ninurta." *Altorientalische Forschungen* 1 (1974): 55–89.

Friedman, A. *The Ballad Revival: Studies in the Influence of Popular on Sophisticated Poetry*. Chicago: University of Chicago Press, 1961.

Frye, N. *The Anatomy of Criticism: Four Essays*. Princeton: Princeton University Press, 1971.

———. *The Great Code: The Bible and Literature*. New York: Harcourt Brace Jovanovich, 1982.

Gaballa, G. A. "Three Acephalous Stelae." *JEA* 63 (1977): 122–26.

Gardiner, A. H. *The Admonitions of an Egyptian Sage*. Leipzig: Hinrichs, 1909.

———. *Ancient Egyptian Onomastica*. 3 vols. London: Oxford University Press, 1947.

———. "Inscriptions from the Tomb of Sarenput, Prince of Elephantine." *ZÄS* 45 (1908): 123–41.

———. "The Instruction Addressed to Kagemni and His Brethren." *JEA* 32 (1946): 71–74.

———. *Late Egyptian Miscellanies.* Bibliotheca aegyptiaca 7. Brussels: Édition de la Fondation égyptologique Reine Élisabeth, 1932.

———. *Late Egyptian Stories.* Bibliotheca aegyptiaca 1. Brussels: Éditions de la Fondation égyptologiqe Reine Élisabeth, 1932.

———. *The Library of A. Chester Beatty: The Chester Beatty Papyri, No. 1.* Oxford: Privately printed by J. Johnson at the Oxford University Press and published by E. Walker, 1931.

———. "The Mansion of Life and the Master of the King's Largess." *JEA* 24 (1938): 83–91.

———. "A Pharaonic Encomium." *JEA* 41 (1955): 30; *JEA* 42 (1956): 8–20.

———. "The Tomb of a Much-Travelled Theban Official." *JEA* 4 (1918): 28–38.

———. "The Tomb of Amenemhet, High-priest of Amon." *ZÄS* 47 (1910): 87–99.

Gardiner, A. H., and J. Černý. *Hieratic Ostraca.* Oxford: Griffith Institute, 1957.

Garnot, J. S. F. *L'Appel aux vivants dans les textes funéraires égyptiens des origines à la fin de l'ancien empire.* Cairo: Institut français d'archéologie orientale, 1938.

Genette, G. *Narrative Discourse: An Essay in Method.* Translated by J. E. Lewin. Ithaca, N.Y.: Cornell University Press, 1980.

Gerardi, P. "The Arab Campaigns of Aššurbanipal: Scribal Reconstruction of the Past." *SAAB* 6 (1992): 67–103.

Gianto, A. "Script and Word Order in EA 162: A Case Study of Egyptian Akkadian." *Or* 66 (1997): 426–33.

Gilliard, R. D. "More Silent Reading in Antiquity: *Non Omne Verbum Sonabat.*" *JBL* 112 (1993): 689–94.

Glanville, S. R. K. *The Instructions of Onchsheshonqy.* Vol. 2 of *Catalogue of Demotic Papyri in the British Museum.* London, 1955.

Glotz, G. *Ancient Greece at Work: An Economic History of Greece from the Homeric Period to the Roman Conquest.* Translated by M. R. Dobie. London: Routledge & K. Paul, 1965 (1st ed., 1926).

Gnirs, A. "Die ägyptische Autobiographie." Pp. 191–241 in *Ancient Egyptian Literature: History and Forms.* Edited by A. Loprieno. Probleme der Ägyptologie 10. Leiden: Brill, 1996.

———. "(Auto)biographies." In *Oxford Encyclopedia of Ancient Egypt.* Edited by D. B. Redford. New York: Oxford University Press, forthcoming.

Goedicke, H. "Diplomatical Studies in the Old Kingdom." *JARCE* 3 (1964): 31–42.

―――. *Königliche Dokumente aus dem Alten Reich.* Ägyptologische Abhandlungen 14. Wiesbaden: Harrassowitz, 1967.

―――. *The Quarrel of Apophis and Seqnenre.* San Antonio, Tex.: Van Siclen, 1986.

―――. "Quotations in Old Kingdom Inscriptions." Pp. 93–106 in *Ägyptologische Studien: Hermann Grapow zum 70. Geburtstag.* Edited by O. Firchow. Berlin: Akademie-Verlag, 1955.

―――. *The Report about the Dispute of a Man with His Ba: Papyrus Berlin 3024.* Baltimore: Johns Hopkins Press, 1970.

Goedicke, H., and E. F. Wente. *Ostraka Michaelides.* Wiesbaden: Harrassowitz, 1962.

Goelet, O. "The Term *stp-s3* in the Old Kingdom and Its Later Development." *JARCE* 23 (1986): 85–98.

Goetze, A. *Old Babylonian Omen Texts.* YOS 10. New Haven: Yale University Press, 1947.

Goldwasser, O. *From Icon to Metaphor: Studies in the Semiotics of the Hieroglyph.* OBO 142. Fribourg: University Press; Göttingen: Vandenhoeck & Ruprecht, 1995.

Golka, F. W. *The Leopard's Spots.* Edinburgh: T&T Clark, 1993.

Gomaa, F. *Die Besiedlung Ägyptens während des Mittleren Reiches.* 2 vols. Beihefte zum Tübinger Atlas des Vorderen Orients, Reihe B, Geisteswissenschaften, 66. Wiesbaden: L. Reichert, 1986–87.

Goody, J. *The Interface between the Written and the Oral.* Cambridge and New York: Cambridge University Press, 1987.

―――. *The Logic of Writing and the Organization of Society.* Cambridge and New York: Cambridge University Press, 1986.

Goody, J., and I. Watt. "The Consequences of Literacy." Pp. 27–68 in *Literacy in Traditional Societies.* Edited by J. Goody. Cambridge and New York: Cambridge University Press, 1968.

Gordon, R. P. "'Converse Translation' in the Targums and Beyond." *JSP* 19 (1999): 3–21.

Grabbe, L. L. *Priests, Prophets, Diviners, Sages: A Socio-Political Study of Religious Specialists in Ancient Israel.* Valley Forge, Pa.: Trinity Press International, 1995.

Grandet, P. *Le Papyrus Harris I, BM 9999.* Cairo: Institut français d'archéologie orientale, 1994.

Grapow, H. *Grundriß der Medezin der alten Ägypter.* Berlin: Akademie-Verlag, 1959.

―――. *Sprachliche und schriftliche Formung ägyptischer Texte.* Leipziger ägyptologische Studien 7. Glückstadt: J. J.Augustin, 1936.

Gray, J. *Joshua, Judges, and Ruth.* NCB; London: Nelson, 1967.

Grayson, A. K. "The Chronology of the Reign of Assurbanipal." *ZA* 70 (1980): 227–45.

Grayson, A. K., and W. G. Lambert. "Akkadian Prophecies." *JCS* 18 (1964): 7–30.

Griffith, F. Ll. *Catalogue of the Demotic Papyri in the John Rylands Library, Manchester.* 3 vols. Manchester, 1909.

──────. *Hieratic Papyri from Kahun and Gurob.* London: Bernard Quaritch, 1898.

──────. *The Inscriptions of Siût and Dêr Rîfeh.* London: Trübner, 1889.

──────. *Stories of the High Priests of Memphis.* 2 vols. Oxford: Clarendon, 1900.

Grimal, N.-C. *La Stèle triomphale de Pi(ankh)y au musée de Caire.* Cairo: Institut français d'archéologie orientale, 1981.

Grimm, A. *Die altägyptischen Festkalender in den Tempeln der griechisch-römischen Epoche.* Wiesbaden: Harrassowitz, 1994.

Guglielmi, W. "Der Gebrauch rhetorischer Stilmittel in der ägyptischen Literatur." Pp. 465–98 in *Ancient Egyptian Literature: History and Forms.* Edited by A. Loprieno. Probleme der Ägyptologie 10. Leiden: Brill, 1996.

Guichard, M. *NABU* 1994, 105.

Guksch, H. *Königsdienst: Zur Selbstdarstellung der Beamten in der 18. Dynastie.* Heidelberg: Heidelberger Orientverlag, 1994.

Gunkel, H. *Die israelitische Literatur.* Darmstadt: Wissenschaftliche Buchgesellschaft, 1963.

──────. "Propheten II.B." Pp. 1538–54 in vol. 4 of *Die Religion in Geschichte und Gegenwart.* Edited by H. Gunkel et al. 2d ed. 5 vols. Tübingen: Mohr, 1909–13.

──────. "Die Propheten als Shriftsteller und Dichter." Pp. xxxvi–lxxii in *Die großen Propheten.* Edited by H. Schmidt. Göttingen: Vandenhoeck & Ruprecht, 1915.

Gunn, B. "A Sixth Dynasty Letter from Saqqara." *ASAÉ* 25 (1925): 242–45.

Gunn, D. M. "David and the Gift of the Kingdom (2 Sam 2–4, 9–20, 1 Kgs 1–2)." *Semeia* 3 (1975): 14–45.

──────. "Narrative Patterns and Oral Tradition in Judges and Samuel." *VT* 24 (1974): 286–317.

──────. "On Oral Tradition: A Response to John Van Seters." *Semeia* 5 (1976): 155–61.

──────. "Traditional Composition in the 'Succession Narrative.'" *VT* 26 (1976): 214–29.

Habachi, L. "The Naos with the Decades (Louvre D 37) and the Discovery of Another Fragment." *JNES* 11 (1952): 251–63.

290 *Writings and Speech in Israelite and Ancient Near Eastern Prophecy*

_____. *The Sanctuary of Heqaib.* Mainz am Rhein: P. von Zabern, 1985.

Hallo, W. W. "Akkadian Apocalypses." *IEJ* 16 (1996): 231–42.

Harari, J. "Nature de la stèle de donation de fonction du roi Ahmôse à la reine Ahmôse Nofretari." *ASAÉ* 56 (1959): 139–202.

Harris, W. V. *Ancient Literacy.* Cambridge, Mass., and London: Harvard University Press, 1989.

Hartman, G. *Saving the Text: Literature, Derrida, Philosophy.* Baltimore: Johns Hopkins Press, 1984.

Hassan, S. *The Mastabas of Ny-ankh-pepy and Others.* Cairo: Institut français d'archéologie orientale, 1974.

Havelock, E. A. "The Linguistic Task of the Presocratics." Pp. 7–82 in *Language and Thought in Early Greek Philosophy.* Edited by K. Robb. Monist Library of Philosophy. La Salle, Ill.: Hegeler Institute, 1983.

_____. *The Literate Revolution in Greece and Its Consequences.* Princeton: Princeton University Press, 1982.

_____. *The Muse Learns to Write: Reflections on Orality and Literacy from Antiquity to the Present.* New Haven: Yale University Press, 1986.

Hayes, J. H., and S. I. Irvine. *Amos, the Eighth Century Prophet: His Times and Preaching.* Nashville: Abingdon, 1987.

Hayes, W. C. "A Much-Copied Letter of the Early Middle Kingdom." *JNES* 7 (1948): 1–10.

_____. *A Papyrus of the Late Middle Kingdom in the Brooklyn Museum (Papyrus Brooklyn 35.1446).* Brooklyn: Brooklyn Museum, 1955.

Heintz, J.-G. "La 'fin' des prophètes bibliques? Nouvelles théories et documents semitiques anciens." Pp. 195–214 in *Oracles et prophéties dans l'antiquité: Actes du Colloque de Strasbourg, 15–17 Juin 1995.* Edited by J.-G. Heinz. Université des sciences humaines de Strasbourg, Travaux du Centre de recherche sur le Proche-Orient et la Grèce antiques 15. Paris: De Boccard, 1997.

Helck, W. *Die 'Admonitions' Pap. Leiden I 344 recto.* Wiesbaden: Harrassowitz, 1995.

_____. *Altägyptische Aktenkunde des 3. und 2. Jahrtausends v. Chr.* Munich: Deutscher Kuntsverlag, 1974.

_____. "Die Erzählung vom Verwunschenen Prizen." *Form und Mass: Beiträge zur Literatur, Sprache und Kunst Ägypten: Festschrift Gerhard Fecht zum 65. Geburtstag,* Ägypten und Altes Testament 12. Edited by J. Osing and G. Dreyers, 218–25. Wiesbaden: Harrassowitz, 1987.

_____. "Gedanken zum Ursprung der ägyptischen Schrift." Pp. 395–408 in *Mélanges Gamal Eddin Mokhtar I.* Edited by P. Posener-Krieger. Bibliotheque d'étude 97. Cairo: Institut français d'archéologie orientale, 1985.

————. *Historische-biographische Texte der 2. Zwischenzeit und neue Texte der 18. Dynastie.* Wiesbaden: Harrassowitz, 1983.

————. "*Jnk we jm:tn.*" *ZÄS* 104 (1977): 89–93.

————. "Kultstatue." Pp. 859–65 in vol. 3 of *Lexikon der Ägyptologie.* Edited by W. Helck, E. Otto, and W. Westendorf. Wiesbaden: Harrassowitz.

————. *Die Lehre des Djedefhor und die Lehre eines Vaters an seinen Sohn.* Wiesbaden: Harrassowitz, 1984.

————. *Die Lehre des Dwɜ-Htjj.* 2 vols. Wiesbaden: Harrassowitz, 1970.

————. *Die Lehre für König Merikare.* Wiesbaden: Harrassowitz, 1977.

————. *Die Prophezeiung des Nfr.tj.* Wiesbaden: Harrassowitz, 1970.

————. *Der Text der Lehre Amenemhets I. für seinen Sohn.* 2d ed. Wiesbaden: Harrassowitz, 1986.

————. *Untersuchungen zu den Beamtentiteln des ägyptischen Alten Reiches.* Glückstadt: J. J. Augustin, 1954.

————. *Untersuchungen zur Thinitenzeit.* Ägyptologische Abhandlungen 45. Wiesbaden: Harrassowitz, 1987.

————. "Zur Herkunft der Erzählung des sog. 'Astartepapyrus.'" Pp. 215–23 in *Fontes atque pontes: Eine Festgabe für Hellmut Brunner.* Edited by M. Görg. Wiesbaden: Harrassowitz, 1983.

Henaut, B. W. *Oral Tradition and the Gospels: The Problem of Mark 4.* JSNTSup 82. Sheffield: Sheffield Academic Press, 1993.

Herder, J. G. *The Spirit of Hebrew Poetry.* 2 vols. Translated by J. Marsh. Burlington, Vt.: Edward Smith, 1833.

Herrmann, S. *A History of Israel in Old Testament Times.* Translated by J. Bowden. Philadelphia: Fortress, 1975.

Hershbell, J. P. "The Oral-Poetic Religion of Xenophanes." Pp. 125–33 in *Language and Thought in Early Greek Philosophy.* Edited by K. Robb. Monist Library of Philosophy. La Salle, Ill.: Hegeler Institute, 1983.

Hoch, J. E. *Semitic Words in Egyptian Texts of the New Kingdom and Third Intermediate Period.* Princeton: Princeton University Press, 1994.

Hodge, R. *Literature as Discourse.* Baltimore: Johns Hopkins Press, 1990.

Hodjache, S. I., and O. D. Berlev. "La père fondateur de la dynastie des princes de *Tjḥḥj* en Nubie." Pp. 183–88 in *Ägypten und Kusch: Fritz Hintze zum 60. Geburtstag.* Edited by E. Endesfelder et al.. Berlin: Akademie-Verlag, 1977.

Hoftijzer, J., and G. Van der Kooij. *Aramaic Texts from Deir ʿAllā.* Documenta et Monumenta Orientis Antiqui 19. Leiden: Brill, 1976.

Holbek, B. "What the Illiterate Think of Writing." Pp. 183–96 in *Literacy and Society.* Edited by K. Shousboe and M. T. Larsen. Copenhagen: Akademisk Forlag, 1989.

Holladay, W. *Jeremiah 2. A Commentary on the Book of the Prophet Jeremiah Chapters 26–52.* Hermeneia. Minneapolis: Fortress, 1989.

Hollis, S. T. *The Ancient Egyptian "Tale of Two Brothers": The Oldest Fairytale in the World.* Norman: University of Oklahoma Press, 1990.

―――. "Tales of Magic and Wonder from Ancient Egypt." Pp. 2255–64 in *Civilizations of the Ancient Near East.* Edited by J. M. Sasson. 4 vols. New York: Scribner, 1995.

Home, H., Lord Kames. *Sketches of the History of Man.* 2d ed. 4 vols. Edinburgh, 1778.

Honko, L. "Epic and Identity: National, Regional, Communal, Individual." *Oral Tradition* 11 (1996): 18–36.

Hornung, E. *Der ägyptische Mythos von der Himmelskuh: Eine Ätiologie des Unvollkommenen.* OBO 46. Freiburg: Universitätsverlag; Göttingen: Vandenhoeck & Ruprecht, 1982.

Hornung, E., and O. Keel, eds. *Studien zu altägyptischen Lebenslehren.* OBO 28. Freiburg: Universitätsverlag; Göttingen: Vandenhoeck & Ruprecht, 1979.

Huffmon, H. B. "Ancient Near Eastern Prophecy." Pp. 477–82 in vol. 5 of *The Anchor Bible Dictionary.* Edited by D. N. Freedman et al. Garden City, N.Y.: Doubleday, 1992.

―――. "The Expansion of Prophecy in the Mari Archives: New Texts, New Readings, New Information." Pp. 7–22 in *Prophecy and Prophets: The Diversity of Contemporary Issues in Scholarship.* Edited by J. Gitay. SBLSS. Atlanta: Scholars Press, 1997.

Husbands, J. *A Miscellany of Poems by Several Hands.* Oxford, 1731.

Husson, G., and D. Valbelle. *L'État et les institutions en Égypte des premiers pharaons aux empereurs romains.* Paris: A. Colin, 1992.

Israelit-Groll, S., ed. *Studies in Egyptology Presented to Miriam Lichtheim.* 2 vols. Jerusalem: Magnes, 1990.

Iversen, E. "The Chester Beatty Papyrus No. 1, recto XVI, 9 – XVII, 13." *JEA* 65 (1979): 78–88.

Jacobsohn, H. *Die dogmatische Stellung des Königs in der Theologie der alten Ägypter.* Ägyptologische Forschungen 8. Glückstadt: J. J. Augustin, 1939.

James, T. G. H. *The Mastaba of Khentika Called Ikhenkhi.* London: Egyptian Exploration Society, 1953.

Jamieson-Drake, D. W. *Scribes and Schools in Monarchic Judah: A Socio-archaeological Approach.* JSOTSup 109. Sheffield: Sheffield Academic Press, 1991.

Jansen-Winkeln, K. *Ägyptische Biographien der 22. und 23. Dynastie.* Ägypten und Altes Testament 8. 2 vols. Wiesbaden: Harrassowitz, 1985.

————. "Zwei Jenseitsklagen." *BSÉG* 17 (1993): 41–47.

Janssen, J. *De traditioneele Egyptische Autobiographie voor het Nieuwe Rijk.* Leiden: Brill, 1946.

Jay, P., ed. *The Greek Anthology and Other Ancient Epigrams: A Selection in Modern Verse Translations.* Harmondsworth: Penguin, 1981.

Johnson, A. R. *The Cult Prophet in Israel.* Cardiff: University of Wales, 1962.

Jones, B. A. *The Formation of the Book of the Twelve: A Study in Text and Canon.* SBLDS 149. Atlanta: Scholars Press, 1995.

Junker, H., ed. *Giza.* Vol. 8. Vienna and Leipzig: Holder–Pichler–Tempsky, 1947.

Kadish, G. E. "British Museum Writing Board 5645: The Complaints of Kah-Kheper-Re-Senebu." *JEA* 59 (1973): 77–90.

Kahn, C. H. "Philosophy and the Written Word: Some Thoughts on Herakleitos and the Early Greek Use of Prose." Pp. 110–24 in *Language and Thought in Early Greek Philosophy.* Edited by K. Robb. Monist Library of Philosophy. La Salle, Ill.: Hegeler Institute, 1983.

Kaiser, O. *Isaiah 1–12.* Translated by J. Bowden. OTL. London: SCM, 1983.

Kaiser, W. "Zur Entstehung des gesamtägyptischen Staates." *MDAI* 46 (1990): 287–300.

Kákosy, L. "Prophecies of Ram Gods." *Studia Aegyptiaca* 7 (Budapest, 1981): 139–54.

Kákosy, L., and Z. I. Fabian. "Harper's Song in the Tomb of Djehutimes (TT 32)." *SAK* 22 (1993): 211–26.

Kamal, A. "Fouilles à Deir Dronka et à Assiout." *ASAÉ* 16 (1916): 65–114.

Kanawati, N. "New Evidence on the Reign of Userkaf?" *GöM* 83 (1984): 31–38.

Kaplony, P. "Die Definition der schönen Literatur im alten Ägypten." Pp. 289–314 in *Fragen an die altägyptische Literatur: Studien zum Gedenken an Eberhard Otto.* Edited by J. Assmann et al. Wiesbaden: Reichert, 1997.

Keane, W. "Religious Language." *Annual Review of Anthropology* 26 (1997): 47–71.

Keil, C. F., and F. Delitzsch. *Biblical Commentary on the Old Testament: Joshua, Judges, Ruth.* Translated by J. Martin. Grand Rapids, Mich.: Eerdmans, 1950.

Kelber, W. H. *The Oral and the Written Gospel: The Hermeneutics of Speaking and Writing in the Synoptic Tradition, Mark, Paul, and Q.* Philadelphia: Fortress, 1983. Repr., with a new introduction, Bloomington: Indiana University Press, 1997.

Kennedy, G. *The Art of Persuasion in Greece.* Princeton: Princeton University Press, 1963.

294 *Writings and Speech in Israelite and Ancient Near Eastern Prophecy*

Kermode, F. *The Sense of an Ending*. Oxford: Oxford University Press, 1967.

Kestner Museum. *Die ägyptischen Reliefs im Kestner-Museum Hannover: 100 Jahre Kestner-Museum Hannover, 1889–1989*. Hannover, 1989.

Klasens, A. *A Magical Statue Base (Socle Behague) in the Museum of Antiquities at Leiden*. Leiden: Brill, 1952.

Klasens, P. "An Amuletic Papyrus of the Twenty-fifth Dynasty." *Oudheidkundige Mededelingen uit het Rijksmuseum van Oudheden te Leiden* 56 (1975): 20–28.

Kloth, N. "Beobachtungen zu den biographischen Inschriften des Alten Reiches." *SAK* 25 (1998): 189–205.

Knauf, E. A. *Midian: Untersuchungen zur Geschichte Palästinas und Nordarabiens am Ende des 2. Jahrtausends v. Chr.* Abhandlungen des Deutschen Palästina-Vereins 101. Wiesbaden: Harrassowitz, 1988.

Knox, B. M. W. "Silent Reading in Antiquity." *Greek, Roman, and Byzantine Studies* 9 (1968): 421–35.

Koch, G. M. *Zum Verhältnis von Dichtung und Geschichtsschreibung: Theorie und Analyse*. Frankfurt am Main: P. Land, 1983.

Koch, R. *Die Erzählung des Sinuhe*. Brussels: Éditions de la Fondation égyptologique Reine Élisabeth, 1990.

Koemoth, P.-P. "La plante, *m3tt*, le feu et la puissance virile." *BSÉG* 17 (1993): 57–62.

Koenen, L. "Prophezeiungen des 'Topfers.'" *ZPE* 2 (1968): 178–209.

Koenig, Y. "Les Effrois de Kenikerkhepeshef." *RdÉ* 33 (1981): 29–37.

Kruchten, J.-M. *Le Décret d'Horemheb*. Brussels: Éditions de l'Université de Bruxelles, 1981.

Kugel, J. *The Idea of Biblical Poetry*. New Haven: Yale University Press, 1981.

Kuhn, T. S. *The Copernican Revolution: Planetary Astronomy in the Development of Western Thought*. Cambridge, Mass.: Harvard University Press, 1957.

Kurth, D. "Bébon und Thoth." *Studien zur altägyptischen Literatur* 19 (1992): 225–30.

Laato, A. "The Royal Covenant Ideology in Judah." Pp. 95–99 in *"Laßet uns Brücken bauen . . .": Collected Communications to the XVth Congress of the International Organization for the Study of the Old Testament, Cambridge, 1995*. Edited by K.-D. Schunck and M. Augustin. BEATAJ 42. Frankfurt am Main: P. Lang, 1998.

Labat, R. *Traité akkadien de diagnostics et prognostics médicaux*. Leiden: Brill, 1951.

Labrique, F. "Rapiecage ou reécriture? La porte d'Évergète, le temple d'Esna." Pp. 897–901 in *Egyptian Religion: The Last Thousand Years: Studies*

Dedicated to the Memory of Jan Quaegebeur. Edited by W. Clarysse, A. Schoors, and H. Willems. Leuven: Peeters, 1998.

Lacau, P., and J.-P. Lauer. *Fouilles à Saqqarah: La Pyramide à degrès. V: Inscriptions à l'encre sur les vases.* Cairo: Institut français d'archéologie orientale, 1965.

Lafont, B. "Le Roi de Mari et les prophètes du dieu Adad." *RA* 78 (1984): 7–18.

Lamberton, R. "Homer in Antiquity." Pp. 33–54 in *A New Companion to Homer.* Edited by I. Morris and B. Powell. Leiden: Brill, 1997.

Landsberger, B. *Brief des Bischofs von Esagila an König Asarhaddon.* Mededelingen der Koninklijke Nederlandse Akademie van Wetenschappen, afd. Letterkunde. Nieuwe Reeks 28/6. Amsterdam: Noord-Hollandsche Uitgevers Maatschappij, 1965.

Lange, H. O., and H. Schäfer. *Grab- und Denksteine des mittleren Reiches im Museum von Kairo.* Berlin: Reichsdruckerei, 1902–25. [= *CGC*, vols. 5, 7, 36, and 78.]

Lanzone, R. V. *Dizionario di mitologia egiziana.* Turin: Litografia fratelli Doyen, 1881–86.

Lass, R. *Historical Linguistics and Language Change.* Cambridge and New York: Cambridge Univresity Press, 1997.

Leclant, J. *Enquètes sur les sacerdoces et les sanctuaires égyptiens à l'époque dite 'éthiopienne' (25e dynastie).* Bibliothèque d'étude 17. Cairo: Institut français d'archéologie orientale, 1954.

———. *Montouemhât, quatrième prophète d'Amon et prince de la ville.* Bibliothèque d'étude 35. Cairo: Institut français d'archéologie orientale, 1961.

Lefebvre, G. *Inscriptions conçernants les grand-prêtres d'Amon, Rôm–Roy et Amenhotep.* Paris: P. Geuthner, 1929.

———. "Textes du tombeaux de Petosiris." *ASAÉ* 22 (1922): 33–48, 139–56.

Legrain, G. "Notes d'inspection XVI: Le protocole royal d'Osorkon II." *ASAÉ* 5 (1905): 281–82.

Lemaire, A. "Oracles, politique et littérature dans les royaumes araméens et transjordaniens (IXe–VIIe s. av. n.è.)," Pp. 188–93 in *Oracles et prophéties dans l'antiquité: Actes du Colloque de Strasbourg, 15–17 Juin 1995.* Edited by J.-G. Heinz. Université des sciences humaines de Strasbourg, Travaux du Centre de recherche sur le Proche-Orient et la Grèce antiques 15. Paris: De Boccard, 1997.

———. "La Disposition originelle des inscriptions sur plâtre de Deir ʿAlla." *SEL* 3 (1986): 79–93.

Lesko, L. H., ed. *Pharaoh's Workers: The Villagers of Deir el-Medina.* Ithaca, N.Y.: Cornell University Press, 1994.

————. "Some Comments on Ancient Egyptian Literacy and Literati." Pp. 656–67 in vol. 2 of *Studies in Egyptology Presented to Miriam Lichtheim.* Edited by S. Israelit-Groll. Jerusalem: Magnes, 1990.

Lewis, D. M. "The Persepolis Tablets: Speech, Seal and Script." Pp. 17–32 in *Literacy and Power in the Ancient World.* Edited by A. K. Bowman and G. Woolf. Cambridge: Cambridge University Press, 1994.

Lewis, T. J. "The Identity and Function of El/Baal Berith." *JBL* 115 (1996): 401–23.

Lichtheim, M. *Ancient Egyptian Autobiographies, Chiefly of the Middle Kingdom: A Study and an Anthology.* OBO 84. Freiburg: Universitätsverlag; Göttingen: Vandenhoeck & Ruprecht, 1988.

————. *Ancient Egyptian Literature.* 2 vols. Berkeley: University of California Press, 1975–76.

————. "Didactic Literature." Pp. 243–62 in *Ancient Egyptian Literature: History and Forms.* Edited by A. Loprieno. Probleme der Ägyptologie 10. Leiden: Brill, 1996.

————. *Moral Values in Ancient Egypt.* OBO 155. Fribourg: University Press; Göttingen: Vandenhoeck & Ruprecht, 1997.

Limme, L. *Stèles égyptiennes.* Brussels: Musées royaux d'art et d'histoire, 1979.

Lipiński, E. "Royal and State Scribes in Ancient Jerusalem." Pp. 157–64 in *Congress Volume: Jerusalem 1986.* Edited by J. A. Emerton. VTSup 40. Leiden: Brill, 1988.

Lloyd, A. B. *Herodotus Book II: A Commentary.* 3 vols. Leiden: Brill, 1974–1988.

Lodge, D., ed. *Modern Criticism and Theory.* London and New York: Longman, 1988.

Lods, A., and G. Dossin. "Une Tablette inédite de Mari, intéressante pour l'histoire ancienne du prophétisme sémitique." Pp. 103–10 in *Studies in Old Testament Prophecy Presented to Professor Theodore H. Robinson by the Society for Old Testament Study on His Sixty-fifth Birthday.* Edited by H. H. Rowley. Edinburgh: T&T Clark, 1950.

Loprieno, A. "Linguistic Variety and Egyptian Literature." Pp. 515–30 in *Ancient Egyptian Literature: History and Forms.* Edited by A. Loprieno. Probleme der Ägyptologie 10. Leiden: Brill, 1996.

Lord, A. B. "Oral Composition and 'Oral Residue' in the Middle Ages." Pp. 7–29 in *Oral Tradition in the Middle Ages.* Edited by W. F. H. Nicolaisen. Medieval and Renaissance Texts and Studies 112. Binghamton, N.Y.: Center for Medieval and Early Renaissance Studies, State University of New York at Binghamton, 1995.

————. *The Singer of Tales*. Harvard Studies in Comparative Literature 24. Cambridge, Mass.: Harvard University Press, 1960.

Louden, B. "Eumaios and Alkinoos: The Audience and the *Odyssey*." *Phoenix* 51 (1997): 95–114.

Lowth, R. *Lectures on the Sacred Poetry of the Hebrews*. Translated by G. Gregory. London: Thomas Tegg & Son, 1835.

Luft, U. "Zur Einleitung der Liebesgedichte auf Papyrus Chester Beatty I, ro XVI 9 ff." *ZÄS* 99 (1973): 108–16.

Malamat, A. "A Forerunner of Biblical Prophecy: The Mari Documents." *Ancient Israelite Religion: Essays in Honor of Frank Moore Cross*. Edited by P. D. Miller, P. D. Hanson, and S. D. McBride, 33–52. Philadelphia: Westminster, 1987.

————. *Mari and the Bible*. Studies in the History and Culture of the Ancient Near East 12. Leiden: Brill, 1998.

Malinine, M. *Choix de textes juridiques en hiératique anormal et en démotique*. Paris: H. Champion, 1953.

Man, P. de. *Resistence to Theory*. Minneapolis: University of Minnesota Press, 1986.

Manniche, L. *Music and Musicians in Ancient Egypt*. London: British Museum Press, 1991.

Marciniak, M. *Deir el-Bahari I. Les Inscriptions hiératiques du temple de Thoutmosis III*. Warsaw: PWN-Éditions scientifiques de Pologne, 1974.

Margalit, B. "Ninth-Century Israelite Prophecy in the Light of Contemporary NWSemitic Epigraphs." Pp. 515–32 in *"Und Mose schrieb dieses Lied auf": Studien zum Alten Textament und zum Alten Orient: Festschrift für Oswald Loretz*. Edited by M Dietrich and I. Kottsieper. AOAT 250. Münster: Ugarit-Verlag, 1998.

Martínez-Pizarro, J. "Review of *Oral Tradition in the Middle Ages* ed. by W. F. H. Nicolaisen." *Medieval Review* 96.11.16 (http://hti.umich.edu/ b/bmr/ tmr.html).

Massart, A. "The Egyptian Geneva Papyrus MAH 15274." *MDAI* 15 (1957): 172–85.

Mathieu, B. "Études de métrique égyptienne I: La distique heptamétrique dan les chants d'amour." *RdÉ* 39 (1989): 63–82.

————. "Études de métrique égyptienne II: Contraintes métriques et production textuelle dans l'*Hymne à la crue du Nil*." *RdÉ* 41 (1990): 127–41.

Mayer, W. *Nuzi-Studien I: Die Archive des Palastes und die Prosopographie der Berufe*. AOAT 205/1. Kevelaer: Butzon & Bercker; Neukirchen-Vluyn: Neukirchener Verlag, 1978.

McKane, W. *Jeremiah 2: Commentary on Jeremiah xxvi–lii*. ICC. Edinburgh: T&T Clark, 1996.

————. *Proverbs: A New Approach.* OTL. Philadelphia: Westminster, 1970.

McKitterick, R., ed. *The Uses of Literacy in Early Mediaeval Europe.* Cambridge: Cambridge University Press, 1995.

Medinet Habu I: Earlier Historical Records of Ramesses III. Chicago: University of Chicago Oriental Institute, 1930.

Medinet Habu IV: Festival Scenes of Ramesses III. Chicago: University of Chicago Oriental Institute, 1940.

Meeks, D. *Année lexicographique.* 3 vols. Paris: Imprimerie de la Margeride, 1980–82.

Meier, S. A. *The Messenger in the Ancient Semitic World.* HSM 45. Atlanta: Scholars Press, 1989.

de Meulenaere, H. "La stèle Louvre C 117." *OLP* 4 (1973): 77–84.

Meyers, C. *Discovering Eve: Ancient Israelite Women in Context.* New York: Oxford University Press, 1988.

Meyers, C., and E. Meyers. *Haggai, Zechariah 1–8.* AB 25B. New York: Doubleday, 1987.

Michalowski, P. "Orality and Literacy in Early Mesopotamian Literature." Pp. 227–45 in *Mesopotamian Epic Literature: Oral or Aural?* Edited by M. E. Vogelzang and H. L. J. Vanstiphout. Lewiston, N.Y.: Mellen, 1992.

Millard, A. R. "The Knowledge of Writing in Iron Age Palestine." Pp. 33–39 in *"Laßet uns Brücken bauen . . .": Collected Communications to the XVth Congress of the International Organization for the Study of the Old Testament, Cambridge, 1995.* Edited by K.-D. Schunck and M. Augustin. BEATAJ 42. Frankfurt am Main: P. Lang, 1998.

Möller, G. *Hieratische Lesestücke.* Leipzig: Hinrichs, 1927–35.

Montet, P. "Les Tombeaux de Siout et Deir Rifeh." *Kêmi* 6 (1936): 131–63.

Moore, G. F. *A Critical and Exegetical Commentary on Judges.* ICC. Edinburgh: T&T Clark, 1895.

Moran, W. L. *The Amarna Letters.* Baltimore and London: Johns Hopkins Press, 1992.

Moret, A. *Galerie égyptienne: stèles, bas-reliefs, monuments divers. Le Musée Guimet.* Paris: E. Leroux, 1909.

Moursi, M. "Die Stele des Vezirs Re-hotep (Kairo JdE 48845)." *MDAI* 37 (1981): 321–29.

Mowinckel, S. *Psalmenstudien: III. Kultprophetie und prophetische Psalmen.* Oslo: Dybwad, 1922.

Müller, H.-P. "Mantische Weisheit und Apokalyptik." *Congress Volume: Uppsala 1971,* VTSup 22, 268–93. Leiden: Brill, 1972.

Murphy, R. "Wisdom in the OT." Pp. 920–31 in vol. 6 of *The Anchor Bible Dictionary*. Edited by D. N. Freedman et al. Garden City, N.Y.: Doubleday, 1992.

Murray, M. A. *Saqqara Mastabas*. Vol. 1. London: Egypt Exploration Society, 1904.

Musée Granet Aix-en-Provence. *Collection égyptienne*. Aix-en-Provence, n.d.

Nakata, I. "Two Remarks on the So-called Prophetic Texts from Mari." *Acta Sumerologica* 4 (1982): 143–48.

Nasta, M. "Principes d'analyse d'une versification orale." *Les Études classiques* 62 (1994): 101–29; 63 (1995): 197–224.

National Center for Educational Statistics. *Condition of Education*, 1999. NCES 1999022.

Naville, E. *The Funeral Papyrus of Iouya*. Cairo: Institut français d'archéologie orientale, 1908.

———. *The Shrine of Saft el-Henneh and the Land of Goshen*. London: Trubner & Co., 1888.

———. *The Temple of Deir el-Bahari*. 6 vols. London: Egypt Exploration Fund, 1905–8.

Nelson, H. H. "Certain Reliefs at Karnak and Medinet Habu and the Ritual of Amenophis I." *JNES* 8 (1949): 310–48.

Newberry, P. E. *Beni Hasan*. 2 vols. London: Egypt Exploration Society, K. Paul, 1890–92.

———. *El Bersheh*. 2 vols. London: Egypt Exploration Fund: 1892–94.

Nibbi, A. "Remarks on Two Stelae from the Wadi Basus." *JEA* 62 (1976) pl. 10.

Niditch, S. *Oral World and Written Word: Ancient Israelite Literature*. LAI. Louisville, Ky.: Westminster John Knox, 1996.

Niles, J. "Understanding Beowulf: Oral Poetry Acts." *JAF* 106 (1993): 131–55.

Nissinen, M. "Prophecy against the King in Neo-Assyrian Sources." Pp. 157–70 in *"Laßet uns Brücken bauen . . .": Collected Communications to the XVth Congress of the International Organization for the Study of the Old Testament, Cambridge, 1995*. Edited by K.-D. Schunck and M. Augustin. BEATAJ 42. Frankfurt am Main: P. Lang, 1998.

———. *References to Prophecy in Neo-Assyrian Sources*. SAAS 7. Helsinki: The Neo-Assyrian Text Corpus Project, 1998.

———. "Die Relevanz der neuassyrischen Prophetie für die alttestamentliche Forschung." Pp. 217–58 in *Mesopotamica—Ugaritica—Biblica: Festschrift für Kurt Bergerhof*. Edited by M. Dietrich and O. Loretz. AOAT 232. Kevelaer: Butzon & Bercker; Neukirchen-Vluyn: Neukirchener Verlag, 1993.

Ong, W. J. *Rhetoric, Romance and Technology: Studies in the Interaction of Expression and Culture.* Ithaca, N.Y.: Cornell University Press, 1971.

Oppenheim, A. L. "The Archives of the Palace of Mari." *JNES* 11 (1952): 129–39.

Otto, E. "Die Ursprünge der Bundestheologie im Alten Testament und im Alten Orient." *Zeitschrift für altorientalische und biblische Rechtsgeschichte* 4 (1998): 1–84.

———. *Das Deuteronomium: Politische Theologie und Rechtsreform in Juda und Assyrien.* BZAW 284. Berlin and New York: de Gruyter, 1999.

Overholt, T. W. *Channels of Prophecy: The Social Dynamics of Prophetic Activity.* Minneapolis: Fortress, 1989.

———. *Prophecy in Cross-Cultural Perspective: A Sourcebook for Biblical Researchers.* Minneapolis: Fortress, 1989.

Pardee, D. *Handbook of Ancient Hebrew Letters.* SBLSBS 15. Chico, California: Scholars Press, 1982.

Parker, S. B. "Official Attitudes toward Prophecy at Mari and in Israel." *VT* 43 (1993): 50–68.

Parkinson, R. B. *The Tale of the Eloquent Peasant.* Oxford: Griffith Institute, Ashmolean Museum, 1991.

———. "Teachings, Discourses and Tales from the Middle Kingdom." Pp. 91–122 in *Middle Kingdom Studies.* Edited by S. Quirke et al. New Malden, Surrey: SIA, 1991.

———. "Types of Literature in the Middle Kingdom." Pp. 297–312 in *Ancient Egyptian Literature: History and Forms.* Edited by A. Loprieno. Probleme der Ägyptologie 10. Leiden: Brill, 1996.

———. *Voices from Ancient Egypt.* London: British Museum Press, 1991.

Parkinson, R. B., and S. Quirke. *Papyrus.* Austin: University of Texas Press, 1995.

Parpola, S. *Assyrian Prophecies.* SAA 9. Helsinki: Helsinki University Press, 1997.

———. "The Forlorn Scholar." Pp. 257–78 in *Language, Literature, and History: Philological and Historical Studies Presented to Erica Reiner.* Edited by F. Rochberg-Halton. AOS 67. New Haven, Conn.: American Oriental Society, 1987.

———. "*likalka ittatakku:* Two Notes on the Morphology of the Verb *alāku* in Neo-Assyrian." *StudOr* 55 (1984): 183–209.

———. *Letters from Assyrian Scholars to the Kings Esarhaddon and Assurbanipal. Part II: Commentary and Appendices.* AOAT 5/2. Kevelaer: Butzon & Bercker; Neukirchen-Vluyn: Neukirchener Verlag, 1983.

———. "The Man without a Scribe and the Question of Literacy in the Assyrian Empire." Pp. 315–24 in Ana šadî Labnāni lū allik: *Beiträge zu*

*altorientalischen und mittelmeerischen Kulturen: Festschrift für Wolf-
gang Röllig*. Edited by B. Pongratz-Leisten, H. Kühne, and P. Xella.
Kevelaer: Butzon & Bercker; Neukirchen-Vluyn: Neukirchener Verlag,
1997.

Parry, M. *The Making of Homeric Verse*. Edited by A. Parry. Oxford:
Clarendon, 1971.

Patane, M. "Existe-t-il dans l'Égypte ancienne une littérature licensieuse?"
BSÉG 15 (1991): 91–93.

Paul, S. M. *Amos*. Hermeneia. Minneapolis: Fortress, 1991.

————. "Heavenly Tablets and the Book of Life." *JANESCU* 5 (1973):
345–53.

Pedersen, O. *Archives and Libraries in the Ancient Near East 1500–300 B.C.*
Bethesda, Md.: CDL, 1998.

Peet, T. E. *The Cemeteries of Abydos*. 3 vols. London: Egypt Exploration Fund,
1914.

————. *The Great Tomb Robberies of the Twentieth Egyptian Dynasty*.
Oxford: Clarendon, 1930.

Penzl, H. "Did Henrik van Veldeken (1145–ca. 1200) Write in a 'German
Dialekt'?" Pp. 57–66 in *The Berkeley Conference on Dutch Linguistics,
1989: Issues and Controversies, Old and New*. Edited by T. F. Shannon
and J. P. Snapper. Lanham, Md.: University Press of America, 1991.

Perdu, O. "Ancient Egyptian Autobiographies." Pp. 2243–54 in *Civilizations of
the Ancient Near East*. Edited by J. M. Sasson. 4 vols. New York:
Scribner, 1995.

Perdue, L. G., et al. *Families in Ancient Israel*. Louisville, Ky.: Westminster
John Knox, 1997.

Pernigotti, S. *La Statuaria egiziana nel museo civico archaelogico di Bologna*.
Bologna: Instituto per la storia di Bologna, 1980.

Person, R. F., Jr. "The Ancient Israelite Scribe as Performer." *JBL* 117 (1998):
601–9.

Petersen, D. L. *Haggai and Zechariah 1–8*. OTL. Philadelphia: Westminster,
1984.

————. *The Roles of Israel's Prophets*. JSOTSup 17. Sheffield: JSOT Press,
1981.

————. "The Temple in Persian Period Prophetic Texts." Pp. 125–44 in
Second Temple Studies 1: Persian Period. Edited by P. R. Davies.
JSOTSup 117. Sheffield: Sheffield Academic Press, 1991.

Petrie, W. M. F. *Dendereh*. London: Egypt Exploration Society, 1900.

————. *Deshasheh*. London: Egypt Exploration Fund, 1898.

————. *Heliopolis*. London: London School of Archaeology in Egypt, 1912.

Pinkerton, J. *Scottish Tragic Ballads*. London, 1781.

Pleyte, W. *Chapitres supplémentaires du Livre des Morts, 162 à 174, publiés d'après les monuments de Leide, du Louvre et du Musée Britannique.* 2 vols. Leiden: Brill, 1881.

Pletyte, W., and F. Rossi. *Papyrus de Turin.* Museo egizio di Torino. Wiesbaden: LTR–Verlag, 1981.

Posener, G. *Catalogue des ostraca hiératiques littéraires de Déir el-Medina,* Vol. II. Cairo: Institut français d'archéologie orientale, 1972.

———. "Le Conte de Néferkarê et du général Siséné (Recherches Littéraires 6)." *RdÉ* 11 (1957): 119–37.

———. "L'Exorde de l'instruction educative d'Amennakhte." *RdÉ* 10 (1955): 61–72.

———. "Fragment littéraire de Moscou." *MDAI* 25 (1969): 101–6.

———. *Le Papyrus Vandier.* Cairo: Institut français d'archéologie orientale, 1985.

———. "Les richesses inconnues de la littérature égyptienne." *RdÉ* 10 (1955): 61–72.

———. "Une stèle de Hatnoub." *JEA* 54 (1968): 67–70.

Posener-Krieger, P. *Les Archives du temple funéraire de Neferikare-Kakai.* Bibliothèque d'étude 65. Cairo: Institut français d'archéologie orientale, 1976.

Posener-Krieger, P., and J. L. de Cenival. *The Abu Sir Papyri.* Hieratic Papyri in the British Museum, Fifth Series. London: Trustees of the British Museum, 1968.

Poulsen, R. C. *Misbegotten Muses: History and Anti-history.* New York: P. Lang, 1988.

Propp, V. *Theory and History of Folklore.* Minneapolis: University of Minnesota Press, 1984.

Quibell, J. E. *Excavations at Saqqara.* Cairo: Institut français d'archéologie orientale, 1908.

Quirke, S. G. "Narrative Literature." Pp. 263–76 in *Ancient Egyptian Literature: History and Forms.* Edited by A. Loprieno. Probleme der Ägyptologie 10. Leiden: Brill, 1996.

Rabinowitz, P. J. "Truth in Fiction: A Re-examination of Audiences." *Critical Inquiry* 4 (1977): 121–41.

Radner, K. "The Relation between Format and Content of Neo-Assyrian Texts." Pp. 63–78 in *Nineveh, 612 BC: The Glory and the Fall of the Assyrian Empire.* Edited by R. Mattila. Catalogue of the 10th Anniversary Exhibition of the Neo-Assyrian Text Corpus Project. Helsinki: Helskini University Press, 1995.

Ramond, P. *Les Stèles égyptiennes du Musée G. Labit à Toulouse.* Cairo: Institut français d'archéologie orientale, 1977.

Ranke, H. *Die ägyptischen Personennamen.* 2 vols. Glückstadt: J. J. Augustin, 1935.

Ray, J. "Literacy in Egypt in the Late and Persian Periods." Pp. 51–66 in *Literacy and Power in the Ancient World.* Edited by A. K. Bowman and G. Woolf. Cambridge: Cambridge University Press, 1994.

Ray, J. D. *The Archive of Hor.* London: Egypt Exploration Society, 1976.

———. "The Emergence of Writing in Egypt." *World Archaeology* 17 (1986): 307–16.

Redford, D. B. "Ancient Egyptian Literature: An Overview." Pp. 2225–39 in *Civilizations of the Ancient Near East.* Edited by J. M. Sasson. 4 vols. New York: Scribner, 1995.

———. *Egypt, Canaan, and Israel in Ancient Times.* Princeton: Princeton University Press, 1992.

———. "Historical Sources: Texts." In *Oxford Encyclopedia of Ancient Egypt.* Edited by D. B. Redford. New York: Oxford University Press, forthcoming.

———. "The Meaning and Use of the Term, *gnwt,* Annals." Pp. 327–42 in *Studien zu Sprache und Religion Ägyptens zu Ehren von Wolfhart Westendorf,* vol. 1. Edited by F. Junge. Göttingen: F. Junge, 1984.

———. *Pharaonic King-lists, Annals, and Daybooks: A Contribution to the Study of the Egyptian Sense of History.* Mississauga, Ont.: Benben, 1986.

———. "Some Observations of the Northern and Northeastern Delta in the Late Pre-dynastic Period." *Essays in Egyptology in Honor of Hans Goedicke.* Edited by B. Bryan and D. Lorton, 201–10. San Antonio, Tex.: Van Siclen, 1994.

———. *A Study of the Biblical Joseph Story, Genesis 37–50.* Leiden: Brill, 1970.

Renz, J. *Die althebräischen Inschriften, Teil 1: Text und Kommentar. Handbuch der althebräischen Epigraphik, Band I.* Edited by J. Renz and W. Röllig. Darmstadt: Wissenschaftliche Buchgesellschaft, 1995.

Reymond, E. A. E. *From Ancient Egyptian Hermetic Writings.* Vienna: Österreichische Nationalbibliothek, 1977.

Richardson, S. "Truth in the Tales of the Odyssey." *Mnemosyne* 49 (1996): 393–402.

Ringgren, H. "Akkadian Apocalypses." Pp. 379–86 in *Apocalypticism in the Mediterranean World and the Near East: Proceedings of the International Colloquium on Apocalypticism, Uppsala, Aug. 12–17, 1979.* Edited by D. Hellholm. Tübingen: Mohr, 1983.

Robins, G., and C. Shute. *The Rhind Mathematical Papyrus.* London: Published for the Trustees of the British Museum by British Museum Publications, 1987.

Roccati, A. "Une Légende égyptienne d'Anat." *RdÉ* 24 (1972): 152–59.

Roeder, G. "Zwei hieroglyphische Inschriften aus Hermopolis (Oberägypten)." *ASAÉ* 52 (1954): 315–442.

Roeder, G., ed. *Ägyptische Inschriften aus dem königlichen Museen zu Berlin*, vol. 2. Leipzig: J. C. Hinrichs, 1901–24.

Rogerson, J., and P. Davies. *The Old Testament World.* Englewood Cliffs, N.J.: Prentice–Hall, 1989.

Römheld, D. *Wege der Weisheit: Die Lehren Amenemopes und Proverbien 22,17–24.* Berlin and New York: de Gruyter, 1989.

Rubel, M. M. *Savage and Barbarian: Historical Attitudes in the Criticism of Homer and Ossian in Britain, 1760–1800.* Amsterdam: North-Holland Publishing Co., 1978.

Russo, J. A. "Oral Theory: Its Development in Homeric Studies and Applicability to Other Literatures." Pp. 7–21 in *Mesopotamian Epic Literature: Oral or Aural?* Edited by M. E. Vogelzang and H. L. J. Vanstiphout. Lewiston, N.Y.: Mellen, 1992.

Sadek, A. I. *Popular Religion in Egypt during the New Kingdom.* Hildesheim: Gerstenberg, 1987.

Sander-Hansen, C. E. *Historische Inschriften der 19. Dynastie.* Brussels: Éditions de la Fondation égyptologique Reine Élisabeth, 1933.

Sandman, M. *The God Ptah.* Lund: C. W. K. Gleerup, 1946.

Sasson, J. M. "Literary Criticism, Folklore Scholarship and Ugaritic Literature." Pp. 81–98 in *Ugarit in Retrospect: Fifty Years of Ugarit and Ugaritic.* Edited by G. D. Young. Winona Lake, Ind.: Eisenbrauns, 1981.

———. "The Posting of Letters with Divine Messages." Pp. 299–316 in *Florilegium mari-anum II: Recueil d'études à la mémoire de Maurice Birot.* Edited by D. Charpin and J.-M. Durand. MNABU 3. Paris: Société pour l'étude du Proche-Orient ancien, 1994.

———. "Some Comments on Archive Keeping at Mari." *Iraq* 34 (1972): 55–57.

———. "Water beneath Straw: Adventures of a Prophetic Phrase in the Mari Archives." Pp. 599–608 in *Solving Riddles and Untying Knots: Biblical, Epigraphic and Semitic Studies in Honor of Jonas C. Greenfield.* Edited by Z. Zevit, S. Gittin, and M. Sokoloff. Winona Lake, Ind.: Eisenbrauns, 1995.

Sauneron, S. "Le Dégagement du temple d'Esne: mur nord." *ASAÉ* 52 (1952): 29–39.

———. *Le Rituel d'embaumement: pap. Boulaq III, pap. Louvre 5.158.* Cairo: Le Caire Imprimerie Nationale, 1952.

———. *Le Temple d'Esna.* 5 vols. Cairo: Institut français d'archéologie orientale, 1962–69.

―――. "Les Travaux de l'Institut français d'archéologie orientale en 1969–1970." *BIFAO* 69 (1971): 283–306.

Säve-Söderbergh, T. "The Paintings in the Tomb of Djehuty-hetep at Debira." *Kush* 8 (1960): 24–44.

el-Sayed, R. *Documents relatifs à Saïs et ses divinités.* Cairo: Institut français d'archéologie orientale, 1975.

Schart, A. "Combining Prophetic Oracles in Mari Letters and Jeremiah 36." *JANESCU* 23 (1995): 77–88.

Schenkel, W. "Wozu die Ägypter eine Schrift brauchten?" Pp. 45–63 in *Schrift und Gedächtnis.* Edited by A. Assmann, J. Assmann, and C. Hardemeir. Beiträge zur Archäologie der literarischen Kommunikation 1. Munich: W. Fink, 1983.

Schlott, A. "Einige Beobachtungen zu Mimik un Gestik von Singenden." *GöM* 152 (1996): 55–70.

Schmitt, J. J. "Preexilic Hebrew Prophecy." Pp. 482–89 in vol. 5 of *The Anchor Bible Dictionary.* Edited by D. N. Freedman et al. Garden City, N.Y.: Doubleday, 1992.

Schott, S. *Bücher und Bibliotheken im alten Ägypten: Verzeichnis der Buch- und Spruchtitel und der Termini technici.* Wiesbaden: Harrassowitz, 1990.

Seeligman, I. L. "The Beginning of *Midrash* in the Books of Chronicles." *Tarbiz* 49 (1980): 14–32 (in Hebrew; English summary, pp. ii–iii).

Sethe, K. "Die ägyptische Bezeichungen für die Oasen und ihre Bewohner." *ZÄS* 56 (1920): 44–54.

―――. *Dramatische Texte zu altägyptischen Mysterienspielen.* Leipzig: J. C. Hinrichs, 1928.

―――. *Übersetzung und Kommentar zu den altägyptischen Pyramidentexten.* 5 vols. Glückstadt: J. J. Augustin, 1935–62.

Seyfried, K.-J. *Beiträge zu den Expeditionen des Mittleren Reiches in die Ost-Wüste.* Hildesheim: Pelizaeus-Museum, 1981.

Shea, J. H., and D. B. Cleveland. "History and Foundations of Information Science. *Annual Review of Information Science and Technology* 12 (1977): 249–75.

Shinan, A. תרגום ואגדה בו. Jerusalem: Magnes, 1992.

Shirun-Grumach, I. *Offenbarung, Orakel und Königsnovelle.* Wiesbaden: Harrassowitz, 1993.

Shupak, N. *Where Can Wisdom Be Found? The Sage's Language in the Bible and in Ancient Egyptian Literature.* OBO 130. Fribourg: University Press; Göttingen: Vandenhoeck & Ruprecht, 1993.

Simpson, W. K. *Inscribed Material from the Pennsylvania-Yale Excavations at Abydos.* New Haven: Peabody Museum of Natural History of Yale

University; Philadelphia: University of Pennsylvania Museum of Archaeology and Anthropology, 1995.

———. *Mastabas of the Western Cemetery.* Boston: Department of Egyptian and Ancient Near Eastern Art, Museum of Fine Arts, 1980.

Skehan, P. W., and A. A. DiLella, O.F.M., *The Wisdom of Ben Sira: A New Translation with Notes.* AB 39. New York: Doubleday, 1987.

Slings, S. R. "Orality and the Poet's Profession." *Acta Antiqua* 33 (1990–92): 9–14.

Slusser, M. "Reading Silently in Antiquity." *JBL* 111 (1992): 499.

Smith, H. S. "The Rock Inscriptions at Buhen." *JEA* 58 (1972): 43–82.

Smith, H. S., and W. J. Tait. *Saqqâra Demotic Papyri I.* London: Egypt Exploration Fund, 1983.

D'Souza, D. *Illiberal Education.* New York: Free Press, 1992.

Spalinger, A. J. *Aspects of the Military Documents of the Ancient Egyptians.* New Haven: Yale University Press, 1982.

Speleers, L., ed. *Recueil des inscriptions égyptiennes des musées royaux cinquantainaire à Bruxelles.* Brussels: Musées royaux d'art et d'histoire, 1923.

Spiegelberg, W. *Demotische Texte auf Krügen.* Leipzig: J. C. Hinrichs, 1912.

———. "The Hieratic Text in Mariette KARNAK, pl. 46: A Contribution of the History of the Viziers of the New Empire." *Proceedings of the Society of Biblical Archaeology* 24 (1902): 320–24.

Steindorff, G. *Catalogue of the Egyptian Sculpture in the Walters Art Gallery.* Baltimore: The Trustees of the Walters Art Gallery, 1946.

Steiner, G. "Critic/Reader." *New Literary History* 10 (1979): 423–52.

Stewart, H. M. *Egyptian Stelae, Reliefs and Paintings from the Petrie Collection.* 3 vols. Warminster: Aris & Phillips, 1976–83.

Strudwick, N. *The Administration of Egypt in the Old Kingdom: The Highest Titles and Their Holders.* London: KPI, 1985.

Sugirtharajah, R. S., ed. *The Postcolonial Bible.* The Bible and Postcolonialism 1. Sheffield: Sheffield Academic Press, 1998.

Svenbro, J. *Phrasikleia: An Anthology of Reading in Ancient Greece.* Translated by J. Lloyd. Ithaca, N.Y.: Cornell University Press, 1993.

Sweet, R. F. G. "Writing as a Factor in the Rise of Urbanism." Pp. 35–49 in *Aspects of Urbanism in Antiquity: From Mesopotamia to Crete.* Edited by W. Aufrecht, N. A. Mirau, and S. W. Gauley. JSOTSup 244. Sheffield: Sheffield Academic Press, 1997.

Tannen, D. "Introducing Constructed Dialogue in Greek and American Conversational and Literary Narrative. Pp. 311–32 in *Direct and Indirect Speech.* Edited by F. Coulams. Trends in Linguistics: Studies and Monographs 31. Berlin and New York: de Gruyter, 1986.

Thomas, R. *Literacy and Orality in Ancient Greece*. Cambridge: Cambridge University Press, 1992.

——. "Literacy and the City-State in Archaic and Classical Greece." Pp. 33–50 in *Literacy and Power in the Ancient World*. Edited by A. K. Bowman and G. Woolf. Cambridge: Cambridge University Press, 1994.

——. *Oral Tradition and Written Record in Classical Athens*. Cambridge: Cambridge University Press, 1989.

——. "Orality." P. 1072 in *The Oxford Classical Dictionary*. 3d ed. Edited by S. Hornblower and A. Spawforth. Oxford: Oxford University Press, 1996.

Thompson, P. *The Voice of the Past: Oral History*. Oxford: Oxford University Press, 1978.

Tigay, J., ed. *Empirical Models for Biblical Criticism*. Philadelphia: University of Pennsylvania Press, 1985.

Tov, E. "Special Layout of Poetical Units in the Texts from the Judean Desert." Pp. 115–28 in *Give Ear to My Words: Psalms and Other Poetry in and around the Hebrew Bible: Essays in Honour of Professor N. A. van Uchelen*. Edited by W. Dijk. Amsterdam: Kamp Societas Hebraica, 1996.

——. *Textual Criticism of the Hebrew Bible*. Minneapolis: Augsburg, 1992.

Tresson, P. *Mélanges Maspero IV*. Cairo: Institut français d'archéologie orientale, 1934.

Tylor, J. *Wall Drawings and Monuments of El Kab: The Tomb of Sebeknekht*. London: B. Quaritch, 1896.

VanderKam, J. C. "The Prophetic-Sapiential Origins of Apocalyptic Thought." Pp. 163–76 in *A Word in Season: Essays in Honour of William McKane*. Edited by J. D. Martin and P. R. Davies. JSOTSup 42. Sheffield: Sheffield Academic Press, 1986.

van der Toorn, K. "Old Babylonian Prophecy between the Oral and the Written." *JNSL* 24 (1998): 55–70.

——. "L'Oracle de victoire comme expression prophétique au Proche-Orient ancien." *RB* 94 (1987): 63–97.

van de Walle, J. M. *La Transmission des textes littéraires égyptiens*. Brussels: Fondation égyptologique Reine Élisabeth, 1948.

Vandier, J. "La Légende de Baba (Bebon) dans le Papyrus Jumilhac." *RdÉ* 9 (1952): 121–23.

——. *Mo'alla. La Tombe d'Ankhtifi et la tombe de Sebekhotep*. Bibliothèque d'étude 18. Cairo: Institut français d'archéologie orientale, 1950.

——. *Le Papyrus Jumilhac*. Paris: Centre national de la recherche scientifique, 1953.

————. *Tombes de Deir el-Medineh: La Tombe de Nefer-abou.* Mémoires publiés par les membres de l'Institut français d'archéologie orientale du Caire 69. Cairo: Institut français d'archéologie orientale, 1935.

Van Seters, J. *Abraham in History and Tradition.* New Haven: Yale University Press, 1975.

————. *In Search of History: Historiography in the Ancient World and the Origins of Biblical History.* New Haven: Yale University Press, 1983.

————. *The Life of Moses: The Yahwist as Historian in Exodus—Numbers.* Louisville, Ky.: Westminster John Knox, 1994.

————. "Oral Patterns or Literary Conventions in Biblical Narrative." *Semeia* 5 (1976): 139–54.

————. "Problems in the Literary Analysis of the Court History of David." *JSOT* 1 (1976): 22–29.

————. "Review of *Oral World and Written Word* by Susan Niditch." *JAOS* 118 (1998): 436–37.

Vanseveren, S. "La Formule homérique: problèmes de définition." *Les Études classiques* 66 (1998): 225–36.

Vansina, J. "Once upon a Time: Oral Traditions as History in Africa." Pp. 413–39 in *Historical Studies Today.* Edited by F. Gilbert and S. R. Graubard. New York: W. W. Norton, 1972.

————. *Oral Tradition as History.* Madison: University of Wisconsin Press, 1985.

Vanstiphout, H. J. L. "Memory and Literacy in Ancient Western Asia." Pp. 2189–96 in *Civilizations of the Ancient Near East.* Edited by J. M. Sasson. 4 vols. New York: Scribner, 1995.

————. "Repetition and Structure in The Aratta Cycle: Their Relevance for the Orality Debate." Pp. 247–64 in *Mesopotamian Epic Literature: Oral or Aural?* Edited by M. E. Vogelzang and H. L. J. Vanstiphout. Lewiston, N.Y.: Mellen, 1992.

————. "Some Remarks on Cuneiform *écritures.*" Pp. 217–34 in *Scripta Signa Vocis: Studies about Scripts, Scriptures, Scribes, and Languages in the Near East,* Festschrift for J. H. Hospers. Edited by H. J. L. Vanstiphout et al. Groningen: Egbert Forsten, 1986.

Veenhof, K. R., ed. *Cuneiform Archives and Libraries.* Leiden: Nederlands Historisch-Archaeologisch Instituut te Instanbul, 1986.

Veldhuis, N. "Tin.tir = Babylon, the Question of Canonization and the Production of Meaning." *JCS* 50 (1997): 77–85.

Vercoutter, J. "Une Épitaphe Royale inédite du Serapéum." *MDAI* 16 (1958): 333–45.

———. "La Prédynastie égyptienne. Anciens et nouveaux concepts." *Cahiers de Recherches de l'Institut de Papyrologie et d'Égyptologie de Lille* 13 (1991): 137–46.

———. *Textes biographiques du Serapéum de Memphis: Contributions à l'étude des stèles votives du Serapéum.* Paris: Librarie ancienne H. Champion, 1962.

Vernus, P. "La Formule 'souffle de la bouche' au Moyen Empire." *RdÉ* 28 (1976): 139–45.

———. "Langue littéraire et diglossie." Pp. 555–64 in *Ancient Egyptian Literature: History and Forms.* Edited by A. Loprieno. Probleme der Ägyptologie 10. Leiden: Brill, 1996.

———. "La Naissance de l'écriture dans l'Égypte ancienne," *Archéo-Nil* 3 (1993): 75–108.

Vittmann, G. "Die Hymne des Ostrakons Wien 6155 und Kairo CG 25214." *Wiener Zeitschrift für die Kunde des Morgenlandes*, 1980.

Vogelsang, F. *Kommentar zu den Klagen des Bauern.* Untersuchungen zur Geschichte und Altertumskunde Ägyptens 6. Leipzig: Hinrichs, 1913.

Vogelzang, M. E., and H. L. J. Vanstiphout, eds. *Mesopotamian Epic Literature: Oral or Aural?* Lewiston, N.Y.: Mellen, 1992.

Volten, A. *Studien zur Weisheitsbuch des Anii.* Copenhagen: Levin & Munksgaard, Ejnar Munksgaard, 1937.

von Rad, G. *Deuteronomy.* OTL. Philadelphia: Westminster, 1966.

———. *Das Gottesvolk im Deuteronomium.* BWANT 47. Stuttgart: W. Kohlhammer, 1929.

———. *Old Testament Theology.* 2 vols. Trans. D. M. G. Stalker. New York: Harper & Row, 1962.

———. *Studies in Deuteronomy.* Trans. D. Stalker. London: SCM, 1953.

von Soden, W. "Dolmetscher und Dolmetschen im alten Orient." Pp. 351–57 in *Aus Sprache, Geschichte und Religion Babyloniens.* Edited by L. Cagni and H.-P. Müller. Naples: Istituto universitario orientale, Dipartimento di studi asiatici, 1989.

———. *Grundriß der akkadischen Grammatik.* Rome: Pontificium Institutum Biblicum, 1952. 3d ed. (*GAG³*) with suppl., 1969.

Wahl, H. M. *Die Jakobserzählungen.* BZAW 259. Berlin and New York: de Gruyter, 1997.

Walton, J. M. *Greek Theatre Practice.* Contributions in Drama and Theatre Studies 3. Westport, Conn.: Greenwood, 1980.

Warburton, W. *The Divine Legation of Moses Demonstrated.* 3 vols. London, 1738–41.

Ward, W. "Neferhotep and His Friends." *JEA* 63 (1977): 63–66.

Weinfeld, M. *Deuteronomy and the Deuteronomic School.* Oxford: Oxford University Press, 1972. Repr., Winona Lake, Ind.: Eisenbrauns, 1992.

Weippert, M. "Assyrische Prophetien der Zeit Asarhaddons und Assurbanipals." Pp. 71–115 in *Assyrian Royal Inscriptions: New Horizons in Literary, Ideological, and Historical Analysis*, Orientis Antiqui Collectio 17. Edited by F. M. Fales. Rome: Istituto per l'Oriente, 1981.

—————. "The Balaam Text from Deir ʿAlla and the Study of the Old Testament." Pp. 151–84 in *The Balaam Text from Deir ʿAlla Re-evaluated: Proceedings of the International Symposium Held at Leiden, 21–24 August 1989.* Edited by J. Hoftijzer and G. van der Kooij. Leiden: Brill, 1991.

—————. "'Das Frühere, siehe, ist eingetroffen . . .': Über Selbstzitate im Prophetenspruch." Pp. 147–69 in *Oracles et prophéties dans l'antiquité: Actes du Colloque de Strasbourg, 15–17 Juin 1995.* Edited by J.-G. Heinz. Université des sciences humaines de Strasbourg, Travaux du Centre de recherche sur le Proche-Orient et la Grèce antiques 15. Paris: De Boccard, 1997.

—————. "Prophetie im Alten Orient." *Neues Bibel-Lexikon* 3 (1997): 196–200.

Wellek, R. "The Term and Concept of Classicism in Literary History." Pp. 55–89 in *Discriminations: Further Concepts of Criticism.* New Haven and London: Yale University Press, 1970.

Wellhausen, J. *Prolegomena to the History of Ancient Israel.* Gloucester, Mass.: Peter Smith, 1973.

Wente, E. F. "Egyptian 'Make Merry' Songs Reconsidered." *JNES* 21 (1962): 118–28.

—————. *Letters from Ancient Egypt.* Atlanta: Scholars Press, 1990.

—————. "A Misplaced Letter to the Dead." *OLP* 6/7 (1976): 595–601.

—————. "The Scribes of Ancient Egypt." Pp. 2211–21 in *Civilizations of the Ancient Near East.* Edited by J. M. Sasson. 4 vols. New York: Scribner, 1995.

Wessetzky, V. "Anmerkungen über das Gottesbuch des Königs." Pp. 963–65 in *Studien zu Sprache und Religion Ägyptens zu Ehren von Wolfhart Westendorf.* Edited by F. Junge. Göttingen: F. Junge, 1984.

West, M. L. *Early Greek Philosophy and the Orient.* Oxford: Clarendon, 1971.

—————. "Rhapsodes." Pp. 1311–12 in *The Oxford Classical Dictionary.* 3d ed. Edited by S. Hornblower and A. Spawforth. Oxford and New York: Oxford University Press, 1996.

Westendorf, W. "*hwj.t-sdd,* das Schlagwort." *GöM* 72 (1984): 37–38.

—————. *Koptisches Handwörterbuch. Bearbeitet auf Grund des Koptischen Handwörterbuchs von Wilhelm Spiegelberg.* Heidelberg: C. Winter Universitätsverlag, 1977.

Westermann, C. *Roots of Wisdom*. Louisville, Ky.: Westminster John Knox, 1995.

Wiedmann, A. K. *The German Quest for Primal Origins in Art, Culture, and Politics 1900–1933: Die "Flucht in Urzustände."* Studies in German Thought and History 16. Lewiston, N.Y.: Mellen, 1995.

Whitney, L. "English Primitivistic Theories of Epic Origins." *Modern Philology* 21 (1924): 337–78.

———. *Primitivism and the Idea of Progress in English Popular Literature of the Eighteenth Century*. Baltimore: Johns Hopkins Press, 1934.

Whybray, R. N. *The Intellectual Tradition in the Old Testament*. BZAW 135. Berlin and New York: de Gruyter, 1974.

Wild, H. "L'«Adresse aux visiteurs» du tombeaux de Ti." *BIFAO* 58 (1959): 101–14.

Wildberger, H. *Isaiah 1–12*. Translated by T. H. Trapp. Minneapolis: Fortress, 1991.

Wildung, D. *Die Rolle ägyptischer Könige im Bewüsstsein ihrer Nachwelt*. Berlin: B. Hessling, 1969.

———. *Sesostris und Amenemhet: Ägypten im Mittleren Reich*. Munich: Hirmer, 1984.

Wilhelm, G. *Grundzüge der Geschichte und Kultur der Hurriter*. Darmstadt: Wissenschaftliche Buchgesellschaft, 1982.

Williams, R. J. "Scribal Training in Ancient Egypt," *JAOS* 92 (1972): 214–21.

Williamson, H. G. M. *Variations on a Theme: King, Messiah, and Servant in the Book of Isaiah*. Carlisle: Paternoster, 1996.

Wilson, R. R. *Prophecy and Society in Ancient Israel*. Philadelphia: Fortress, 1980.

Winlock, H. E. *Bas-Reliefs from the Temple of Ramesses I at Abydos*. New York (City) Metropolitan Museum of Art; Papers, v. 1, pt. 1, no. 5. New York: Arno, 1973.

Wood, R. *An Essay on the Original Genius and Writings of Homer*. London, 1775.

Wreszinski, W. *Ägyptische Inschriften aus dem K. K. Hofmuseum in Wien*. Leipzig, 1906.

Young, I. M. "Israelite Literacy: Interpreting the Evidence. Part I." *VT* 48 (1998): 239–53.

———. "Israelite Literacy: Interpreting the Evidence. Part II." *VT* 48 (1998): 408–22.

Youtie, H. C. "*Agrammatos:* An Aspect of Greek Society in Egypt." *Harvard Studies in Classical Philology* 75 (1971): 161–76.

———. "Between Literacy and Illiteracy." Pp. 481–83 in *Akten des xiii. internationalen Papyrologenkongresses, Marburg/Lahn, 2–6. August 1971.* Edited by E. Kiessling and H.-A. Rupprecht. Munich: Beck, 1974.

———. "P. Mich. inv. 855: Letter from Heraklides to Nemesion." *ZPE* 27 (1977): 147–50.

Žaba, Z. *Les Maximes de Ptahhotep.* Prague: Éditions de l'Academie tshécoslovaque des sciences, 1956.

Zevit, Z. "Cognitive Theory and Memorability in Biblical Poetry." *Ma'ariv* 8 (1992): 199–212.

Ziegler, C. *Catalogue des instruments de musique égyptiens.* Musée du Louvre, Département des antiquités égyptiennes. Paris: Éditions de la Réunion des Musées Nationaux, 1979.

Zimmern, H. "Gilgameš-Omina und Gilgameš-Orakel." *ZA* 24 (1910): 166–71.

Zivie, A. P. "Un Fragment inédit de coudée votive." *BIFAO* 71 (1971): 181–88.

———. *Hermopolis et le nome de l'Ibis.* Cairo: Institut français d'archéologie orientale, 1975.

Zumthor, P. *Oral Poetry: An Introduction.* Theory and History of Literature 70. Trans. K. Murphy-Judy. Minneapolis: University of Minnesota Press, 1990.

Index of Scripture Citations

Daniel

1:4	132
5:5	7 n. 14, 42
9:1–27	37
9:2	7 n. 18, 8 n. 22
9:11	7 n. 15
9:13	7 n. 15
12:1	13 n. 36

Ezra

3:2	7 nn. 15 & 19
3:4	7 n. 19

Nehemiah

8	10 n. 28, 18 n. 53
8:1	7 n. 16
8:13–17	26 n. 74
8:15	7 n. 19
9:3	7 n. 15
10:35	7 n. 19
10:37	7 n. 19

2 Chronicles

17:7–9	10 n. 28, 18 n. 53
17:9	7 n. 15
21:12	72
21:12–15	84
26:11	133
30:5	7 n. 19
30:18	7 n. 19
31:3	7 n. 15
34:14	7 n. 16
34:30	10 n. 28
35:26	7 n. 15

2 Maccabees

4:9–14	132

Sirach

6:18–37	6 n. 10
38:24–39:11	6
38:24–39:3	7 n. 18, 8 n. 22, 18
49:10	19
51:23	132